my revision notes

Pearson Edexcel International GCSE (9–1)

HISTORY

Rob Bircher
Kirsty Taylor
Alec Fisher
Rob Quinn

In order to ensure that this resource offers high-quality support for the associated Pearson qualification, it has been through a review process by the awarding body. This process confirms that this resource fully covers the teaching and learning content of the specification or part of a specification at which it is aimed. It also confirms that it demonstrates an appropriate balance between the development of subject skills, knowledge and understanding, in addition to preparation for assessment.

Endorsement does not cover any guidance on assessment activities or processes (e.g. practice questions or advice on how to answer assessment questions), included in the resource nor does it prescribe any particular approach to the teaching or delivery of a related course.

While the publishers have made every attempt to ensure that advice on the qualification and its assessment is accurate, the official specification and associated assessment guidance materials are the only authoritative source of information and should always be referred to for definitive guidance.

Pearson examiners have not contributed to any sections in this resource relevant to examination papers for which they have responsibility.

Examiners will not use endorsed resources as a source of material for any assessment set by Pearson. Endorsement of a resource does not mean that the resource is required to achieve this Pearson qualification, nor does it mean that it is the only suitable material available to support the qualification, and any resource lists produced by the awarding body shall include this and other appropriate resources.

Acknowledgements
Every effort has been made to trace all copyright holders, but if any have been inadvertently overlooked, the Publishers will be pleased to make the necessary arrangements at the first opportunity.

Although every effort has been made to ensure that website addresses are correct at time of going to press, Hodder Education cannot be held responsible for the content of any website mentioned in this book. It is sometimes possible to find a relocated web page by typing in the address of the home page for a website in the URL window of your browser.

Hachette UK's policy is to use papers that are natural, renewable and recyclable products and made from wood grown in well-managed forests and other controlled sources. The logging and manufacturing processes are expected to conform to the environmental regulations of the country of origin.

Orders: please contact Hachette UK Distribution, Hely Hutchinson Centre, Milton Road, Didcot, Oxfordshire, OX11 7HH. Telephone: +44 (0)1235 827827. Email education@hachette.co.uk
Lines are open from 9 a.m. to 5 p.m., Monday to Friday. You can also order through our website: www.hoddereducation.co.uk

ISBN: 978 1 3983 0069 9

© Rob Bircher, Kirsty Taylor, Alec Fisher and Rob Quinn 2020

First published in 2020 by

Hodder Education,

An Hachette UK Company

Carmelite House

50 Victoria Embankment

London EC4Y 0DZ

www.hoddereducation.co.uk

The authorised representative in the EEA is Hachette Ireland, 8 Castlecourt Centre, Dublin 15, D15 XTP3, Ireland (email: info@hbgi.ie)

Impression number   10 9 8 7

Year   2025

All rights reserved. Apart from any use permitted under UK copyright law, no part of this publication may be reproduced or transmitted in any form or by any means, electronic or mechanical, including photocopying and recording, or held within any information storage and retrieval system, without permission in writing from the publisher or under licence from the Copyright Licensing Agency Limited. Further details of such licences (for reprographic reproduction) may be obtained from the Copyright Licensing Agency Limited, www.cla.co.uk

Cover photo © SERGEJ SVERDELOV - stock.adobe.com
Illustrations by Aptara Inc.
Typeset in Bembo Std 11/13 pts. by Aptara Inc.
Printed in the UK by Bell and Bain Ltd, Glasgow

A catalogue record for this title is available from the British Library.

Get the most from this book

This book will help you revise for the Pearson Edexcel IGCSE History specification. It covers the following options:

Paper 1: Depth Studies

- Germany: development of dictatorship, 1918–45
- A world divided: superpower relations, 1943–72
- A divided union: civil rights in the USA, 1945–74

Paper 2: Section A Historical Investigations

- Russia and the Soviet Union, 1905–24
- The USA, 1918–41

Paper 2: Section B Breadth Studies

- Changes in medicine, c1848–c1948
- China: conflict, crisis and change, 1900–89

You can use the revision planner on pages 4 and 5 to plan your revision, topic by topic. Tick each box when you have revised and understood a topic.

You can also keep track of your revision by ticking off each topic heading throughout the book. Be a scribbler, make notes as you learn. You will need an exercise book for most of the revision tasks, but you can also write in this book.

Tick to track your progress

Revision tasks

Use these tasks to make sure that you have understood every topic and to help you think about what you are revising. If you do the tasks you will have to use the information in the book. If you use the information you will remember it better. The more you use it, the better you will remember it.

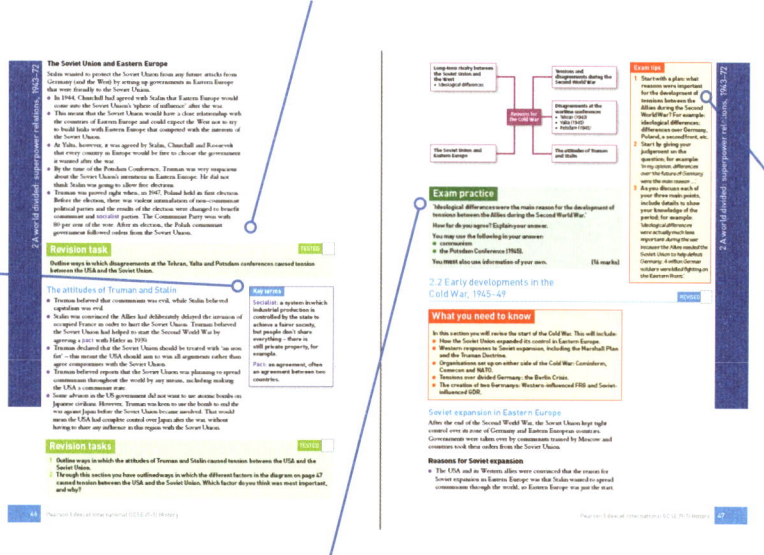

Key terms

Key terms are highlighted the first time they appear in the chapter, with an explanation nearby in the margin.

Exam tips

Throughout the book there are tips that explain how you can boost your final grade.

Exam practice

Sample exam questions are provided for each topic. Use them to consolidate your revision and practise your exam skills.

Pearson Edexcel International GCSE (9–1) History   3

My revision planner

Introduction

Section 1 Depth Studies

1 Germany: development of dictatorship, 1918–45
- 13   1.1 The establishment of the Weimar Republic and its early problems
- 18   1.2 The recovery of Germany, 1924–29
- 21   1.3 The rise of Hitler and the Nazis to January 1933
- 25   1.4 Nazi Germany, 1933–39
- 36   1.5 Germany and the occupied territories during the Second World War

2 A world divided: superpower relations, 1943–72
- 42   2.1 Reasons for the Cold War
- 47   2.2 Early developments in the Cold War, 1945–49
- 54   2.3 The Cold War in the 1950s
- 61   2.4 Three crises: Berlin, Cuba and Czechoslovakia
- 69   2.5 The Thaw and moves towards Détente, 1963–72

3 A divided union: civil rights in the USA, 1945–74
- 74   3.1 The Red Scare and McCarthyism
- 79   3.2 Civil rights in the 1950s
- 86   3.3 The impact of civil rights protests, 1960–74
- 96   3.4 Other protest movements: students, women, anti-Vietnam
- 103   3.5 Nixon and Watergate

Section 2A Historical Investigations

4 Russia and the Soviet Union, 1905–24
- 107   4.1 Tsarist rule in Russia, 1905–14
- 115   4.2 Opposition to Tsarist rule, 1914–17: the impact of war and the February Revolution
- 120   4.3 Provisional Government and the Bolshevik Revolution
- 127   4.4 The Bolshevik consolidation of power and the Civil War
- 137   4.5 War Communism and the New Economic Policy (NEP)

5 The USA, 1918–41
- 143   5.1 The Roaring Twenties
- 150   5.2 Increased social tensions in the 1920s
- 157   5.3 The USA in Depression, 1929–33
- 165   5.4 Roosevelt and the New Deal, 1933–41
- 171   5.5 The opposition to the New Deal

Section 2B Breadth Studies

6 Changes in medicine, c1848–c1948

- 175 6.1 Progress in the mid-nineteenth century; Nightingale, Chadwick, Snow and Simpson
- 180 6.2 Discovery and development, 1860–75; Lister and Pasteur
- 186 6.3 Accelerating change, 1875–1905; Ehrlich, Koch and chemistry
- 191 6.4 Government action and war, 1905–20
- 198 6.5 Advances in medicine, surgery and public health, 1920–48; the NHS

7 China: conflict, crisis and change, 1900–89

- 206 7.1 The fall of the Qing dynasty, warlordism and chaos, 1900–34
- 213 7.2 The triumph of Mao and the CCP, 1934–49
- 220 7.3 Change under Mao, 1949–63
- 229 7.4 The Cultural Revolution and its impact, 1965–76
- 233 7.5 China, 1976–89

Introduction

How to revise   REVISED ☐

There is no single way to revise, but here are some good ideas.

1 Make a revision timetable

For a subject like history, which involves learning large amounts of factual detail, it is essential that you construct a 'revision plan':

- **Start early** – you should start by looking at the dates of your exams and working backwards to the first date you intend to start revising, probably six to eight weeks before your exam.
- **Be realistic** – work out a realistic revision plan to complete your revision; don't try to do too much. Remember that you have to fit in your history revision alongside your other GCSE subjects. Plan to include breaks to give yourself a rest.
- **Revise regularly** – regular, short spells of 20–40 minutes are better than long slogs of several hours.
- **Plan your time carefully** – test yourself to see what you know and give more revision time to topic areas you find difficult. Spend longer on the sections you feel less confident about.
- **Track your progress** – keep to your timetable, and use the revision planner on pages 4 and 5 to tick off each topic as you complete it. Give yourself targets and reward yourself when you have achieved them.

2 Revise actively

Different people revise in different ways and you will have to find the methods which best suit your learning style. The best revision techniques are active. Here are some techniques which students have used to help them revise:

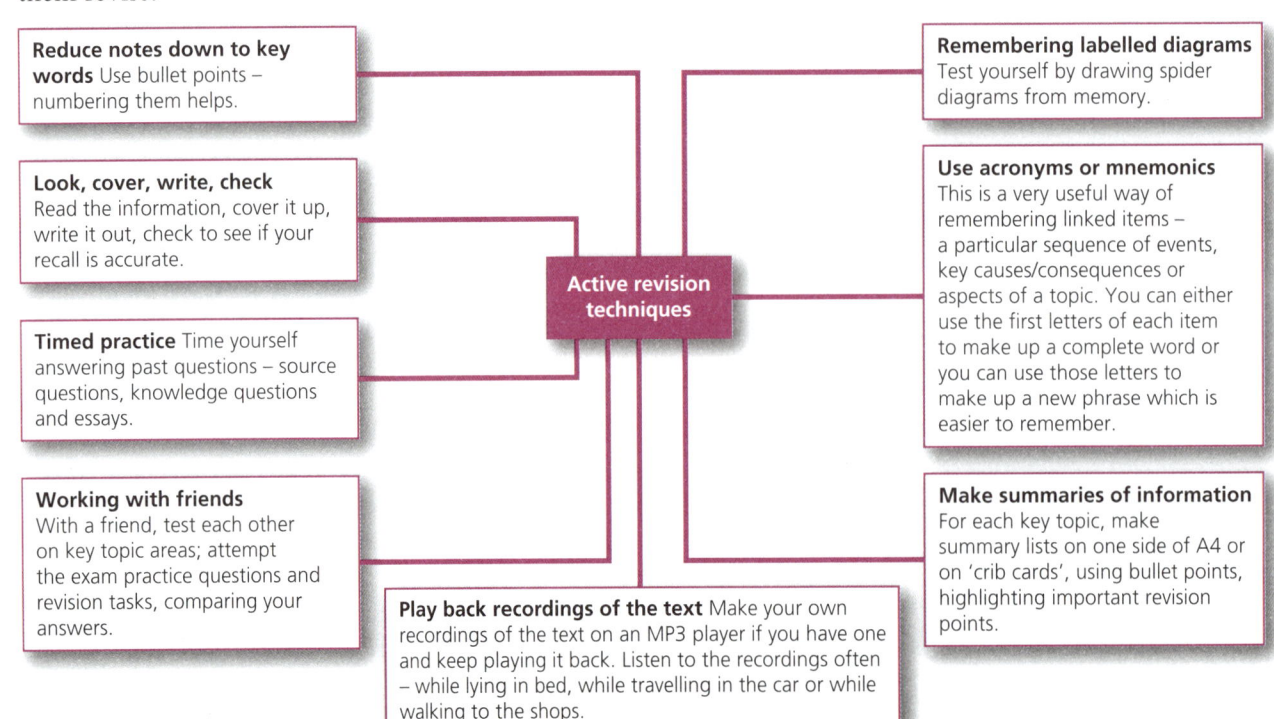

Reduce notes down to key words Use bullet points – numbering them helps.

Look, cover, write, check Read the information, cover it up, write it out, check to see if your recall is accurate.

Timed practice Time yourself answering past questions – source questions, knowledge questions and essays.

Working with friends With a friend, test each other on key topic areas; attempt the exam practice questions and revision tasks, comparing your answers.

Play back recordings of the text Make your own recordings of the text on an MP3 player if you have one and keep playing it back. Listen to the recordings often – while lying in bed, while travelling in the car or while walking to the shops.

Remembering labelled diagrams Test yourself by drawing spider diagrams from memory.

Use acronyms or mnemonics This is a very useful way of remembering linked items – a particular sequence of events, key causes/consequences or aspects of a topic. You can either use the first letters of each item to make up a complete word or you can use those letters to make up a new phrase which is easier to remember.

Make summaries of information For each key topic, make summary lists on one side of A4 or on 'crib cards', using bullet points, highlighting important revision points.

Guide to the Pearson Edexcel IGCSE History examination

You will be examined on two units for Paper 1, one unit for Paper 2, Section A and one unit for Paper 2, Section B.

When answering the exam questions, always bear in mind the following:
- The more marks the question has, the longer you should spend answering it.
- Only include information that is directly relevant to the question.
- Be specific; avoid generalised comments.
- Try to include specific details such as names, dates, events, organisations and activities.
- Always support your statements with examples.

Paper 1: Depth Studies

REVISED

This paper tests your knowledge on the key features and characteristics of the historical period.

You will be tested on your historical interpretation skills and will need to be able to make judgements about historical events and periods studied, using second-order historical concepts. The second-order concepts assessed in Paper 1 are causation, consequence and significance.
- Paper 1 is worth 50 per cent of your total IGCSE marks.
- The exam lasts 1 hour 30 minutes.
- You need to answer two questions, one on each of the depth studies you have studied.
- Each question consists of three parts:
  - (Part a) This is worth 6 marks.
  - (Part b) This is worth 8 marks.
  - (Part c) This is worth 16 marks.
- Try to spend 40 minutes on each full question. Ideally, you want to allow five to ten minutes at the end of the exam to read through and check your answers.

How to answer the 6-mark question – 'What impression?'

Six-mark questions on Paper 1 ask you to analyse a secondary extract. The question will look like:

What impression does the author give about …?

You *must* use Extract A to explain your answer.

The question requires you to infer the impression given by the author of the extract. This goes beyond simply repeating what the author has written. You will need to infer what impression is given and support this by considering the following:
- **Tone** – what tone does the author use in the extract? Is it positive or negative? Supportive, critical or balanced etc?
- **Language** – what language is used to give this impression? Focus on the vocabulary used. What does it explicitly state? What can you infer?

Make direct reference to the extract and use short quotes to highlight key phrases and words used.
- **Content** – what information about the topic has the author selected? How does this affect the impression it gives?
- Remember, this is a six-mark question so don't spend too long answering it.

How to answer the 8-mark question – 'Explain TWO effects'

Eight-mark questions on Paper 1 require you to explain **two** effects of something. The question will look like:

Explain two effects of … on …

- You must look at *two* effects. If you only explain one effect you will only receive a maximum of half the marks available.
- You don't need to write a full essay for the answer. Write two separate paragraphs – one for each effect.
- To reach the highest marks, you must go beyond simply describing an effect. Make sure you explain the consequences of each effect on the situation at the time.
- Select relevant and specific information to support your explanation.

How to answer the 16-mark question – 'How far do you agree?'

Sixteen-mark questions carry the most marks and therefore require a longer and more detailed answer. The question will start with a statement in quotation marks and you are required to judge how far you agree with it:

'[Statement]' How far do you agree? Explain your answer.

You may use the following in your answer:
- Stimulus point 1
- Stimulus point 2

You ***must*** also use information of your own.

- Sixteen-mark questions carry the most marks and therefore require a carefully planned and detailed answer.
- You will be rewarded for answers that are well organised, well structured and coherent.
- The stimulus points are there to help get you started. You must also use your own knowledge and go beyond the points that you've been given.
- Make sure you choose accurate and relevant information.
- Remember the rules of essay writing: ensure your answer has an introduction that briefly outlines your view, at least three paragraphs of discussion and a reasoned conclusion which provides a judgement on the statement in the question.
- Your conclusion is a crucial part of your answer. Make sure that you include clear criteria for your overall judgement, which you have backed up with convincing evidence and argument. This is not as simple as saying you totally agree or disagree with the statement. It also means avoiding sitting on the fence and not having an opinion! Instead, you must make a considered judgement as to *how far* you agree.

To a very small extent → To a small extent → To some extent → To a large extent → To a very large extent

Structuring your conclusion

JUDGEMENT: Start with your judgement – try to incorporate words from the question into this sentence.

COUNTER: Show that you are aware that there is some evidence to counter this and give the best example.

SUPPORT: Explain why, overall, you have reached the judgement you have. Outline your key criteria or reasons why.

Paper 2: Investigation and Breadth Studies

REVISED

- This is worth 50 per cent of your total IGCSE marks.
- The exam lasts 1 hour 30 minutes.
- There are two sections for this paper:
  - Section A: Historical Investigation (30 marks)
  - Section B: Breadth Study in Change (30 marks)
- You need to answer two questions; one question on your Historical Investigation and one on your Breadth Study.
- Each question consists of three parts:
  - (Part a) This is worth 6 marks
  - (Part b) This is worth 8 marks
  - (Part c) This is worth 16 marks
- Try to spend 40 minutes on each full question. Ideally, you want to allow five or ten minutes at the end of the exam to read through and check your answers.

Section A: Historical Investigation

Section A tests your knowledge and understanding of the key features and characteristics of historical periods and your ability to use a range of source material to comprehend, interpret and cross-refer sources. You will also be tested on how well you can analyse and evaluate historical interpretations in the context of historical events studied.

How to answer the 6-mark question – 'Describing two features'

Six-mark questions on Paper 2 Section A ask you to describe two features of an event. You will have a choice of two events. The question will look like this:

Describe TWO features of EITHER … OR …

- Bear in mind this is an 'Either/Or' question – you don't have to answer both!
- Make sure you describe *two* features. If you only describe one feature you will only receive a maximum of half the marks available.
- To help structure your answer, write two paragraphs – one for each feature.
- Use specific and detailed knowledge to describe each feature.

How to answer the 8-mark question – 'two sources describing two features'

Eight-mark questions on Paper 2 Section A ask you to cross reference two sources. The question will look like this:

How far does Source A support the evidence of Source B about …?

- Don't just paraphrase the sources.
- Read the sources carefully and pick out points from each source to show where they agree/disagree.
- To gain top marks, you must identify both agreement and disagreement.
- Write three paragraphs to help structure your answer:
  - Paragraph 1 – explain how the sources agree.
  - Paragraph 2 – explain how the sources disagree.
  - Paragraph 3 – give a brief conclusion explaining *how far* the sources support one another.

| To a very small extent | To a small extent | To some extent | To a large extent | To a very large extent |

NB: You are **not** required to evaluate the utility or reliability of the sources.

How to answer the 16-mark question – 'two sources and an extract'

For 16-mark questions on Paper 2 Section A you need to reach a judgement relating to an Interpretation.

The question will take the following form:

Extract C suggests … How far do you agree with this Interpretation? Use Extract C, Sources A and B and your own knowledge to explain your answer.

- Sixteen-mark questions carry the most marks and therefore require a carefully planned and detailed answer. Make sure you create a quick plan of how you are going to answer the question *before* you start writing.
- Read the extract carefully and pick out the main points that it makes.
- Compare these to what Source A and Source B reveal, and explain how they agree/disagree with the extract. Next, use detailed and specific examples from your own knowledge to agree/disagree with the extract.
- Finish with a conclusion that makes a judgement based on the sources and your own knowledge. Make sure you weigh up the evidence to help formulate *how far* you agree with the interpretation.

| To a very small extent | To a small extent | To some extent | To a large extent | To a very large extent |

Section B: Breadth Study in Change

Section B tests your knowledge and understanding of the key features and characteristics of historical periods and your ability to explain, analyse and make judgements about historical events and periods studied, using second-order historical concepts. The second-order concepts assessed in Section B are: change, continuity, causation, significance, similarity and difference.

How to answer the 6-mark question – 'similarity/difference'

Six-mark questions on Paper 2 Section B ask you to compare two different periods. The question will always look like this:

Explain TWO ways in which [X] was similar to/different from [Y].

- Make sure you aim for two clear points. By only dealing with one similarity/difference you will only be able to gain three out of the six marks.
- You will not gain extra credit for giving a third point.
- For a top answer, you will need to choose specific information about both the periods to support the comparison.
- Remember, this is a six-mark question so don't spend too long answering it. You won't need to write an introduction or a conclusion.

How to answer the 8-mark question – 'causes'

Eight-mark questions on Paper 2 Section B require an explanation of causes. The question takes the following form:

Explain TWO causes of …

- You don't need to write a full essay for the answer. Write two separate paragraphs – one for each cause.
- Don't simply describe the cause; make sure you *explain how* the causes led to the outcome.
- Select relevant and detailed information to support the explanation.

How to answer the 16-mark question – 'change over time / significance'

Sixteen-mark questions on Paper 2 Section B require a judgement relating to one of the following: causes of change / extent of change. The question will be in one of the following styles:

- How far did … change in the years …?
- How far did … change … in the years …?
- How significant was … in changing … in the years to …?
- How far was the … the key turning point in … in the years …?

You may use the following in your answer:

- Stimulus point 1
- Stimulus point 2

You **must** also use information of your own.

- Sixteen-mark questions carry the most marks and therefore require a carefully planned and detailed answer.
- You will be awarded marks for answers that are well organised, well structured and coherent.

- The stimulus points are there to help get you started. You must also use your own knowledge and go beyond the points that you've been given.
- Make sure you choose accurate and relevant information.
- Remember the rules of essay writing: ensure your answer has an introduction that briefly outlines your view, at least three paragraphs of discussion and a reasoned conclusion which provides a judgement on the statement in the question.
- Your conclusion is a crucial part of your answer. Make sure that you include clear criteria for your overall judgement, which you have backed up with convincing evidence and argument. This is not as simple as saying you totally agree or disagree with the statement. It also means avoiding sitting on the fence and not having an opinion! Instead, you must make a considered judgement as to *how far* you agree.

To a very small extent → To a small extent → To some extent → To a large extent → To a very large extent

Section 1 Depth Studies

1 Germany: development of dictatorship, 1918–45

1.1 The establishment of the Weimar Republic and its early problems

REVISED

> **What you need to know**
>
> In this section you will revise the massive political, social and economic consequences for Germany after its defeat in the First World War. This will include:
> - The abdication of the Kaiser and the German revolution.
> - The strengths and weaknesses of the new Republic and its Constitution.
> - The challenges facing the new Weimar **Republic**, including reactions to the Treaty of Versailles and political threats from the left and right.
> - The French invasion and occupation of the Ruhr, and the hyperinflation crisis of 1923.

The abdication of the Kaiser and the German revolution of 1918–19

- By November 1918, the First World War had lasted for four years; 1.8 million German soldiers had died and the army had been forced to retreat.
- Low domestic production led to hunger. Moreover, a naval blockade imposed by the Allies prevented the import of food, fuel and medicines. Increasingly, Germans blamed **Kaiser Wilhelm II**.
- In October 1919, German sailors at Kiel mutinied and refused an order to attack British naval forces. Strikes and protests spread across Germany and soldiers mutinied.
- The Kaiser had lost control. In some cities, ordinary Germans set up workers' councils as an alternative to the Kaiser's authority.
- It was clear Germany could not fight on, but the Allies refused to make peace unless the Kaiser **abdicated**.
- On 9 November, the Kaiser was forced to abdicate and flee to Holland. The following day, a new republic was set up under President Ebert. On 11 November 1918, Germany signed an **armistice** with the Allies.

> **Key terms**
>
> **Republic:** a state without a monarch.
>
> **Abdicate:** to give up the throne.
>
> **Armistice:** formal agreement of opposing forces to stop fighting.

> **Kaiser Wilhelm II (1859–1941)**
> - Wilhelm was Kaiser from 1888 to 1918.
> - He was the grandson of Queen Victoria.
> - He was determined to increase German naval power and build an empire like Britain's.
> - He supported Austria in 1914 and invaded France.
> - He died in exile in the Netherlands, in 1941.

The strengths and weaknesses of the new Republic and its constitution

In January 1919, a new democratic constitution was drawn up for Germany. Democracy was new to Germany and therefore was not immediately welcomed. The unpopularity of the new government grew as it became closely linked to the numerous difficulties facing Germany following the First World War, therefore undermining the Republic from the start. Moreover, the Weimar constitution, despite its democratic credentials, included weaknesses that would also help create later instability.

> **Key term**
>
> **Constitution:** a list of rules on how a country is governed.
>
> **Coalition:** a government formed of more than one political party working together.

Strengths of the Weimar constitution	Weaknesses of the Weimar constitution
Everybody aged over 20 could vote. (In Britain the age was 21 for men and 30 for women.)	Article 48 – in an emergency, the President could take action without consulting the Reichstag. This gave the President too much power, making it possible he might act undemocratically (see page 25).
The President was elected every seven years and had the power to appoint the Chancellor (head of the government).	
Proportional representation in elections meant the percentage of votes won by a party directly determined the percentage of seats they won in the Reichstag (parliament). This was fairer and more democratic than other electoral systems.	Proportional representation made it difficult for any single party to get an overall majority. Therefore, there were coalition governments and these tended to be weak, unstable and short lived.
The Reichstag was elected every four years and served a fixed term. It passed or rejected changes in the law.	Proportional representation allowed small extremist parties to win seats in the Reichstag. These parties were often anti-democratic.
All Germans enjoyed freedom of speech and freedom of religious beliefs. Their civil rights were protected.	

Revision tasks

1 Here are some key terms, events and people. Imagine that these are answers and it is your job to come up with a suitable question for each one. Try to make each question as detailed as possible so that you are using specific knowledge to phrase it.

   a) Kaiser
   b) Kiel
   c) Proportional representation
   d) Article 48
   e) President
   f) Constitution
   g) Naval blockade
   h) Allies
   i) Reichstag
   j) Coalition governments

2 When was it clear that the Kaiser would have to abdicate?
3 How did the Weimar constitution make later instability more likely?

> **Exam practice**
>
> Study Extract A.
>
> What impression does the author give about the impact of proportional representation on Weimar Germany?
>
> You **must** use Extract A to explain your answer. (6 marks)

> **Exam tip**
>
> Remember that the examiner wants you to explain the impression the author gives. You can support your ideas using short quotations that focus on key phrases or even key words.

> **Extract A**
>
> The Weimar constitution was based on proportional representation: any political party winning more than 60,000 votes was entitled to a member in the Reichstag. One result of this was the growth of several parties. All the governments of the Weimar period were coalitions of two or more parties. Coalitions meant that party politicians had to make compromises with each other in order to govern. Many Germans despised the frequent changes of government and the wheeling and dealing that was involved.
>
> Adapted from *Nazi Germany 1933–1945* by Christopher Culpin and Steve Mastin, 2013, Hodder.

German reactions to the Treaty of Versailles, June 1919

Following the armistice of November 1918, the Allies (Britain, France and the United States) began to draw up a peace treaty. The German people hoped for a fair treaty as the Kaiser had been replaced by a democratic republic. However, the Germans were not even invited to the Paris Peace Conference and had no say in the negotiations.

The key terms of the Treaty of Versailles and German reaction

The resulting Treaty of Versailles punished Germany harshly. However, President Ebert had no choice but to sign the Treaty in June 1919. Opponents angrily described it as a 'diktat' (dictated peace).

Key terms of Treaty	Reactions in Germany
Germany was forced to accept full blame for starting the war (Article 231: the War Guilt clause).	This was a national humiliation for Germany. The public resented it and felt responsibility was shared by all the nations involved.
Because Germany had to accept full blame for the war, the Allies could make Germany pay reparations (compensation for war damages), mostly to France and Belgium. A total amount of £6.6 billion was set in 1921, to be paid in annual instalments.	Many Germans felt reparations were too high. They felt that the payments would further weaken the economy which was already damaged by war.
Germany was not allowed tanks, submarines or aircraft. The army was limited to 100,000 soldiers and the navy to six battleships and 15,000 men. The Rhineland was demilitarised. Conscription was banned.	This made many Germans feel insecure. Germany had been a strong and proud nation. Now it seemed that the Allies were deliberately trying to weaken them.
Germany lost 10 per cent of its land, including all of its overseas colonies. The land lost contained 13 per cent of the population, as well as important raw materials and industry.	These terms robbed Germany of its key industrial areas including Alsace-Lorraine (iron) and the Saar (coal). Critics argued that this undermined the economy even further.

The 'stab in the back' myth and the 'November Criminals'

Some returning soldiers and senior commanders believed, wrongly, that Germany could have fought on in the war and that the front-line troops had been 'stabbed in the back' by weak politicians, communists and Jewish people.
- They regarded the government as traitors for agreeing the armistice and signing the Treaty of Versailles, labelling them the 'November Criminals'.
- This 'stab in the back' myth soon became popular with those who opposed the new democratic republic.

Challenges to the Weimar Republic from the left and right

Although most Germans supported the new constitution and Republic, there were still powerful opponents who rejected democratic ideals. This came from both the **communist** left-and **nationalist** right-wing of German politics.

Challenge from the left: the Spartacist Rising, January 1919

- The Spartacist League (later the KPDD – the German Communist Party) was a communist group led by Rosa Luxemburg and Karl Liebknecht. They believed that President Ebert would not improve the lives of working people. They wanted a full-scale revolution like the one in Russia in 1917.
- In January 1919, an uprising began in Berlin. Spartacists took over government telegraph and newspaper offices. They hoped protesters would seize other buildings, but this failed to happen.
- The uprising was badly planned and did not attract support from other left-wing groups. The government ordered the army, helped by the *Freikorps*, to restore order. Liebknecht and Luxemburg were killed and the rising was crushed.

Challenge from the right: the Kapp Putsch, March 1920

- The *Freikorps* were furious about the Treaty of Versailles and government plans to reduce the size of the army.
- *Freikorps* units refused to disband or hand back their weapons after defeating the Spartacists and a similar communist rising in the Ruhr. In 1920, they attempted a takeover of Berlin. The plan was to form a new right-wing government, led by Wolfgang Kapp.
- 12,000 *Freikorps* marched on Berlin. The army refused to fire on former soldiers and so the government was forced to flee Berlin for the sleepy town of Weimar.
- The government appealed for a general strike. Workers and civil servants stopped working and refused to cooperate with Kapp. The country was paralysed. Kapp was unable to govern and the putsch collapsed in just four days. Kapp fled the city and the government returned (now forever known as the 'Weimar' government).

> **Key terms**
>
> **Communists:** believed that as the workers created the wealth in society, they should have a more equal share in it. The communists had little faith that democracy would improve the lives of German workers and so wanted a full-scale revolution.
>
> **Nationalists:** believed in a strong Germany with a powerful leader; often anti-democratic.
>
> *Freikorps:* a force of irregular military volunteers. They were anti-democratic, anti-communist and strongly nationalist in their beliefs. Following the war, many former soldiers joined. They were armed by the Weimar government and used to crush the communist uprising.

Revision tasks

1 Make your own copy and complete the concept map below.

2 Use the look, cover, write and check method to help you learn the terms.
3 Write a simple definition of the 'stab in the back' myth.
4 Explain which was more of a threat to the Weimar government: the Spartacist Rising or the Kapp Putsch.

The French occupation of the Ruhr, January 1923

The First World War had brought Germany close to bankruptcy and the Treaty of Versailles made things even worse. In 1922, the Weimar government announced it could not afford to pay reparations. France did not believe this and was determined to make Germany pay.

- In January 1923, 60,000 French and Belgian troops marched into the Ruhr, an important industrial area of Germany. Troops occupied the area for ten months, taking industrial products and raw materials to meet the value of the reparations owed.
- The Weimar government ordered workers to begin passive resistance. This meant going on strike and refusing to cooperate with the French. Some workers even flooded mines or set fire to factories.
- French occupation of the Ruhr meant Germany lost income from one of its main industrial areas. Moreover, the striking workers still needed to be paid. This added to the Weimar government's economic problems.

Causes and effects of hyperinflation, 1923

Causes

- The German government had printed more banknotes to help pay for the cost of the war and the reparations payments. However, the more notes in circulation, the more their value dropped.
- In 1923, the government was forced to print even more money to pay the striking workers in the Ruhr. This caused hyperinflation, when prices rose at an incredible rate as the value of the currency collapsed.

Effects

Short-term effects of hyperinflation	Long-term effects of hyperinflation
Many workers' wages did not keep up with rising prices as these were increasing so quickly. They could no longer afford daily necessities. In 1918, a loaf of bread in Berlin cost 0.63 marks. By July 1923, this had risen to 3,465 marks and by November it was 201,000,000,000 marks!	The Weimar Republic was severely weakened by hyperinflation. Millions of Germans had lost savings and there was widespread poverty.
Those on fixed incomes, such as pensioners, were hit hardest. Soon their monthly incomes became worthless.	Many Germans blamed the government for the crisis. Those who lost their savings were never compensated.
People with savings found that the value of their money was wiped out almost overnight. Millions of middle-class Germans were plunged into poverty.	In future years, few people would forget the damage caused by hyperinflation. Their faith in democracy was never fully restored.

While the great majority of Germans suffered during the period of hyperinflation, some did benefit:
- People with loans and mortgages could pay back the money owed more quickly. This especially helped some business owners.
- People who owned possessions such as land or buildings were protected as these rose in value in line with inflation.
- Some businesses benefited from high profits as prices tended to increase more than wages.

Revision tasks

TESTED

1. How did the occupation of the Ruhr further damage the German economy?
2. Explain why the following would have been winners or losers during the hyperinflation of 1923:
   - a farmer
   - a factory worker
   - a business owner who took out a loan to buy a factory in 1914.

Exam practice

Explain **two** effects of hyperinflation in 1923 on Germany. (8 marks)

Exam tip

Eight-mark questions on Paper 1 require you to explain **two** effects of something. This goes beyond simply describing an effect. To reach the highest level, you must explain the consequences of each effect on the situation at the time.

1.2 The recovery of Germany, 1924–29

REVISED

What you need to know

In this section you will revise the period from 1924 to 1929. This is seen as a period of recovery for Germany, largely due to the efforts of **Gustav Stresemann**, but serious problems persisted. This section will include:
- The strengths and weaknesses of Stresemann's domestic policy.
- The strengths and weaknesses of Stresemann's foreign policy.

Gustav Stresemann (1878–1929)

- Stresemann was a hugely influential German politician who served as Chancellor in 1923 (for a brief period of 102 days) and Foreign Minister from 1923 to 1929.
- He ended the hyperinflation crisis and the French occupation of the Ruhr.
- He restored some of Germany's reputation on the international stage.
- In 1926, he won the Nobel Peace Prize for his efforts to improve German relations with France.

The strengths and weaknesses of Stresemann's domestic policy

Stresemann tried to find solutions to the difficult economic and political problems facing the Weimar Republic.

A new currency

Hyperinflation had made the German mark worthless. Stresemann introduced a temporary currency called the Rentenmark. One Rentenmark replaced 1,000 billion marks. The old notes were recalled and destroyed. In 1924, the temporary currency was replaced by the permanent Reichsmark.

Positives and negatives

+ The new currency was quickly accepted by Germans and other countries that traded with Germany. Inflation was brought under control.
− Those who had lost their savings were never compensated by the government. They felt cheated and disillusioned with the Weimar Republic.

The Dawes Plan, 1924

Stresemann organised loans from the USA as part of the Dawes Plan. These loans gave a massive boost that helped kick-start the German economy.

Positives and negatives

+ US loans made to the Weimar Republic were invested in German industry. By 1928, German industrial production had reached pre-war levels. Wages and pensions rose. The cost of living went down and confidence in the economy was restored.
+ The German government also improved housing, hospitals, schools and roads.
+ Reparations were linked to Germany's economic performance and Germany was given longer to pay.
+ Stresemann ended passive resistance and could now promise to keep up reparation payments to France. The French agreed to remove their troops from the Ruhr.
− Food prices were low and so farmers remained poor. Many supported extremist groups such as the Nazis, who promised to help them.
− Some Germans criticised the Dawes Plan and felt the government was accepting blame for the war by continuing reparations payments. Right-wing nationalists regarded this, and Stresemann's decision to call off passive resistance, as a betrayal. This was one of the causes of the Munich Putsch (see pages 21–23).
− The loans made the German economic recovery dependant on the USA. If there were economic problems in the USA, this would have severe knock-on effects for Germany (see page 23).

The Young Plan, 1929

The Young Plan reduced the amount of reparations Germany had to pay and supported further economic recovery.

Positives and negatives

+ The amount Germany had to pay in reparations was reduced from a total of £6.6 billion to under £2 billion.
+ The Young Plan led to the final removal of British, French and Belgian troops from the Ruhr.
+ Lower reparations payments saved the government money which it used to cut taxes and invest to create more jobs.
− Nationalist groups were once again angry that the German government had agreed to continue paying reparations, even at a reduced rate. However, only 14 per cent of Germans voted against the Young Plan in a referendum.

– Under the Young Plan, Germany would still be paying reparations in 1988. Some argued that this would endanger Germany's progress as a nation.

The strengths and weaknesses of Stresemann's foreign policy

Stresemann realised that Germany was in no military position to challenge the Treaty of Versailles. Instead he relied on diplomacy to improve Germany's position and relationships with other countries.

Foreign policy	Outcome
Locarno Pact, 1925	Britain, France, Italy and Belgium agreed to respect the existing borders between Germany, Belgium and France. + This began a period of improved relations and cooperation between Britain, France and Germany – the 'Locarno honeymoon'.
League of Nations, 1926	The League of Nations was an international organisation set up in 1920 to ensure peace. + Initially, Germany was forbidden from joining, but this changed in 1926 when Germany was given a permanent seat on the Security Council. This marked Germany's return to 'great power' status and the improved trust it had on the international scene.
Kellogg–Briand Pact, 1928	Germany signed the Pact with 64 other nations who all agreed to solve international disputes 'by peaceful means'. Armies would be kept, but only for self-defence rather than for aggression. + The Pact further improved international trust in Germany, especially with the USA and the leading European nations, while confirming Germany's status as a great power.

Many Germans felt let down by Stresemann's foreign policies. They still regarded the Treaty of Versailles as a 'diktat' and felt that diplomacy only confirmed the worst aspects of the Treaty.

Revision tasks

TESTED

1 Fill in your own copy of the table below using the information on pages 18 to 20 to help you. Tick to show how successfully Stresemann dealt with the big problems facing Germany and then give reasons to support your judgement.

Problem	Failure	Mixed	Success	Reasons
Reparations				
Hyperinflation				
Weakened economy				
Lack of trust from other countries				

2 Next, write a paragraph that makes an overall judgement on *how far* Stresemann solved Germany's problems between 1924 and 1929. Support your judgement.

1.3 The rise of Hitler and the Nazis to January 1933

REVISED

What you need to know

In this section you will revise how Hitler and the Nazi Party changed from operating at the fringes of German political life, as late as 1928, to Hitler becoming Chancellor in 1933. This will include:
- Hitler's involvement in the German Workers' Party (later the Nazi Party).
- The Munich Putsch of 1923, and subsequent reorganisation of the Nazi Party, 1924–29.
- The impact of the Great Depression and other factors that helped the Nazis become popular after 1929.
- The political deal that resulted in Hitler being offered the Chancellorship in 1933.

Hitler and changes to the German Workers' Party, 1920–22

Hitler joined the small German Worker's Party in 1919. Its leader, Anton Drexler, recognised Hitler's flair for communication and put him in charge of party propaganda. In 1920, a Twenty-Five Point Programme was launched, along with a new party name, the National Socialist German Workers' Party – Nazis for short. The most important points of the Programme were:
- a strong central government in Germany to replace the 'weak' democratic republic
- the abolition of the Treaty of Versailles, with Germany rearming and recovering lost land
- union between Germany and Austria
- no Jewish person could be a citizen, only 'true' ethnic Germans
- state ownership of large businesses and industries
- generous payments for pensioners.

By 1921, Hitler had replaced Drexler as leader of the Party and was attracting attention with his fiery speeches. He controlled the Party like a military commander, demanding unswerving loyalty. The swastika became the Party emblem and the distinctive arm salute was introduced. The Nazis launched their own newspaper – *The People's Observer* (*Völkischer Beobachter*) – to help promote their views.

The SA

In 1921, Hitler established the *Sturmabteilung* (SA) – stormtroopers. These men were the official 'muscle' of the Nazi Party and they wore brown uniforms, earning the nickname 'Brownshirts'.

Many had previously belonged to the *Freikorps* (see page 16) and so were violently anti-communist and anti-democratic. The SA controlled crowds at Nazi events and frequently disrupted the meetings of their political opponents using threats and violence.

The causes, events and results of the Munich Putsch, 1923

Causes

The Weimar government was already unpopular due to the national humiliation caused by the occupation of the Ruhr and the economic chaos of hyperinflation. When Stresemann called off passive resistance (see page 19) to persuade the French to leave, this was seen as the ultimate betrayal by nationalists.

Events

On 8 November, Hitler hijacked a meeting of local nationalist politicians and announced he was taking over the government of Bavaria. He was joined by the well-known Erich Ludendorff who had been Germany's second highest ranking general at the end of the war and who had strongly objected to the Armistice.
- Nazi stormtroopers began taking over official buildings.
- The next day, 2,000 Nazis marched on Munich but armed police blocked their path. In an exchange of fire, sixteen Nazis were killed.
- The putsch collapsed into chaos. Hitler escaped in a car, while Ludendorff and others were arrested. Hitler was arrested two days later.

Results

The trial in 1924 was a media sensation which Hitler turned to his advantage. He glorified his attempt to overthrow the 'November Criminals' who, he argued, had betrayed Germany. His passionate speech impressed many nationalists who now saw him as a potential leader. A sympathetic judge found Hitler guilty of high treason, but sentenced him to just five years' imprisonment – with the prospect of early release. He served only nine months.

Reorganisation of the Nazi Party, 1924–28

In the *short term*, the Munich Putsch was a disaster for the Nazis, but in the *longer term* it was much more positive. Its failure made Hitler realise that the Nazis could never win power through force alone. While in prison, Hitler wrote, 'If out-voting them takes longer than outshooting them, then at least the results will be guaranteed by their own constitution'. Therefore, a radical change of approach was needed.

Hitler reorganised the *structure* of the Nazi Party:
- Local branches were set up in every part of the country. The Nazis became a legally recognised and legitimate political party.
- The SA deliberately appealed to young, unemployed men. After joining the Party, they were provided with a uniform, lodgings and food.
- Nazi associations were set up to appeal to different groups in society. The *NS-Frauenschaft* (a women's organisation) was established alongside the National Socialist German Students' League. In 1926, the Nazis created the Hitler Youth in an attempt to win over future generations of supporters.
- In 1926, Hitler established the cult of the Führer (leader). No loyal Party member questioned Hitler's leadership and the 'Heil Hitler' greeting became compulsory.
- The SS were set up as Hitler's private protection squad. These men were his most fanatical supporters and swore an oath of loyalty to him personally.

Hitler also adapted the *tactics* used by the Nazis to win support:
- Joseph Goebbels was appointed to spread the Nazi message through greater use of propaganda. He organised rallies and coordinated the production of posters, leaflets and radio broadcasts.
- The SA were instructed to tone down their violent tactics and encouraged to demonstrate order and strength. This attracted middle-class supporters who wanted a party strong enough to resist the communists.
- The Nazis appealed to farmers who were suffering from falling agricultural prices by promising higher prices for their produce. The Nazis also contrasted the purity of rural life against supposed moral decadence in the cities.

Hitler's reorganisation of the Party and change in tactics may not have won the Nazis any more voters, but it certainly increased Party membership which rose from 27,000 in 1925 to over 100,000 by 1928.

Revision tasks

TESTED

1 Draw a timeline of the changes and events affecting the German Workers Party (later the Nazi Party), 1919–24.
2 Make a list of the positive and negative outcomes of the Munich Putsch for Hitler and the Nazi Party.

Exam practice

Study Extract A.

What impression does the author give about Hitler's role in the Munich Putsch?

You **must** use Extract A to explain your answer.   (6 marks)

Extract A

Hitler proved singularly ineffective. Nothing had been properly planned. He remained shut up in the Beer Hall unable to make up his mind whether or not to risk a demonstration. It was Ludendorff who decided for him and at noon the next day, led Hitler and the other Nazi leaders at the head of a column of several thousand men, which marched into the centre of the city. While Ludendorff marched on and pushed through the [police] cordon, Hitler, after being pulled to the ground and dislocating his arm, scrambled to his feet and fled.

A historian describing the Munich Putsch. Adapted from *Hitler and Stalin: Parallel lives*, Alan Bullock, Knopf, 1992.

> **Exam tip**
>
> You should not spend too much time on six-mark questions. The most you should spend on a question is one and a half minutes per mark, so that equates to a maximum of nine minutes.

The impact of the Great Depression

In 1928, the Nazis were little more than an extreme party at the fringe of German political life. They polled just 2.6 per cent of the vote. However, by 1932, the Nazis were the largest party in the Reichstag, and by January 1933, Hitler was Chancellor. Hitler's message had not changed, but an economic depression meant more people were willing to listen to him.

- In October 1929, the US stock market collapsed, triggering a worldwide economic depression. US banks recalled their loans to Germany (see the Dawes Plan on page 17). German businesses closed and by 1932, unemployment reached 6 million.
- Under Chancellor Brüning (1930–32), the government had cut spending on welfare payments in order to avoid hyperinflation. Traditional politicians seemed unable to tackle the Depression and there were deep divisions between the parties in the Reichstag.
- Brüning was nicknamed the 'hunger Chancellor' as more and more people felt democracy had let them down. Increasing numbers of Germans started supporting anti-democratic parties (especially the **KPD** and the Nazis). Brüning resigned in May 1932, by which time the Nazis had enjoyed increased success in regional and general elections.

> **Key term**
>
> **KPD:** the German Communist Party (previously the Spartacist League). Led by Ernst Thalman, it became widely supported during the Depression. The Party was effectively banned by the Nazis following the Reichstag Fire in 1933. Thalman was sent to a concentration camp in 1933, and executed in 1944.

Nazi methods to win support

The Nazis were skilled at using propaganda. Posters, meetings and speeches repeated simple and deliberately vague promises that appealed to a wide audience. One of the most well-known slogans was *'Arbeit und Brot'* – meaning 'Work and Bread'.

- Hitler was portrayed as a strong leader and the country's 'last hope', while the democratic parties were accused of weakly allowing Germany to lurch from one crisis to another.
- As support for the KPD grew, Nazi propaganda highlighted the 'Bolshevik menace' and threat of revolution. Business leaders, worried by the chances of a communist takeover, were quick to donate large sums to Nazi electoral campaigns. Middle-class voters flocked to the Nazis.
- The Nazis took advantage of modern technology. In the 1932 presidential election, Hitler was able to speak at five cities on the same day, flying from one venue to the next as part of his 'Hitler over Germany' campaign. This made the leader look dynamic and different.
- The Nazis set up homeless shelters and soup kitchens to feed the unemployed and vulnerable. This was effective propaganda, portraying the Nazis as able to get things done, in contrast with the divided parties in the Reichstag.

The role of the SA

The SA provided protection at Nazi meetings, but also disrupted the activities of their political opponents, especially the KPD. They were led by **Ernst Röhm**.

- By 1931, the SA had around 3 million members, many of them drawn from the growing ranks of young, unemployed men.
- The Red Front, the KPD's own fighting unit, frequently fought with the police as well as the SA. Hitler knew disorder on the streets alarmed many middle-class Germans and exploited this by presenting the SA as the guardians of order.

Ernst Röhm (1887–1934)

- Röhm served as a Captain in the First World War.
- He established the SA along with Hitler in 1921.
- He was arrested and imprisoned following the Munich Putsch.
- Röhm became Head of the SA in 1931.
- He criticised Hitler for not being radical enough after 1933.
- He was shot during the 'Night of Long Knives' in June 1934.

The events of 1932–33 and the political deal

Despite the economic crisis and the calculated ways in which the Nazis exploited the unpopularity of the Weimar Republic, it was never inevitable that Hitler would become chancellor. In the November 1932 election, the Nazis lost 2 million votes and 38 seats in the Reichstag. The Party was almost bankrupt and unlikely to afford another expensive election campaign. At a time when support for the Nazis was actually falling, it was a back-room political deal that handed Hitler the chancellorship.

Since 1930, President **Paul von Hindenburg** had ruled by decree, using the emergency powers granted by the Weimar constitution (see page 14). He used this power to dismiss or appoint a chancellor as he saw fit:

- Following the November 1932 elections, the Nazis remained the largest single party in the Reichstag. However, Hindenburg still refused to make Hitler chancellor and appointed Kurt von Schleicher in December 1932. Without sufficient support in the Reichstag, von Schleicher was forced to resign within a month.
- Behind the scenes, conservative politician and former chancellor, **Franz von Papen** conspired with wealthy industrialists who feared communism more than they feared the Nazis.
- In January 1933, von Papen convinced Hindenburg to appoint Hitler chancellor. Hindenburg was persuaded that, with von Papen as vice-chancellor and only two other Nazis in the cabinet, Hitler could be controlled. The SA would be used, much like the *Freikorps* in 1919, to crush the communists. Then Hitler would be quietly dropped. The plan backfired spectacularly (see page 26).

Paul von Hindenburg (1847–1934)

- Hindenburg was German Chief of Staff during the First World War.
- He was elected president of Germany in 1925, largely due to his status as a war hero, and re-elected in 1932.
- He was strongly anti-communist and authoritarian in outlook.

Franz von Papen (1879–1969)

- Von Papen was born in 1879 into a wealthy family.
- He was a strongly nationalist and conservative politician.
- He served as chancellor in 1932, before being replaced by von Schleicher.
- Von Papen boasted to Hindenburg that as vice-chancellor, he would 'push Hitler so far into a corner' that he would 'squeak'.

Revision tasks

1 What were the main effects of the Depression on Germany?
2 How did the Nazis exploit these problems?
3 What role did the SA play in the growing popularity of the Nazis?
4 Why was the political deal so important to Hitler and the Nazis?

TESTED

Exam practice

'The economic depression was the main reason Hitler became chancellor in January 1933.'

How far do you agree? Explain your answer.

You may use the following in your answer:
- the economic depression
- Nazi propaganda.

You **must** also use information of your own. (16 marks)

Exam tips

Sixteen-mark questions include two bullet points. These are intended to help get you started. One can be used to support the statement and the other one to challenge it. However, if you want to achieve the highest marks you must go beyond these points and include aspects of your own knowledge.

1.4 Nazi Germany, 1933–39

REVISED

What you need to know

In this section you will revise how Hitler and the Nazis dominated politics and transformed life in Germany before the Second World War. This will include:

- How Hitler transformed Germany from a democratic state to a dictatorship.
- The methods used by the Nazis to control the lives of ordinary Germans.
- Nazi policies towards women, education, young people and the Churches.
- Nazi racial policies and treatment of Jewish people.
- Unemployment and the workers in the Nazi state.

Setting up the Nazi dictatorship, 1933–34

Hitler had made no secret of his desire to sweep away democracy. However, when he became chancellor in January 1933, Hitler was in a weak position. Certain challenges had to be overcome if he was to establish a Nazi dictatorship:

- The Nazis lacked an overall majority in the Reichstag, despite being the largest single party.
- There were only two other Nazis in the Cabinet and they were outnumbered by conservative nationalists. As vice-chancellor, Franz von Papen planned to control Hitler.
- President Hindenburg had appointed Hitler as chancellor, but could also remove him at any time.
- The armed forces distrusted the Nazis. They resented the SA with its 4 million members, fearing it might take over the army. Despite being small, the army remained capable of removing Hitler by force.
- Strong opposition from the KPD and the Social Democrats continued. They could rely on the support of Germany's many highly organised trade unions.

How Hitler established a dictatorship

Event	How Hitler used this to strengthen his power
February 1933, Reichstag Fire: The Reichstag was set on fire by Marinus Van Der Lubbe, a Dutch communist who was arrested at the scene. Hitler declared that the fire marked the beginning of a communist uprising.	Hitler was granted Emergency Powers by Hindenburg. This allowed him to: • Arrest 4,000 communists, including many Communist Party leaders. The KPD was effectively leaderless. Other political opponents were also locked up. • Ban political meetings and close newspapers and radio stations. • Search houses and lock up suspects without trial.
March 1933, Enabling Act: Despite not having a majority, Hitler persuaded the Nationalist Party and Centre Party to support a new Enabling Act to give his government special powers for the next four years.	Hitler could make laws, treaties and even change the constitution without consulting the Reichstag. He could rule by decree and began to dismantle the democratic system. By July, Hitler had made decrees banning trade unions and all other political parties. Germany was now a one-party state.
June 1934, 'Night of the Long Knives': Hitler used the SS to arrest 400 SA leaders, including Ernst Röhm, who Hitler accused of plotting to remove him. Röhm and the other leaders were shot.	Röhm had been a potential rival to Hitler within the Party. He had wanted Hitler to introduce more socialist policies. By removing him in such a ruthless way, Hitler deterred any further disagreement. Hitler won the trust of the German army who were satisfied that the threat from the SA was ended.
August 1934, Hitler as Führer: Hindenburg died on 2 August 1934. Hitler wanted to change the constitution and combine the roles of President and Chancellor. He decided to seek the approval of the German people. In the referendum that followed, more than 90 per cent of voters (38 million) agreed with his action.	Hitler was now officially Führer of Germany. The German army now swore a personal oath of loyalty to Adolf Hitler, making his position virtually unassailable.

> **Revision tasks**   TESTED

1. Fill in your own copy of the table below using the information on pages 25 and 26 to help you. The first one has been started for you.

Hitler's weakness	When this weakness was solved	How this was solved
Continued opposition to the Nazis from the KPD, Social Democrats and trade unions.	By July 1934.	Hitler had used his new powers under the Enabling Act to ban the trade unions and other political parties.
The Nazis lacked an overall majority in the Reichstag.		
There were only two other Nazis in the Cabinet and von Papen was Vice-Chancellor. Hindenburg and von Papen planned to control Hitler.		
As President, Hindenburg had appointed Hitler but had the power to remove him as Chancellor at any time.		
The armed forces were distrustful of Hitler and the Nazis.		

2. Looking back at your completed table, which event do you think was the most important in consolidating Hitler's power and moving Germany away from democracy and towards dictatorship? Explain your answer.

Nazi methods of control

The Nazis were determined to win over ordinary Germans using propaganda. However, historians have shown that only those willing to be persuaded and the undecided were strongly influenced in this way. Former political opponents and critics of the Nazis had to be controlled in other ways.

The police state

To establish a **totalitarian** Germany, Hitler relied mainly on **Heinrich Himmler**. His methods were to intimidate and discourage any form of opposition.

> **Heinrich Himmler (1900–45)**
> - Himmler joined the Nazi Party in the early 1920s and took part in the Munich Putsch in 1923.
> - He was obsessed with racial purity in Germany and believed in the superiority of the **Aryan** race.
> - He was responsible for the SS, Gestapo and concentration camps and later oversaw the 'Final Solution'.
> - Himmler committed suicide after being captured by the Allies in 1945.

> **Key terms**
>
> **Totalitarian:** a system of government in which the ruling party or ruler has total control. Opposition is prohibited.
>
> **Aryan:** the Nazis defined Aryans as north-western Europeans and claimed that these were a superior race. Blonde hair and blue eyes were seen as the ideal characteristics of the Aryan.

1 Germany: development of dictatorship, 1918–45

The SS
Formed in 1925, as Hitler's personal bodyguard. Led by Heinrich Himmler after 1929. It had 50,000 members in 1934, 240,000 in 1939 and 1 million by 1944.

Wore distinctive black uniforms and showed total obedience to Hitler. Highly trained and expected to be pure Aryans (see page 32). Their primary responsibilities were to destroy opposition and carry out Nazi racial policies:
- The Death's Head units ran the concentration camps and later the extermination camps (see page 36).
- The SD (security services) investigated disloyalty in the armed forces and Nazi Party.
- The Waffen SS were special armoured regiments that fought alongside the regular army.

The Gestapo and informers
- Set up in 1933, the Gestapo (secret state police) was greatly feared. They arrested and sent people to concentration camps without trial, opened mail and tapped telephones.
- However, the Gestapo was understaffed and not nearly as powerful as people thought. It relied on networks of informers – members of the public who alerted it to suspect activity. Some Germans used this as an opportunity to settle scores with their neighbours or get back at someone they disliked. The resultant climate of mistrust deterred open criticism of the Nazis.

Concentration camps
These special prisons were used first to isolate social democrats, communists and anyone else brave enough to oppose the Nazis. Conditions were harsh, food limited and hard labour compulsory. Beatings were common and some inmates were killed.

Those not conforming to the ideal Nazi society were also imprisoned (see page 00). By 1939, an estimated 1.3 million Germans had spent at least some time in a concentration camp.

Police and courts
High-ranking police officials reported directly to Himmler and were expected to be loyal Nazis. The Nazis also controlled the courts. Magistrates and judges swore an oath of loyalty to Hitler. Opponents of the regime rarely received a fair trial.

Punishments were very harsh. By 1943, the death penalty was used for 43 different crimes, including telling an anti-Nazi joke.

Revision tasks

TESTED

1 Make your own copy and complete the concept map below.

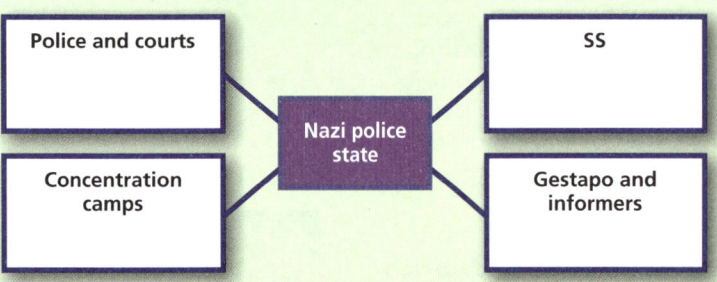

2 Use the look, cover, write and check method to help you learn the terms.

Censorship and propaganda

Hitler and the Nazis could not rule through fear alone, therefore the Nazis strictly controlled all aspects of German media and culture. Propaganda ensured the Nazi vision was widely shared while censorship prevented contrary ideas from emerging. The man charged with the task was **Joseph Goebbels**.

> **Joseph Goebbels (1897–1945)**
> - Goebbels joined the Nazi Party in 1924 and was appointed propaganda chief in 1930.
> - In 1933 he became Minister for Propaganda.
> - He used radio, films, posters and rallies to portray Hitler as the saviour of Germany.
> - He and his wife committed suicide in May 1945, one day after Hitler had taken his own life and a few hours after they had ended the lives of their six children.

	Propaganda value	Censorship measures
Radio	Broadcast Hitler's speeches daily. Nazi ideas and propaganda were repeated constantly. Cheap radios or 'Peoples' Receivers' were made available. Loudspeakers were placed in public spaces and factories for those without radios.	Foreign broadcasts were banned. Listening to an anti-Nazi station such as the BBC was punishable by death. Peoples' Receivers were designed so they did not pick up foreign stations.
Books	*Mein Kampf* became a bestseller. Nazi approved authors could have their books published more easily than ever before.	All books were approved by Goebbels before publication. Books by Jewish people or containing ideas or views disapproved of by the Nazis were banned and removed from libraries. Public book burnings were organised.
Films	Goebbels ordered that films were useful ways of conveying Nazi ideas. This was usually quite subtle as obvious propaganda was less entertaining for audiences. Newsreels shown before each film were strictly pro-Nazi in their message. Audiences were required to arrive before these started.	All foreign films were censored before being shown. Actors and directors who had been critical of the Nazis were forced to work abroad.
Newspapers	The Nazis used their own papers such as the *Völkischer Beobachter* and the violently antisemitic *Der Stürmer* to communicate their ideas. Later, the government bought up most other newspapers. By 1944, 82 per cent of the press was Nazi owned.	Goebbels shut down all anti-Nazi newspapers. Jewish editors and journalists were sacked, as were any who opposed the Nazis politically. Editors were told what they could and could not publish by the Nazi News Agency. Stories invariably had a pro-Nazi bias.
Rallies	Spectacular rallies were held, the most famous of which were at Nuremberg. Thousands of stormtroopers, the army and leading Nazis would gather for parades and speeches. Such events were intended to create the image of power, unity and order.	Nazi rallies were carefully planned and stage managed. Even the lighting was strictly controlled to create a powerful and optimistic impression.

Revision task

TESTED

1 Describe the different roles of Goebbels and Himmler.
2 Why did Hitler have to rely on both these men to ensure Nazi control over ordinary Germans?

Exam practice

'The Nazis relied mainly on censorship to maintain control over ordinary Germans after 1933.'

How far do you agree? Explain your answer.

You may use the following in your answer:
- censorship of the media
- Nazi propaganda methods.

You **must** also use information of your own. (16 marks)

> **Exam tip**
>
> Remember the rule of one and a half minutes per mark means you should spend no more than 24 minutes answering each sixteen-mark question. This should give you time to make a quick plan before starting to write.

Nazi policies towards women, education, the young and the Church, and their impact

The Nazis wanted to control the lives of women, young people and the workers. They also sought to reduce the influence of their main competitor, the Church, for the hearts and minds of Germans.

Nazi policies towards women

The Nazis had strong beliefs about men and women's role in society. They emphasised the need to increase the birth rate, arguing that if Germany did not increase its population, it could never be a great power.

Women were expected to fulfil their biological and domestic duties by:
- Having as many children as possible and raising them as loyal Germans, eager to serve and sacrifice for the national community.
- Looking after their husbands and running homes in an efficient and thrifty manner.
- Prioritising raising a family over having a job and career.
- Avoiding make-up and fashion by dressing more traditionally.
- Staying fit, healthy and fertile.

The Nazis encouraged this in various ways:
- Propaganda emphasised the value of motherhood. Honour Crosses for German Motherhood were awarded: a bronze medal for four children, silver for six and gold for eight.
- Contraception was harder to access and banned altogether in 1941. Dieting, smoking and drinking were discouraged as harmful to fertility.
- Marriage loans encouraged women to stop work and start a family. Repayments were substantially reduced each time a child was born.
- Divorces became easier to obtain so women could remarry and have more children.

Despite these policies, the Nazis only partly achieved their aims for German women. See the table below.

Evidence the Nazis achieved their aims for women	Evidence the Nazis failed to achieve their aims for women
In 1933, 970,000 babies were born. By 1939, this had risen to 1,413,000.	Despite the increase, birth rates remained stubbornly below those of the Weimar Republic.
Women were restricted in certain careers. Married female doctors and civil servants were sacked in 1933. There was also a drop in the number of women teachers. By 1936, women lawyers could not argue cases or sit as judges.	Total numbers of women working increased between 1933 and 1939. When war broke out, this increased further as they filled the jobs vacated by men (see page 39).
The number of women at university was reduced from one in five in 1933 to one in ten by 1935.	Many women, especially in the cities, continued to follow fashion, wear make-up, smoke and drink alcohol.

Revision tasks

TESTED

1. Summarise the main aims the Nazis had for German women.
2. Choose the assertion you most agree with below and turn it into an argument, supporting it using the information on page 30.

   The Nazis were totally successful / partially successful / quite unsuccessful / totally unsuccessful in achieving their aims for German women.

Nazis policies on education

As a means of ensuring the loyalty of future generations, the Nazis strictly controlled the education system.

- Teachers joined the National Socialist Teachers' League and taught a Nazi-controlled curriculum. Those who refused were sacked.
- Racial Science lessons deliberately emphasised that there was a hierarchy of races. Jewish people were inferior and a threat to the purity of the German race. In contrast, the Aryan race was superior to all others
- History lessons emphasised how Germany had been 'stabbed in the back' during the First World War. Geography lessons focused on the land 'unfairly' taken from Germany after the Treaty of Versailles.
- PE lessons were increased to create healthy Germans for the future. Boys would need to be fit for military service and girls for motherhood.
- Girls were given lessons on how to do housework and run a home.

Nazi policies towards young people

The Nazis focused much of their propaganda on the young. Children would be the first generation to grow up in the Third Reich and so the Nazis wanted to ensure fanatical loyalty. Outside school, children were encouraged to join Nazi-run Hitler Youth groups:

Boys
- Young Folk (ages 10–14), Hitler Youth (ages 14–18).
- Encouraged discipline, obedience, courage and physical fitness.
- Military-style activities included hiking, camping, map reading, mock battles and target practice.
- Competitive sports were encouraged, including swimming and boxing.
- Regular propaganda talks were given and Hitler's speeches carefully studied.

Girls
- Young Maidens (ages 10–14), League of German Maidens (ages 14–18).
- Encouraged physical fitness for future motherhood.
- Focus on domestic life including childcare, nutrition, crafts and housework.
- Propaganda talks.

Despite this emphasis on young people, the Nazis never totally achieved their aims. See the table below.

Evidence the Nazis achieved their aims for young people	Evidence the Nazis failed to achieve their aims for young people
By 1936, the Hitler Youth had 5.4 million voluntary members. This increased when membership became compulsory.	Even after joining a youth group was made compulsory, many boys and girls avoided it. The endless marching was dull for some boys, while many others were bored by the long propaganda talks.
82 per cent of German children and teens belonged to the Hitler Youth or its female equivalent, the League of German Girls.	Some young people joined unofficial groups like the Edelweiss Pirates. Others showed their defiance through their musical tastes and fashion choices (see page 40).

Revision tasks

TESTED

1. What similarities were there between Nazi approaches towards German girls and boys?
2. What differences were there?

Nazi policies towards religion and the Churches

The majority of Germans were Christian, including some 40 million Protestants and 22 million Catholics. Therefore, the Church was the biggest non-Nazi organisation in Germany. Hitler wanted to remove Christianity's influence, but could not afford to alienate public opinion by offending people's religious beliefs.

Religion	What the Nazis did	How effective was Nazi control?
Protestants	A 'Reich Church' was set up, with the slogan, 'With a swastika on our chests and the cross in our hearts'. This combined Nazi symbols with Christian services. Many Jewish elements of Christianity were removed.	Some pastors, led by Martin Niemöller and Dietrich Bonhöffer, formed the Confessing Church in opposition to the Reich Church. They openly criticised some Nazi policies. In 1937, the Nazis briefly arrested some 700 pastors for disobeying government guidance on their sermons. Niemöller and Bonhöffer were both sent to concentration camps. Bonhöffer was executed in 1945, after being associated with the July Bomb Plot (see page 40). However, the majority of Protestant pastors kept out of politics and never openly criticised the Nazis.
Catholics	In 1933, Hitler signed the Concordat – this allowed freedom of worship and meant Catholic youth groups and schools stayed open. In return, the Pope agreed Catholics would not interfere in politics. Hitler soon broke the agreement. Crucifixes were removed from schools and Catholic newspapers were censored. In 1936, Catholic youth groups and schools were closed.	A few Catholic priests made sermons criticising certain Nazi policies. In 1941, Cardinal Galen openly attacked the policy of killing people with mental and physical disabilities. Most Catholic priests and bishops kept quiet. The few Catholic priests who did speak out were sent to concentration camps. However, Galen was too popular and high profile for the Nazis to risk arresting him.

Exam practice

Explain **two** effects of Nazi policies on young people, 1933–39. (8 marks)

Exam tip

Remember that even a very detailed answer will only get four marks if you look at just one effect. Two paragraphs, one for each effect, will work best.

Nazi racial policies and the increasing persecution of Jewish people

Hitler's racism shaped the Nazi world view. He argued that some racial groups were superior to others. The ideal members of the 'master race' were Aryan – blond-haired, blue-eyed Germans. In contrast, other groups, especially Jewish people, were regarded as sub-human.

Racial policies

The Nazis wanted to remove those groups they felt were a burden on society. Those not regarded as racially pure or 'socially useful' were harshly dealt with. (See the table on page 33.)

Group persecuted	Why persecuted	How persecuted
People with mental and physical disabilities	The Nazis believed such conditions were hereditary and therefore a threat to future racial health.	**1933:** Compulsory sterilisation of people with disabilities. **1939:** Following the outbreak of war, children with disabilities started to be euthanised. Adults followed in 1940, but the policy was abandoned in 1941 after criticism from the Catholic Church.
Roma people and Germans of African ancestry	Both groups were regarded as racially inferior and a threat to the purity of German blood.	**1937:** Around 500 Germans of African ancestry were sterilised. **1938:** Roma people were rounded up and sent to concentration camps.
Homeless people, poor people, sex workers, those who committed crimes, habitual criminals and gay people	Homeless people, poor people, sex workers, those who committed crimes were seen as a burden rather than as contributors to society. Some Nazis believed their behaviour was hereditary. Gay people would not produce children and therefore were not seen as socially useful.	Some were compulsorily sterilised after 1933. **1936:** Rounded up and sent to concentration camps.

Persecution of Jewish people, 1933–39

Despite them making up about one per cent of the population, the Nazis regarded Jewish people as the biggest threat to the strength of the German race.

Hitler blamed the Jewish people for Germany's defeat in the First World War and subsequent economic depression. He closely associated them with communism while also blaming them for the worst abuses of big business. **Antisemitic** persecution unfolded in several stages:

- **1933:** Jewish people were immediately banned from government employment. Jewish judges and some lawyers were prohibited from practising law. The SA organised a nationwide boycott of shops and businesses owned by Jewish people.
- **1935:** Jewish people were banned from serving in the army. They were also prohibited from using public spaces such as swimming pools, parks and cinemas.
  - **September** – Nuremberg Laws were introduced. These ensured there was no interracial mixing of German blood:
    - Jewish people could not marry or have sex with non-Jewish people.
    - Aryan Germans who were married to Jewish people were encouraged to get a divorce or they themselves would be treated as Jewish.
    - Most significantly, Jewish people also lost their status as German citizens. They no longer had any rights and could not vote or hold a passport.
- **1938:** Jewish people had to register their possessions with the government. These could now be confiscated at any time. Jewish people were also forced to carry cards identifying them as Jewish, which they had to present to an official whenever asked. This made them easier to identify if the authorities wanted to question or imprison them. Jewish doctors and lawyers were prohibited from taking on non-Jewish people as clients or patients.
  - **8–9 November** *Kristallnacht* ('Night of the Broken Glass'): In protest at Nazi antisemitism, a Jewish student had shot and killed a German diplomat in Paris.

> **Key term**
>
> **Antisemitic:** being hostile and prejudiced towards Jewish people.

- On 8 and 9 November, Nazi leaders encouraged plain-clothed SS and SA men to attack Jewish people and smash up their homes, businesses and synagogues (places of worship). The police were ordered to do nothing.
- 191 synagogues were vandalised or set on fire and 91 Jewish people were killed; 20,000 Jewish people were rounded up and sent to concentration camps.

- **1939:** The Reich Office for Jewish Emigration was set up to encourage Jewish people who were able to leave the country. However, many had nowhere to go and there were limits on how many refugees other countries were willing to accept. Those who did leave had to surrender all of their property and possessions to the Nazi state. Those who remained faced an increasingly hostile environment, especially after the outbreak of war in 1939.

> **Revision tasks**
> 1 Draw your own timeline of key events in Jewish persecution, 1933–39.
> 2 What turning points can you identify in Nazi persecution of the Jewish people? Highlight these on your timeline. TESTED

Exam practice

Study Extract A.

What impression does the author give about the difficulties facing Jewish people wanting to leave Nazi Germany in 1938?

You **must** use Extract A to explain your answer. (6 marks)

Extract A

In the summer of 1938, delegates from thirty-two countries met at the French resort of Evian … Delegate after delegate rose to express sympathy for the refugees. But most countries, including the United States and Britain, offered excuses for not letting in more refugees. The German government was able to state with great pleasure how 'astounding' it was that foreign countries criticised Germany for its treatment of the Jewish people, but none of them wanted to open their doors to them.

From the United States Holocaust Memorial Museum website.

> **Exam tip**
> To get the highest marks, your answer will need to consider how the author has selected certain information. Is there anything further about the topic in question that the extract does not include that affects the impression given?

Unemployment and the workers in the Nazi state

The Nazis rose to power on the back of massive unemployment and had made much of their slogan 'Work and Bread'. Now they would have to try to deliver on their promises. Nazi aims were simple:
- Reduce the high unemployment caused by the Depression.
- Prepare Germany for war and ensure the nation was self-sufficient, and no longer vulnerable to blockades as it had been in the First World War (see page 13).
- Bring German workers more firmly under their control.

Reducing unemployment

In 1933, unemployment in Germany was 6 million, but by 1939, it had fallen to around half a million. To some this seemed almost an economic miracle. The Nazis had introduced the following policies:
- They doubled spending on public works as part of the **New Plan**. Jobs were created including the construction of the autobahns (motorways) and the Olympic Stadium.
- They broke the Treaty of Versailles and increased the army from 100,000 to 900,000 men by 1938.
- They invested money in private businesses to help create new jobs.

> **Key term**
> **New Plan:** plan by finance minister Hjalmar Schacht in 1933. Trade agreements with other countries ensured a supply of raw materials needed for rearmament. Public construction projects such as roadbuilding helped reduce unemployment.

HOWEVER, this fall in unemployment is not as impressive as it first appears. Some historians describe 'the hidden unemployed', as the Nazis were deliberately selective in who they counted in the official statistics:
- Women and Jewish people were not included in the unemployment figures.
- Temporary workers or seasonal workers were counted as being in full employment. This brought down unemployment statistics by about 1 million.
- After 1935, unemployed men had to serve six months in the National Labour Service (RAD). These men were used on public building projects as cheap labour. They were no longer counted as unemployed.

Ensuring self-sufficiency

It was the task of Herman Goering and the **Four-Year Plan** to make Germany self-sufficient in preparation for war. There were some successes:
- Scientists were able to use coal to make oil and artificial rubber; paper pulp to produce textiles; and flour to create cosmetics. Even a coffee substitute was manufactured from acorns.
- Germany was self-sufficient in bread, potatoes and sugar by 1939.
- Domestic production of iron, coal and steel increased dramatically.

HOWEVER, Germany was still far from self-sufficient:
- Food rationing became necessary even before 1939, by which time 15 per cent of the country's food was still being imported.
- Imports of raw materials such as iron ore led to an overall rise in imports from 4.5 million tonnes in 1933, to 21 million tonnes in 1938. Artificial rubber never made up more than 5 per cent of Germany's needs.

> **Key term**
>
> **Four-Year Plan:** intensive economic plan from 1936, led by Herman Goering, to make Germany self-sufficient and reduce unemployment. Propaganda campaigns urged people to buy only German goods and food. German farmers were paid subsidies to grow more food. Scientists were tasked with creating synthetic alternatives for materials that were in short supply.

Bringing the workers under Nazi control

The Nazis had banned trade unions in 1933, and these were replaced by the German Labour Front (DAF). The DAF included employers and employees and was established to ensure the efficient running of German industry. The DAF had many different functions which all added up to greater Nazi control over workers' employment and their leisure time. (See the table below.)

How the Nazis controlled working conditions	How the Nazis controlled leisure time
The organisation Beauty of Labour (SDA) encouraged employers to provide: - canteens serving hot meals - improved toilets and showers - improved ventilation - sport and leisure facilities. Workers' wages increased during the 1930s.	The Strength Through Joy (KDF) organisation aimed to create satisfied and therefore productive workers. They offered: - subsidised holidays, including cruises - cheap tickets for the theatre, sports events and concerts - subsidised train travel and discounted hotels.
HOWEVER Working hours also increased by around 10 per cent. With the increased cost of living, workers' wages were worth less in 1939 than in 1933. The costs of improvements to the workplace were often deducted from workers' wages.	**HOWEVER** By 1939, there was some disillusionment. All KDF activities included some propaganda content such as political lectures. The KDF created the Volkswagen scheme. Workers made weekly payments towards a car. However, the Second World War stopped production and no cars were ever delivered.

Revision tasks

TESTED

1 Here are some key terms, events and people. Imagine that these are answers and it is your job to come up with a suitable question for each one. Try to make each question as detailed as possible so that you are using specific knowledge to phrase it.
   - New Plan
   - 900,000
   - Volkswagen
   - National Labour Service
   - 21 million tonnes
   - Strength Through Joy
   - Four-Year plan
   - Acorns
   - DAF
   - 'hidden unemployed'

2 How successfully did the Nazis achieve each of their aims for the German economy? Explain your answer.

1.5 Germany and the occupied territories during the Second World War

REVISED

What you need to know

In this section you will revise the profound effect that the Second World War had on life in Germany and the occupied territories. This will include:
- The intensification in the persecution of the Jewish people which culminated in the Holocaust.
- The effects of the Second World War on the German home front.
- The growth of opposition to Hitler as the war progressed.

Nazi policies towards Jewish people, 1939–45

Hitler's conquest of Eastern Europe was part of his programme of obtaining *Lebensraum* (living space) for Germans. This involved removing or enslaving those who lived there already, including Jewish people. By the end of the Second World War, around 6 million Jewish people had been murdered.

Ghettos

When the German army occupied Poland, over 2 million Polish Jewish people came under Nazi control. The first ghettos, walled-off slum areas in cities where Jewish people were forced to live, were established in 1940. Conditions were awful:
- The Nazis withheld food, medicine and fuel. Starvation was common.
- Ghettos were massively overcrowded and lacked adequate water supply and sanitation. Diseases such as typhus spread rapidly.
- In the largest ghetto, in Warsaw, approximately 100,000 Jewish people died in two years.
- From 1941, the Nazis started sending German Jewish people to the ghettos.
- From July 1942, any Jewish people still in the ghettos were rounded up and sent to extermination camps.

Einsatzgruppen

Following the invasion of the Soviet Union in June 1941, 4 million additional Jewish people fell under Nazi control. The ghettos could not accommodate such numbers. Therefore, *Einsatzgruppen* (special task

forces) followed the German army into the occupied territories. Put simply, these task forces were death squads.
- In the summer of 1941, four *Einsatzgruppen* squads followed the German army into the Soviet Union. They were responsible for shooting thousands of Jewish men, women and children.
- Most often, local Jewish people would be rounded up and marched to large pits, where they were shot and buried. Approximately 1.3 million Soviet Jewish people were killed in this way.

Mass shootings required a lot of manpower, guns, ammunition and transport. Concerns arose over the high numbers of Jewish people in Nazi-occupied territory and the inefficiency of the shootings. Himmler was also concerned for the mental well-being of the men involved and started a search for another means of mass murder.

The Final Solution

At the Wannsee Conference in January 1942, when the Second World War was at its height, leading Nazis finalised their plans for a 'final solution to the Jewish problem'.
- Specially constructed extermination camps were built, mainly in Poland.
- Prisoners arrived by train from all over occupied Europe.
- Upon arrival, inmates were separated into those fit for work and those who would be killed straightaway. Older people, mothers with small children and children under ten were sent to gas chambers disguised as shower blocks and murdered.
- Those who could work suffered terrible conditions in the camp. Those who did not die from starvation and disease were gassed when they could no longer work.
- Bodies were disposed of in specially designed crematoria.

Revision tasks

1 What turning points can you identify in the Nazi treatment of Jewish people after 1939?
2 Explain why Nazi persecution of Jewish people intensified after 1939.

Exam practice

Explain **two** effects of the Second World War, 1939–45, on the Nazis' treatment of Jewish people. (8 marks)

Exam tip

You should not spend too much time on eight-mark questions. The most you should spend on a question is one and a half minutes per mark, so that equates to twelve minutes maximum. That gives you six minutes for each paragraph dealing with an effect.

The Home Front during the war

Initially, there had been enthusiastic support for the war. Hitler's early successes in western Europe created confidence among the German public. However, as the war dragged on, this enthusiasm waned.

Evacuation

Mass evacuation of children began in Germany in 1942, when Allied bombers started targeting civilian areas.
- About 2.5 million children were evacuated from cities to more rural areas.
- Evacuees were housed in special camps supervised by Hitler Youth (see page 31) leaders and teachers. These allowed the Nazis to extend their indoctrination of German children.

Rationing

Rationing began before the outbreak of war in 1939. At first, bread, dairy products and meat were rationed, along with soap. Civilians were issued with food stamps.

- In the first phases of the war, when the army was rapidly occupying other countries, some goods and supplies could be shipped back to Germany. There was a particular demand for tobacco and toilet paper.
- The longer the war dragged on, the more rationing hit ordinary Germans. In May 1942, the government cut rations per person to around half a loaf of bread a day and just 40 grams of meat.
- In the final months of the war, as the Soviet army advanced into Germany, refugees fled west into areas already suffering a food shortage. Starvation resulted.

'Total war'

Following defeats in the Soviet Union it became clear that Germany's resources were under great strain. In a speech in 1943, Goebbels made it clear that the German people were involved in 'total war'. Propaganda made it clear – more sacrifices would have to be made if Germany was to achieve the final victory:

- Places of entertainment including sports venues were closed. All non-essential businesses were closed down. Cinemas were kept open and continued to spout propaganda.
- The Nazis tried to mobilise more women into the war effort (see below).
- Shortages of essentials intensified. In 1943, clothing production ended. Germans used exchange centres where they could swap clothes instead.
- In August 1944, the working week was increased to 60 hours and holidays were banned.
- In October 1944, the Nazis set up the *Völkssturm* (Home Guard) to protect Germany from invasion. All males aged 16 to 60 and not already in military service had to join. By the end of the war, boys as young as twelve were forced to fight.

The effects of Allied bombing

In 1942, the British and Americans started targeting civilian areas in Germany for bombing raids. This was a clear attempt to destroy German morale.

- In 1943, 40,000 civilians were killed in Hamburg as half the city was destroyed. When Dresden was bombed in 1945, about 25,000 people were killed. Other cities were also bombed.
- Nazi propaganda emphasised the bravery of civilians in the face of Allied bombing. The government set up welfare organisations to provide food and shelter for those who had lost their homes.
- Bombing clearly had a negative impact on German morale. However, most people had no choice except to get on with their daily lives.

The changing role of women

The Nazis believed that the ideal German woman was a stay-at-home mother (see page 30). However, the demands of the war led to a change in Nazi policy.
- In 1941, women without children and with previous experience of employment were required to register for work.
- By 1943, 'total war' meant all women aged between 17 and 45 had to register for work.
- By the end of the war, women made up around 60 per cent of the German workforce.
- Some women worked as auxiliaries in the armed forces, operating searchlights and even anti-aircraft guns.

The war had a massive impact on German women. Years spent worrying about absent fathers, husbands and sons, along with bombing raids and food shortages, would have taken a toll. As the Soviet army advanced into Germany, tens of thousands of women were raped. Some even committed suicide to avoid such a fate.

Revision tasks
TESTED

1 Copy and complete the concept map below.

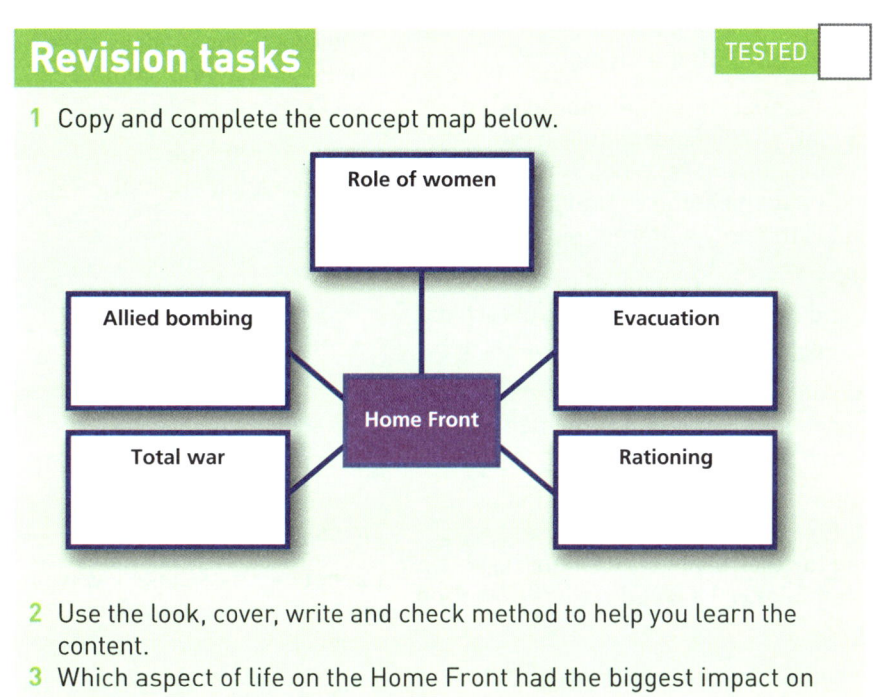

2 Use the look, cover, write and check method to help you learn the content.
3 Which aspect of life on the Home Front had the biggest impact on Germans? Explain your answer.

The growth of opposition to Hitler

During the 1930s, open opposition to the Nazi regime was almost impossible. All other political parties and the trade unions were banned in 1933; the Gestapo, SS and the threat of the concentration camp were an effective deterrent. However, as the military situation deteriorated, some Germans began to oppose the regime. Some posed more of a risk to the Nazis than others. (See the table on page 40.)

Opponents	Who they were and what they did	How they were dealt with
Swing Youth	Young people who rejected joining the Hitler Youth and being told what to think. More of a cultural movement than an organised group. Listened to American swing and jazz music, which the Nazis disapproved of as 'negro music'. Often grew their hair long and wore American fashions.	Dance halls were raided and closed down. Some youths were rounded up and given short sentences in concentration camps.
The White Rose Group, 1942–43	A small group of university students in Munich led by Hans Scholl, Sophie Scholl and Christoph Probst. Printed and distributed six leaflets criticising Hitler's leadership and the murder of civilians and Jewish people on the Eastern Front. Painted anti-Nazi slogans on walls.	Hans and Sophie Scholl were arrested and executed. They were given an unfair trial and found guilty of treason. Both were executed by guillotine.
The July Bomb Plotters, July 1944	A small group of army officers horrified by the violence of the SS in the occupied territories. They resented Hitler meddling in military strategy and blamed him for a series of defeats. The plan, Operation Valkyrie, was to kill Hitler, take control of Berlin and make peace with the Allies. On 20 July 1944, Colonel von Stauffenberg left a bomb (inside a leather briefcase) under a table at Hitler's military headquarters. When Hitler arrived, Stauffenberg left and the bomb exploded. Four people died, but Hitler only suffered minor injuries. The plotters were too slow and failed to take control of the phones and radio stations in Berlin. Word got out that Hitler had survived and the plot collapsed. The overwhelming majority of army officers remained supportive of Hitler and remained committed to their oath of loyalty (see page 26).	Around 5,000 people were executed in the weeks that followed, as a savage warning to others. The remaining leaders of the plot were hanged on meat hooks. There were no further assassination attempts.
The Edelweiss Pirates, 1937–44	A mainly working-class youth group originally founded in the Rhineland two years before the war started. Spread to other parts of Germany as war progressed. Members wore an Edelweiss flower on their clothing. Rejected Nazi culture and, like the Swing Youth, listened to forbidden foreign music. They hated the Hitler Youth which they saw as overly militaristic. The Pirates organised their own hikes and camping trips. Some Pirates beat up Hitler Youth members. Wrote anti-Nazi graffiti on walls and printed flyers critical of the regime. As the war progressed, their activities became more serious: • They hid army deserters and escapees from concentration camps. • They committed acts of sabotage, such as derailing trains carrying ammunition. • In 1944, a group of Pirates in Cologne planned to blow up a Gestapo building but were captured.	Some were arrested and sent to concentration camps. Saboteurs and those involved in the Cologne plan were publicly hanged.

Hitler's death and the end of Third Reich

By 1945, Germany faced total defeat.
- The Americans and British had advanced into Germany from the west, while the Soviet Red Army did the same from the east.
- The Allies had intensified their bombing of German cities, causing huge casualties and making thousands homeless.
- Millions of refugees, fearful of the brutality of the Red Army and the destruction of the bombing raids, were displaced. Up to 1 million German civilians perished from hunger, disease or the cold.
- The German army fought on to the bitter end, as did many in the *Volkssturm* (see page 38).

On 28 April, Adolf Hitler married his long-term girlfriend Eva Braun. Shelling could be heard and the Soviets were just a few shattered streets away. Two days later, the newly-weds swallowed cyanide capsules and shot themselves. Germany was in ruins and on 7 May 1945, finally surrendered to the Allies.

Revision tasks

TESTED

1 Rank the opponents of the Nazis on page 40 to show how serious a threat they posed to the Nazi regime. Explain your choices.
2 What reasons can you think of why so many Germans fought on until the bitter end?

2 A world divided: superpower relations, 1943–72

2.1 Reasons for the Cold War

REVISED

What you need to know

In this section you will revise the reasons why the **Cold War** started. This will include:
- Ideological differences between the Soviet Union and the USA: communism and capitalism.
- Tensions between the Soviet Union and its allies during the Second World War.
- The agreements made about post-war Europe in the wartime conferences.
- The way the Soviet Union took control in Eastern Europe.
- The clash between the post-war leaders of the USA and the Soviet Union: Truman and Stalin.

Long-term rivalry between the Soviet Union and the West

Leaders in the West were against the Soviet Union from its very beginning. This was because the Soviet Union completely rejected the West's capitalist **ideology** and wanted to encourage ordinary people in the West to overthrow **capitalism** and get rid of the rich.

Ideological differences between communism and capitalism

Communism and the Soviet Union

- The Soviet Union was formed soon after a revolution in the Russian Empire in 1917. The revolution was led by communists, who wanted the Soviet Union to develop into the world's first communist state.
- In a communist state there would be no private property or inequality: everyone would work for the benefit of everyone else. The rights of individuals would be seen as less important than the good of society as a whole.
- The first step to **communism** was for the state to take control of everything. Only one party was allowed: the Communist Party. This controlled the state.
- However, the Soviet Union needed other countries to become communist too: otherwise it did not have the **industrial base** it required. Consequently, the Soviet Union worked to encourage communist revolutions in other countries.

Capitalism and the USA

- The USA was built on the idea that every American had the chance to make a great life for themselves based on their own effort: the American Dream. The rights of individuals, and their individual freedoms, were the most important thing.
- Freedom was an essential core belief for the USA: this included the freedom to vote in democratic elections, freedom of speech and freedom of religion (to believe what you wanted).

Key terms

Cold War: a state of tension and conflict between the USA and its allies (the West) and the Soviet Union and its allies (the East).

Ideology: a system of ideas about how things should be run, and how people should behave.

Communism: there is no individual ownership. All production happens for the benefit of everyone rather than just a few. In order to try to achieve communism, the government of the Soviet Union took over all production and planned what every factory and farm should produce.

Capitalism: individuals own the businesses and property and aim to make as much profit as they can by selling their products in a competitive market. Customer demand determines what products businesses produce and how high prices can be.

Industrial base: all the industries in a country; very industrialised countries would have a very large and strong industrial base while countries that were developing would have a smaller, weaker industrial base.

- The USA was a capitalist state. This meant individuals owned businesses and worked to make them as profitable as possible because the bigger the profits, the richer they became. By doing this, these individuals created jobs for others.
- However, capitalism also created inequalities: poor people whose lives were not as good as rich people's. The USA was worried that its poor people would like the sound of communism, which took everything away from the rich and shared it among everyone.

Revision task

TESTED

Outline one way in which ideological differences caused tension between the USA and the Soviet Union.

Tensions and disagreements during the Second World War

- **Joseph Stalin** was the leader of the Soviet Union during the Second World War. In June 1941, after Hitler invaded the Soviet Union, Stalin joined the Allies in fighting against Nazi Germany: this put the USA and the Soviet Union on the same side.
- The Soviet Union suffered terribly from the German invasion. It is estimated that 27 million Soviet citizens were killed in the Great Patriotic War (the Soviet name for the Second World War). At the same time, over 4 million German soldiers were killed fighting on the Eastern **Front** against the Soviet Union. The Soviet Union eventually defeated the Germans in Berlin in May 1945.
- The Allied invasion of German-occupied France in 1944 meant Germany was now fighting on two fronts. But Stalin had been demanding this invasion go ahead since 1941. He was convinced the Allies wanted to see the Soviet Union weakened by fighting Germany. Stalin thought the Allies left the invasion of France for as long as they could in order to achieve this – possibly with the plan of attacking the Soviet Union as soon as it had defeated Germany.
- There were also tensions between the Allies over what should happen to Germany once it had been defeated. The Soviet Union wanted to make sure Germany could never be a threat to it again. The USA and Britain, in particular, did not want to see Germany destroyed.
- Churchill, the British leader, was suspicious about Stalin's plans for Eastern Europe after the war. As the Soviet Union's Red Army advanced on Germany, it took control in Eastern European countries such as Poland which had been occupied by the Germans. Churchill thought Stalin planned to keep hold of these countries after the war.

Key term

Front: in a war, a front is the place where armies are fighting against each other.

Joseph Stalin (1878–1953)

- Stalin was born in Georgia, then part of the Russian Empire.
- He became Soviet leader after the death of Lenin in 1924.
- He was a dictator who oversaw brutal policies that killed millions.
- Stalin made the Soviet Union an industrial superpower and a nuclear power.
- His wartime leadership began with near defeat, but ended in the Soviet Union defeating Nazi Germany.

Revision task

TESTED

Outline one way in which disagreements during the Second World War caused tension between the USA and the Soviet Union.

Key features of the conferences at Tehran, Yalta and Potsdam

The Tehran Conference

Stalin, Churchill and Roosevelt (the President of the USA) met at the Tehran **Conference**, Iran, in November 1943. They agreed that:
- The USA and Britain would invade France in May 1944, opening up a second front that would help the Soviet Union against Germany.
- The Soviet Union would join the USA in fighting Japan once Germany was defeated.
- A new organisation called the **United Nations (UN)** would be set up after the war to sort out disagreements between countries and help to prevent more wars.
- Part of eastern Poland would become a part of the Soviet Union after the war.

The Yalta Conference

Stalin, Roosevelt and Churchill met again in Yalta, in the Soviet Union, in February 1945. At this point, the war was nearly won – the Red Army was only 65 kilometres from Berlin. The Allies agreed that:
- Germany would be divided into four **occupied** zones after it was defeated: a Soviet zone, a US zone, a British zone and a French zone.
- In the same way, the German capital Berlin would be divided into four zones (Soviet, US, British, French) – even though the city was located in the Soviet zone of Germany.
- Countries that the Allies **liberated** from German occupation (for example, Poland) would choose the sort of government they wanted after the war had ended, in **free elections**.
- The Soviet Union agreed to join the USA to fight Japan once Germany was defeated. In return, the Soviet Union would get territory taken from Japan.

There was one main area of disagreement between the Allies at Yalta: Poland.
- Stalin said he wanted a strong Poland (to help protect the Soviet Union from any future attack by Germany), but the Soviet Union would not give up the eastern part of the country. Instead, he said Poland should be given some of Germany's territory to the west.
- The other Allies were not happy about this, but agreed because Stalin promised that Poland would have free elections after the war. Stalin also said the Soviet Union would not support communists trying to lead a revolution in Greece (see page 49, the Truman Doctrine).

The Potsdam Conference

This conference was held in the German city of Potsdam, in July 1945 – Germany had surrendered on 8 May 1945. Several important changes had occurred since Yalta:
- US President Roosevelt died in April 1945. The new president was **Harry Truman**. While Roosevelt and Stalin had had a good relationship, Truman did not trust the Soviet leader.
- During the Potsdam Conference, Winston Churchill lost a general election. The new British prime minister was Clement Attlee.

> **Key terms**
>
> **Conference**: a formal meeting in which ideas and opinions are discussed.
>
> **United Nations (UN)**: an international organisation that aims to keep world peace by sorting out disputes between countries, in a peaceful way if possible, but with military force as a last resort. It was founded in 1945, following the end of the Second World War.
>
> **Occupied**: when a country or area is taken over by the armed forces of another country.
>
> **Liberated**: set free.
>
> **Free elections**: democratic elections in which people are free to choose to vote for whichever candidate they want. An example of an election that was not free would be if there was only one political party to vote for, or if voters were intimidated or bribed into voting for a particular candidate.

- Nazi Germany had been defeated. The USA and Britain began bringing their troops home: for example, US troops in Europe decreased from 3 million in 1945, to 300,000 in 1946. The Soviet Union did not pull its troops out of Eastern European countries, however.
- During the conference, Truman told Stalin that the USA had a 'powerful new weapon': on 6 August 1945 (four days after the conference had finished), the USA dropped the first **atomic bomb** on the Japanese city of Hiroshima. On 9 August, a second atomic bomb was dropped on Nagasaki. Japan surrendered six days later. As many as 226,000 people were killed – half killed by the bomb, the rest dying from radiation and burns over the following months and years.

Agreements at the Potsdam Conference

- The Allies agreed where the new border would be between Poland and Germany. Stalin achieved his goal of gaining territory from eastern Poland, while in return Poland gained territory from Germany.
- They also agreed to ban the Nazi Party and to put its leaders on trial as war criminals.

Disagreements at the Potsdam Conference

- Stalin wanted very high **reparations** payments from Germany ($10 billion) to pay for all the damage done by Germany to the Soviet Union. The USA and Britain did not want to do this because setting high reparations in the First World War had been bad for international peace and for trade.
- Britain and the USA wanted reconstruction for Germany – to rebuild its economy, which would mean more trade and stronger capitalist economies. Stalin suspected his allies wanted to make Germany strong again so it could help them control or destroy the Soviet Union.
- Poland remained a divisive issue: the British had hosted the Polish non-communist government during the war and believed it should now be restored to power there. However, in 1947, Stalin put a communist government in charge of Poland.
- Stalin wanted a base for the Soviet navy in the Mediterranean. The USA and Britain refused to agree to this. Stalin saw this as more proof that his former allies were against the Soviet Union becoming more powerful.

> **Key terms**
>
> **Atomic bomb**: a nuclear weapon where atoms of plutonium or uranium are split apart, releasing enormous amounts of nuclear energy.
>
> **Reparations**: compensation payments.

> **Harry Truman, US President (1945–53)**
>
> - Truman was vice president to President Roosevelt, becoming president when Roosevelt died in 1945.
> - He was strongly opposed to communism. The Truman Doctrine (1947) declared that the USA would oppose communist aggression everywhere.
> - Truman supported the Marshall Plan (1947), which funded the recovery of Western Europe after the war ($13 billion in loans).
> - Truman was criticised when China also became a communist country in 1949. His critics said he had allowed communism to spread.
> - Truman was president during the Berlin Crisis (1948) and oversaw the formation of NATO (1949) and the USA's development of the hydrogen bomb.

The Soviet Union and Eastern Europe

Stalin wanted to protect the Soviet Union from any future attacks from Germany (and the West) by setting up governments in Eastern Europe that were friendly to the Soviet Union.

- In 1944, Churchill had agreed with Stalin that Eastern Europe would come into the Soviet Union's 'sphere of influence' after the war.
- This meant that the Soviet Union would have a close relationship with the countries of Eastern Europe and could expect the West not to try to build links with Eastern Europe that competed with the interests of the Soviet Union.
- At Yalta, however, it was agreed by Stalin, Churchill and Roosevelt that every country in Europe would be free to choose the government it wanted after the war.
- By the time of the Potsdam Conference, Truman was very suspicious about the Soviet Union's intentions in Eastern Europe. He did not think Stalin was going to allow free elections.
- Truman was proved right when, in 1947, Poland held its first election. Before the election, there was violent intimidation of non-communist political parties and the results of the election were changed to benefit communist and **socialist** parties. The Communist Party won with 80 per cent of the vote. After its election, the Polish communist government followed orders from the Soviet Union.

Revision task

Outline ways in which disagreements at the Tehran, Yalta and Potsdam conferences caused tension between the USA and the Soviet Union.

The attitudes of Truman and Stalin

- Truman believed that communism was evil, while Stalin believed capitalism was evil.
- Stalin was convinced the Allies had deliberately delayed the invasion of occupied France in order to hurt the Soviet Union. Truman believed the Soviet Union had helped to start the Second World War by agreeing a **pact** with Hitler in 1939.
- Truman declared that the Soviet Union should be treated with 'an iron fist' – this meant the USA should aim to win all arguments rather than agree compromises with the Soviet Union.
- Truman believed reports that the Soviet Union was planning to spread communism throughout the world by any means, including making the USA a communist state.
- Some advisors in the US government did not want to use atomic bombs on Japanese civilians. However, Truman was keen to use the bomb to end the war against Japan before the Soviet Union became involved. That would mean the USA had complete control over Japan after the war, without having to share any influence in this region with the Soviet Union.

Key terms

Socialist: a system in which industrial production is controlled by the state to achieve a fairer society, but people don't share everything – there is still private property, for example.

Pact: an agreement, often an agreement between two countries.

Revision tasks

1. Outline ways in which the attitudes of Truman and Stalin caused tension between the USA and the Soviet Union.
2. Through this section you have outlined ways in which the different factors in the diagram on page 47 caused tension between the USA and the Soviet Union. Which factor do you think was most important, and why?

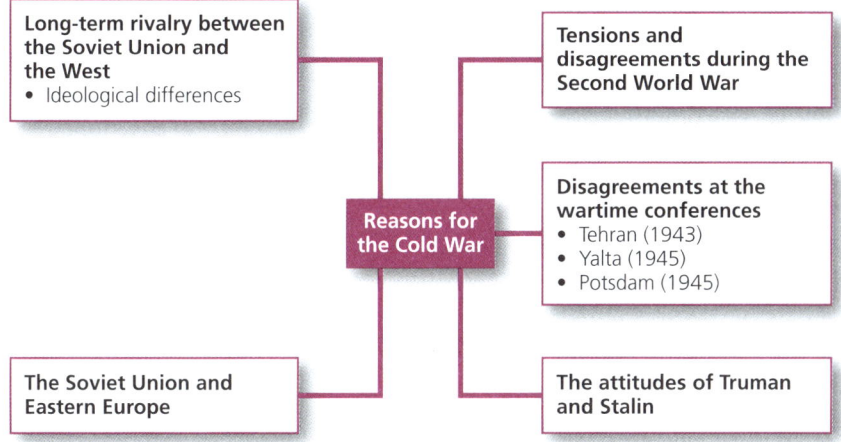

Exam tips

1. Start with a plan: what reasons were important for the development of tensions between the Allies during the Second World War? For example: ideological differences; differences over Germany, Poland, a second front, etc.
2. Start by giving your judgement on the question; for example: 'In my opinion, differences over the future of Germany were the main reason …'
3. As you discuss each of your three main points, include details to show your knowledge of the period; for example: 'Ideological differences were actually much less important during the war because the Allies needed the Soviet Union to help defeat Germany: 4 million German soldiers were killed fighting on the Eastern Front.'

Exam practice

'Ideological differences were the main reason for the development of tensions between the Allies during the Second World War.'

How far do you agree? Explain your answer.

You may use the following in your answer:
- communism
- the Potsdam Conference (1945).

You **must** also use information of your own. (16 marks)

2.2 Early developments in the Cold War, 1945–49

REVISED

What you need to know

In this section you will revise the start of the Cold War. This will include:
- How the Soviet Union expanded its control in Eastern Europe.
- Western responses to Soviet expansion, including the Marshall Plan and the Truman Doctrine.
- Organisations set up on either side of the Cold War: Cominform, Comecon and NATO.
- Tensions over divided Germany: the Berlin Crisis.
- The creation of two Germanys: Western-influenced FRG and Soviet-influenced GDR.

Soviet expansion in Eastern Europe

After the end of the Second World War, the Soviet Union kept tight control over its zone of Germany and Eastern European countries. Governments were taken over by communists trained by Moscow and countries took their orders from the Soviet Union.

Reasons for Soviet expansion

- The USA and its Western allies were convinced that the reason for Soviet expansion in Eastern Europe was that Stalin wanted to spread communism through the world, so Eastern Europe was just the start.

- Evidence for this was the 'Long **Telegram**'. This was sent by George Kennan who worked at the US Embassy in Moscow. Kennan warned that Stalin was determined to expand Soviet power.
- However, Stalin's reasons for expanding Soviet control were more about defending the Soviet Union from any attack by the West.
- In the First World War, Germany had attacked the Russian Empire. In the Second World War, Germany had invaded the Soviet Union. Attacks had usually come through Poland. Stalin's plan was to have a zone of Eastern European countries loyal to the Soviet Union between Germany and the Soviet Union, to help protect it from an attack from the West.
- The Allies had also agreed, towards the end of the Second World War, that Eastern European countries would be in the Soviet Union's 'sphere of influence' – that is, friendly towards the Soviet Union.

> **Key terms**
>
> **Telegram**: Telegraphs used an electric current to send messages over long distances. Messages sent by telegraphs were called telegrams.
>
> **Iron curtain**: a metaphor used to describe the division in Europe between Western-influenced countries and countries controlled by the Soviet Union.

Churchill and the 'iron curtain'

- The phrase '**iron curtain**' was used by the West to describe the way Soviet control came down over Eastern Europe after the end of the Second World War.
- The phrase was first used by Winston Churchill in a speech he made in 1946, while he was on a trip to the USA.
- Churchill described the area behind the 'iron curtain' as not only being influenced by the Soviet Union, but also being under Moscow's *control*.
- During the war, Churchill and Roosevelt had accepted that Eastern Europe would be in the Soviet Union's sphere of influence. But they were shocked when the Soviet Union went on to dominate these Eastern European countries; for example, by the way the Soviet Union controlled elections in Poland.

Revision task   TESTED

What do you think was the main reason for Soviet expansion in Eastern Europe? Explain your answer.

Exam practice

Study Extract A.

What impression does the author give about Western views of Soviet expansion in Eastern Europe?

You **must** use Extract A to explain your answer.   (6 marks)

> **Extract A**
>
> From 'Access to History Europe and the Cold War 1945-91', published in 2006.
>
> Roosevelt and Churchill privately accepted that Eastern Europe was a Soviet sphere of influence, with Western Europe as an Anglo-American sphere of interest from which Soviet influence was excluded. They hoped that Stalin would eventually tolerate democratic governments in Eastern Europe. They accepted that the USSR had special interests in Poland, but it was Stalin's ruthless defence of these interests that already, by the summer of 1945, had begun to alienate the West.
>
> www.wcmo.edu/about/history/iron-curtain-speech.html

> **Exam tips**
>
> 1 Be careful not to simply describe what the extract says. Your answer needs to consider the impression that the extract makes about the topic in the question.
>
> 2 Consider the language that the author of the extract uses. For example, the phrase 'iron curtain' suggests a hard, heavy barrier – a negative impression.
>
> 3 Consider what the extract does not mention about the topic, but which you do know about. For example, that, because of its history of conflict, Stalin had wanted a buffer between the Soviet Union and Germany.

The Truman Doctrine and the Marshall Plan

- The USA and its Western allies were worried that Soviet control would expand further into Europe.
- Many countries had been devastated by the war; their people had lost everything. Communism was an attractive ideology. The Soviet Union had become a world power by following communist ideology in which everyone was equal. Many people who had been left with nothing following the war found this equality appealing.
- The USA was therefore worried about Soviet influence spreading to countries such as Greece, Italy and France.

The Truman Doctrine

- A terrible **civil war** took place in Greece between 1946 and 1949. The country was divided between monarchists (supporters of the king) and communists, who wanted Greece to follow the Soviet Union.
- British troops stayed in Greece after the Second World War. They helped to keep the monarchists in power, but the government was very weak.
- In 1947, President Truman announced that the USA would help Greece to stay free of communism. The USA would not send military troops, but it would give $400 million direct to the Greek government, which it could use to fight the communists.
- In fact, Truman pledged that the USA would help *any country* where freedom was under threat from 'armed **minorities** or outside pressures'. This meant the USA would send money, equipment and **advisors** to stop the spread of communism.
- This policy aimed to contain the spread of communism – to stop it spreading any further. It did not aim to roll back the spread of communism. This was known as **containment**.
- The policy became known as the Truman **Doctrine**. In lots of ways the announcement of the Truman Doctrine is when the Cold War 'officially' started. The Truman Doctrine also led directly to the formation of NATO.

> **Key terms**
>
> **Civil war**: when people in a country fight a war against each other rather than against another country.
>
> **Minorities**: a smaller group of people who are different in some way from most of the population of a country.
>
> **Advisor**: an expert – in the Cold War these advisors were often military experts.
>
> **Containment**: stopping the spread of something.
>
> **Doctrine**: principles announced by a government about its policies.
>
> **Congress**: the parliament of the USA.

The Marshall Plan

- In 1948, the USA decided to give around $13 billion ($200 billion in today's money) to European countries to help them recover from the devastation caused by the Second World War.
- This was because Truman believed communism was much more attractive to people when they had nowhere to live, no job to go to, and not much to eat. The faster European countries could recover, the less attractive communism would seem.
- This $13 billion fund was officially called the European Recovery Program (ERP), but it became known as Marshall Aid or the Marshall Plan, after George Marshall, the American secretary of state in charge of the programme.
- In return for the Marshall Plan's aid, countries agreed to buy US products and allow US companies to invest in their industries – so the Marshall Plan made economic sense for the USA.
- A year before, the US **Congress** had refused to agree to the Marshall Plan – it was such a huge sum of money. But then, in 1948, communists took control of Czechoslovakia's government. This convinced Congress to support the Marshall Plan because of fears that communism was spreading.

- Stalin quickly decided that the Marshall Plan money could weaken Soviet control over Eastern Europe. He told governments there to refuse to accept it because, he said, the Marshall Plan was actually about the USA making countries dependent on it for money.
- Seventeen western European countries, including West Germany, took part in the Marshall Plan. Over the next four years, these countries received shares in the $13 billion fund. Countries joined together as the OEEC (Organisation for European Economic Cooperation) to organise how best to use the money for economic recovery. In time, West Germany was also allowed into the OEEC.

> **Revision task** TESTED
>
> Explain why Stalin did not want countries in Eastern Europe to take part in the Marshall Plan.

Cominform and Comecon

Cominform, 1947

- Cominform was an alliance of nine European communist parties that Stalin set up in 1947, at least partly in response to the Marshall Plan.
- Cominform existed to make sure that other European communist parties followed the approach set out by the Soviet Union, and by Stalin in particular.
- The communist parties in countries such as France and Italy were told to try to block the take up of the Marshall Plan in their countries. They failed to do this.
- Cominform ended in 1956, following new leadership in the Soviet Union after Stalin's death.

Comecon, 1949

- Comecon was an economic organisation that aimed to coordinate economic development between the Soviet Union and its Eastern European allies.
- At first it was mainly about setting up trade links between the six original members – the Soviet Union, Bulgaria, Czechoslovakia, Hungary, Poland and Romania.
- After Stalin's death, in 1953, Comecon began to encourage its Eastern European members to specialise in different types of production: so one country would produce oil, for example, that it would exchange with another for machinery.
- The aim of Comecon was, like Cominform, to prevent Eastern European countries from being attracted away from the Soviet sphere of influence by Western policies, like the Marshall Plan.
- However, differences between countries made Comecon very difficult to organise. In fact, all the Eastern European countries increased trade with Western countries more than with the Soviet Union through the Cold War.

Disagreements over Germany

- The Soviet Union wanted Germany to be as weak as possible after the war, so that it would not threaten the Soviet Union with invasion again.
- But the USA and its Western allies wanted Germany to recover. The USA wanted a Germany it could trade with. Also, Britain and France did not have the resources to keep feeding the German people. They needed Germany to be more **self-sufficient**.

> **Key term**
>
> **Self-sufficient**: when a society is able to meet its needs from its own resources, for example, when a country can grow enough food to feed its people.

- The Allies had agreed to divide Germany after the war into four zones of occupation. The different Soviet and western views about Germany meant the Soviet zones and western zones of Germany quickly became very different.
- The Soviets were supposed to supply the western, industrial parts of Germany with food from rural eastern Germany in return for machinery. The western zones started to send machinery in 1946, but the Soviet Union did not send food.
- In January 1947, the USA and Britain merged their two separate zones into one zone, known as Bizonia. The western Allies' aim was to make Bizonia self-sufficient. In August 1948, the French zone was added to Bizonia, too, to become Trizonia.

The Berlin Crisis (1948–49)

Causes of the Berlin Crisis

- Because Berlin was located in the Soviet zone of Germany, the decision to divide Berlin into four zones, or sectors, meant that the USA and its western allies occupied areas deep within the Soviet zone.
- The western Allies were allowed access to their sectors of Berlin by specific road, rail, canal and air routes.
- Berlin had its own city government. The western powers prevented the Soviet Union from installing a socialist city government in Berlin. This frustrated Stalin, who wanted Berlin's government to be under Soviet control.
- The formation of Bizonia (1947) increased tensions between the superpowers over Germany. The Soviet Union wanted to keep Germany divided and weak. Stalin believed that the USA wanted Germany to recover in order for it to help control the Soviet Union.
- The western zones of Germany received $1.4 billion from the Marshall Plan (1948). This helped the western zones of Germany, and the western sectors of Berlin, to recover quickly from the war. The Soviet Union did not want Germany to recover so its zones of occupation had much lower **standards of living**. But, at the same time, Stalin did not want a successful capitalist West Berlin showing up the low living standards of East Berlin.
- In 1948, the US and British zones of occupation were merged to form Bizonia. In June 1948, without telling the Soviet Union, Bizonia introduced a new **currency** to their zones – including West Berlin: the Deutschmark.
- The Soviets said this broke the Potsdam agreement over Germany because the Allies had agreed that they would not govern Germany in different ways. The Soviet Union liked Germany having its old, weak, **devalued** currency (the Reichsmark) because it prevented the country from recovering. The new Deutschmark threatened this – and, besides, the Soviet Union had been kept out of planning this new currency.
- In response, Soviet troops **blockaded** all rail, road and water routes used to reach the western sectors of Berlin.

> **Key terms**
>
> **Standards of living**: living standards measure how comfortable life is: how good the housing is, how much money people have to spend, what job opportunities there are, how healthy and educated people are, etc.
>
> **Currency**: the money system used in a country or area, for example, the Deutschmark.
>
> **Devalued**: not worth much; a devalued currency has lost its value compared to other currencies.
>
> **Blockade**: to block access to something.

Revision task [TESTED]

Explain how the Marshall Plan (1948) led to the Berlin Crisis (1948–49). You could draw your answer as a flow chart.

Events of the Berlin Crisis

- In March 1948, the Soviet Union pulled out of the Allied Control Council. This was the organisation set up by the Soviet Union, USA and Britain to run Germany. There had been friction between the Allies since 1946, but the creation of Bizonia and plans to introduce a new currency had crossed a line for the Soviet Union and it refused to return to the Council.
- When the western sectors of Berlin were included in Marshall Plan funding in April 1948, Soviet troops began to stop road and rail traffic coming into Bizonia so they could search it. These delays impacted on life in Bizonia, which was dependent on imports from western zones of Germany.
- On 18 June 1948, the western powers announced their plans to create a new West Germany and to introduce a new currency. In response, the Soviet Union announced, on 22 June that it would introduce a new currency of its own in Soviet-controlled areas: the Ostmark.
- On 24 June 1948, the Soviet leadership blocked all routes into western Berlin by road, rail and canal. Soviet food supplies to West Berlin were ended and electricity supplies were shut off. West Berlin only had enough food to last one month, and enough coal for a month and a half, so the situation was very serious.
- Stalin offered to drop the blockade if the West stopped the Deutschmark being used in Berlin. Instead, the USA and its allies organised the Berlin **airlift**.
- The Berlin airlift started on 26 June 1948 and lasted until 30 September 1949. It involved the USA, Britain and other allies bringing in supplies for West Berlin's population by air.
- The airlift was very challenging to organise. Every day, 4,000 tonnes of supplies needed to be flown in to meet the needs of West Berlin's population. At one point in the airlift campaign, one plane landed every 45 seconds at Berlin's Tempelhof airport. But the USA and its allies showed that they could keep the airlift going indefinitely. West Berlin was not going to starve.
- On 11 May 1949, the Soviet Union lifted the blockade of West Berlin. Stalin had failed to force the western allies out of Berlin.

> **Key terms**
>
> **Airlift**: to transport supplies into an area by aircraft – usually because other ways of getting into the area by land are not possible.
>
> **Democracy**: where everyone in a country (or almost everyone) gets to have a say in how the country is governed by voting in an election for someone to represent them.

Results of the Berlin Crisis

- The Berlin Crisis was the first major crisis of the Cold War. It greatly increased tensions between the Soviet Union and the USA. Truman saw it as a great victory in which the West had stood together against the Soviet Union's threats.
- Berlin became an important symbol of the Cold War. West Berlin symbolised freedom and **democracy**, deep in the heart of Soviet-controlled Eastern Europe.

NATO

- War between the USA and its allies and the Soviet Union seemed very likely during the Berlin Crisis. Berlin was surrounded by over 1 million Soviet troops: at any moment, Stalin could have ordered them to take over all of Berlin.
- On 4 April 1949, just before the Soviet Union ended the blockade, NATO – the North Atlantic Treaty Organization – was set up by the western Allies. It had twelve members to begin with, including the USA, Britain, France and Italy.

- NATO was a defensive military alliance. It did not aim to start any attack itself. Instead, any armed attack on one of the members of NATO was to be considered an attack on them all, and they would all come to the aid of the attacked country.
- The formation of NATO meant the USA was now committed to defending Western Europe from Soviet expansion. Any Soviet move to take control of a NATO member, for example, Norway, would mean war with the USA.
- The Soviet leadership did not agree that NATO was defensive: Stalin saw it as an 'aggressive alliance'. When West Germany was allowed to join (in 1955), this increased Soviet fears about NATO – the idea of arming Germans again was very alarming for the Soviet Union.
- NATO increased Cold War tensions. In response to NATO, the Soviet Union set up the Warsaw Pact in 1955 (see page 55).

West Germany and East Germany

- In May 1949, two weeks after the end of the Berlin Crisis, the state of West Germany was created out of the occupied zones of the Western allies: the Federal Republic of Germany (FRG).
- Soon after, in October 1949, the Soviets responded by overseeing the creation of the state of East Germany out of their occupation zone: the German Democratic Republic (GDR).
- The USA refused to recognise the GDR as a state and declared that they would support the FDR in its aim of reunifying all Germany as a free and democratic state.

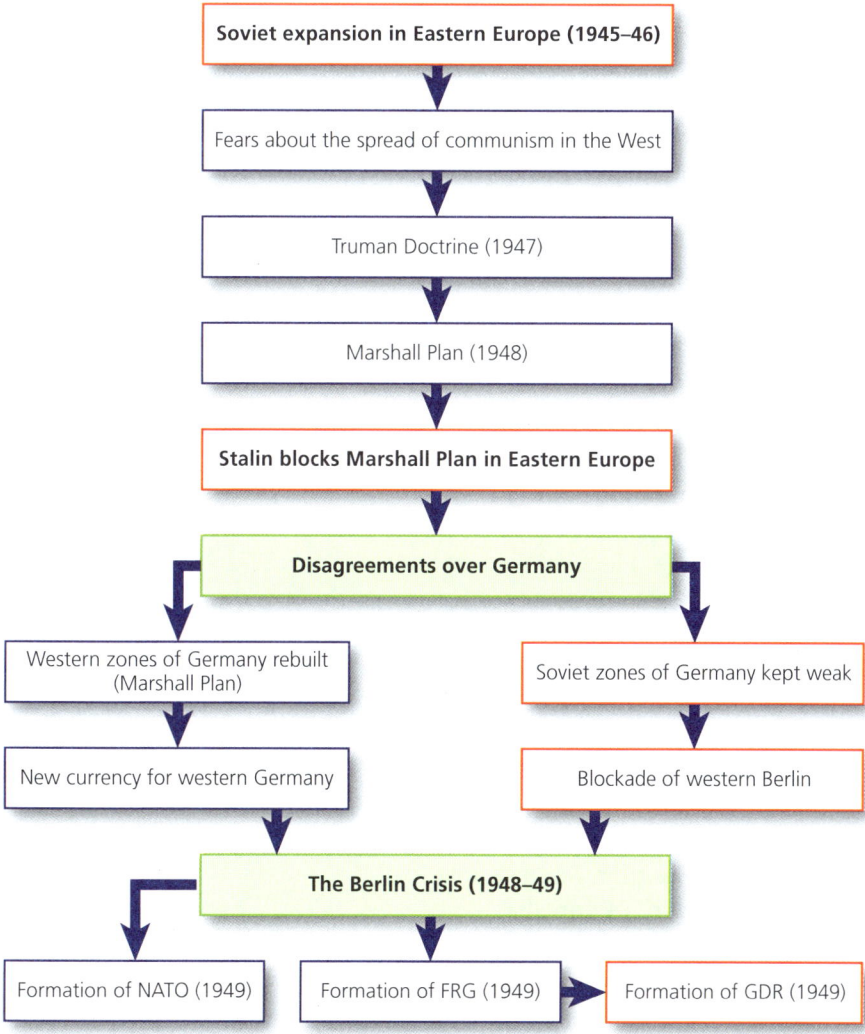

Early developments in the Cold War, 1945–49

2.3 The Cold War in the 1950s

REVISED

What you need to know

In this section you will revise the events of the Cold War in the 1950s. This will include:
- The impact of the Korean War on Cold War tensions.
- Changes to Soviet attitudes towards the West under Khrushchev's leadership.
- The Hungarian Revolution of 1956 and the Soviet invasion of Hungary.
- The nuclear arms race and its impact on relations between the superpowers.

The impact of the Korean War and the formation of the Warsaw Pact

The Korean War (1950–53)

How did the Korean War start?

- In the Second World War, the USA had **liberated** the south of Korea from the Japanese. The USSR had liberated the north of Korea. The leader in the North, Kim Il-Sung, followed Stalin's orders.
- In 1950, Stalin agreed to Kim Il-Sung's plan to invade South Korea and unite the country under his rule. There were three main reasons why Stalin agreed:
  1. The Soviet Union now had atomic weapons: this meant the USA no longer had an overwhelming advantage over the Soviet Union.
  2. China was now communist and could help North Korea's invasion.
  3. The USA had pulled most of its troops out of South Korea.
- However, Stalin would not send Soviet troops to Korea in case this caused a war between the USA and the Soviet Union.
- On 25 June 1950, the North attacked. The South Korean forces retreated. Within weeks, the North had almost complete control of Korea.

The USA's response

- At the time the Korean War began, in 1950, the USA was deeply concerned about the spread of communism. In 1950, a US senator called McCarthy began a campaign against communists in the USA, whom he blamed for weakening the country.
- China had become a communist country in 1949. The USA had spent millions of dollars supporting the Nationalists – the opposition to the Chinese Communist Party. The USA blamed the Soviet Union for helping the communists win in China. President Truman was determined not to let communism spread to South Korea as well.
- President Truman ordered the US navy and army to organise troops and supplies to be sent to aid South Korea.
- Truman also pressured the United Nations to take military action against North Korea. The UN agreed that North Korea had broken world peace and ordered it to withdraw its troops from South Korea.
- When North Korea did not obey, the **UN's Security Council** agreed to send troops to Korea. Sixteen UN countries were involved, but the USA provided 50 per cent of the UN troops and 90 per cent of the naval and air forces.

> **Key terms**
>
> **Liberated**: set free from control by something or someone.
>
> **UN Security Council**: the part of the UN that can authorise military actions.

Key features of the war

- In September 1950, UN forces launched attacks on the North Korean army and forced it back to North Korea. South Korea was free again. However, the UN forces continued to advance into North Korea. This was partly because Truman wanted to defeat communism in the North and see the whole of Korea become an ally of the USA.
- Truman's military chiefs were very confident that neither the Soviet Union nor China would stop the UN's invasion of North Korea. However, on 20 October 1950, when UN forces approached the border between North Korea and China, 300,000 Chinese soldiers attacked them and drove them back to South Korea. This was a disaster for the USA because many US soldiers were killed. A communist army had defeated the USA.
- The Korean War continued with fighting along the border between North Korea and South Korea. In March 1953, Stalin died. The North Koreans and Chinese could not be sure if a new Soviet leader would keep supporting the war. They agreed to a **ceasefire** agreement with the UN on 27 July 1953.

Impact of the Korean War

- For the Soviet Union, the Korean War was a failure. South Korea did not become communist. Stalin had not expected the USA to fight to save South Korea, so the strong US response was bad news – it meant the USA was not bluffing in its determination to stop communism spreading.
- For the USA, some Americans felt Truman had failed in Korea: when Chinese troops attacked in the North, he should have used the USA's full military force, including nuclear weapons, to defeat them and roll back communism in Asia.
- For others, the Korean War showed that the USA and Soviet Union could fight each other by supporting opposing sides in another country's civil war. This is called a **proxy war**. Proxy war had the advantage of avoiding direct military conflict between the superpowers, which could lead to a nuclear conflict. The Korean War set a pattern for more Cold War proxy conflicts, such as the Vietnam War (1955–75).
- After the Korean War, the USA encouraged the formation of other organisations similar to NATO in different global regions, which also aimed to stop communism spreading: for example, SEATO (South East Asia Treaty Organization, 1954), CENTO (an organisation of Middle Eastern countries) and ANZUS (Australia and New Zealand).
- The Korean War also showed how the United Nations could take action to stop one country from invading another. The United Nations could be used to intervene to stop or reduce conflict between the superpowers.

The formation of the Warsaw Pact

- In 1955, six years after NATO was created (see pages 52–53), the Soviet Union set up its own military alliance – the Warsaw Pact.
- As well as the Soviet Union, the Pact included Albania (which withdrew in 1968), Bulgaria, Czechoslovakia, East Germany, Hungary, Poland and Romania.
- The Warsaw Pact was a mutual defence organisation – like NATO. It also meant that Soviet troops were stationed in all the Warsaw Pact countries, and set up a single military command for the armed forces of all the member countries (led by the Soviet Union).
- The main reason for the Warsaw Pact was West Germany becoming a member of NATO (1955). The Soviet Union also felt surrounded and threatened by the new anti-communism organisations set up after the Korean War (for example, SEATO). The Warsaw Pact was its response.

Key terms

Ceasefire: an agreement between two sides in a war that fighting should stop.

Proxy war: when two countries which are enemies both support different sides in a war rather than fighting directly against each other.

> **Revision task** TESTED
>
> What were the three most important effects of the Korean War on relations between the superpowers? Explain your choices.

Khrushchev and peaceful co-existence

Stalin died in 1953. By 1955, a new leader, **Nikita Khrushchev**, was fully in control of the Soviet Union. He rejected Stalin's methods ('**de-Stalinisation**') and indicated that he wanted to reduce Cold War tension. Instead, he argued for 'peaceful **co-existence**' with the West. This meant encouraging good trade and diplomatic relations between the Soviet Union and capitalist countries.

- One reason for 'peaceful co-existence' was that the Soviet Union was spending huge amounts on its military. Khrushchev wanted to spend less on the military and invest more on improving living conditions for the Soviet people, but this meant reducing the threat of war with the West and improving trade with western countries.
- However, leaders in the West were not convinced by 'peaceful co-existence'. After all, Khrushchev was still completely committed to communist ideology, which saw the destruction of capitalism as a necessary first step to the development of communism in every country.
- Also, the Soviet Union responded with force in Eastern Europe when people there protested against Soviet rule, as happened in Hungary in 1956.

> **Revision task** TESTED
>
> Identify two reasons why Khrushchev wanted 'peaceful co-existence' with the West.

The impact of Soviet rule on Hungary

Hungary had been an ally of Germany in the Second World War, which meant that once the Soviet Union took control of Hungary, it treated the country very harshly.

- Even though Hungary was devastated by the war, the Soviet Union insisted on $200 million in reparations from Hungary.
- It also held 1 million Hungarians as prisoners of war for many years after the war.
- The Soviet Union also required Hungary to **collectivise** its farming in 1948, which produced a widespread famine.
- Despite another political party, the Smallholders' Party, winning 57 per cent of the vote in elections in 1945, the Soviet Marshal in charge of the Soviet occupation of Hungary refused to let them become the government. Instead, a **coalition** government was set up, including the Communist Party which had won only 17 per cent of the vote.
- This all meant that the Communist Party was not popular in Hungary, and neither was the Soviet Union.

Nikita Khrushchev (1894–1971)

- Khrushchev was leader of the Soviet Union from 1958 to 1964.
- He joined the Bolshevik Party in 1918.
- He became a close colleague (henchman) of Joseph Stalin.
- As Soviet leader, Khrushchev led criticism of Stalin's crimes (without implicating himself), tried to reduce tensions with the West and attempted to improve the Soviet Union's agricultural productivity.
- He was forced out of power for a number of failures: the Cuban Missile Crisis, the break between China and the Soviet Union and declining agricultural productivity.

Key terms

De-Stalinisation: Khrushchev's policy of criticising the crimes and mistakes of Stalin. It caused problems for the Soviet Union in Eastern Europe: if Stalin had been wrong then what gave the Soviet Union the right now to tell all other communist parties how to run their countries?

Co-existence: when two different or opposing groups put up with each other rather than fighting.

Collectivise: Stalinist collectivisation involved forcing individual farms to join together into much larger collective farms, on which everyone worked for the benefit of the state rather than only for themselves and their families.

Coalition: an alliance of different political parties to form a government.

Rákosi

- The Soviet Union chose Mátyás Rákosi to lead the Hungarian Communist Party after the Red Army occupied Hungary in 1945.
- Rákosi followed Stalin in everything: he said he was 'Stalin's best pupil'.
- Rákosi made the Communist Party the only political party in Hungary. Like Stalin, he ordered the arrest of anyone likely to be against the Communist Party.
- A **secret police** force called the AVH was set up: its brutality meant it was detested and feared by Hungarians. There were also Soviet troops stationed in Hungary.
- By 1956, 350,000 Hungarians had been put in prison and over 2,000 had been executed.

De-Stalinisation

- When Stalin died in 1953, the new Soviet leadership launched a policy of 'de-Stalinisation', which meant removing all the negative aspects of Stalinism from Soviet politics, economics and society.
- For example, Stalin was accused of a 'cult of personality'. This meant using propaganda to create an image of the leader as almost like a god. For example, whatever Stalin said was what everyone else immediately agreed with.
- Stalin also imposed totalitarian control (total control over every aspect of life) and used his secret police force to arrest anyone suspected of any kind of criticism or opposition to his leadership – even joke telling.
- In 1956, Khrushchev gave a 'Secret Speech' to the Twentieth Congress (meeting) of the CPSU (the Communist Party of the Soviet Union). It became known as the 'Secret Speech' because it was delivered at an unpublicised, closed session of delegates, with guests and members of the press excluded. This speech strongly criticised Stalin – although he did not mention Stalin's greatest crimes, which Khrushchev had helped carry out.
- The Secret Speech was designed to clear the way for political, economic and social reforms. One of the first and biggest reforms was the release of millions of political prisoners, arrested under Stalin and sent to *gulags* – forced labour camps. The KGB, the Soviet secret police, was also no longer able to sentence criminals without a court, or torture people to make them confess.
- In the Soviet Union and across Eastern Europe, Khrushchev's 'Secret Speech' led to a relaxation of the strict controls on people's lives. This was called the 'Thaw'. Across the Soviet Union and Eastern Europe, people (especially young people) took advantage of the new sense of freedom to enjoy new music, films, books and fashions. Conservatives were worried that this freedom was quickly getting out of control.

Nagy and his demands

- After Stalin's death, the Soviet leadership was worried that Rákosi's brutal leadership would cause unrest in Hungary. In 1953, Imre Nagy was installed as leader instead. Nagy was a Communist Party member who had introduced popular farming reforms.
- Nagy's attempts at introducing reforms to Hungary were wrecked by Rákosi. Rákosi was able to convince the Soviet leadership to make another conservative, Gero, Hungary's leader instead.
- Then came Khrushchev's 'Secret Speech', in February 1956. Rákosi was sent to Moscow and Nagy was again made leader.

> **Key term**
>
> **Secret police**: police who do not wear a uniform so they can spy on people and discover if they are acting against the state. Dictatorships rely heavily on secret police forces.

- The relaxation of Soviet control triggered changes across Eastern Europe. In Hungary, the 'Thaw' meant more **freedom of speech**. There was criticism of Rákosi's crimes. Victims of his purges were reburied in public ceremonies in October 1956.
- Following the reburials, students began demonstrating in Hungary's capital city, Budapest.
- On 22 October, students read out a list of sixteen demands on national radio. These included free elections, free speech, the return of prisoners of war from the Soviet Union, trials of all those involved in Rákosi's purges, trade links with the West and that Soviet troops should immediately leave Hungary.
- A giant statue of Stalin was pulled down – point thirteen of the sixteen points. Protestors fought with Soviet troops stationed in Hungary. Members of Hungary's secret police, the AVH, were lynched (hanged) in the streets. The Hungarian Revolution of 1956 had begun.
- Nagy was told to sign a request for help from the Soviet Union to put down the unrest. He refused to do this. Instead, he came out as a supporter of the students' demands.
- Nagy announced on radio that he was going to discuss with the Soviet Union:
  - the removal of all Soviet troops from Hungary
  - the introduction of **multi-party democracy** in Hungary
  - Hungary withdrawing from the Warsaw Pact.
- On 3 November, Nagy announced that a coalition government would be formed.

> **Key terms**
>
> **Freedom of speech**: the right to say or write what you think, without fear of being arrested for it.
>
> **Multi-party democracy**: where people have a choice of different political parties to vote for in elections

Revision task

TESTED

Explain one way in which Khrushchev's 'Secret Speech' might have influenced Nagy's demands.

Reasons for the Soviet invasion of Hungary

On 31 October 1956, the Soviet leadership decided to use massive force to crush the Hungarian Revolution.

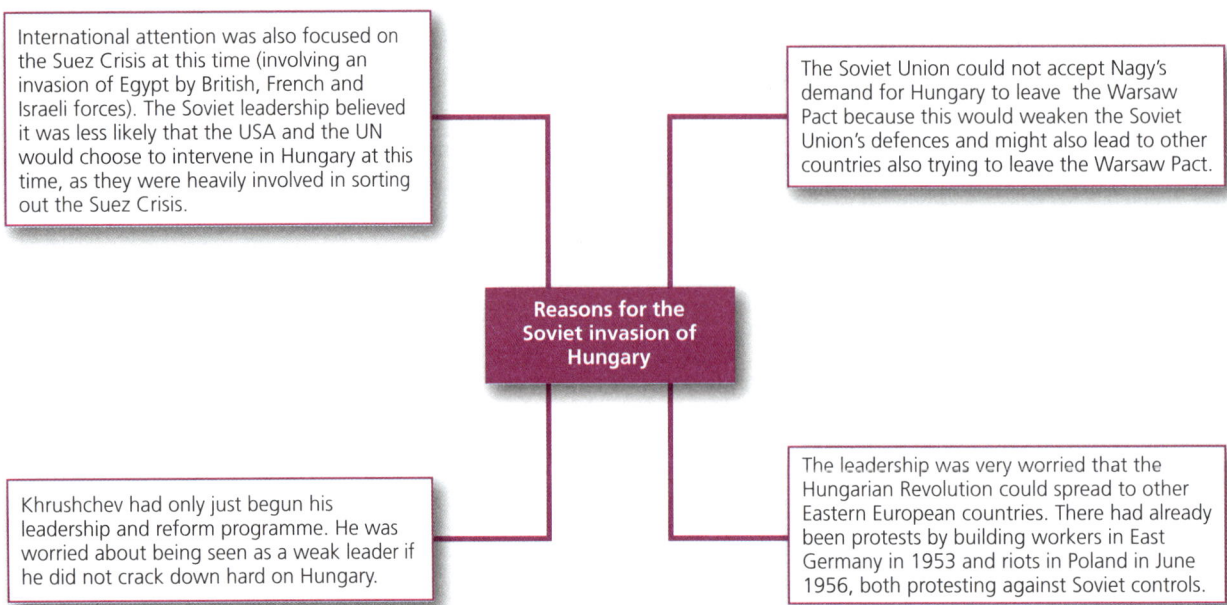

- International attention was also focused on the Suez Crisis at this time (involving an invasion of Egypt by British, French and Israeli forces). The Soviet leadership believed it was less likely that the USA and the UN would choose to intervene in Hungary at this time, as they were heavily involved in sorting out the Suez Crisis.
- The Soviet Union could not accept Nagy's demand for Hungary to leave the Warsaw Pact because this would weaken the Soviet Union's defences and might also lead to other countries also trying to leave the Warsaw Pact.
- Khrushchev had only just begun his leadership and reform programme. He was worried about being seen as a weak leader if he did not crack down hard on Hungary.
- The leadership was very worried that the Hungarian Revolution could spread to other Eastern European countries. There had already been protests by building workers in East Germany in 1953 and riots in Poland in June 1956, both protesting against Soviet controls.

Effects of the invasion

- On 4 November, 200,000 Soviet troops and 6,000 tanks entered Hungary. They quickly took control of the country's communications.
- Hungarians fought against the Soviet troops, even though they had little chance against the tanks and heavily armed soldiers: 2,500 Hungarians were killed and 20,000 were wounded; 200,000 Hungarians fled the country.
- On 10 November, a ceasefire was agreed and fighting stopped. Communist Party control was re-established under a new leader, Kádár, who was loyal to the Soviet Union. Around 100,000 people were arrested for taking part in the Revolution, 26,000 were put in prison and more than 300 people were executed, including Nagy.

International reactions to the invasion

- International reaction from the West was very critical of the Soviet invasion. There were demonstrations in the USA and UK against the invasion, and millions of dollars in donations were made to an appeal to help Hungarian refugees. Many communists in Western countries ended their support for the Soviet Union.
- The United Nations set up a special enquiry into the Revolution and invasion, but both the Soviet Union and Hungary's new government refused to take part.
- Hungarians had counted on the USA and its allies to help it fight against the Soviet occupation. US President Eisenhower had previously talked about 'rolling back' communism and many Hungarians thought that Radio Free Europe (a radio station funded by the USA) had promised that Western powers would intervene to stop the Soviet invasion.
- However, unlike in Korea, this time the USA and its allies did not take any action to stop the invasion. The UN's enquiry was very critical of the Soviet Union and Hungary's new government, but it also took no action.
- The Suez Crisis was one reason why nothing was done by the West. Britain and France had invaded another country (Egypt), telling lies to try to cover up their actions. This made it very difficult for the USA to act against one invasion but not the other.
- The main reason for inaction was that the USA was worried that taking military action against the invasion might start a nuclear war with the Soviet Union.

> **Revision task** TESTED
>
> List the reasons for the Soviet invasion of Hungary in 1956. Which of your reasons do you think was most important? Explain why.

The nuclear arms race and its impact on superpower relations

The nuclear arms race was a period during which both Soviet and US governments tried to get a military advantage over the other by spending vast amounts of money developing more and better weapons.

The nuclear arms race: from 1945 to the 1970s

- The USA was the first to develop nuclear weapons. It exploded two atomic bombs on Japanese cities in 1945, winning the war against Japan.
- Stalin immediately put teams of scientists and spies to work to develop a Soviet atomic bomb. This was achieved in 1949.

- US scientists began developing a much more powerful nuclear weapon, the hydrogen bomb. This was successfully tested in 1952.
- The Soviet Union followed with its own hydrogen bomb in 1953.
- The next development was **intercontinental ballistic missiles (ICBMs)**. Instead of bombs dropped from aircraft, these rockets could be launched from one continent and fly to targets on another continent. Such missiles carried nuclear **warheads**. Both sides invested massively in rocket technology – much of it developed using the expertise of former Nazi scientists.
- In 1957, the Soviet Union was the first to successfully test an intercontinental ballistic missile: the SS-6. This was also the year when the Soviet Union launched the first man-made **satellite**, Sputnik.
- The USA was shocked by the Soviet successes and piled investment into their own ICBM programme to bring out ICBMs in 1958: the budget for missile development increased by 20 per cent.
- Both these first ICBMs were actually shorter in range than true ICBMs and needed to be stationed closer to their targets: in Britain for the US's Thor and Jupiter missiles, and in the north of Russia for the SS-6s. They also took about an hour to fuel, meaning launching these ICBMs was not immediate.
- Both sides then began developing quicker launching ICBMs, with longer ranges. By the 1960s, the USA had the Minuteman I ICBM, and the Soviets the SS-13. Both these had solid fuel systems – very much quicker to launch – and ranges of over 8,000 kilometres. At the same time, both sides developed SLBMs: submarine-launched ballistic missiles. The Soviets were, again, the first to launch an SLBM: the SS-N-4 in 1958.
- The USA then intensified development of their Polaris SLBM, which launched in 1960. This had a much longer range than the Soviet SLBM.
- The late 1960s and 1970s arms race focused on multiple **thermonuclear** warheads: one missile containing multiple mini-hydrogen warheads that could then either spread out to hit multiple targets or hit the same target multiple times. Again, this technology was first successfully developed by the Soviet Union (SS-9) in 1967.
- The USA took this concept further with guided multiple warheads, so each warhead could be independently targeted to hit different targets accurately. These were called MIRVs: multiple independently targetable re-entry vehicles. The US's Minuteman III (1970) was the first. (The USSR's first MIRV was not until 1978.)

> **Key terms**
>
> **Intercontinental ballistic missiles (ICBMs):** guided missiles with a minimum range of 5,500 kilometres, meaning they can be launched in one continent and guided to hit a target in another continent.
>
> **Warhead:** the part of a missile that explodes.
>
> **Satellite:** something placed in orbit around the Earth for communications or to gather information from space.
>
> **Thermonuclear:** using high-temperature nuclear fusion (the hydrogen bomb) to create a nuclear reaction rather than nuclear fission (the atomic bomb).

Revision task TESTED

Use the information in this section to create an arms race timeline.

The impact of the arms race on superpower relations

- The arms race demanded huge levels of investment. This was a drain on the budgets of both countries. It reduced the amount that could be spent on other priorities, such as improving living standards.
- Both sides wanted to achieve a technological breakthrough that would give their side a devastating military advantage, such as the USA had enjoyed in 1945–9 as the world's only nuclear power. But neither achieved this: as soon as one development was achieved, the other side would very quickly catch up.

- Both sides used extensive spying networks to find out what the other was working on. For the USA this was achieved with spy planes, such as the U-2, which flew too high to be shot down by Soviet missiles (until the 1960s). The Soviets used human spies. Both types of spying caused conflict when the spies were caught.
- The sides were fairly evenly matched after 1949. By the 1960s and 1970s, the USA had more 'nukes' but the Soviets' 'nukes' were more destructive. Whichever side launched their missiles first didn't really matter: the response from the other side would mean both the USA and the Soviet Union would be devastated by multiple nuclear strikes.
- This was known as MAD – mutually assured destruction. MAD meant that the Cold War never went 'hot': the risks were far too high. However, there was always the chance that a nuclear war could start because of a mistake, an accident or a misunderstanding. This risk actually meant communications between the superpowers had to improve after one of the three major crises of the Cold War: the Cuban Missile Crisis (see pages 63–66).

Exam practice

'The main reason for worsening relations between the USA and the Soviet Union in the 1950s was the Soviet invasion of Hungary in 1956.'

How far do you agree? Explain your answer.

You may use the following in your answer:
- the Soviet Invasion of Hungary in 1956
- the Warsaw Pact.

You **must** also use information of your own. (16 marks)

Exam tip

- Sixteen-mark questions also include two bulleted 'stimulus points'.
- These stimulus points are there to help get you started: one can be used to support the statement in the question ('The main reason ...') and the other one can be used to challenge the statement.
- To achieve your best answer, go further than these two points and include one of your own. You don't need to use both or either of the stimulus points if you have relevant points of your own to use instead – but do aim to make three points in total.

2.4 Three crises: Berlin, Cuba and Czechoslovakia

REVISED

What you need to know

In this section you will revise the three crises of the Cold War. This will include the causes, key events and outcomes of:
- The Berlin Crisis of 1961.
- The Cuban Missile Crisis of 1962.
- The Soviet invasion of Czechoslovakia in 1968.

The Berlin Crisis, 1961

There are two Berlin crises to revise in your course: the first Berlin Crisis of 1948–49 (Berlin airlift), and the second Berlin Crisis of 1961. This is the second!

- Tensions between the superpowers over Berlin were building up throughout the 1950s: in 1955, West Germany joined NATO and West Berlin became a showcase for the capitalist redevelopment of Germany.
- In contrast, living conditions in East Germany were poor and there was little personal freedom. Large numbers of East Germans left their state for West Germany through Berlin – 4 million people between 1949 and 1961.
- Berlin was also a problem for East Germany and the Soviets because large numbers of western spies operated there, getting information from East Germans.

- In 1958, Khrushchev told the Western allies to leave West Berlin in six months so that the whole city could become a neutral city – the Berlin **Ultimatum**. President Eisenhower was not against this idea. He was interested in the United Nations taking control of Berlin.

> **Key terms**
>
> **Ultimatum**: a final demand which will have consequences if it is not met.
>
> **Nuclear disarmament**: a process of reducing the number of nuclear weapons or getting rid of nuclear weapons completely.

The Paris Summit Conference, 1960

- Khrushchev and Eisenhower planned to meet at the Paris Summit on 14 May 1960 – Berlin would certainly have been discussed, as well as talks about **nuclear disarmament**.
- However, on 1 May, just before the summit began, an American U-2 spy plane was shot down by the Soviets over the city of Sverdlovsk. The American pilot, Gary Powers, was captured.
- The Soviets had known about the spy flights before, but had not been able to shoot them down until the development of a new, long-range, surface-to-air missile.
- At first, Eisenhower said it was not a spy plane but a weather plane, then he was forced to admit publicly that the USA had been spying on the Soviet Union with spy planes for several years. This increased tensions further.
- As a result, Khrushchev declared the Soviet Union would not take part in the Paris Summit.

Reasons for the construction of the Berlin Wall in 1961

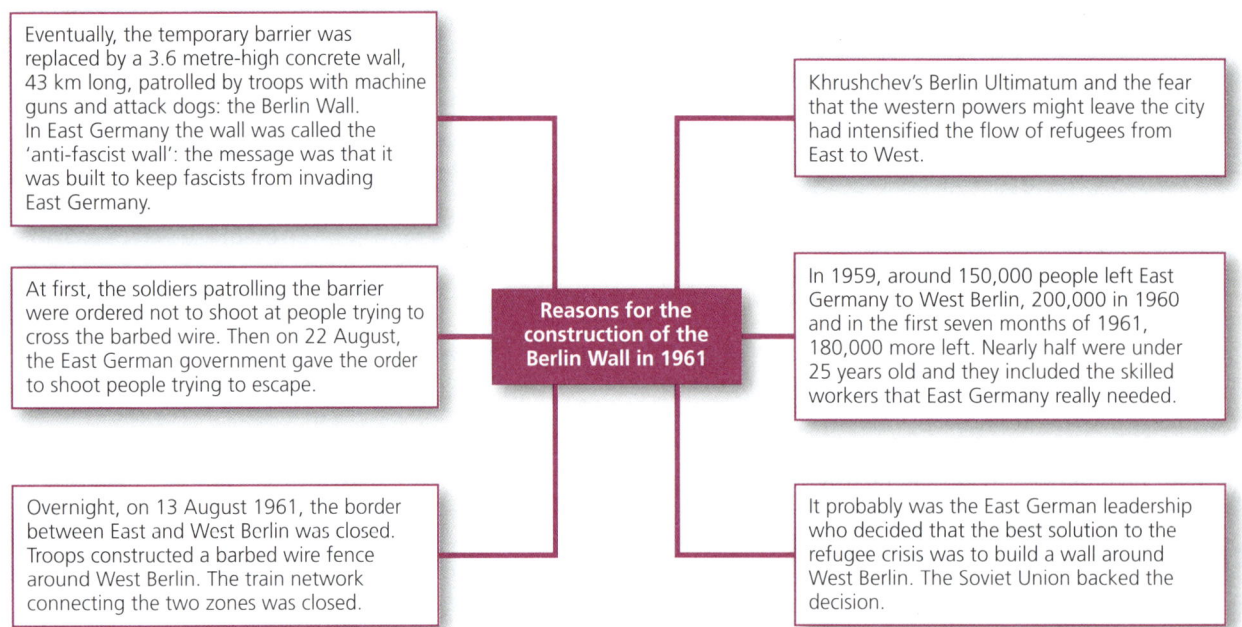

The effects of the Berlin Wall

Effects on relations between East and West Germany

- The construction of the wall caused serious problems for Berliners. East Berliners with jobs in West Berlin lost their jobs. Families with relations in both parts of the city were split apart. For many it was not possible to meet again.
- West Germany felt let down by the USA. The Soviet Union had broken the 1949 agreement over Berlin, and yet the USA took no action against the wall.

- East Germans did not believe that the wall was to keep **fascists** out of East Berlin – if that was true, why were the machine guns in the lookout towers pointing *towards* East Berlin rather than outwards at the 'fascists'? There were thousands of escape attempts.

Effects on relations between the superpowers

- The building of the wall immediately intensified tensions between the USA and Soviet Union.
- Soviet troops were used to guard checkpoints along the wall. The USA objected to this. American troops and tanks were brought in to guard the western side of the checkpoints. In response, the Soviets brought tanks up to their side of the checkpoint. For eighteen hours both sides waited to see what the other would do – war could easily have started at this crisis point.
- However, the new US President, **John F. Kennedy**, helped reduce the tensions by agreeing with Khrushchev that the USA would remove its troops from the checkpoints if the Soviet Union did the same with their troops.
- Although Kennedy chose peaceful means to reduce tensions over Berlin, he did also order that **nuclear testing** should start again in 1962.

> **Key terms**
>
> **Fascists**: people following far-right ideologies that see race and nation as more important than individuals.
>
> **Nuclear testing**: testing new nuclear weapons by exploding them, for example, exploding them underground where the radiation can be contained.

John F. Kennedy (1917–63)

- John F. Kennedy (JFK) was US President from 1961 to 1963.
- He was a young president, and there were concerns that he lacked experience.
- His time as president was mostly taken up with Cold War crises: the Berlin Crisis (1961), the Bay of Pigs and the Cuban Missile Crisis, and increased American involvement in Vietnam.
- JFK was assassinated in 1963 by an American, Lee Harvey Oswald.

Revision task

TESTED

Identify two effects of the Berlin Wall on relations between East and West Germany, and two effects of the Berlin Wall on relations between the superpowers.

The Cuban Missile Crisis, 1962

- In 1959, there was a revolution in Cuba. The pro-America government of Fulgencio Batista was replaced by a socialist state led by **Fidel Castro**.
- Many US businesses had invested in Cuba. Castro took over all the American property in Cuba.
- The USA responded by banning the import of sugar from Cuba. Sugar was Cuba's main export and the USA was its main market, so this was an economic disaster for Cuba.
- The Soviet Union offered to buy Cuba's sugar instead. Links between Cuba and the Soviet Union increased. The USA saw this as unacceptable: Cuba was only 145 kilometres from the USA.

> **Fidel Castro (1926–2016)**
> - Castro was leader of the Republic of Cuba from 1965 to 2011.
> - He was a revolutionary who led the Cuban Revolution which eventually overthrew Batista in 1959.
> - He helped create the first socialist state in the West.
> - Castro was the target of a number of US plots to remove him as Cuba's leader.
> - The USA refused to trade with socialist Cuba, and Castro therefore turned to the Soviet Union for trade deals and support.

The Bay of Pigs invasion, April 1961

- President Kennedy approved a plan for an invasion of Cuba that aimed to remove Castro and return the island to supporting the USA.
- In this plan, the CIA trained around 1,400 Cuban exiles – men who had left Cuba because of the revolution – as the invasion force, and equipped them with US weapons and equipment.
- The invasion took place in April 1961. First, on 16 April, old US bomber planes, painted to look like Cuban air force planes, attacked the actual Cuban air force. The bombing was not accurate and not all the Cuban planes were destroyed. Then, on the following day (17 April) the Cuban exiles landed at the Bay of Pigs in Cuba.
- The exiles (and the USA) had anticipated that the Cuban people and, especially, parts of the Cuban army, would help them to get rid of Castro. But in fact the Cuban people supported Castro. The 1,400 exiles faced a Cuban army force of around 20,000 men, plus Cuban air force planes, and were defeated.

Effects of the Bay of Pigs invasion

- The defeat of the invasion made Castro's position more secure because the attack from the USA united the Cuban people behind his government. He negotiated $53 million of baby food and medicines from the USA in return for the US prisoners seized during the Bay of Pigs invasion.
- The defeated invasion was very embarrassing for Kennedy, who had only been president since January 1961. He became even more determined to remove Castro from power, even allowing the CIA to make plans to assassinate Castro, and to make sure that communism did not spread to other countries in Latin (South) America.
- The defeated invasion was positive news for Khrushchev. Castro was sure that the USA would attack again, and the Soviet Union was happy to send military advisors to Cuba to help Castro increase his defences. Cuba was pushed further towards the Soviet Union.

The causes of the Cuban Missile Crisis

- Khrushchev was concerned that the Soviet Union was falling behind in the arms race. He was also worried about US missile bases positioned close to the Soviet Union, in Italy and Turkey. Cuba was a good opportunity to restore the balance: positioning Soviet missiles close to the USA.
- Castro was keen to have a strong **deterrent** against further US attacks. He requested that Soviet nuclear missiles should be installed on Cuba. In September 1962, Soviet specialists began secretly building a number of missile bases there.
- US suspicions about what was happening on Cuba were confirmed on 14 October 1962, when an American U-2 spy plane took photographs of Soviet strategic missile launch pads in Cuba.

> **Key term**
>
> **Deterrent**: something designed to stop or discourage something from being done or attempted.

- President Kennedy also received reports that twenty Soviet ships were on their way to Cuba, and these ships were very probably carrying nuclear missiles for the Cuban missile base.
- This was a very serious situation for the USA: the bases meant that medium-range nuclear missiles could be launched from Cuba that could very quickly hit anywhere in the USA.
- The President had to decide quickly how to respond – once the missiles reached Cuba, military experts thought they would be ready to launch in just two weeks' time. Options for Kennedy included: an invasion of Cuba; air strikes to destroy the bases; a blockade of Cuba to stop Soviet ships reaching the island (all three of which could have triggered a nuclear conflict); involving the United Nations in **diplomacy**; or do nothing. His decision (made on 20 October) was to order a blockade of Cuba.

> **Key terms**
>
> **Diplomacy**: representatives of a country who discuss issues with representatives of other countries in an attempt to sort out issues or problems without conflict.
>
> **DEFCON**: a series of five levels of alert used by the US armed forces. DEFCON 1 (the most severe) is all-out nuclear war, DEFCON 2 is the highest level ever used to date.

Revision task

TESTED

Make an argument that it was the USA's actions that were the main reason for Cuba allowing Soviet missile bases to be constructed there in 1962. What other reasons might also be important?

Key events of the Cuban Missile Crisis in 1962

- **16 October:** Kennedy informed about the missile bases on Cuba.
- **22 October:** Kennedy announced a blockade of Cuba by the US Navy. US military bases around the world were put on **DEFCON** 2: one step down from maximum readiness for an ICBM attack.
- **23 October:** Kennedy received a letter from Khrushchev announcing that the Soviet ships would continue to Cuba, regardless of the blockade.
- **24 October:** The Soviet ships approached the blockade – then turned back or stopped.
- **26 October:** A long letter from Khrushchev reached Kennedy. Khrushchev said that the missiles on Cuba would only ever be used to defend Cuba. He stated that if the USA promised not to attack Cuba again, then there could be negotiations about removing the missiles.
- **27 October:** A second personal letter to Kennedy from Khrushchev arrived in which the Soviet leader said the USA would need to remove their missiles from bases in Turkey before the Soviet Union would remove its missiles from Cuba.
- A U-2 spy plane was shot down over Cuba; the pilot was killed. Kennedy was advised to launch an attack on Cuba. Instead, Kennedy communicated to Khrushchev that the USA would agree not to attack Cuba again in return for the removal of the missiles from Cuba. But if Khrushchev didn't take this deal, the USA would attack.
- **28 October:** Khrushchev accepted the deal and said the Soviet Union would dismantle the missile systems and take them back to the Soviet Union. The crisis was over.

Outcomes of the Cuban Missile Crisis

- Kennedy was seen as having stood up to the Soviet Union and forced Khrushchev to back down. He was also recognised internationally as a great **statesman** because he had chosen peaceful means to deal with the crisis instead of launching attacks on Cuba and the Soviet Union, which risked nuclear war.
- In the Soviet Union, Khrushchev was seen to have failed as leader because he had been forced to back down over the missile bases. It did not look as though the Soviet Union had gained anything from the deal – a US agreement to remove missiles from Turkey was kept a secret. Khrushchev's failure over the crisis was one reason why he was forced out as Soviet leader in 1964.
- Both sides recognised that there were points in the crisis where nuclear war nearly happened, not because either side wanted it, but because communications to clarify the situation took too long. As a result, a **hotline teleprinter** link was installed that connected the US president in Washington directly to the Soviet general secretary in Moscow. This made accidental nuclear war a lot less likely to happen because now the two leaders could communicate directly with one another.
- The superpowers also agreed **treaties** to reduce the numbers of nuclear weapons and the ways new nuclear weapons could be tested.
  - In 1963, the USA and Soviet Union signed the Limited Test Ban Treaty: this meant no testing of nuclear weapons in the atmosphere.
  - In 1968, the superpowers and other nuclear allies signed the Outer Space Treaty, which agreed not to position nuclear weapons on satellites in orbit around the Earth.
  - In 1968, the Nuclear Non-proliferation Treaty was signed: countries with nuclear weapons promised not to help other countries to develop nuclear weapons of their own. The spread (proliferation) of nuclear powers was reduced, as was the risk of a nuclear war that wasn't started by the superpowers.
- The Cuban Missile Crisis therefore meant a reduction in tension between the superpowers because of how close the crisis had come to turning into a nuclear conflict that would have devastated both countries and many others.
- However, despite treaties to reduce nuclear proliferation and control testing, both superpowers continued the arms race.

> **Key terms**
>
> **Statesman**: a leader who has shown that they are skilled and experienced at getting good results in international negotiations or discussions.
>
> **Hotline**: a direct communication link that is only used for a specific purpose.
>
> **Teleprinter**: a machine for sending telegraph messages: a keyboard is used to type in the message, and a printer at the other end prints out the message.
>
> **Treaty**: a formal agreement made between states.

> **Revision task** [TESTED]
>
> Did the Cuban Missile Crisis increase tensions between the superpowers or reduce them (or both)? Explain your answer.

The Soviet invasion of Czechoslovakia, 1968

Causes of the Soviet invasion

- A new leader in Czechoslovakia brought in reforms that promised more freedoms and better standards of living to the Czechoslovakian people.
- The reforms encouraged others within Czechoslovakia to demand more radical changes.
- The Soviet leadership was increasingly concerned about Czechoslovakia leaving the Warsaw Pact and about demands for change in Czechoslovakia spreading to other Eastern European countries.

Dubček's reforms

- In January 1968, Dubček (pronounced Dub-check) became the leader of Czechoslovakia's Communist Party. The old leader, Novotny, was unpopular because of purges under his leadership in the 1950s.
- Dubček was a committed communist, but he wanted to reform communism from within: to make it more democratic and to make the economy work for the people.
- Czechoslovakia's economy was declining in the 1960s, mainly because it was being forced to send the steel it made to the Soviet Union, which meant its own industries lacked materials. Nor were Czechoslovak factories producing the things that people wanted to buy – **consumer goods** such as fridges and furniture.
- Dubček's economic reforms brought in an Action Programme in April 1968, which increased investment in consumer goods and reduced central controls on what was produced. Better working conditions in factories were introduced to motivate workers to be more productive.
- His political reforms were extensive: other parties were allowed to share some power in Czechoslovakia with elections planned within a ten-year period, victims of Novotny's purges were freed from imprisonment and **censorship** controls were almost completely removed. Travel restrictions on Czechoslovaks were dropped and there were more contacts with the West.

Key terms

Consumer goods: products that consumers (ordinary customers) want to buy.

Censorship: stopping the publication or broadcast of things that the state considers to be unacceptable.

Reactions to Dubček's reforms

- Removing censorship meant free speech. Czechoslovaks used their new freedom to criticise the Communist Party and the Soviet Union.
- There were student demonstrations demanding more change. Intellectuals also published a programme for further reforms.
- On 17 July 1968, Soviet leader **Leonid Brezhnev** and the leaders of Bulgaria, East Germany (GDR), Hungary and Poland sent Dubček a letter warning him of their concern that if radical changes continued in Czechoslovakia, there was a threat to communism in their countries.
- Dubček replied that he was loyal to socialism and the Warsaw Pact. He agreed not to allow other political parties and tried to bring back censorship in Czechoslovakia.
- Dubček's actions led to huge demonstrations. When police broke up the demonstrations, national strikes – where everyone in the country would stop work – began to be organised. To Brezhnev and the other Warsaw Pact leaders, this looked like an uprising against the Communist Party and Soviet control.

Leonid Brezhnev (1906–1982)

- Brezhnev was leader of the Soviet Union from 1964 to 1982.
- He rejected Khrushchev's reforms of socialism and returned the Soviet Union to stable politics.
- In foreign relations, Brezhnev was successful at improving relations with the USA.
- Under his leadership, the Soviet Union also reached the same level of nuclear weapons technology as the USA.
- His lack of reform led to political and economic stagnation in the Soviet Union.

Events of the Soviet invasion

- On 20 August 1968, 120,000 Soviet troops and 80,000 troops from other Warsaw Pact countries invaded Czechoslovakia – Brezhnev had run out of patience with Dubček's attempts to restore control.
- **Petrol bombs** were thrown at Soviet tanks, some Czechoslovak students even climbed onto tanks to try to convince the Soviet soldiers to turn back. Around 100 people were killed. The Czechoslovak army did not join the protests against the invasion.
- **Martial law** was declared; Dubček was arrested and taken to Moscow. In August 1968, the Moscow Agreement required the Czechoslovak Party to reverse the reforms and agree to Soviet troops staying in Czechoslovakia.
- Protests continued into April 1969 – in January 1969 a student, Jan Palach, set himself on fire to protest against the invasion.
- In 1969, Brezhnev was frustrated by the slow rate of change in Czechoslovakia. He said that the Czechoslovaks should 'learn to do what they were told' by the Soviet Union: restore order, bring back censorship, stop any talk of sharing power with other political parties – or expect the Soviet Union to invade again.

Impacts of the Soviet invasion of Czechoslovakia

- In Czechoslovakia, the Communist Party demoted Dubček and chose a new leader, Husák. Husák oversaw a crackdown: reformers were expelled from the Communist Party (including Dubček), censorship was brought back, the secret police had their **surveillance** powers increased, and traditional Soviet **central planning** of the economy was restored.
- Relations between the superpowers did not change. This was because the USA was becoming more deeply involved in the Vietnam War. US President Johnson had an agreement with Brezhnev that the USA would not intervene in Czechoslovakia if the Soviet Union did not intervene in Vietnam.
- Relations between the Soviet Union and China did worsen: this was because China's ruling Communist Party did not like the idea of the Soviet Union invading a fellow communist country.

The Brezhnev Doctrine

- Brezhnev first announced what came to be known as the Brezhnev Doctrine before the invasion of Czechoslovakia, on 3 August 1968. He made it mainly because of his concerns about Dubček's reforms and their likely consequences for Eastern Europe.
- The Brezhnev Doctrine stated that although socialist nations were free to choose their own path, no socialist nation should be allowed to damage socialism itself or damage the interests of other socialist nations.
- One effect of the Brezhnev Doctrine was a justification for the Soviet invasion. The invasion had been necessary, according to the Brezhnev Doctrine, because Czechoslovakia's 'counter revolution' against socialism weakened socialism against the capitalist countries (what if Czechoslovakia became a western ally?) and risked spreading uprisings to other socialist countries (such as Poland).
- A second effect of the Brezhnev Doctrine was that it meant no other Eastern European country risked making significant reforms until the 1980s. This was important because it meant Soviet-style economies in Eastern Europe stagnated, while young people in these countries felt disconnected from socialism.

> **Key terms**
>
> **Petrol bomb**: a bottle filled with petrol which is set on fire and thrown.
>
> **Martial law**: when ordinary laws are suspended (put on hold for a while) and a military government takes charge.
>
> **Surveillance**: putting people under very close observation, e.g. by the secret police.
>
> **Central planning**: when the state takes control of planning what industry and agriculture produce (instead of the market).

Revision task

TESTED

Identify three effects of the Soviet invasion of Czechoslovakia in 1968. Which do you think was most important for Cold War relations? Explain your answer.

Exam practice

Study Extract A.

What impression does the author give about the Soviet invasion of Czechoslovakia?

You **must** use Extract A to explain your answer. (6 marks)

Extract A

Dubček repeatedly made the case that Czechoslovakia remained a loyal member of the Warsaw Pact, and took steps to re-impose censorship, but events were beyond his control. Huge demonstrations were dispersed by police violence, national strikes were called. The Warsaw Pact Five [Soviet Union, Bulgaria, GDR, Hungary and Poland] ran out of patience with Dubček's inability to restore control. The invasion was a great shock, not least to Dubček, who said, 'I, who have devoted my whole life to cooperation with the Soviet Union, now they do this to me! This is the tragedy of my life!'

From *The Crisis of Communism: The USSR and the Soviet Empire 1953–2000*, by Rob Bircher, OUP, 2015, p. 136.

Exam tips

1. Start by summing up the overall impression the extract gives about the topic in question. Is it positive or negative? Supportive, critical or balanced?
2. What language is used to give this impression? Focus on the vocabulary used. What does it explicitly state? What can you infer? Make direct reference to the extract and use short quotes to highlight key phrases and words used.
3. What information about the topic has the author selected? Is there anything further about the topic that they have not included that might give a different impression?

2.5 The Thaw and moves towards Détente, 1963–72

REVISED

What you need to know

In this section you will revise Khrushchev's 'Thaw' in control over people in the Soviet Union, which also influenced Eastern Europe, and about moves towards Détente – the reduction of Cold War tensions. This will include:
- Khrushchev's Thaw and what happened when Brezhnev took over the Soviet leadership.
- The reduction in tensions between the superpowers known as Détente: features of Détente, reasons for Détente and the extent of Détente by 1972.

The Thaw

Khrushchev's reforms as leader began with the release of political prisoners from the Stalin era, and a relaxation of strict controls on people in the Soviet Union by the security services. Leaders across Eastern Europe followed the same approach, and it was this 'Thaw' in the Cold War that encouraged demands for more freedoms from Soviet and Party control which led to the revolution in Hungary in 1956 (see pages 57–59).

When Brezhnev fully took over the leadership of the Soviet Union in 1964, Khrushchev's reforms were stopped and the Thaw ended. Under Brezhnev, there was a strong campaign to shut down any criticism of the Soviet Union from Soviet citizens. However, in his foreign policy, Brezhnev wanted to reduce tensions with the USA. This was partly to allow more trade between the Soviet Union and the West.

Moves towards Détente

- Détente is a term used to describe the reduction of tensions during the Cold War. The main period of Détente was between 1967 and 1979, beginning with US President Johnson suggesting talks to limit the arms race in 1967, and ending with the Soviet invasion of Afghanistan in 1979.
- Moves towards Détente began with the installation of the 'hotline' in 1963, between the Pentagon and the Kremlin: a teleprinter line that meant the leaders of the USA and Soviet Union could communicate directly and immediately. The hotline was installed as a result of the Cuban Missile Crisis. Tension had increased during the Crisis because of delays in communications. Because the hotline was designed to reduce tension between the Cold War sides, it can be seen as a move towards Détente.
- In 1963, the Soviet Union, USA and Britain signed the Test Ban Treaty. This banned all testing of nuclear weapons apart from testing them underground. Previous tests created nuclear fallout, which spread radioactive particles from the explosion over wide areas, affecting human populations and also contaminating the environment. This led to protests against nuclear testing in the atmosphere. The Test Ban Treaty also made developing new nuclear weapons a little more difficult, so it did slow the arms race slightly. It was a move towards Détente because it involved the USA and Soviet Union meeting and agreeing a treaty to slow the arms race.
- In 1967, the USA, Soviet Union, Britain and several other countries signed the Outer Space Treaty. This treaty banned putting nuclear weapons in space – for example, in orbit around the Earth, or on the Moon. Again, it is significant because the two Cold War enemies had to cooperate together to agree the terms of the treaty, and it closed off any possibility of a Cold War in space.
- In 1968, the United Nations agreed a US–Soviet treaty called the Non-Proliferation Treaty. Under this treaty, the USA, Soviet Union and Britain all agreed not to help any other state obtain or develop the technology to make nuclear weapons. Instead, states with nuclear weapons would help other countries to develop **nuclear power**. Another part of the treaty was that nuclear states would try to agree ways to disarm. Despite the Treaty's terms, disarmament did not follow and other states, such as India and Pakistan, did develop nuclear weapons. However, the intention behind the treaty was another example of the USA and Soviet Union working together to reduce Cold War tensions.

> **Key term**
>
> **Nuclear power**: using a nuclear reactor to generate electricity through controlled nuclear reactions.

Reasons for Détente

Reasons for Détente included:
- **The arms race**: the cost of always having to develop new technologies and keep on increasing military investment was becoming unsustainable, especially for the Soviet Union. Reducing tensions through Détente was a way of reducing spending on the arms race.
- **The oil crisis (1973)**: the international price of oil increased by 400 per cent between 1972 and 1973. This was because of the 1973 oil crisis, when important Arab oil-producing countries in the Middle East stopped selling oil to countries, including the USA, which supported Israel in its war with a coalition of Arab states led by Egypt. The USA needed to import oil to meet its energy needs, so higher import prices were making it weaker. The Soviet Union had large supplies of oil and gas and became the world's biggest producer in the 1970s. This enabled it to invest more in military spending, making it stronger. The USA was therefore keen to reduce superpower tensions at this time.
- **The Vietnam War**: the USA was involved in a civil war in Vietnam that was very unpopular with many Americans, and also extremely expensive.
  - President Johnson launched major, expensive social reforms in the USA, but the cost of the Vietnam War made these much more difficult to achieve.
  - By the time Nixon became US President in 1969, the USA wanted to find a way out of the Vietnam War, and wanted the Soviet Union's help to achieve this. Brezhnev assisted the negotiations between the USA and North Vietnam (the USA's enemy) which produced a peace treaty in Vietnam in 1973.
- **West Germany**: the leader of West Germany, Willy Brandt, wanted to reduce tensions between East and West Germany. The Soviet Union supported this, because they believed that more trade between East Germany and West Germany would mean West Germany would become less closely tied to the USA.

SALT

- SALT stands for Strategic Arms Limitation Talks.
- SALT involved negotiations between the USA and the Soviet Union with the aim of reducing the arms race.
- President Johnson suggested the talks in 1967, both sides agreed to have them in 1968, and the negotiations began in 1969.
- The talks, which were held in Helsinki and in Vienna, continued for nearly three years.

SALT treaties

- There were two main agreements as a result of SALT, signed in Moscow in 1972 by Nixon and Brezhnev:
  1 The Treaty on Anti-Ballistic Missile (ABM) Systems.
  2 The **Interim** Agreement on Limitation of Strategic Offensive Weapons.
- Anti-ballistic missile systems were designed to destroy incoming enemy ICBMs before they could hit their targets by firing **interceptor** missiles at them. The Treaty on ABM Systems said that each superpower could only have one area that was protected by an ABM, and that an ABM could only have 100 interceptor missiles.

> **Key terms**
>
> **Interim**: temporary, not permanent.
>
> **Interceptor**: something that stops something else reaching its target.

- The reason for the Treaty on ABM Systems was that if one superpower thought its ABMs protected it completely from the ICBMs of the other, then it would be much more likely to risk launching its own nuclear weapons. The Treaty kept the deterrent of MAD – mutually assured destruction (see page 61).
- Each side was allowed to use satellites to check the other was not breaking the Treaty.
- The Interim Agreement imposed a five-year freeze on the numbers of ICBMs and SLBMs (see page 60) that each side could have. It was a temporary agreement until a new round of talks (SALT 2) could be completed. This Interim Agreement was designed to reduce the arms race.

Limitations of SALT

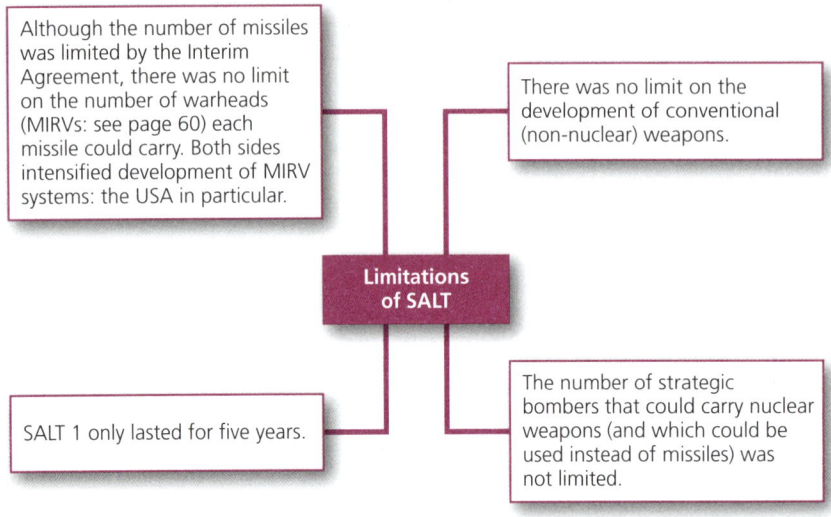

The extent of Détente in 1972

- Both sides in the Cold War had important reasons to reduce Cold War tensions: the USA needed the help of the Soviet Union in agreeing a peace treaty in Vietnam, and both the USA and Soviet Union wanted to spend less money on the arms race and more on improving life for their citizens.
- Fears of nuclear conflict had been significantly reduced from the time of the Cuban Missile Crisis. The Nuclear Non-proliferation Treaty (1968) helped limit the spread of nuclear weapons to other countries, however SALT only slowed the arms race slightly: both sides found ways to get round the Interim Agreement.
- By 1972, Détente had produced important increases in communication and respect between the two sides. However, neither side gave up their ideological commitments: Brezhnev continued to declare that it was inevitable that communism would defeat capitalism. Each side continued to build up for an attack on the other. Some historians suggest that Détente was just a less risky way for both sides to continue to fight the Cold War.

- In 1972, US President Nixon visited China, a communist ally of the Soviet Union: this diplomatic visit suggested that the USA was willing to be more friendly towards communist governments. However, it is possible that the USA did this in order to increase the split between the Soviet Union and China, which would weaken the Soviet Union.

Revision task

TESTED

Which of the reasons given for Détente in this book do you think was the most important one and which one was the least important? Explain your decision for both.

Exam practice

Explain **two** effects of Détente (1963–72) on superpower relations.

(8 marks)

Exam tips

- Eight-mark questions require you to explain two effects of something. This goes beyond simply describing an effect.
- To reach the highest level, you should explain the *consequences* of each effect on the situation at the time – the impacts it had.
- Follow the same approach for each of your two effects: describe the effect using specific information and then explain its consequences.

3 A divided union: civil rights in the USA, 1945–74

3.1 The Red Scare and McCarthyism

REVISED

What you need to know

In this section you will revise the importance of the 1950s Red Scare. This will include:
- Reasons for the Red Scare.
- What McCarthyism was and the methods used by McCarthy.
- The reasons for McCarthy's downfall.
- The significance of McCarthyism and the Red Scare for the USA.

Reasons for the Red Scare

The Cold War, 1945–50

- The USA was **capitalist**, promoting the idea of democracy and the freedom for people to make as much money as possible.
- The Soviet Union was **communist**, arguing that everyone should be made to be equal and that all property should be owned by the state; communism seemed to be a direct threat to American freedom.
- The capitalist USA was allied with the communist Soviet Union against Germany and Japan during the Second World War.
- In 1945, rivalry between the USA and the Soviet Union began as they argued about how to deal with post-war Europe.
- They agreed that the countries of Western Europe would be free under US influence, while the countries of Eastern Europe would have communist governments under the influence of the Soviet Union.
- Germany and Berlin were both divided between the USA, Britain, France and the Soviet Union.

Competition between these two **superpowers** became known as the Cold War, as both countries tried to prove that they were better than the other.

Key terms

Capitalist: the belief that people should be free to make as much money as they want.

Communist: the belief that everyone should be equal.

Superpower: a country that is so powerful it can influence events in other countries.

Reasons for increased tensions between the USA and the Soviet Union

- The USA had developed nuclear weapons in secret and used them against Japan in 1945; by 1949, the Soviet Union had developed its own nuclear weapons.
- Churchill had highlighted the divisions in Europe in his 'iron curtain' speech in 1946; the US government feared communism would start to spread quickly from country to country.
- The Soviet Union had tried to force US allies out of West Berlin with a transport blockade in 1948; the USA had flown supplies in to keep their section of Berlin open.
- With his Truman Doctrine in 1947, President Truman promised military support to protect countries threatened by communist takeovers; the Marshall Plan offered billions of dollars to countries in Western Europe to remain capitalist.

However, with the communist takeover of China in 1949, and the invasion of South Korea by communist North Korea in 1950, it seemed to many Americans that they were losing the Cold War. They believed that communists were working to take over the USA. This became known as the **Red Scare**.

> ### Revision task
> TESTED
>
> Draw a spider diagram to show the different reasons for the increasing suspicion of communist activity in the USA in the 1940s.

The role of the Federal Bureau of Investigation

From 1945, there was a growing concern that there were communist spies working in the USA:
- A raid on the offices of the communist *Amerasia* magazine found confidential documents from the US **State Department**.
- The 1946 Atomic Energy Act – the Federal Bureau of Investigation (**FBI**) gained the power to investigate the loyalty of workers in the American atomic industry.
- The 1947 National Security Act – the US army, navy and air force were combined into the Department of Defence; President Truman played upon politicians' fears of communist spies.

J. Edgar Hoover, Director of the FBI, told Truman in 1947 that he was concerned about communist conspiracies. The President issued Executive Order 9835, which allowed the FBI to set up and run Federal Loyalty Boards. This meant that employees of the **federal government** could be removed from their jobs if they were suspected of being disloyal to the US government. Between 1947 and 1951, 3 million federal employees were investigated, 3,000 were forced to resign and 300 were fired.

Individual states and businesses also removed people they considered to be disloyal to the USA. Over 150 organisations were investigated for having links to communism, including the NAACP (see page 80). Many of them were banned.

> ### The government of the USA
>
> Each US state has its own government, but the government of the USA as a whole is known as the federal government. The federal government is made up of three parts:
> - **The Presidency** – the President signs laws to enact them, and can also veto them (refuse to sign them).
> - **Congress** – the two Houses of **Congress** (Representatives, who are elected for two years; Senators, who are elected for six years) pass laws and investigate issues using committees to question witnesses.
> - **The Supreme Court** – nine judges who make sure that the laws of the states or Congress and the actions of the President do not break the rules of the **Constitution**.
>
> The set of rules that US government has to follow are known as the Constitution. Any changes to the Constitution since it was set up in 1787 are known as **Amendments**.

Key terms

Red Scare: the belief that communists are trying to overthrow the government of a country.

FBI: the Federal Bureau of Investigation was set up to find people working against the US government and way of life.

Federal government: the central government of the whole of the USA, based in Washington DC, and run by the President and his advisors. See box below.

State Department: the department of the federal government responsible for US relations with other countries.

Congress: the law-making part of the US government, made up of two Houses – the Representatives, and the Senate.

Constitution: the 1787 document that laid down the rules for how the US government should be run.

Amendments: changes to the Constitution that have been added in since 1787.

The House Un-American Activities Committee and the Hollywood Ten

- In 1938, the House Un-American Activities Committee (HUAC) was set up to monitor extreme political groups like the Nazis who might be operating in the USA.
- In 1947, HUAC had begun public hearings about communism. Suspects were asked, 'Are you, or have you ever been, a member of the Communist Party?' Hoover, director of the FBI, appeared as a witness and the FBI began to secretly pass information on suspects for the Committee to investigate.
- There had been strikes by General Motors workers and coal miners immediately after the Second World War. After a HUAC investigation, Congress passed the Taft–Hartley Act in 1947, forcing trade union leaders to swear that they were not communists and giving the President the power to declare strikes illegal.
- The most notorious HUAC investigation was into the Hollywood movie industry. Film-makers were accused of making propaganda to brainwash Americans into supporting communism. Writers and producers were called to testify before the Committee and explain their political views. Anyone who refused to answer was sent to prison.
- Some actors including Ronald Reagan and Gary Cooper were happy to support these investigations. Others, like British-born Charlie Chaplin, left the USA to avoid being forced to appear. Walt Disney appeared to provide evidence against his own employees who had recently gone on strike. Nineteen of the 41 writers and producers originally called before HUAC were identified as communists.
- Writers, such as **Dalton Trumbo**, and producers, referred to as 'the **Hollywood** Ten', were sacked from their jobs and sent to prison for a year for contempt of Congress. They argued that the First Amendment of the US Constitution allowed them the freedom to hold whatever views they liked. They were blacklisted – banned from working in the movie industry – until the 1960s. Many of them never worked in Hollywood again. A further investigation in 1954 added 350 people to the blacklist.

> **Key term**
>
> **Hollywood**: the area of California where the US film industry is based.

> **Dalton Trumbo (1905–76)**
>
> - Trumbo was one of the Hollywood Ten who was imprisoned and blacklisted in 1947 by HUAC.
> - He wrote under false names in the 1950s, winning Oscars for *Roman Holiday* and *The Brave One*.
> - He received a screen credit for his re-writing of *Spartacus* in 1960, which helped to end the blacklist.

Revision task

Explain two reasons why the FBI and Congress wanted to find communist spies and sympathisers in the 1940s and 1950s.

Hiss and Rosenberg cases

Spy scandals hit the USA and Britain, including one involving British physicist Klaus Fuchs, who was accused of giving nuclear secrets to the Soviet Union. Many believed that communist spies had enabled the Soviets to develop atomic bombs so quickly. Fuchs confessed and was sentenced to fourteen years in a British prison. He named David Greenglass as another spy in the USA. Greenglass named his relatives, the Rosenbergs, as fellow spies.

Julius and Ethel Rosenberg were scientists. They were accused of giving atomic secrets to the Soviet Union that had been stolen from the secret US nuclear laboratory at Los Alamos by Greenglass, who worked as a soldier there. Greenglass testified to save his own wife from being investigated and was sent to prison for nine and a half years. The Rosenbergs were both executed as **traitors** in 1953.

Alger Hiss was a member of the State Department who had worked closely with President Roosevelt during the war. Whittaker Chambers, editor of *Time* magazine, accused Hiss of helping the communists get an advantage over the USA after the war. Hiss was called before HUAC in 1948, but denied being a communist.

Richard Nixon, one of the members of HUAC, was determined to prove that Hiss had been giving secret information to the Soviet Union. These accusations led to Hiss going on trial in 1949. He was convicted of lying to the court and sent to prison for five years. Hiss was never convicted of spying, but his case convinced many people that communists had infiltrated the highest levels of the US government.

> **Key terms**
>
> **Traitors**: people who betray their country, especially during times of war.
>
> **McCarthyism**: the mistaken belief that communist spies were everywhere in the USA, and that they needed to be found and removed.
>
> **Senate committee**: a group of senators who investigate a particular issue.

Revision task

TESTED

Do you think it was fair that the Rosenbergs were executed? Explain your answer.

Methods used by McCarthy

Joe McCarthy

Joe McCarthy was a US senator for Wisconsin. In February 1950, he told a ladies' Republican club in Wheeling, West Virginia, that communists working for the State Department had persuaded the USA to follow a pro-communist foreign policy. He held up a list of the 205 people he claimed were responsible for this. Senator Joseph McCarthy quickly made himself the country's leading expert in rooting out communist spies. His actions against communists became known as '**McCarthyism**'.

McCarthyism

In 1950, McCarthy became a member of the Senate Internal Security Sub-committee (SISS), leading it in 1953 and 1954. This was the **Senate's main committee** for investigating communist activity. McCarthy used it to make his attacks on alleged communists.

HUAC and the FBI helped provide the committee with material. Some producers, directors and screen writers refused to testify as the committee demanded that witnesses name others they suspected, providing an ever-expanding list of suspects to be summoned.

McCarthy's methods were simple, but effective. He would:
- interview witnesses in public, bullying them to confess to wild accusations without any evidence
- make accusations one after another that the suspect would not know how to answer
- assume any refusal to answer was a sign of guilt.

Nothing needed to be proved. Just being accused was enough to destroy someone's reputation. If anyone stood up to him or questioned his methods, McCarthy questioned their loyalty to the USA.

McCarthy became very popular. He had supporters among the veterans of the American Legion, as well as Christian fundamentalists who thought that communism was the work of the devil. Poorer people were more easily won over as his conspiracies were seen by them as attacks on more well-educated and well-off Americans.

The growth of opposition and reasons for McCarthy's downfall

McCarthy's aggressive approach towards the military undermined people's faith in him. He investigated respected figures like George Marshall, who was accused of encouraging the spread of communism in Europe with his Marshall Plan (see page 49). In 1954, he accused the US army of being the hiding place of a large number of communists, even though the army had just fought a three-year war against the communist takeover of Korea.

Millions of people watched McCarthy's hearings on television. They did not like his bullying tactics, his lack of any concrete evidence for his accusations or that he often seemed to be drunk. The US army's attorney attacked McCarthy for having no evidence to back up his accusations.

Television journalist Ed Murrow devoted an episode of his programme 'See It Now' to criticising McCarthy. McCarthy's lies were being uncovered. The 205 names of communist suspects that had formed the basis for his original claim was just a random sheet of paper pulled from his briefcase. The photograph he used to accuse a US general of collaborating with communists was cropped from a larger photograph showing he was part of an official US delegation.

President Eisenhower came out in support of the army. McCarthy was accused of trying to get someone who worked for him into the army. He was criticised by the Senate in December 1954 for not following established rules. He remained a senator and carried on his investigations, but the media had now lost interest in them. He died from alcoholism in 1957.

> **Revision task** TESTED
>
> Make a table to show three reasons why people supported McCarthy, and three reasons why his influence came to an end.

Overall impact of McCarthyism on the USA

- No one was ever convicted of spying as a result of McCarthy's accusations. However, 9,500 federal workers were dismissed and a further 15,000 resigned while being investigated. The State Department lost many intelligent and experienced employees. Hundreds of scientists, as well as university and school teachers, lost their jobs.
- People were accused of being communist if they held different views from most Americans – any radical, socialist or moderately left-wing views were immediately condemned.

- **Trade union** influence was reduced by the accusations that strikes were communist activity, and union membership declined as workers feared they would be considered communist by association.
- The anti-communist hysteria that gripped the American people took a long time to calm down. People continued to look for 'the Reds under the bed', and swore that they would rather be 'dead than red'.
- The 1950 McCarran Internal Security Act forced all communist organisations to register with the US government and banned communists from working in the defence industry, while the 1954 Communist Control Act made it illegal to communicate communist ideas in any form.

> **Key term**
>
> **Trade union**: an organisation that represents the interests of the workers to their bosses.

Exam practice

Explain **two** effects of the Red Scare on American society between 1945 and 1954. (8 marks)

> **Exam tips**
>
> You should break your answer down into two short paragraphs, one for each effect:
> 1. Choose one effect of the event in the question and write about this.
> 2. Use specific information from your knowledge to describe this consequence of the event.
> 3. Make sure that you clearly link the consequence back to the question – 'X led to Y because ...'
> 4. Choose another effect of the event in the question and write about this, repeating steps 2 and 3 above.

3.2 Civil rights in the 1950s

REVISED

> **What you need to know**
>
> In this section you will revise the campaign for **civil rights** for black Americans in the 1950s. This will include:
> - Black American experience of segregation and discrimination.
> - The importance of the *Brown vs Topeka* Supreme Court case in challenging segregation in education.
> - Increasing violence against black Americans by the Ku Klux Klan.
> - The significance of the Montgomery Bus Boycott in ending segregation on public transport.
> - The influence of the 1957 Civil Rights Act.

Segregation and discrimination

The American Civil War in the 1860s was a battle between the southern states who wanted to keep **slavery**, and the northern states who wanted slavery to end. The North won the war and slavery was abolished in 1865. The Fourteenth Amendment to the Constitution guaranteed equal treatment, and the Fifteenth Amendment guaranteed the right to vote. However, discrimination towards black Americans continued.

The southern states introduced the **Jim Crow laws** to segregate black and white Americans in public places, in education and on public transport.

> **Key terms**
>
> **Civil rights**: guarantees of equal treatment and opportunities for the citizens of a country.
>
> **Slavery**: when a human being is treated as if they are someone else's property.
>
> **Jim Crow laws/Segregation laws**: laws that forced black Americans to use separate public facilities from white Americans.

They also tried to prevent black Americans from voting, or from marrying white Americans.

Beginning with the 1896 *Plessy vs Ferguson* case, the US Supreme Court argued that these **segregation laws** were constitutional, provided that black Americans were treated equally if they were separate. Black Americans could not:
- go to the same schools, the same cinemas or restaurants as white Americans
- ride in the same railway carriages as white Americans
- keep their seat on buses if white Americans needed to sit down.

This separation enabled white Americans to ensure that education and facilities for black Americans were inferior to those that white Americans enjoyed. This was not the 'separate but equal' that the Supreme Court had agreed in 1896.

Black Americans in the South were worse off than many white Americans:
- On farms, they were **sharecroppers**, paying the rent for their land by selling a share of their crops.
- Some ended up in domestic service, as the cleaners or cooks of richer white Americans.
- Those working in shops or factories found that they were paid half what white Americans were paid for the same job.

The police, juries and judges of the southern states were all white Americans. Black Americans could not elect politicians who could help them because they were prevented from voting by literacy tests, taxes or the 'grandfather' clause – you were only eligible to vote if your grandfather had been able to vote. Any black Americans who tried to challenge this system found that they and their families became victims of racial violence.

The northern states did not have segregation laws, but black Americans still faced discrimination. They lived in poorer neighbourhoods where black Americans were concentrated, known as **ghettos**. They were still likely to be paid less than white Americans and if a business needed to let go of some workers, black Americans would be the first to be fired. However, black Americans could at least vote if they lived in the North.

> **Key terms**
>
> **Sharecroppers**: black American farmers who paid for the rent of their farms with a share of the crops they grew.
>
> **Ghetto**: a part of a town or city with very poor-quality housing.
>
> **Supreme Court**: the highest court in the USA whose rulings have to be followed by everyone, including the government.

> **Revision task** TESTED
>
> Draw a spider diagram to summarise the problems faced by black Americans in the 1950s.

The influence of the Supreme Court and Congress on the lives of black Americans

The Constitution guaranteed equal treatment and the right to vote after the Civil War. However, the **Supreme Court**'s support for segregation in the 1890s led to the Jim Crow laws being imposed throughout the southern states.

The National Association for the Advancement of Colored people (NAACP) had been campaigning against the Jim Crow laws and discrimination since it was founded in 1909. It had focused on persuading Congress to pass laws to end segregation and prevent lynching. Southern

Democrats had been elected to Congress by racist white voters and did not want things to change.

In the 1940s, the NAACP changed its tactics to challenge segregation in the law courts.

The importance of *Brown vs Topeka*, 1954

In 1951, the parents of Linda Brown applied for her to move to Summer Elementary School in Topeka, Kansas. It was nearer to where they lived than her current school. The local School Board refused because Linda Brown was a black American, and this school was for white Americans only.

The Brown family asked the NAACP for help. The case was referred to the Supreme Court. NAACP lawyers, led by Thurgood Marshall, argued that segregated education was educationally and psychologically damaging to black American children.

The new Chief Justice, Earl Warren, reached a verdict on 17 May 1954. The Court unanimously decided that segregation in education was unconstitutional as the Constitution did not allow discrimination on the basis of race. A year later, they ruled that desegregation in education should happen as quickly as possible.

This was a great victory for the NAACP and did a lot to raise awareness of the problem of civil rights for black Americans, as well as showing campaigners that challenges to segregation could be successful. More protest movements and legal challenges followed as a wider movement for civil rights started to campaign for change.

There were limits to this victory:
- By 1957, more than 300,000 black children went to desegregated schools in the southern states, but over 2 million black American children were still being taught in segregated schools.
- Southern politicians backed the Southern Manifesto – a document that argued against **integration** in education and passed hundreds of laws to try to stop the *Brown* decision being put into practice.
- By the 1970s, 8 per cent of black American children in the southern states still went to segregated schools.
- Many black American schools were closed, leading to the loss of a number of jobs.
- Integration was often very difficult for black American children as they faced resistance from the white American communities where they now went to school, as shown in the events at Little Rock High School (see page 84).

> **Key term**
>
> **Integration**: the opposite of segregation, bringing people from different races together, sometimes referred to as desegregation.

Revision task

TESTED

Give three reasons why the Linda Brown court case was an important event for the civil rights movement.

The revival of the Ku Klux Klan (KKK)

Many white Americans in the South remained convinced that black Americans were inferior to them. A White Citizen's Council (WCC) was set up in Mississippi to pressure politicians to resist integration. WCCs began to appear across the southern states.

The white supremacist group, the Ku Klux Klan (KKK), had been revived during the First World War, but its membership had dropped in the 1920s due to a number of scandals. Membership began to grow again after the *Brown* decision, and continued to grow in response to the increasing number of civil rights protests.

Klan members:
- wore white robes and hoods to hide their identities
- intimidated anyone who resisted segregation or supported civil rights for all
- put burning crosses outside people's house as a warning
- beat up or lynched their opponents
- began to bomb the houses and churches of those who opposed them.

As many local lawyers and policemen were members, they did not worry about getting caught or being prosecuted.

The importance of the death of Emmett Till, 1955

The racially motivated murder of fourteen-year-old Emmett Till, in 1955, was an example of this increasing violence against black Americans:
- Emmett Till was a northerner from Chicago. In August 1955, he was visiting relatives in the town of Money, Mississippi. He boasted he had a white girlfriend back in Chicago, so local teenagers dared him to go into Bryant's grocery store and talk to the white owner's wife.
- Carolyn Bryant later claimed that Till flirted with her. The teenagers claimed he whistled at her. A few days later, Roy Bryant, Carolyn's husband, and his half-brother, dragged Emmett Till out of his bed in the middle of the night. They beat him, shot him in the head and dumped his body in the river.
- The Mississippi authorities wanted Till to be buried quickly, but his mother insisted his body be sent back to her in Chicago. She had his open coffin displayed in public so that people could see what had been done to him. Photographs were published across the United States. People were shocked by his horrific injuries.
- The trial of Bryant and his half-brother J.W. Milam was widely reported across America. Despite the evidence, the all-white jury took just one hour to decide they were not guilty. Bryant and Milam both confessed to the murder after the trial in a magazine article, but the 'double jeopardy' law in the United States does not allow people to be tried twice for the same crime.
- Acquitting white Americans for racial violence was typical in this period of time, but the publicity that followed this case was something new. White Americans living in the North saw the racism that black Americans were suffering in the South for the first time. For black Americans it encouraged them to become involved in the **civil rights movement**.

> **Key term**
>
> **Civil rights movement**: a number of different organisations that work together to improve the civil rights of black Americans.

> **Revision task** TESTED
>
> In five bullet points, explain why the Klan and their supporters were able to get away with violence against black Americans.

The key events and significance of the Montgomery Bus Boycott, 1955–56

Black Americans depended on public transport as many could not afford a car of their own. In Alabama, the bus laws said that black Americans had to give up their seats for white passengers if the bus was full, and that they must stand even if there was an empty seat next to a white passenger.

- **1 December 1955:** in Montgomery, Alabama, Rosa Parks and three other black Americans on their way home from work, were told to stand to allow a white passenger to sit down. Rosa Parks refused. The driver stopped the bus and called the police, who arrested her.
- **5 December 1955:** Rosa Parks, who was secretary of the Montgomery NAACP, and the Montgomery Women's Political Council decided to call a **boycott** of the buses. Seventy per cent of bus passengers were black Americans and on that day 90 per cent of those did not use the bus.
- Campaigners met at the Holt Street Baptist Church and set up the Montgomery Improvement Association (MIA), led by local Baptist minister, Martin Luther King. They supported the boycott and demanded that black American passengers be treated with respect – they should not have to give up their seats for white passengers.
- **8 December 1955:** the MIA met the bus companies, who refused their demands. The boycott continued, despite white supporters being discouraged from giving lifts and taxi fares being increased. The MIA changed their demand to complete desegregation of the buses.
- The MIA set up a carpooling system, organised by local churches. They borrowed or bought cars that were used as an alternative to the bus system to get people around town.
- **30 January 1956:** Martin Luther King's house was bombed, as were the houses and churches of other boycott supporters.
- **22 February 1956:** 90 of the leading protesters were arrested for organising an illegal boycott. They avoided prison by paying fines. Helped along by inspirational speeches from Martin Luther King and the support of the carpool, the boycott lasted 381 days.

> **Key term**
>
> **Boycott:** not using a service as a protest against something.

As the US media picked up on the story and it began to be reported across the country, the NAACP stepped in, hoping for a court ruling that would end segregation on transportation, just as it had with education.

The Supreme Court case, *Browder vs Gayle*, began in February 1956, arguing that segregation was a violation of the equal treatment guaranteed by the Fourteenth Amendment. A majority of the Supreme Court judges ruled that segregation on buses was unconstitutional and, in December 1956, the boycott came to an end.

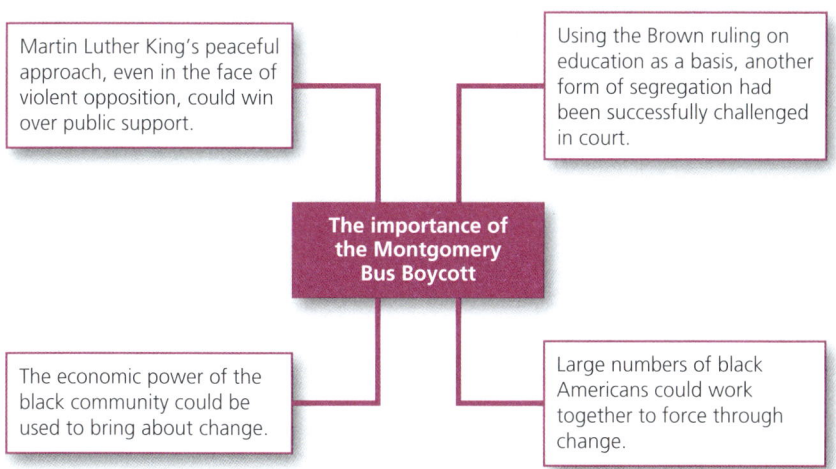

Change was limited at first, as this was focused just on public transport. The need for the freedom rides in the 1960s (see page 87) showed that this was a small victory in a much wider battle. It also resulted in increased opposition from groups such as the KKK whose membership increased, and whose campaign of violence resulted in more shootings and bombings against the black American community.

> **Revision task** TESTED
>
> Draw a table to show the important points about the Montgomery Bus Boycott and the *Brown* ruling. Which was more important in improving the lives of black Americans? Explain your choice.

The key events and significance of Little Rock High School, 1957

Following the *Brown* decision, a federal court ruled that Central High School, Little Rock, Arkansas, must become integrated. Nine black American children wanted to study there.

The white community strongly objected to this. Governor Orval Faubus went on television to say that he had ordered state troopers to stop the nine black American students from enrolling at the school. He said that this was for their own protection.

When the Little Rock Nine arrived at school on 4 September, they were met by an angry mob who screamed abuse at them. State troopers stopped them from entering the school. They were taken home under police escort. This was captured by the world's media on television and in photographs, most famously of a white woman screaming abuse at fifteen-year-old Elizabeth Eckford.

It was a national embarrassment. President Eisenhower asked Faubus to change his mind. A federal judge started proceedings against Faubus. The situation continued. After a riot outside the school on 23 September, Eisenhower ordered 1,200 federal troops from the 101st Airborne to protect the children, and on 25 September they were finally able to go to their classes.

The soldiers remained in place for a year. In September 1958, Governor Faubus shut all high schools in Little Rock and took his case to the Supreme Court. The court ordered desegregation to continue and schools re-opened in August 1959. Abuse continued for many years and integration was only really achieved in the 1970s.

Events at Little Rock were significant because:
- It was the first time a President had directly intervened to support the Supreme Court's decision on education.
- It showed that the federal government could overrule state government on civil rights issues.
- Publicising the extreme racism of many in the South was embarrassing when the USA was arguing with other countries that they did not treat their own citizens properly.
- The power of the media to gain support for civil rights struggles was demonstrated again.

The significance of the Civil Rights Act, 1957

While the Supreme Court had been involved in improving civil rights for black Americans, Congress was slow to respond. The southern Democrats were opposed to any attempts to end segregation.

President Eisenhower had said that he was in favour of improving civil rights for black Americans, but he also believed Congress should not interfere in the rights of individual states.

Supreme Court rulings and the Montgomery Bus Boycott had raised awareness. Violent opposition to these changes had damaged the United States' international reputation as the promoter of freedom and equality. A Civil Rights **bill** was unsuccessfully introduced to Congress in 1956.

A second bill was introduced in 1957 – a weakened version was finally passed into law with the support of **Lyndon Johnson**, Democrat leader in the Senate. It was signed into law on 9 September 1957 by President Eisenhower.

The **Act** aimed to improve black American voting rights by setting up a commission to investigate how they were prevented from voting and allowed federal courts to prosecute states that prevented people from voting.

In reality, this did very little to help, as juries did not support civil rights and prosecutions ended with 'not guilty' verdicts. Another Civil Rights Act was passed in 1960, which introduced federal inspections of the voting process and clearer penalties for states preventing people from voting; but this only resulted in a three per cent increase in black Americans registering to vote.

For the first time since the Civil War era, Congress and the federal government had acted to try to improve the civil rights of black Americans. It showed that change was possible and encouraged campaigners to keep on fighting for further change.

> **Key terms**
>
> **Bill**: a proposal for a new law.
>
> **Act**: a law that has been passed by Congress.
>
> **Great Society programme**: President Johnson's plan to help American people out of poverty by improving their education, health and civil rights.

> **Lyndon Johnson (1908–73)**
> - Johnson was a Democrat politician who represented his home state of Texas.
> - He was elected to the House of Representatives in 1937 and the Senate in 1948.
> - Vice President to John F. Kennedy 1961–63 and President from 1963–68, following Kennedy's assassination.
> - As Senate leader, he helped pass the 1957 Civil Rights Act, and as President he helped pass the 1964 Civil Rights Act, the 1965 Voting Rights Act and the 1968 Fair Housing Act.
> - Johnson tried to improve the lives of ordinary Americans with his **Great Society programme**, but was best known for increasing US involvement in the conflict in Vietnam.

> **Revision task** TESTED
>
> How do events at Little Rock High School and the 1957 Civil Rights Act show the limits of what could be done to help black Americans in the 1950s?

Exam practice

What impression does the author give about the 1954 *Brown vs Topeka* case?

You **must** use Extract A to explain your answer. (6 marks)

Extract A

Linda Brown's parents wanted her to attend a neighbourhood school rather than the school for black Americans, which was some distance away. Lawyers from the NAACP, led by Thurgood Marshall, presented evidence to the Supreme Court stating that separate education created low self-esteem and was psychologically harmful. On 17 May 1954 Chief Justice Warren of the Supreme Court gave a closing judgment: 'Separate educational facilities are inherently unequal'. However, the *Brown* v. *Topeka* judgment did not specify how integration should be carried out – apart from a vague notion of 'at the earliest possible speed'.

From *WJEC Eduqas GCSE History: The Development of the USA 1929–2000,* Steve Waugh and John Wright, ed. Paul Evans, Hodder Education, 2016.

Exam tips

1. Make sure you read the extract all the way through.
2. Write down what the author's view on the topic is, and say whether or not it is positive or negative.
3. Explain why you think the author's view is positive or negative using specific examples of words and phrases from the extract.
4. Explain why the author has chosen to include or leave out certain information about the topic. You will need to make specific references to what is included in the extract.

3.3 The impact of civil rights protests, 1960–74

What you need to know

In this section you will revise how civil rights protests led to changes in the lives of black Americans. This will include:
- Civil rights protests such as sit-ins and the freedom rides that challenged segregation.
- The influence of Martin Luther King and new civil rights laws.
- The campaign to ensure voting rights for black Americans.
- The black nationalism of the Nation of Islam and Malcolm X.
- The Black Power Movement and the Black Panthers.

Civil rights protests in the early 1960s

Sit-ins

On 1 February 1960, four black American college students from North Carolina Agriculture and Technology College sat at the whites-only lunch counter at Woolworths store in Greensboro. They were asked to leave, but stayed there until the shop closed. They returned day after day with more and more supporters. This spread to other segregated shops in Greensboro, then across North Carolina, until by August 1961, there were 70,000 people involved in **sit-ins** across the country.

Protesters faced abuse from racist white Americans. They had food and drink thrown over them and were physically attacked. The protesters did not fight back. Thousands of protesters were arrested but they followed a new tactic 'jail not bail' – instead of paying fines they allowed themselves

Key term

Sit-in: when protesters deliberately break a segregation law but refuse to leave the place where they are protesting.

to be sent to prison in large numbers, which led to prison over-crowding. As the media reported their struggle, more and more people joined the protests.

Civil rights organisations, such as the NAACP, the Southern Christian Leadership Council (SCLC), the newly-formed Student Nonviolent Coordinating Committee (SNCC) and the northern group known as the Congress of Racial Equality (CORE), began to support the sit-in protesters and gave them training in how to not respond violently.

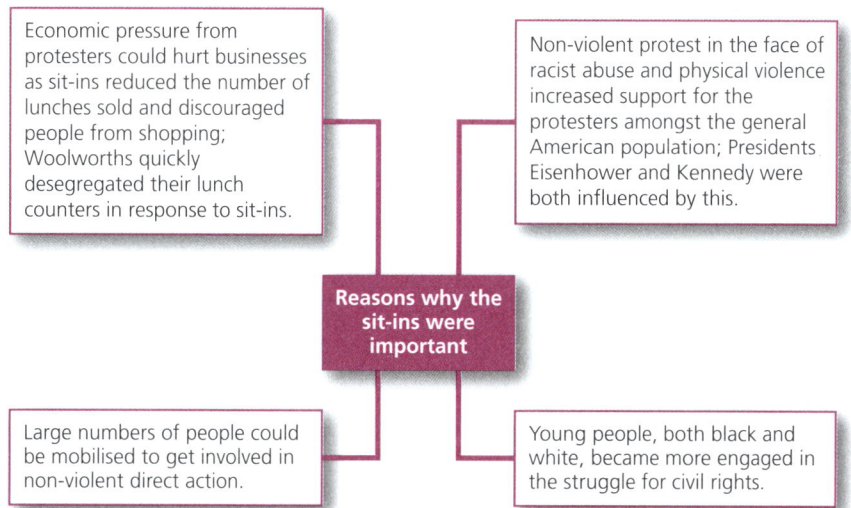

Freedom riders and the Anniston fire bombing

In December 1960, the Supreme Court ordered all interstate bus stations and their facilities to be integrated. CORE protesters organised '**freedom rides**' to show that this ruling was not being implemented. They believed that if they got a violent reaction from white racists, it would make the federal government enforce the Supreme Court ruling.

On 4 May 1961, the first freedom ride began on two buses from Washington DC to New Orleans. CORE protesters used whites-only facilities along the way. To begin with they did not face any problems.

On 14 May 1961, the first bus carrying freedom riders arrived at the bus station in Anniston, Alabama. An angry mob encouraged by William Chappell, a Ku Klux Klan leader, attacked the bus, smashing windows and damaging the tyres. The bus managed to get to the edge of town before it broke down. The white mob followed.

Someone threw a petrol bomb into the bus, holding the door shut while it filled with smoke. The passengers managed to escape. When the second bus got to Anniston it was also attacked. Passengers were dragged off the bus and beaten up. They got back on the bus but were attacked again when they got to Montgomery. The police did little to prevent this. 'Bull' Connor, the chief of police, ordered his men not to help.

Further freedom rides by CORE, joined by the SNCC, resulted in the arrest of over 300 protesters in Jackson, Mississippi. In the end, President Kennedy said he would send **US Marshals** to force states to integrate bus facilities. Bus facilities were desegregated and by the end of 1961, the freedom rides were over.

> **Key terms**
>
> **Freedom ride**: people travelling around the US bus network challenging segregation on the buses and in bus stations.
>
> **US Marshals**: government law enforcement officials.

The Meredith Case

Desegregation of elementary and high schools had begun in the 1950s, but the desegregation of American universities was a lot slower. Mississippi University was one of the universities that resisted this change.

Black American student James Meredith applied for a place at Mississippi University in May 1961, and was rejected. The NAACP helped him to take his case to court, and in June 1962, the Supreme Court ordered the university to admit him. They still refused.

Ross Barnett, the Governor of Mississippi, pressured the **state legislature** to pass a law banning anyone from university who had committed a crime – James Meredith had a conviction for false voter registration, so he was automatically banned.

On 29 September, President Kennedy ordered the university to accept Meredith. White students rioted in protest. Kennedy sent 300 officials, including US Marshals, to escort Meredith to university registration on 30 September. There were more riots in which two people died and more than 300 were injured – this became known as the 'Battle of Oxford'. Two thousand federal troops were sent to break up the rioting.

On 1 October, James Meredith registered to study for a political science degree at Mississippi University. He was protected by 300 state troopers until he graduated, which showed that another President had acted to enforce a judgment by the Supreme Court.

Some state governors, like George Wallace in Alabama, continued to make speeches against integration at universities, but resistance was now broken, even if black students still faced difficulties once they got to university.

> **Key terms**
>
> **State legislature**: the elected body that makes laws for a particular US state.
>
> **Non-violent direct action**: a protest that provokes a violent response from the people who are being protested against, but where the protesters do not respond with violence.

> **Revision task** TESTED
>
> Explain why
> a) sit-ins
> b) freedom rides, and
> c) the Meredith case
>
> were important in improving the lives of black Americans.

The methods and activities of Martin Luther King

Martin Luther King was born in 1929 in Atlanta, Georgia. His family was quite well off as his father was a Baptist preacher. He got his doctorate from Boston University and decided to become a preacher himself. He had been preaching for a year in Montgomery when the bus boycott began in 1955. His inspirational speeches led to him being chosen as the leader of the Montgomery Improvement Association (MIA).

There were a number of qualities about Martin Luther King that led him to become an inspirational leader in the campaign for civil rights:
- He was a devout Christian, a fact which won him a lot of supporters in both black and white communities; he was a founding member of the Southern Christian Leadership Conference, which organised protests.
- He used **non-violent direct action**, as Gandhi had in the struggle for Indian independence. This was simple for campaigners to implement and won the sympathy of the white community; it resulted in a lot of positive coverage in the media.

- His inspirational speeches and writings about civil rights influenced many people to support civil rights campaigns, and have continued to inspire campaigners ever since.

By 1963, Martin Luther King was widely recognised as one of the leaders of the civil rights movement.

The Birmingham 'Children's March'

- In 1963, in Birmingham, Alabama, a number of civil rights groups organised co-ordinated sit-ins, boycotts and marches to end segregation in the state completely. Birmingham was chosen because:
  - It had done nothing to integrate any of its public facilities.
  - Forty-five per cent of its population was black, which meant a large number of protesters.
  - It had a large Klan presence – campaigners referred to it as 'Bombingham' – and a racist chief of police, so the chance of achieving large-scale publicity was high.
- On 3 April 1963, the first march took place. The police closed public parks and playgrounds. Many civil rights leaders, including Martin Luther King, were put in prison for defying the ban on marches.
- On 2 May 1963, the first 'Children's March' took place. The SNCC trained younger protesters. The marchers were mostly teenagers, though some were as young as six. Thousands were arrested.
- On 3 May 1963, Police Chief 'Bull' Connor ordered dogs and water cannon to be used against protesters as prisons were full. Footage of this was broadcast around the world, leading to a huge surge of support for the civil rights campaigners.
- President Kennedy sent his Attorney General, Burke Marshall, to negotiate between the two sides. The Governor of Alabama and the Klan both tried to disrupt these proceedings, but white business owners wanted the conflict to end. By the middle of May, the protests were over. Desegregation began very slowly afterwards.
- President Kennedy decided that a Civil Rights law was needed to make sure this never happened again. On the same day, civil rights campaigner Medgar Evers was shot dead in Jackson, Mississippi, by a white sniper.

The march on Washington and the 'Dream' speech

The centenary of the **emancipation of enslaved people** was on 28 August 1963. President Kennedy's Civil Rights bill was being debated in Congress. It seemed the ideal time for a march on Washington in support of civil rights for black Americans. The NAACP, CORE, the SNCC and the SCLC got as many people to attend the march as possible.

On one side, the civil rights protesters were getting frustrated by the lack of progress. On the other side, there was increasing violence against the protesters. President Kennedy was concerned the march would actually damage the chances of his Civil Rights bill getting passed and asked for it to be called off.

About 250,000 protesters, twice those expected, joined the march on 28 August 1963. They marched through the city peacefully and then gathered at the Lincoln Memorial for prayers, music and speeches.

Martin Luther King was the final speaker of the day. His 'I have a dream' speech has become one of the most famous speeches in history, even though it was mostly improvised. He explained that his dream was for

> **Key term**
>
> **Emancipation of enslaved people**: freeing of all enslaved people by President Lincoln during the Civil War.

black and white children to live together as equals. He linked this to the Bible, to the Constitution, and to the **Declaration of Independence**, to show how the equality he was dreaming of was all part of the idea of the '**American Dream**' anyway.

The march was a huge success because:
- It showed the extent of support for equal civil rights, including among US celebrities such as singer Bob Dylan, and actors Paul Newman and Marlon Brando.
- People were impressed by how such a large number of protesters could remain peaceful.
- It put pressure on politicians to make sure that they addressed the problem.
- It gave worldwide publicity to the civil rights movement.

In the short term, however, the protesters were frustrated. Bombing campaigns against them continued and in November 1963, when Kennedy was assassinated and replaced by southerner Lyndon Johnson, it seemed that change would not happen after all.

> **Revision task** TESTED
>
> Draw a spider diagram to show reasons why Martin Luther King was one of the most influential leaders of the civil rights movement.

Voting rights

The failure of the Mississippi Freedom Summer

In 1962, the US Government's Voter Education Project, staffed by SNCC members, tried to encourage black Americans to register to vote. Even after the 1957 and 1960 Civil Rights Acts, many were still being refused. Campaigners were harassed, beaten and sometimes shot. Many of those who did register to vote found themselves **evicted** from their farms or sacked from their jobs.

There was going to be a presidential election at the end of 1964, so there was renewed interest in improving voter registration. Supported by Bobby Kennedy, the brother of President Kennedy, the NAACP, CORE and SNCC organised a campaign to increase black American voter registration. They called it 'Freedom Summer'.

The focus was on Mississippi as only seven per cent of black Americans were registered to vote there, the lowest proportion in the country. To vote in Mississippi, you had to pass a very difficult **literacy test**. Civil rights groups created the Mississippi Freedom Party to organise their campaign. They set up classes to teach literacy to black Americans and went on to found 30 Freedom Schools to help improve black American education.

Many consider Freedom Summer to be a failure as only 1,600 more black Americans were registered to vote, even though 17,000 had tried. Many still failed the literacy test, or were victims of threat or violence.

> **Key terms**
>
> **Declaration of Independence**: the 1776 document that said that the King of England had no control over Americans as 'all men are created equal'.
>
> **The 'American Dream'**: to live in peace and prosperity with your family.
>
> **Eviction**: being thrown out of a place you have been renting, which could be farm land or a home.
>
> **Literacy test**: a reading and writing test used to try to stop less-educated black Americans from being able to vote.

The Selma march

Selma, Alabama, had a very low rate of black voter registration – only 383 out of 15,000.

- In January 1965, local civil rights groups invited the SCLC to campaign in Selma. The police resisted attempts to increase voter registration.
- On 7 March 1965, a protest march began from Selma to the state capital, Montgomery, to petition Governor Wallace for improved voting rights. The march was stopped by the police at the Edmund Pettus Bridge at the edge of Selma. The police, under orders from Chief Jim Clark, attacked the protesters with tear gas, clubs and cattle prods. This became known as 'Bloody Sunday' and footage was once again shown around the world. Another march was planned, but Martin Luther King called it off as he was concerned about further violence.
- On 17 March 1965, President Johnson put a voting rights bill into Congress for debate. He used the Alabama National Guard to protect the Selma marchers.
- On 21 March 1965, Martin Luther King led 25,000 people peacefully from Selma to Montgomery.
- In August 1965, the Voting Rights Act was passed.

The march did achieve what the civil rights groups set out to do, but it also split the civil rights movement. Some younger protesters, including members of the SNCC such as Stokely Carmichael, began to doubt that non-violence in the face of police brutality was the right approach.

The impact of protest on civil rights legislation of the 1960s

The Civil Rights Act, 1964

Kennedy's Civil Rights bill was stuck in Congress by the autumn of 1963. President Lyndon Johnson used the shock of Kennedy's assassination to bully Congress into passing it. In the end, the Democrat President was helped by Republican votes to balance out the opposition of the southern Democrats. Johnson signed the Civil Rights Act into law on 2 July 1964.

The Act:
- Banned segregation in public places, businesses and all levels of education.
- Stated that the federal government, not individuals, would bring discrimination cases to court.
- Made permanent the Fair Employment Practices Commission from the Second World War – this made sure any businesses working with the government were not breaking the law.
- Created the Equal Employment Opportunity Commission (EEOC) to ensure the law was being enforced.

While this law ended segregation, in reality it did little to deal with the problem of discrimination. Some protesters were very frustrated by this and began to look for other ways to deal with discrimination.

The Voting Rights Act, 1965

Johnson had originally intended voting rights to be included in the Civil Rights Act, but he removed them as he feared they would mean the Act would never have got enough votes to pass. The Selma march convinced him that he needed to do something quickly, so he had Congress pass the Voting Rights Act in just a few months. He signed it into law on 6 August 1965.

The Act:
- Set one simple national test for voter registration for everyone.
- Banned states from using their own voter qualifications without the approval of the federal government.
- Appointed federal agents to monitor registration; they could intervene if they thought there was discrimination.

By the end of 1965, 250,000 black Americans had registered to vote; 750,000 more had registered by the end of 1968. In Mississippi, where in 1964 only 6.7 per cent of black Americans had been registered to vote, by 1968, 67.5 per cent had registered. It was a dramatic increase.

This led to an increase in the number of black political representatives – councillors, mayors, members of Congress. It also meant that politicians had to pay more attention to what black voters wanted if they were going to win elections.

Other civil rights reforms
- The 1967 Supreme Court ruling, *Loving vs Virginia*, declared that state laws forbidding interracial marriages were unconstitutional.
- The 1968 Fair Housing Act banned discrimination in housing based on race, colour, gender, national origin or religion.

Black Power

Reasons for the growth of Black Power

There was increasing frustration with the lack of progress for black Americans after the Civil Rights Act and Voting Rights Act. Some began to look for a different way to bring about change. This was called '**Black Power**' – a more direct and aggressive approach. There were many reasons why support for Black Power grew in the 1960s:
- segregation and discrimination continued, despite changes in the law
- a lack of job opportunities for black Americans
- terrible living conditions in the ghettos
- increased publicity which spread the ideas of Black Power, especially the importance of being proud of black culture and heritage.

The Nation of Islam and the work of Malcolm X

Not all black Americans agreed with the idea of peaceful protest to achieve integration with white Americans. Many were becoming increasingly frustrated by how little their lives were changing. A new idea was emerging – equality could only be achieved if black Americans lived separate lives from the rest of America. This became known as **black nationalism**. Some of its supporters thought that it might be necessary to use violence to achieve it.

The Nation of Islam started in the 1930s. It emphasised the Muslim beliefs that Africans had followed before slavery and argued that full separation of races was the only way that equality could be achieved. In 1952, this black nationalist group only had 500 members, but by 1962, this had grown to 40,000, including celebrity supporters like **Muhammad Ali**.

> **Revision task**
> 1 Draw a table to show the ways in which the Civil Rights laws of the 1960s did and did not improve the lives of black Americans.
> 2 How much did the civil rights laws of the 1960s improve the lives of black Americans? Explain your judgement. TESTED

> **Key terms**
>
> **Black Power**: the idea that black Americans should be proud of their distinct culture and their African heritage.
>
> **Black nationalism**: the belief that black Americans should solve their own problems.

> **Muhammad Ali (1942–2016)**
> - Muhammed Ali was born Cassius Clay in Kentucky.
> - He was a heavyweight boxer, winning the gold medal in the 1960 Olympics in Rome.
> - Influenced by Malcolm X, Ali converted to Islam in 1961 and took the name Muhammad Ali.
> - He was convicted in 1966 for refusing to fight in Vietnam due to religious objections; his conviction was overturned by the Supreme Court in 1971.
> - He became the world heavyweight boxing champion of the world three times.

Malcolm Little joined the Nation of Islam while he was in prison for burglary. He changed his last name to X to get rid of the surname his family had been given by enslavers. Malcolm X became a minister and travelled the USA making passionate speeches. He was critical of the civil rights movement which he dismissed as an attempt to please white people. He argued that black Americans would have to achieve equality 'by any means necessary'.

Malcolm X set up educational programmes for black people living in the northern ghettos. By 1960, more than 75 per cent of the membership of the Nation of Islam was aged between 17 and 35. He had a good understanding of the difficulties faced by poor, young, northern black Americans.

In 1964, Malcolm X left the Nation of Islam. He went on the *hajj*, the pilgrimage to Mecca, and realised that Muslims from all across the world treated each other equally. When he got back to the United States, he set up the Organization of Afro–American Unity to promote civil rights as well as close links with Africa. He was even prepared to work with white Americans. However, he was shot and killed by members of the Nation of Islam while giving a speech in Harlem, New York, on 21 February 1965.

Malcom X is considered to be an important influence on black American civil rights as he did much to promote the idea of black pride, and to highlight the social and economic problems black Americans were facing.

The influence of Stokely Carmichael

Frustrated by his experiences in Freedom Summer, Stokely Carmichael, an SNCC leader, was looking for a new way of protesting for civil rights.

Influenced by Malcolm X, Carmichael argued that black Americans had to solve problems for themselves, not depend on the help of white Americans. He wanted to improve the lives of black Americans, at the same time as celebrating their African heritage. He was harassed so many times by the police that he began to carry a gun to protect himself, and he said that black people should reply with violence if they were attacked.

Carmichael began to use the phrase 'Black Power' to describe the idea that black Americans should be proud of their heritage, should live their own lives in peace, and that they could bring this about through their own actions, without any help. The idea became increasingly popular.

Stokely Carmichael eventually left the SNCC. While he was popular with some, others criticised his more aggressive approach, and his criticism of US involvement in Vietnam. He went to live in Guinea in Africa in 1969, and stayed there for the rest of his life.

The 1968 Olympics

The 1968 Olympics were held in Mexico and broadcast to a global audience of 1 billion people. A number of black Americans were included in the US team, even though there were calls for them to boycott the event as a protest.

The most iconic images of Black Power came from the medal ceremony for the men's 200 metres race. Black American athletes Tommy Smith and John Carlos had come first and third in the race. During the US national anthem, they both gave the Black Power salute – a clenched fist in a black glove. They also wore black socks without shoes to highlight the poverty of black Americans.

They were heavily criticised by the media for bringing politics into sport. Tommy Smith and John Carlos were sent home and banned from future Olympics. It was a very effective protest as it was seen by so many people around the world.

The impact of Black Power

Black Power worried many of the less extreme civil rights supporters and alienated many white supporters. They blamed Black Power for race riots, and for a more aggressive approach to protests by the police.

However, it did result in increasing self-confidence and belief in the black American community, especially among young people.

It also resulted in a new focus for the civil rights movement (and for US presidents), away from legal rights and directed more towards trying to deal with the realities of on-going discrimination:
- In 1966, Martin Luther King and the SCLC began the Chicago Freedom Movement to improve housing in the city.
- In 1968, Martin Luther King was assassinated while supporting a worker's strike for equal pay in Memphis, Tennessee.
- President Johnson introduced bussing, taking children from black areas of cities to go to schools in white areas on buses – the Supreme Court continued to support this policy despite many legal challenges in the 1970s.
- President Johnson also began the policy of affirmative action, encouraging employers or colleges to give black Americans jobs or places to study, even if they did not have the same qualifications as white Americans. President Nixon continued this into the 1970s, and again it was supported by the Supreme Court.

The impact of race riots, especially in the Watts District

In the four years after the signing of the 1964 Civil Rights Act, there were hundreds of race riots across the USA, as black Americans became increasingly frustrated with the lack of change. They were still being discriminated against, and were still more likely to be unemployed and poor.

In August 1965, a race riot involving 30,000 people caused serious damage in the Watts District of Los Angeles. The riot lasted six days, resulting in 34 deaths, 4,000 arrests and $40m worth of damage. It started when a black youth, Marquette Frye, resisted arrest for drink-driving. Rumours started that the police had attacked his family. The National Guard was sent in to end the riots.

> **Revision task**
>
> Explain why there was increasing support among black Americans for the ideas of the Nation of Islam, Malcolm X and Stokely Carmichael.
>
> TESTED

In the summer of 1967, there were riots in 125 US cities. In Newark, it left 26 people dead and 1,000 injured. In Detroit, it left more than 40 people dead and 7,000 arrested. The damage cost more than $700m.

The US government commissioned the Kerner Report into the riots. It was published in 1968, and said that economic problems faced by black Americans were partly to blame, but that the brutality of the police had made this worse. Its recommendations were mostly ignored.

Following the assassination of Martin Luther King in Memphis in April 1968, there was rioting across the USA. The rioting left 46 people dead and 3,000 injured. It seemed as if non-violent protest had finally come to an end.

While the violence alienated some white supporters, it did lead to a renewed focus on economic problems for the civil rights movement. It also highlighted that problems in the North needed to be addressed just like they had been in the South.

The Black Panthers

Huey Newton and Bobby Seale set up the Black Panther Party in Oakland, California, in October 1966. They had both been influenced by Malcolm X. Their followers wore black clothes, including a black beret, and many of them carried guns for self-preservation.

The Black Panthers wanted to replace capitalist society with a version of communism for the black community, which is why they were monitored by the FBI. They followed the police around to make sure they did not abuse black Americans and in the ghettos many considered them to be an effective police force they could trust.

Their Ten-Point Programme demanded jobs, housing and education for black Americans and an end to abuse by the police. Support for the Black Panthers dropped away towards the end of the 1960s as a result of in-fighting. The Party did still achieve a number of things, including:
- free medical clinics for black Americans
- breakfast clubs for black American children
- classes on the history of black Americans
- encouraging black American gangs to reduce levels of violence.

Revision task

TESTED

1. Draw a table to show reasons why the Black Panthers were an important group, but also the limitations of their importance.
2. To what extent were the Black Panthers an important group in improving the lives of black Americans? Explain your answer.

Exam practice

'The work of Martin Luther King was the most important influence on changes in the lives of black Americans in the 1960s.'

How far do you agree? Explain your answer.

You may use the following in your answer:
- the work of Martin Luther King
- the influence of Stokely Carmichael.

You **must** also use information of your own. (16 marks)

> **Exam tips**
>
> 1 Identify the focus of the question, e.g. 'The main achievement of X was Y', and make sure all of your points link back to this focus.
> 2 Write a paragraph about how each of the two features or events you have been given could be linked to the focus of the question; use specific examples to support the points you make.
> 3 Write another paragraph about a relevant feature or event that is not included in the question, making sure you support your points with specific examples and that you link your points back to the specific focus of the question.
> 4 If needed, you could repeat step 3 for another feature or event.
> 5 Write a conclusion to explain how far you agree with the view given in the question, referring back to points you have made in the rest of your answer.

3.4 Other protest movements: students, women, anti-Vietnam

REVISED

> **What you need to know**
>
> In this section you will revise the protest movements against the Vietnam War and in support of improving women's rights. This will include:
> - The reasons for an increase in protest movements in this period.
> - Different aspects of student protest movements.
> - The movement for women's rights and those who opposed it.

> **Key terms**
>
> **Feminism**: campaigning for women to be treated equally to men.
>
> **Generation gap**: when younger and older people have very different opinions.
>
> **The Depression**: the economic downturn that affected the USA in the 1930s and caused a lot of unemployment and hardship.
>
> **New Deal**: President Roosevelt's plan to use government money to get people back to work.

Reasons for the growth of protest movements

There were a number of reasons for the increase in protest movements in the USA in the 1950s and 1960s:

- The growing **'generation gap'** between younger and older Americans – the older generations had more traditional values as they had lived through the hard times of the **Depression** in the 1930s, while younger Americans grew up in an affluent society that gave them a lot more personal freedom.
- As a result of Roosevelt's **New Deal** in the 1930s, there was an increasing expectation that the federal government would step in to try to help people solve their problems.
- Increasing media coverage of protests, especially through television, meant that protesters could get a lot more interest and support for their causes.
- Frustration with the slow pace of change, from women going back to living their pre-war lives in 1945, to black Americans who were not seeing much improvement in their daily lives after years of promises from politicians.
- The success of the civil rights movement inspired anti-war protesters and **feminists** to challenge the discrimination they faced.

> **Revision task** `TESTED`
>
> Draw a spider diagram to show the different reasons why there was an increasing number of protests in the 1960s.

The student movement

The post-war '**baby boom**' had increased the proportion of younger people in society by the early 1960s. They tended to be from white middle-class families. Many of them went to university where they often became involved in political activities. There was a general sense of the injustice of the world, as could be seen in popular music by artists like **Bob Dylan**. They wanted the government to do more to improve people's lives.

There were several issues that grabbed the attention of young people in the USA in this period:
- Civil rights for black Americans – getting involved in protests through new organisations such as the SNCC (see page 87).
- Nuclear disarmament – this generation of young people were the first to grow up with the threat of **nuclear war**.
- The war in Vietnam in which the average age of American soldiers was only nineteen.

> **Key terms**
>
> **Baby boom**: an increase in the birth rate in the years after the Second World War.
>
> **Nuclear war**: a war using atomic weapons that has the potential to kill all human life on Earth.

> **Bob Dylan (1941–)**
> - Bob Dylan is a folk singer whose early songs inspired many young people to join protests.
> - Some songs reflected concerns about civil rights abuses such as 'Only a pawn in their game' about the death of Medgar Evers, which he sang at the March on Washington in 1963.
> - Other songs focused on the threat of war, such as 'Blowin' in the wind' and 'Masters of war'.
> - 'The times they are a-changing' became an anthem of teenage rebellion.

Students for a Democratic Society and the Berkeley Free Speech Movement

The Students for a Democratic Society (SDS) began at the University of Michigan in 1959. It aimed to give students more of a say in the courses that were on offer. This involved sit-ins and mass meetings to challenge the strict rules of the universities. By the end of the 1960s, there were 100,000 SDS members across 150 colleges and universities.

In 1964, protests at the University of California, Berkeley, received more media attention as many members of the SDS from there had been involved in Freedom Summer (see page 90). They returned from campaigning to get black Americans to register to vote, to begin campaigning against racism at the university. The university banned them from protesting.

Students who broke the ban were suspended. Four hundred more filled the university administration building, demanding to be suspended as well. The police were called while SDS members made speeches criticising the university. Eventually the student protesters agreed to leave.

This led to the Free Speech Movement (FSM) which campaigned for students to be able to talk about whatever they wanted while at university. Half the students at the University of California, Berkeley supported FSM.

After another rally and sit-in in December 1964, large numbers of protesters were arrested. The university agreed that students could protest but that they would have to follow strict rules.

While FSM had shown that students could pressure universities into giving in to their demands, their confrontational approach alienated many moderate students and older Americans.

The anti-Vietnam War movement

In 1954, Vietnam had been divided between the North, run by a communist government, and the South, run by a government sympathetic to the USA. Soldiers from the North, who the Americans called the Viet Cong, infiltrated the South to overthrow the government.

The USA sent advisors to help the government of South Vietnam. In 1964, after an apparent attack on a US ship off the coast of Vietnam, the US military began a large-scale operation in Vietnam, with troops on the ground in the South and bombing raids on the North. By 1969, there were half a million US troops in Vietnam.

Anti-war protests

As US military involvement increased, and horrific images of the war filled television news broadcasts, opposition to US involvement in the Vietnam War began to increase. People had many objections to the war:

- The huge cost to the taxpayer with little evidence of success.
- The rising number of deaths and injuries.
- US tactics, which involved indiscriminate aerial bombing and chemical weapons attacks which killed or injured large numbers of civilians.
- The draft, which forced many young men, especially black and poor white Americans, into the US army to fight the war.

In October 1965, the SDS said that it was opposed to the war. Its membership rose rapidly. Media coverage of the devastation caused by the war meant that while young people had begun opposition to the war, more groups of people began to oppose the war as it dragged on, including groups of **veterans**.

> **Key term**
>
> **Veterans**: people who used to be in the armed forces.

Student protests against the war included mass meetings, sit-ins and students openly burning their draft cards in defiance of the law. In the first half of 1968, there were over 100 demonstrations against the war, involving 400,000 students. In 1969, 500,000 people marched in Washington DC against the war.

The most infamous protest took place at Kent State University in Ohio in May 1970. Troops used tear gas against student demonstrators before firing into the crowd. Four students were killed and eleven were injured. Four hundred colleges were closed as 2 million students went on strike in protest against this.

The Vietnam War split American society into those who supported it and those who opposed it. Protests persuaded President Johnson not to stand for re-election in 1968, and may have led people to vote in Republican Richard Nixon rather than his Democrat opponent, Hubert Humphrey.

Nixon began the withdrawal of US troops from Vietnam in 1969, and handed over control of the war to the government of South Vietnam. Opponents of the war seemed unpatriotic and Nixon claimed he was supporting the 'silent majority' of ordinary Americans who just wanted the war to be over.

Hippies

Some young people reacted very differently to the conflict in the 1960s. Instead of getting involved, they decided to drop out of society altogether. They did not work or go to university. Instead they chose to live in communes, or travel around living out of the back of buses or vans.

The hippy **counter-culture** involved experimenting with sex, drugs, music and art, and believing in peace and love above all else. Hippies grew their hair long, wore colourful and often outlandish clothes, as well as having no problem with public nudity.

The greatest celebration of hippy culture was the 1969 rock music festival at Woodstock which was attended by half a million people. Hippies campaigned for civil rights, women's rights and environmental issues, as well as being opposed to the war in Vietnam.

Most Americans were horrified by the hippies and could not understand why they would choose to reject everything that they considered to be great about America. While many young people did not become hippies themselves, hippy ideals about tolerance, sex and drugs did become more mainstream in America.

> **Key terms**
>
> **Counter-culture**: a set of ideas that are different from the ideas that most people believe in.
>
> **Contraceptive pill**: a pill that is taken by women to prevent pregnancy.

> **Revision task**   TESTED
>
> How successful do you think the SDS, FSM and anti-war protests were? Explain your answer.
>
> HINT: consider what each group wanted to achieve and what they actually achieved.

The women's movement

The Second World War brought changes to the lives of women in the USA. It had widened the number of jobs they could do and increased the number of women in work from 12 million in 1940, to 18.5 million in 1945. However, once the war was over, women:
- continued to be paid less than men and were absent from the highest-paid jobs
- were still expected to give up their jobs when they married
- went back to being limited to what were considered by some traditional women's jobs as teachers, secretaries and nurses.

Women continued to be viewed as a cheap source of labour and, by 1960, women made up nearly half of the workforce.

There were changes that began in the 1950s that resulted in some women challenging the traditional roles of being only a wife and a mother:
- Labour-saving devices such as washing machines and refrigerators meant that there was less for women to do at home, but also meant that more money was needed to pay for these devices.
- The development of the **contraceptive pill** from 1960 gave women much greater control over when to have children. This was only available to all women across the USA after the Supreme Court *Eisenstadt vs Baird* ruling in 1972.

- Women were much better educated, with 1.3 million women in university by 1960, and there were many who were now qualified for professional careers.
- The public profile of the civil rights movement and the student protest movement convinced many women that they should campaign for increased rights as well.

> **Revision task** TESTED
>
> Give three reasons why women began to protest for equal rights. Which reason do you think is the most important? Explain your choice.

Eleanor Roosevelt

Eleanor Roosevelt, the widow of President Roosevelt, had been campaigning for women's rights since the 1930s. As First Lady, she would only allow women to interview her so that newspapers and radio stations had to employ female journalists if they wanted to interview her.

After her husband died, she continued to be an important figure in the Democrat Party. She helped to get John F. Kennedy nominated as the Democrat candidate for President in 1960, and in return he set up the **President's Commission** on the status of women in 1961. Eleanor Roosevelt was put in charge, although she died before the final report was published.

The Commission's report was published in 1963, and showed how badly women were treated at work, how they were stuck in low-paid jobs and were paid less than 60 per cent of what men were paid for the same job.

As a result of the Commission, President Kennedy passed the Equal Pay Act in 1963, which made it illegal to pay people different wages for doing the same job. It was also an influence on the 1964 Civil Rights Act which made all discrimination in jobs illegal.

Betty Friedan

Journalist Betty Friedan researched how women felt about married life. She discovered that many well-educated women found being housewives made them bored and unhappy. She described their family homes as being comfortable prisons. In 1963, she published her findings in *The Feminine Mystique*. Her book quickly became a best-seller.

Friedan argued that women should have equal rights to men in all aspects of their lives, but she was frustrated that the changes in the law in 1963 and 1964 (see above) had not done enough to end discrimination against women. As a result, she was one of the founding members of the National Organisation for Women (NOW), set up to campaign for the government to enforce women's equal rights.

National Organisation for Women (NOW)

NOW was set up in June 1966 by feminists, many of whom were white and middle class, who realised that the Equal Pay and Civil Rights Acts had done little to tackle discrimination against women.

Betty Friedan became NOW's first president, and at the first national conference in 1967, NOW set out its demands in their Bill of Rights:
- the Equal Rights Amendment to become part of the Constitution (see below)

> **Key term**
>
> **President's Commission:** a group of experts who research a particular issue dictated by the President.

- maternity rights, including maternity leave, welfare payments and help paying for childcare
- equal access to education and training
- an end to employment discrimination
- removal of laws limiting contraception and abortion.

By the early 1970s, NOW had 40,000 members. They used marching, strikes, petitions, lobbying politicians and legal cases to try to bring about change:
- Between 1966 and 1971, they won $30 million for women in disputes over equal pay.
- In February 1970, NOW disrupted a Senate discussion by demanding the Equal Rights Amendment be passed.
- In August 1970, NOW's Women's Strike for Equality was supported by thousands of women across the USA, with 50,000 in New York alone.

Some people thought that NOW was too extreme and was doing little to improve the lives of poorer women. Others thought that NOW had not gone far enough.

> **Revision task** — TESTED
>
> Draw a table to show what Eleanor Roosevelt and Betty Friedan each did to help improve women's rights. Who did more to improve the rights of women in this period? Explain your choice.

Women's Liberation Movement

The Women's Liberation Movement was the name given to a group of women who had more far-reaching demands than NOW. The most extreme feminists wanted to free themselves from anything to do with men at all.

The methods of the Women's Liberation groups were much more aggressive than those of NOW. They:
- refused to wear make-up or bras as they were symbols of male control
- held sit-ins to highlight businesses they thought were sexist
- tried to force their way into bars and clubs that were for men only.

In 1968, at the Miss America beauty pageant in Atlantic City, members of the Liberation Movement protested. Their placards and leaflets, shouting of feminist slogans, and throwing away of bras and make-up, grabbed the attention of the world's media. They also crowned a sheep Miss America to show how degrading beauty contests were.

However, much of this publicity was negative and made the supporters of Women's Liberation seem too extreme for the wider American population to support. More moderate feminist campaigners thought this was too much of a distraction from working for equal pay and better job opportunities.

Abortion

In 1960, **abortion** was illegal in every state in the USA, unless the life of the mother was endangered by the pregnancy. NOW and the Women's Liberation Movement wanted to change this. They wanted women to be able to choose what happened to their bodies. They argued that dangerous illegal abortions were happening, whatever the law said.

> **Key term**
>
> **Abortion**: a medical procedure to artificially end a pregnancy.

Campaigns to allow abortion did start to result in changes. In 1970, New York allowed abortions on demand up to 24 weeks of pregnancy and several other states followed this example. Abortion remained illegal in most states.

In 1970, Norma McCorvey, using the name Jane Roe, went to court in Dallas, Texas, to claim the right to an abortion. The court allowed it, but only in her case. McCorvey's lawyers, including feminist Sarah Weddington, decided to take the case to the Supreme Court so it would apply in every state. The case was known as *Roe vs Wade* (the Dallas District Attorney).

In January 1973, the Supreme Court ruled that abortion laws broke a women's right to privacy and choice of family matters, as defined in the Fourteenth Amendment. They said abortion should be limited to a maximum of six months into the pregnancy. It meant that abortion was now available in every state in the USA.

Phyllis Schlafly and opposition to the women's movement

Not everyone supported the women's movement. Media coverage was often very negative and it was not taken as seriously as the civil rights movement or student protests.

The most common objection to equality for women was the strongly held belief that women were weaker than men and were meant to be housewives, protected by men because men were stronger. There was concern that equality would be very damaging to family life.

An anti-feminist movement began, led by Phyllis Schlafly. She was a wife and a mother of six children who believed that women were meant to be housewives, and she was opposed to abortion because of her Catholic beliefs. Her powerful speeches led a lot of women to support her movement.

In 1972, Congress finally passed the Equal Rights Amendment (ERA) Bill which had first been proposed in 1923. This would mean that equal rights for women would be written into law.

Phyllis Schlafly founded 'Stop ERA' – an organisation to help stop states agreeing to the amendment, as 38 states had to agree to it before it could be put in the Constitution. She argued that not only would it damage families, but it would mean that women would have to serve in the military and divorced wives would no longer get money from their ex-husbands. She was successful. By the time the deadline for agreement was reached in 1982, only 35 of the required 38 states had agreed to ERA.

The impact of the women's movement

There were a number of laws and legal decisions that helped to improve the situation for women beyond the Equal Pay and Civil Rights Acts and abortion rights:
- The 1971 *Reed vs Reed* Supreme Court case ruled that laws that discriminate against women were unconstitutional.
- The 1972 Educational Amendment Act outlawed discrimination against girls and women in education.
- The 1974 Equal Credit Opportunity Act made it illegal for women to be refused loans on the grounds of their gender.

Gradually, it came to be accepted that women could have a career as well as having children, even though much more needed to be done to deal with issues of pay and opportunities.

> **Exam practice**
>
> 'The work of Betty Friedan was the most important influence on women's lives between 1945 and 1974.'
>
> How far do you agree? Explain your answer.
>
> You may use the following in your answer:
> - the work of Betty Friedan
> - the Women's Liberation movement.
>
> You **must** also use information of your own. (16 marks)

> **Exam tips**
>
> Begin with the focus of the question, '*The most important influence on women's lives between 1945 and 1974 was ...*', and make sure all of your points link back to this focus. For further guidance, see page 95.

> **Revision task**
>
> How successful do you think the women's liberation movement was? Explain your judgement.
> TESTED

3.5 Nixon and Watergate

REVISED

What you need to know

In this section you will revise the Watergate scandal and its importance in US politics. This will include:
- The reasons why the Watergate scandal happened.
- What happened in the Watergate scandal.
- The impact of the scandal on US politics.
- The significance of President Ford's pardoning of former President Nixon.

Reasons for the Watergate scandal

- 1968: Nixon was given the Republican **nomination** for the 1968 presidential election, which he won.
- Nixon became very suspicious of those around him, holding grudges against those who opposed him, but also rewarding those loyal to him. He installed tape recorders in the Oval Office that would eventually prove his own wrong-doing.
- Nixon used 'dirty tricks' to deal with his opponents. In 1971, he sent the 'White House Plumbers', a group whose job was to prevent leaks of sensitive information, to dig up information on Daniel Ellsberg, a Pentagon official who had given sensitive information about the war in Vietnam to the *New York Times* newspaper.
- In 1972, Nixon decided to stand for re-election. He was not convinced he would win in a straight fight. He set up the Committee to Re-Elect the President (known as CREEP) to raise funds for his election campaign. It was headed by John Mitchell, who had been **Attorney General**. Nixon gave them a secret budget of $350,000 to help the White House Plumbers spy on his opponents.
- CREEP seemed to be very successful. Democratic candidate Edmund Muskie was reduced to tears on the campaign trail by false stories that CREEP had planted in the press about his wife and lost the Democratic nomination.
- This changed when five men were arrested in the Democratic Party office in the Watergate Centre on 17 June 1972. The burglars were discovered repairing bugging devices that had been planted on 28 May. Some of them had connections to CREEP. Nixon remained very popular and easily won re-election in November 1972.
- Two separate investigations uncovered the connections between the burglars and the White House:
  1 Woodward and Bernstein, reporters for the *Washington Post* newspaper, found connections between CREEP and the burglars, even though the White House had denied any such connection. They continued to investigate, and with the help of an FBI insider known as 'Deep Throat', they were able to provide proof of these connections.
  2 The FBI found links between the burglars and CREEP – Liddy and Hunt were White House Plumbers who had planned the break-in, and CREEP Director of Security, James McCord, was one of the burglars. The money to pay for the sabotage operation against the Democrats had come from CREEP as well. It took two years to uncover all of this.

Key terms

Donors: people who give money to support the campaign of a candidate in an election.

Nomination: the process by which political parties chose who their candidates are in elections.

Attorney General: the government's most senior legal advisor.

Revision task

Explain why the capture of the Watergate burglars was a serious problem for President Nixon. TESTED

Key features of the Watergate Scandal

- Nixon appeared to be unconcerned by these stories. He said that both political parties tried to get an advantage over each other, and this was nothing new. He said that the White House had nothing to do with the break-in and people believed him.
- However, Nixon immediately began a cover-up operation. In the Oval Office, he discussed using the CIA to stop the FBI investigation into CREEP. When the CIA refused to help, he bribed the burglars to remain silent. Both of these actions were obstructing justice – a federal crime.
- In January 1973, the Watergate burglars went on trial. James McCord said that there had been a White House cover-up, which Nixon denied. They were all convicted. Nixon did admit that two of his advisors, Bob Haldeman and John Ehrlichman, had been involved, so they resigned on 30 April 1973. Vice-President Agnew was also forced to resign over charges of evading income tax.
- The Select Committee on Presidential Campaign Activities was set up to investigate the accusations against Nixon. Its proceedings were televised between May and November 1973. Nixon's approval ratings plummeted. It became clear that White House officials had been involved in a cover-up; some of them, including John Dean, openly admitted it.
- During the Senate investigations it was revealed that Nixon used a tape machine to record meetings in the Oval Office. Nixon refused to hand over the tapes because he said it would threaten national security. In November 1973, he handed over nine tapes that had been heavily edited – one of them had eighteen minutes missing. In July 1974, the Supreme Court ruled that Nixon had to hand over unedited copies of the tapes.
- The 'Smoking Gun' tape of 23 June 1972 proved Nixon's guilt as he could be heard trying to stop the FBI investigation. The tapes also showed that he had known about the 'dirty tricks' campaign (see page 103), and that he had repeatedly lied about it. Americans were horrified to hear their president swearing repeatedly (in written versions this was covered by the phrase 'expletive deleted').

The House of Representatives decided to **impeach** Nixon for:
- **obstruction of justice**, because of the cover-up
- abuse of power, because of using the CIA and other government agencies to help in the cover-up.
- This would involve a trial in the Senate which could result in the President being removed from office and sent to prison. Nixon knew he had lost the support of the Republicans in the Senate, so on 8 August 1974, he resigned.

> **Key terms**
>
> **Impeachment**: when Congress accuses the President of breaking the law or behaving inappropriately, to stop the President abusing their position of power.
>
> **Obstruction of justice**: when a President uses their power to try and prevent law enforcement officials from investigating a crime.

Revision task
TESTED

Which event in the Watergate scandal do you think was the most important? Explain your choice.

Impact on US politics

There were a number of consequences of the Watergate Scandal, as shown below.

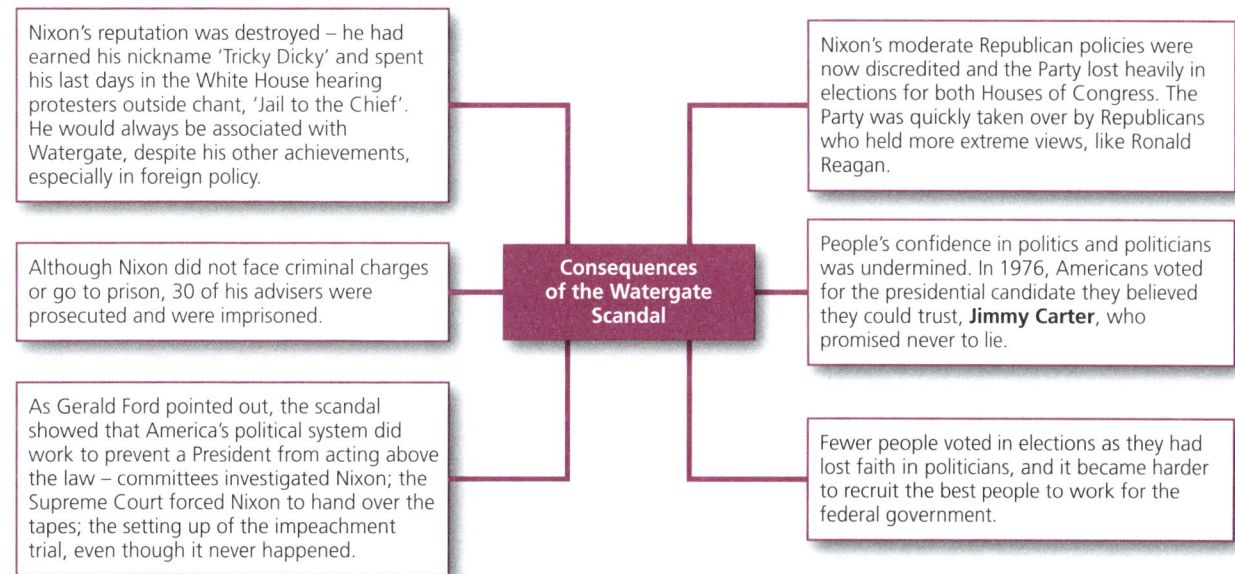

Throughout the twentieth century, US presidents had appeared to increase their power, creating what some people called the 'imperial presidency' – a president so powerful, he thought he could do whatever he wanted. Now Congress acted to try to reduce some of those presidential powers:

- The War Powers Act (1973) prevented the President from going to war without the approval of Congress.
- The Election Campaign Act (1974) limited contributions to political campaigns to $5,000 a person to prevent corruption.
- The Privacy Act (1974) allowed US citizens access to information that the federal government held about them, and controlled how information could be collected by the government.
- The Congressional Budget Control Act (1974) established rules for how the President was able to use government money.

Over the following years, more and more restrictions were also put on the President's ability to issue orders to the FBI and the CIA. It was hoped that these changes would prevent another Watergate and would restore people's faith in the federal government.

Jimmy Carter (1924–)

- Carter served on submarines in the US Navy before taking over his family peanut-farming business in the 1950s.
- He was the Senator for Georgia, 1963–67 and Governor of Georgia, 1971–75.
- He served as the 39th US President between 1977 and 1981, having promised the US electorate that he would never lie to them.

Revision task

TESTED

What do you think was the most important consequence of the Watergate Scandal? Explain your choice.

Gerald Ford and the presidential pardon

Nixon was the first President to resign. Recently appointed Vice-President Gerald Ford became President, saying 'our long national nightmare is over'. Ford used the presidential **power of pardon** to issue a decree on 8 September 1974, pardoning Nixon for any criminal acts that he had taken part in. This meant that Nixon would not face any prosecution for his wrong-doing. Ford argued that this action was to put an end to the scandal so that the nation could move on. This was a very unpopular decision and may have contributed to Ford's failure to be re-elected in 1976.

> **Key term**
>
> **Power of pardon**: the Second Article of the US Constitution gives the President the power to forgive criminals convicted of federal crimes.

Revision task   TESTED

Do you think that President Ford should have pardoned Nixon? Explain your answer.

Exam practice

Explain **two** effects of the Watergate Scandal in the 1970s.   (8 marks)

> **Exam tips**
>
> 1. You should break your answer down into two short paragraphs, one for each effect.
> 2. Choose one effect of the event in the question and write about this.
> 3. Use specific information from your knowledge to describe this consequence of the event.
> 4. Make sure that you clearly link the consequence back to the question – 'X led to Y because ...'
> 5. Choose another effect of the event in the question and write about this, repeating steps 2 and 3 above.

Section 2A Historical Investigations

4 Russia and the Soviet Union, 1905–24

4.1 Tsarist rule in Russia, 1905–14

REVISED

> **What you need to know**
>
> In this section you will revise how the Tsar ruled Russia in this period and how and why some people rebelled against his rule. This includes:
> - Tsarist rule in Russia in 1905 and reasons for discontent in Russia.
> - The *Potemkin* Mutiny and the setting up of Soviets.
> - The 1905 Revolution, including the October Manifesto and why Nicholas survived.
> - The attitude of Nicholas to the first four Dumas.
> - The growth of opposition groups.
> - Stolypin's policy of repression and land reform.
> - The Lena Goldfield strike.

Tsarist rule in Russia in 1905

In 1905, the huge Russian Empire was the largest country in the world.
- It included people of many different nationalities, ethnicities, languages and religions.
- The late nineteenth century had seen the growth of towns, cities and industry. St Petersburg and Moscow were by far the largest urban areas.
- Despite the industrial growth, Russia was still largely a rural, farming society. Up to 80 per cent of the population were peasants. It had only been a little over 40 years since the 1861 **emancipation of the serfs** and life for most peasants had not improved much since then.
- The **aristocracy** made up only 1.5 per cent of the population, but held much of its wealth and all political power after the Tsar himself. They owned huge country estates and grand houses in the cities.

How was Russia ruled?

Russia was ruled by **Tsar Nicholas II**. His family had controlled Russia for centuries and Nicholas wanted to continue to rule as they had.

The Tsar was an **autocrat**. This meant that, unlike in many other countries at this time, the Tsar could do whatever he wanted – there was no parliament or legal court which could question his decisions or challenge him.
- The Tsar had an Imperial Council of ministers to advise him, but he could choose whether or not to take their advice and he could appoint and dismiss these ministers as he wanted. Many of these advisors were Nicholas' family and friends – all were from the aristocracy or the Church.

> **Key terms**
>
> **Emancipation of the serfs**: serfdom is a form of slavery where people have to work for a landowner in return for being able to farm some land for themselves. Russian serfs were only officially freed (emancipated) in 1861.
>
> **Aristocracy**: upper class.
>
> **Autocrat**: a ruler with absolute power.

- The Russian Orthodox Church was very powerful and supported autocracy. It taught that the Tsar was chosen and guided by God.
- Members of the Russian armed forces all swore an oath of loyalty to the Tsar and his family. The army was used to put down disorder.
- Political parties were banned. Political opponents were arrested by the police. The **Okhrana** spied on people, looking for anyone who might be against the Tsar's regime. Thousands were imprisoned or exiled to **Siberia**. Some were executed.
- Newspapers and books were **censored**.
- Regions of the countryside were run by governors, appointed by the Tsar. Local 'land captains' dealt with smaller areas of the countryside.
- In towns, there was some **democracy** as people (mostly from the middle classes) were elected to the **zemstva** which ran some of the local services.

Tsar Nicholas II (1868–1918)

- Nicholas II was devoted to his wife, Alexandra, and family (they had four daughters and a son).
- He worked hard but did not possess the skills to be an effective ruler. He did not like making decisions and refused to delegate tasks to others. He even did his own filing!
- He strongly believed in autocracy and therefore resisted all political reform.
- He was forced to abdicate in 1917, and was killed, along with his family, by the Bolsheviks in 1918.

Long-term reasons for discontent

Many people from all classes and parts of the Russian Empire were afraid of the police and *Okhrana* but different groups had their own reasons for discontent as well.

Key terms

Okhrana: the Tsar's secret police.

Siberia: a large, very cold and hostile province in the north east of the Russian Empire.

Censored: checked before being published – anything unacceptable would be removed or changed.

Democracy: where rulers of a country are elected by the population of that country.

Zemstva: council. Socialism: and Trade unions: definitions, each on new line.

Socialism: a system where the state owns most businesses and land and the profits are shared by everyone.

Trade union: an organisation made up of workers, usually from one trade or a group of trades, which can negotiate things such as better pay with business owners.

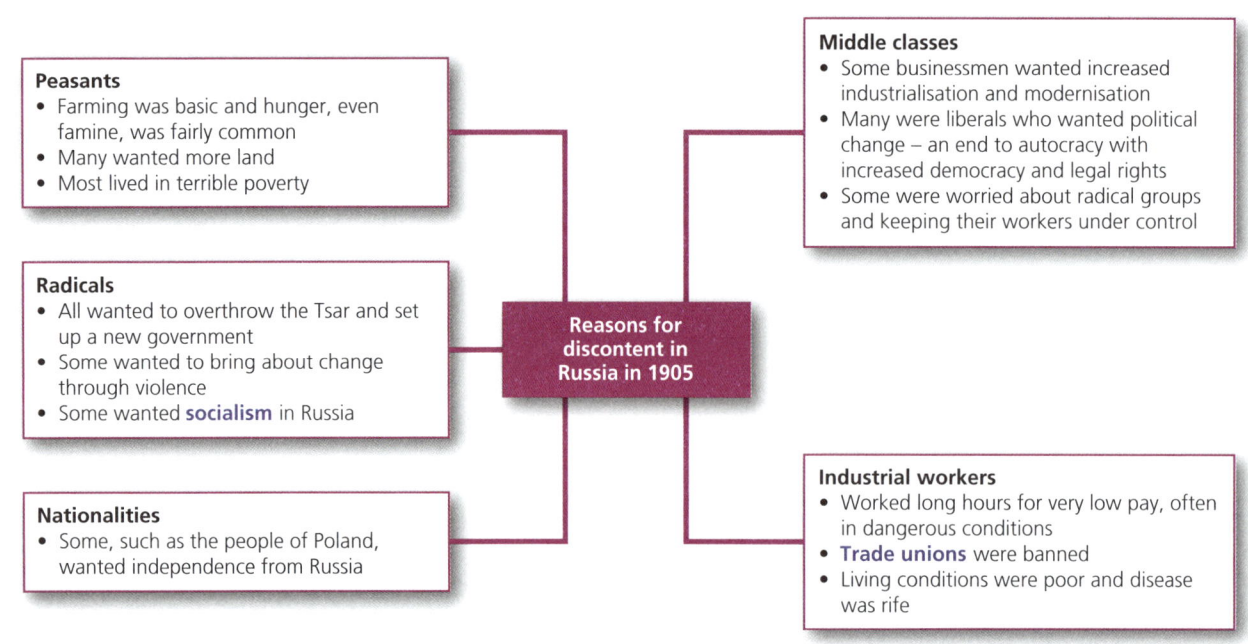

Peasants
- Farming was basic and hunger, even famine, was fairly common
- Many wanted more land
- Most lived in terrible poverty

Radicals
- All wanted to overthrow the Tsar and set up a new government
- Some wanted to bring about change through violence
- Some wanted **socialism** in Russia

Nationalities
- Some, such as the people of Poland, wanted independence from Russia

Middle classes
- Some businessmen wanted increased industrialisation and modernisation
- Many were liberals who wanted political change – an end to autocracy with increased democracy and legal rights
- Some were worried about radical groups and keeping their workers under control

Reasons for discontent in Russia in 1905

Industrial workers
- Worked long hours for very low pay, often in dangerous conditions
- **Trade unions** were banned
- Living conditions were poor and disease was rife

Revision task

TESTED

Sources written by people from different groups are likely to give different reasons for the discontent of Russian people in 1905. Complete the following table to show which groups wanted political change, economic change and improved living and working conditions. Then, write a paragraph explaining which types of people were demanding which type of change, and why.

	Political change	Economic change	Improved living and working conditions
Peasants			
Industrial workers			
Middle classes			
Nationalities			
Radicals			

The 1905 Revolution

Although there was widespread discontent in Russia at this time, there were triggers which turned this discontent into a revolution.

Short-term causes of the 1905 Revolution

1. **Poor harvest, 1901**: Most areas of Russia were struck with famine in 1901–02 because of the poor harvest. This increased hardship and discontent among peasants, as they were still expected to provide grain for export, even though they did not have enough to feed themselves and their families.
2. **Russo–Japanese War, 1904–05**: The Tsar took Russia to war with Japan over Manchuria, because Japan was looking to take over the territory that bordered Russia. The war caused food shortages and taxes were raised to pay for it, adding to people's hunger and poverty. The Russian armed forces lost several battles and looked very weak. People blamed the Tsar's government.
3. **Bloody Sunday, 22 January 1905**: Throughout January, discontent among workers in St Petersburg mounted. It came to a head on 22 January, when a large crowd of protesters, led by a priest called Father Gapon, brought a petition to the Tsar's Winter Palace. The petition asked for reduced working hours and for trade unions to be allowed. The army charged and fired into the crowd, injuring many and killing over 100. People throughout Russia were horrified and most blamed the Tsar.

The setting up of Soviets

Bloody Sunday triggered revolutionary activity across Russia:
- In the countryside, peasants rioted, attacking their landlords' houses and taking their land. Some landlords were killed.
- In the towns and cities, industrial workers went on strike and demonstrated in the streets.
- Some nationalist groups declared independence.

From May, workers in towns and cities began electing people to small councils (**Soviets**) to help organise strikes and other protests. Revolutionaries began returning from **exile**. The St Petersburg Soviet was the largest. It and others in large cities were formed to help co-ordinate a general strike which had begun in September.

Key terms

Soviet: an elected council of workers.

Exile: a punishment when people have to leave their country and cannot come back to it.

The General Strike brought Russia to a complete standstill as all important industries, including railway workers, joined the strike.

The St Petersburg Soviet and its chair – Leon Trotsky, returning from exile – would play an important role in the events of 1917 (see page 122).

The *Potemkin* Mutiny

One of the main methods the Tsar used to keep control over Russia was through the armed forces, which were loyal to their leader. However, there were problems within the armed forces which led to discontent:
- Living conditions on navy ships were very poor.
- Very strict discipline was maintained. The officers, who were all from the upper classes, were in total control.
- Morale was low due to defeats in the Russo–Japanese War.

Some sailors became interested in socialism, including a low-ranked officer on the battleship *Potemkin* called Afanasi Matyushenko. He planned to lead a **mutiny** by the Russian navy which would then join the peasants and workers (see below) in order to take down the Tsar and his government.

> **Key terms**
>
> **Mutiny**: a rebellion by members of the armed forces against their leaders.
>
> **Asylum**: protection by a country.
>
> **Duma**: elected parliament.

The mutiny began on the *Potemkin* on 14 June 1905. Leading mutineers began to disobey orders and refused to eat meat that had been cooked for them as it had maggots in it.

↓

As this continued, one of the officers shot and killed one of the mutineers which led to the mutineers attacking the rest of the officers. The officers were either killed or locked up.

↓

The mutineers formed a socialist 'committee' led by Matyushenko to take control of the ship and sailed to Odessa, where workers' protests were taking place.

↓

In Odessa there were demonstrations to support the mutiny and rioting began in the city. The Tsar ordered the army to bring back control to Odessa, which it did through violence – over 1,000 people were killed.

↓

The mutineers on the *Potemkin* tried and failed to get other navy ships to mutiny. They sailed to Romania where they sank the ship and stayed on to seek **asylum**.

Revision task

TESTED

Explain why the *Potemkin* Mutiny was particularly serious for the Tsar.

The October Manifesto

Although he was extremely reluctant to give up any of his power, the situation had become so bad that the Tsar had little choice but to accept the advice of some of those around him and grant some concessions to try to restore control. In the October Manifesto, the Tsar promised:
- a **Duma**, which would have to approve any new laws
- freedom of speech and religion
- the right to form political parties
- the right to form trade unions.

Some people, especially the middle classes, were very happy with the manifesto. Other groups did not think the manifesto went far enough as it said nothing about land ownership or worker's rights. Radicals still wanted the Tsar overthrown.

Why Nicholas survived

- The October Manifesto did address some of people's concerns. Its publication led to the end of the General Strike.
- Because the different protesters all had very different aims, the October Manifesto satisfied some and not others. This divided the protesters.
- The Tsar ensured the majority of the armed forces stayed loyal to him by promising improved conditions and better pay.
- The Tsar negotiated peace with Japan which meant that he could use the returning troops to forcefully stop the protests. Huge numbers of troops brutally put down uprisings in both towns and the countryside. Some protesters were killed and many were imprisoned.
- Many members of Soviets were arrested and some imprisoned. The St Petersburg and Moscow Soviets were closed down and the leaders arrested and exiled to Siberia.

The attitude of Nicholas to the first four Dumas

Nicholas had agreed to a Duma only very reluctantly. The Fundamental Laws of 1906 ensured that the Tsar could:

- close the Duma whenever he wanted
- rule without the Duma when it was not in session
- change who could vote in elections to the Duma
- appoint whomever he wanted as his ministers – they didn't have to be members of the Duma.

Moreover, the Tsar remained supreme leader of the armed forces so could call on them to put down any rebellions. Four Dumas were held between 1906 and 1914. Nicholas paid little attention to the criticisms of the Duma and dismissed each one when it became an obstacle to his demands.

The first Duma

Opening just four days after the Fundamental Laws in April 1906, the first Duma was openly hostile towards the Tsar. It demanded **land reform** and the release of political prisoners. The Tsar dissolved it after just 73 days.

The second Duma

More members of extreme parties stood for election to the second Duma – including some that supported autocracy. The Duma argued very heatedly for over three months before the Tsar dissolved it.

The third Duma

This began in November 1907, after the Tsar had changed voting laws so only the most wealthy male Russians could vote – those most likely to support candidates who were more supportive of the Tsar. This Duma was therefore much more favourable to Nicholas' government, for example, it passed several of Stolypin's reforms (see below). However, even this Duma was becoming more hostile to the Tsar by 1912, so Nicholas dissolved it.

> **Revision task**
>
> 1 List five reasons why Nicholas survived in order of importance. Explain why you have chosen your first reason as the most important.
> 2 Looking back at the task on page 109, decide which groups (peasants, industrial workers, the middle class, nationalities and radicals) were most likely to be satisfied / partly satisfied / unsatisfied with the changes brought about by the October Manifesto. Give reasons why.
>
> TESTED

> **Key term**
>
> **Land reform**: a process of breaking up big estates owned by landlords and handing out the land to the people who actually farmed it.

The fourth Duma

Those elected to the fourth Duma, which began in November 1912, were still quite critical of the Tsar. This criticism grew during the First World War until the Tsar dissolved the Duma in 1915.

The growth of opposition groups

The period 1905–14 saw the growth of opposition groups to the Tsar.
- **Kadets** were mostly liberals who wanted a constitutional monarchy – they wanted to keep the Tsar but reduce his power. They grew more disillusioned with the Tsar as time went on.
- **Octobrists** were also mostly liberals from the middle and upper classes. They supported the Tsar and the ideals of the October Manifesto, but became more opposed to the Tsar as it became obvious that he would not stick to the promises of the October Manifesto.
- **Social Democrats** were radical socialists who wanted a **Marxist** society and to completely remove the Tsar. They existed in secret before 1905. In 1903, they split into Mensheviks and Bolsheviks. Both believed in Marxist revolution but disagreed on the timing and path this should take.
- **Social Revolutionaries (SRs)** were another radical party. Some were socialist but before 1905 used violence to try to overthrow the Tsar. The party was supported by many peasants because of their ideas of land reform.

Stolypin's policies

Pyotr Stolypin was appointed prime minister by the Tsar in 1906. He wanted to reform industry and agriculture so the economy would grow. The hope was that these improvements would also prevent any further revolutions from occurring.

> **Pyotr Stolypin (1862–1911)**
> - Stolypin was born into a very wealthy, aristocratic family who owned huge amounts of land.
> - He studied agriculture at university in St Petersburg and shortly after worked for the government, where he rapidly rose through the ranks. He was appointed prime minister by the Tsar in 1906.
> - He was seen as too liberal by the Tsar's supporters and too conservative by opposition groups, and was therefore hated by many! He was assassinated in 1911.

Repression

In order to prevent possible revolution, the police and *Okhrana* became even more important during Stolypin's time in charge. Over 20,000 people deemed to be 'revolutionary' were exiled. Over 1,000 people were hanged (the hangman's noose became known as 'Stolypin's necktie').

Many trade unions had formed after the October Manifesto but Stolypin's policy of repression led to over 600 unions closing. Censorship was tightened and hundreds of newspapers stopped publishing altogether. This meant that the most extreme opposition groups were effectively repressed, but they went underground rather than disappearing altogether.

> **Revision task**
>
> Sum up Nicholas II's attitude to the first four Dumas. Give examples to support your summary. TESTED

> **Key term**
>
> **Marxist**: the economic and political theories of nineteenth-century philosopher Karl Marx, which include the idea of organising society so that the means of production are owned and run by workers.

Land reform

Stolypin tried to improve industry. He was partially successful. Heavy industry grew rapidly and the economy did grow during his time in power, but still lagged behind western powers. He was hampered as the Tsar blocked some of his reforms, such as introducing laws to protect factory workers.

He was more successful with agricultural reform. He introduced laws which allowed peasants to remove themselves from the **mir** and buy more land. Peasants' Land Banks were introduced, which loaned wealthier peasants money to buy land. This benefited **kulaks** who managed to create larger, more efficient farms. Agricultural production significantly increased, though most peasants still lived in great poverty.

> **Key terms**
>
> **Mir**: village communes which all peasants joined and which divided up land between them all.
>
> **Kulaks**: wealthier peasants.

Revision task TESTED

1. Write two lists: one of ways in which people may have felt that Stolypin was an effective prime minister and another of ways in which people may have felt that he was ineffective.
2. What do you think? Was Stolypin an effective prime minister or not?

The Lena Goldfield strike

There had been some progress made in improving the lives of industrial workers. Some trade unions did continue and successfully forced the introduction of safety inspectors into factories in 1912.

However, many workers continued to work in dangerous conditions for long hours and low pay. This was the case at the Lena Goldfield mines in Siberia:

- Shifts were often fifteen or sixteen hours long.
- Workers were given little or no safety equipment.
- Injuries were common due to the lack of safety measures and long hours.
- Pay was low and workers were heavily fined for even very minor offences.

In 1911, wages were reduced and workers were given some payment in the form of meals from the company's canteen. In late February 1912, the only food available in the canteen was horse meat, which was rotting! In response, 6,000 Lena Goldfield workers formed a strike committee. They demanded:

- the introduction of an eight-hour working day
- an increase in wages
- the abolition of company fines
- better food in the canteen.

When the company rejected their demands, the workers went on strike. As the strike continued, the company asked the government to send army troops to break it up. The soldiers arrived in early April and quickly arrested the leaders of the strike committee. On 5 April, a large demonstration took place where 2,500 workers marched to the company's headquarters to demand the release of their leaders. The army troops opened fire. Many were injured and over 250 workers were killed.

The response of the Tsar's government to the strike illustrated that little had changed in Russia since Bloody Sunday of 1905. The massacre led to around 750,000 workers going on strike throughout Russia. The Lena Goldfield strike carried on until mid-August when most of the workers left and the company was forced to close down.

Revision task

TESTED

Complete the table below to help you describe at least two features of the Lena Goldfield strike.

Feature of the Lena Goldfield strike	Supporting detail of this feature

Exam practice

Study Sources A and B.

How does Source A support the evidence of Source B about the reasons for discontent during the 1905 Revolution?

Explain your answer. (8 marks)

Source A

From a petition to Nicholas II from peasants from Kherson province, in Ukraine, in May 1905.

Our needs are great, Your Majesty! For two and a half centuries we endured servitude [being serfs] and thereby made it possible for the privileged classes to live in clover [luxury]; we alone carried the burden of harsh military service; for many centuries we have had to pay an unbearable amount in taxes and dues. For our unfailing centuries-old service to the state we received a wretched allotment of land with high redemption dues [repayments], we were deprived of all rights; for centuries we stagnated in ignorance and we remain in that condition today.

Adapted from *The Revolution of 1905: Russia in disarray*, Abraham Ascher, 1988, Stanford University Press, p. 165.

Source B

From a petition by Father Gapon to be presented to Nicholas II on what turned into Bloody Sunday, 9 January 1905.

SIRE

We are impoverished; we are oppressed, overburdened with excessive toil [work], contemptuously treated ... We are suffocating in despotism [cruel treatment by a government] and lawlessness. O SIRE we have no strength left, and our endurance is at an end. We have reached that frightful moment when death is better than the prolongation [continuation] of our unbearable sufferings.

A People's Tragedy: The Russian Revolution 1891–1924, Orlando Figes, 1996, Jonathan Cape, p. 175.

Exam tips

1. Start by reading the sources twice.
2. Then annotate parts of the sources that are especially important to the exam question to help you identify the reasons given for discontent.
3. In your answer, you should give a judgement on how far A supports B. You could use phrases such as '*totally supports / partially supports / does not support at all ...*' to help you do this.
4. You should state any reasons that are the same or similar.
5. Then state any reasons that are different.

4.2 Opposition to Tsarist rule, 1914–17: the impact of war and the February Revolution

REVISED

What you need to know

In this section you will revise the different opposition to the Tsar in this period and the reasons for and results of this. This will include:
- The economic, social and political effects of the First World War on Russia.
- The influence of Rasputin.
- The immediate causes of the February Revolution, especially events in Petrograd.
- The army mutiny.
- The abdication of the Tsar.
- The setting up of the Provisional Government.

The effects of the First World War on Russia

There were very few Russians who did not agree with the Tsar's decision to enter the First World War in August 1914, on the side of the Allies (Britain and France). Briefly at least, the Tsar was very popular as the vast majority threw their support behind the war effort.
- The Duma immediately voted to allow war credits to pay for military equipment and transport, with little debate.
- The German embassy was attacked by Russian students.
- St Petersburg was renamed Petrograd (as St Petersburg sounded too German).
- Most people seemed to accept that some hardships would follow but that this was necessary for victory. For example, most accepted without question the government's ban on the sale of vodka.

However, it was not long before the effects of the First World War would directly lead to another revolution.

Economic effects of the war

The war had a huge impact on the Russian economy and the incomes of individuals:
- Huge numbers of men were drafted into the armed forces. This meant the countryside lost agricultural workers and towns lost industrial workers and skilled craftsmen.
- To finance the war, the Tsar borrowed vast sums of money from other countries and raised some taxes. This still wasn't enough to cover everything. For example:
  - Widows and orphans of those soldiers who were killed were entitled to state war pensions, but casualties were so high that the state could not afford to pay everyone, leaving many in poverty.
  - The government was not always able to pay for food, reducing peasants' incomes and adding to food shortages in towns and cities.
- As the war began to go badly for Russia, territory was lost to both Germany and Austria–Hungary. This included important coal fields and mines, which led to shortages of fuel throughout Russia and shortages of raw materials for industry.
- The increased need for manufacturing military equipment led to more jobs being available in towns and cities. Urbanisation and employment therefore increased. However, wages remained low.

- Increased military production and military transport was achieved at a huge cost to civilian industry and transport. This led to shortages of food, fuel and other essentials in many towns and cities. The price of food rocketed. Many Russians were threatened with starvation.

Social effects of the war

- Russian military defeats during the war negatively affected morale among both troops and civilians. This effect increased as it became apparent that the war was not going to be over quickly.
- Nearly 2 million Russian troops were killed and nearly 5 million were wounded, leaving many families devastated.
- Many civilians were also killed, especially in the western territories which had been invaded.
- Peasants were affected by the loss of agricultural workers as men were sent to fight or went to cities in search of work. This left more work for those left behind.
- For industrial workers, pay remained low but the cost of goods rose, making life harder.
- As more people moved to towns and cities looking for work, this added to the problem of overcrowding and made living conditions worse.
- Lack of food and the high price of what food was available left many urban Russians hungry, some on the edge of starvation.

Political effects of the war

- The large numbers of Russian deaths in the war were at least partly due to poor military leadership, tactics and planning. The army was led by aristocrats who were appointed by the Tsar. Normal soldiers were treated very badly. This increased discontent among the lower classes.
- In September 1915, the Tsar made himself Commander-in-Chief of the armed forces and moved to the front line – this made the Tsar directly responsible for the military defeats and deaths, adding to his unpopularity.
- The lack of equipment – there were only two rifles for every three soldiers – and poor medical facilities were other reasons for the large number of deaths. This was again blamed on the Tsar and his government.
- Many middle-class people set up medical organisations and war committees to provide better supplies for the troops. They were generally more effective than the government's efforts, which increased disillusionment with autocracy and the Tsar himself.
- As the war continued to go badly, many members of the Fourth Duma (known as the **Progressive Bloc**) believed the Tsar should relinquish some control to the Duma. Representatives were sent to talk to the Tsar but Nicolas II simply dismissed the Duma, further alienating many of its members.
- As the Tsar was away with the army from September 1915, the **Tsarina**, Alexandra, was put in charge of civilian government. This was very unpopular as Alexandra was German and increasingly she only took the advice of Rasputin, who was distrusted and despised by many Russians (see page 117).
- Military defeats and poor leadership combined with people's economic and social problems to increase discontent with the autocratic system and with the Tsar himself.

> **Key terms**
>
> **Progressive Bloc**: a large group within the Duma, mostly Kadets and Octobrists.
>
> **Tsarina**: the Tsar's wife, empress of Russia.

> **Revision task** TESTED ☐
>
> Complete the following table to evaluate how the First World War increased opposition to the Tsar. Some reasons will apply to more than one group. You can use the following list to help you get started. You will need to give details for each reason.
> - Military defeats
> - Food shortages
> - Shortages of military equipment
> - Huge casualties
> - Poor treatment in the army
> - The Tsar's dismissal of the Duma
> - Poor governance at home

Reasons why the war increased opposition to the Tsar	How this affected peasants	How this affected industrial workers	How this affected the middle classes

The influence of Rasputin

In April 1907, Tsarina Alexandra asked **Grigori Rasputin**, a monk from Siberia who had a reputation as a great healer, to help her son Alexis. Alexis, heir to the Russian throne, suffered from **haemophilia**. On several occasions it was believed that Rasputin saved Alexis' life. Alexandra was very religious and was convinced that Rasputin was sent by God to control her son's illness.

Both Alexandra and Tsar Nicholas began to ask and take Rasputin's political advice. This damaged the Tsar's reputation further and was one of the reasons for his downfall in 1917, because:

- Rasputin was a great supporter of autocracy and constantly gave advice that meant the Tsar and Tsarina would not relinquish any power to anyone or anything else. This meant that he was always going to clash with the Duma.
- His drunken lifestyle and womanising ways were scandalous to most Russians. They distrusted him and did not believe that such a man should have influence over the Tsar. This became worse as Alexandra became increasingly close to Rasputin, sparking rumours they were having an affair.
- The Tsarina refused to give up her friendship and reliance on Rasputin, calling him 'our friend'. The Tsar supported her decision. For many Russians, this illustrated the royal couple's poor judgement.
- Nicholas left Alexandra in charge of Russia in order to lead the army in September 1915. She relied almost totally on Rasputin for guidance. When the Duma complained about his influence, Alexandra introduced laws that would further limit the Duma's power. When members of the Duma complained to the Tsar, he dismissed it, further alienating Duma members.
- With nobody to challenge Rasputin, he held audiences on matters of state and became involved in the war plans. The Tsarina, on Rasputin's advice, dismissed several ministers and replaced them with those who would not question her or Rasputin.

> **Key term**
>
> **Haemophilia**: a genetic disorder that affects the ability of blood to clot, so sufferers bleed longer than usual, meaning that injuries that are usually minor can be life-threatening.

> **Grigori Rasputin (1871–1916)**
>
> - Rasputin was a monk from Siberia who was famous for his ability to heal people and infamous for his debauched lifestyle.
> - Rasputin became a political advisor to both the Tsar and Tsarina from 1907, when it appeared that he helped control their son's haemophilia.
> - There were rumours of an affair between Alexandra and Rasputin. These were probably untrue but he certainly held considerable influence over her.
> - After the Tsar left St Petersburg to lead the armed forces in 1915, Rasputin was effectively ruling Russia through the Tsarina. He was murdered in December 1916 by a Russian aristocrat.

- Rasputin was assassinated by a Russian aristocrat, Prince Yusipov, in December 1916, but he had already done lasting damage to the Tsar's reputation. The Tsarina's poor judgement continued as she insisted Rasputin was given a state funeral – something that only royals or senior aristocrats would normally receive.

Revision tasks

TESTED

1. Create a mind map of the ways in which Rasputin damaged Russian autocracy.
2. Select three points from the diagram and write a paragraph outlining how they explain the ways in which Rasputin damaged the Russian autocracy.

The February Revolution

By January 1917, many Russians had reached new levels of desperation. There were huge queues for food and fuel throughout the country. Even when food was available, rising prices meant that few could afford all they needed. The immediate causes of the February Revolution were largely due to events in Petrograd. This time revolution was successful largely because of the actions of the army.

January 1917
- Around 150,000 people took part in a demonstration on the streets of Petrograd in remembrance of Bloody Sunday.
- Many industrial workers throughout Russia went on strike, demanding food and fuel, higher pay and the Tsar's abdication.
- The Duma re-opened to widespread support – 80,000 people took to the streets of Petrograd to welcome its return, again calling for the Tsar to abdicate.

Events in Petrograd, February 1917
- 22 February – around 40,000 strikers from the Putilov steelworks took to the streets of Petrograd in a demonstration.
- 23 February (International Women's Day) – tens of thousands of women took part in a march in Petrograd, protesting about food and fuel shortages. They were joined by many strikers.
- 24 February – more went on strike, more factories were occupied by workers and there were several food riots in the city. People started voting for deputies for a new Petrograd Soviet.
- By 25 February – all of Petrograd was on strike. Protesters demanded food and peace.

The army mutiny
- 26 February – the army garrison in Petrograd received orders to use force to stop the demonstrations. Around 40 demonstrators were shot but the protests continued. The Tsar dissolved the Duma.
- 27 February – many in the army mutinied – soldiers not only refused to shoot protesters, they joined the demonstrators, shot some of their officers and even started voting their own army deputies to the Petrograd Soviet.
- 28 February – nearly all remaining members of the army in Petrograd joined the demonstrators.
- 1 March – soldiers mutinied in Moscow and sailors mutinied in the naval base at Kronstadt.

Abdication of the Tsar
- 27 February – the Tsar dismissed the Duma but some members formed a Provisional Committee. The new Petrograd Soviet met for the first time.
- 28 February – the Tsar tried to return to Petrograd but railway workers and soldiers stopped him. Some of his advisors suggested political reform but the Tsar refused to relinquish any of his power.
- 2 March – the Provisional Committee declared itself the Provisional Government of Russia. The Tsar abdicated in favour of his brother. His brother refused. Autocracy in Russia was at an end.

> **Revision tasks**
>
> TESTED
>
> 1 The table below lists causes of the February 1917 Revolution. Decide whether each of these causes is long-term, medium-term or immediate. Then write an explanation of how each factor helped lead to revolution. Add any more factors you can think of.
>
> | Factor | Long-term/medium-term/immediate cause? | How it helped lead to revolution |
> |---|---|---|
> | Food and fuel shortages | | |
> | Rasputin | | |
> | Poor living and working conditions for industrial workers | | |
> | Russian defeats and heavy losses of the First World War | | |
> | The growth of organised opposition groups to the Tsar | | |
> | Strikes, demonstrations and riots in Petrograd | | |
> | The unwillingness of the Tsar to share power with the Duma | | |
> | The army mutiny | | |
> | | | |
>
> 2 Explain why the army mutiny was the decisive factor in making the February Revolution successful.

Setting up the Provisional Government

The Provisional Government was formed of a mixed group of men who had been elected to the last Duma. Most were Octobrists or Kadets, some were Social Revolutionaries or belonged to no political party. Almost all of them were from the upper or middle classes. The leading members of the Provisional Government were initially:
- Prince Georgy Lvov, an aristocrat of no party, who became Prime Minister
- Pavel Milyukov, leader of the Kadets, who became Foreign Minister
- **Alexander Kerensky**, an SR and member of both the Provisional Committee and the Petrograd Soviet, who became Justice Minister.

Many Russians seem to have been initially supportive of the Provisional Government and pleased that the Tsar was no longer in power. The government was mainly supported by landowners, army officers and business owners. Many people were encouraged by the first actions of the Provisional Government, which were incredibly liberal for the time:
- Elections would be held for a permanent government – *every* person over the age of twenty had the right to vote in a **secret ballot**.
- Freedom of speech was allowed and censorship of the press was abolished.
- The *Okhrana* was disbanded.
- All political prisoners, whatever their views, were released from prison or allowed to return from exile.
- Trade unions and strikes were allowed.

> **Alexander Kerensky (1881–1970)**
> - Kerensky was a socialist lawyer who defended revolutionaries in trials.
> - In 1912, he was elected to the Duma (the Fourth Duma).
> - After the February Revolution (1917), he became Minister for Justice in the Provisional Government, the Minister of War and, in July 1917, he became Prime Minister.
> - Kerensky was not able to stop the rising popularity of the Bolshevik Party or prevent the Bolshevik Revolution.
> - He fled Petrograd during the Revolution and left Russia in June 1918, living the rest of his life in exile.

> **Key term**
>
> **Secret ballot**: voting anonymously so nobody knows who people vote for, so people cannot be pressured into voting for someone.

- Workers could not be forced to work for more than eight hours a day.
- Discrimination because of race, gender or religious belief was made illegal.

However, these initial promises included little to resolve the most pressing concerns for the majority of Russians – access to food, improved living conditions and an end to the war.

Revision task

1. Historians disagree on the main cause of the Revolution of February 1917. Give one reason in support of each of the following as a main cause of the Revolution:
   - The Tsar's refusal to share power.
   - The actions of industrial workers.
   - The action of the Duma supported by the middle and upper classes.
   - The actions of the Russian army.
2. Which do you think was the main cause of the February Revolution in 1917? Write a paragraph explaining why.

Exam practice

Describe **TWO** features of **EITHER** the 1905 Revolution **OR** the February Revolution of 1917. (6 marks)

Exam tips

1. Decide which event you are going to pick – you only need to write about one.
2. Then identify two features of this event. You won't get any more marks if you identify more than two. If you only identify one feature you can only receive a maximum of three marks.
3. Write two paragraphs – one on each feature. For each feature you need to give supporting details to show your knowledge and understanding.

4.3 Provisional Government and the Bolshevik Revolution

What you need to know

In this section you will revise the rule of the Provisional Government and how this contributed to the Bolshevik Revolution, as well as the events of the Revolution and why it was successful. This will include:
- The weaknesses and mistakes of the Provisional Government.
- The impact of the Petrograd Soviet.
- The activities of Lenin and the Bolsheviks, including the April Theses and the July Days.
- The nature and impact of the Kornilov Revolt.
- Key events of the Bolshevik takeover.
- Reasons for the success of the Bolsheviks, especially the roles of Lenin and Trotsky.

Weaknesses and mistakes of the Provisional Government

The Provisional Government was set up on 2 March 1917. 'Provisional' means 'temporary' – it was only supposed to govern Russia until elections could take place for a proper, permanent **Constituent Assembly**. It was in a weak position, mainly because its authority was shared with the Petrograd Soviet. It also made mistakes, which weakened it further.

Weaknesses of the Provisional Government

- **Dual Power**: the Provisional Government had to share power, so it had less power than a proper government. The best example is Soviet Order Number 1: soldiers and sailors would only obey orders from the Provisional Government *if* the Petrograd Soviet agreed with those orders.
- **Unelected**: unlike the Petrograd Soviet, the Provisional Government was not elected. That made it harder for people to support its decisions.
- **The war**: the Provisional Government wanted to continue the First World War, but this was very unpopular with many Russians.
- **Land reform**: the Provisional Government was mainly middle class. Many of its supporters did not want land reform because they were landlords and reform would take their land away. But the peasants wanted land and had started to take it – encouraged by the Bolsheviks.

> **Key terms**
>
> **Constituent Assembly**: one of the demands of the 1905 Revolution in Russia was that Russia should have a constitution (a document setting out the powers of the government, the rights of the people, etc.). The Constituent Assembly was going to be an elected group of people who would put together this new constitution.
>
> **Deserters**: soldiers who run away from the fighting during a war.

Mistakes of the Provisional Government

Continuing the war
The Provisional Government continued the war, including launching attacks such as the June Offensive, 1917. If this had succeeded, the government would probably have become very popular. But it failed and made the government even less popular: the high number of **deserters** also showed that the Provisional Government was not trusted by its armed forces.

Freedom of speech
By allowing freedom of speech, the Provisional Government showed it was a modern, democratic government. But it also meant all its critics could point out its weaknesses and mistakes. For example, the Bolsheviks' promise of 'Peace, Bread and Land' became increasingly popular.

Elections for the Constituent Assembly
The Provisional Government was supposed to organise elections for the Constituent Assembly within six months, but it kept delaying them because of all the other problems Russia was facing. This frustrated people.

Land reform
The Provisional Government put off starting land reform because its members thought this should be done by the Constituent Assembly. But in the meantime, peasants took land anyway, causing disorder which the Provisional Government could do little to stop. That made the Provisional Government look weak, even to its supporters: it couldn't defend people's property. It also meant peasants did not support the Provisional Government.

Revision tasks

TESTED

1. Describe two weaknesses of the Provisional Government.
2. Complete the table below. Explain why each mistake of the Provisional Government was not popular with ordinary Russians. Then give each a mark out of ten, according to how important each was in explaining the unpopularity of the Provisional Government.

Mistakes of the Provisional Government	Why this was not popular with ordinary Russians	Mark out of 10
Putting off elections		
Putting off land reform		
Allowing freedom of speech		
Continuing the war		

3. Using your completed table, explain which of the Provisional Government's mistakes you think was the most important in respect to its lack of popularity with ordinary Russians.

The impact of the Petrograd Soviet

The Petrograd Soviet had around 3,000 members by March 1917. Many of these were revolutionaries, but most were Mensheviks and Social Revolutionaries, rather than Bolsheviks. This was important because Mensheviks believed the middle classes (the Provisional Government) needed some time in power before Russia would be ready for a socialist revolution. The Bolsheviks wanted workers to take control straight away, but they were a minority within the Petrograd Soviet. That meant the impact of the Soviet was quite moderate in the first half of 1917.

- The Petrograd Soviet did not block the Provisional Government or try to overthrow it. Instead, the Soviet saw its role as influencing the Provisional Government so that it took into account what workers, peasants, soldiers and sailors wanted.
- Soviet Order Number 1 was a significant limitation on the Provisional Government's powers. However, the Soviet did not stop the Provisional Government from launching the June Offensive – despite most Soviet members being against offensives (most thought Russia should just defend its borders).
- The impact of the Soviet on the Provisional Government was also lessened because Alexander Kerensky was a member of both. The June Offensive was his idea as Minister of War (for the Provisional Government).

The June Offensive turned out to be a disaster for Russia. This helped increase support for the Bolsheviks. The Bolshevik leader, **Vladimir Lenin**, saw the potential of the Petrograd Soviet to increase Bolshevik power and influence so that it could be used as the basis for a revolution. He therefore got more and more Bolsheviks to stand for election to the Soviet. Many were elected. By September 1917, the Petrograd Soviet was under Bolshevik control.

The activities of Lenin and the Bolsheviks

Vladimir Lenin (1870–1924)

- When Lenin was seventeen, his brother Alexander was executed for taking part in an attempted assassination of Tsar Alexander III. This event is thought to have radicalised Lenin.
- Lenin was the leader of the Bolshevik part of the Russian Social Democratic Labour Party. He was also an important and influential writer on Marxism.
- While Marx had said that a peasant country like Russia was not ready for a socialist revolution, Lenin argued that Russia could become socialist if a revolutionary party, such as the Bolsheviks, seized power in the name of the workers and peasants. This is what happened in October 1917.
- Lenin took on the leadership of Russia. One of his first acts was to pull Russia out of the First World War. The terms of the peace agreed with Germany were very harsh. Lenin's actions triggered a civil war in Russia, which the Bolsheviks eventually won.

The April Theses

In April 1917, Lenin returned to Russia from exile in Switzerland with help from Germany. His party, the Bolsheviks, was not popular. But Lenin had developed a very clear and radical programme for his party, which was published as the April **Theses**.

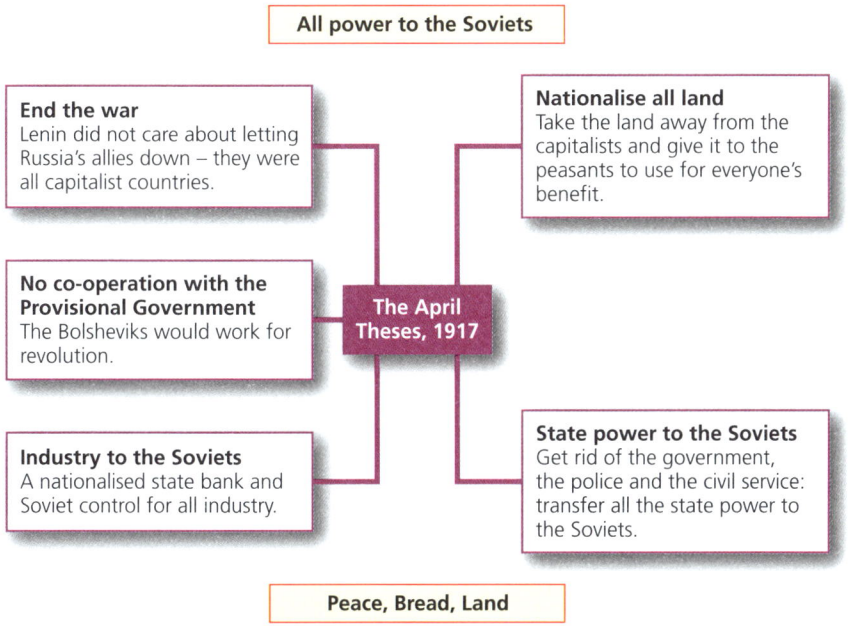

> **Key term**
>
> **Theses**: sets of ideas, set out for people to read and think about.
>
> **Red Guards**: the Red Guard was initially the militia of the Petrograd Soviet – workers who were armed and able to fight. It later increased across many parts of Russia and became part of the Red Army – the Communist army in 1918.
>
> **Spontaneous**: happening without any particular organisation or planning.

The April Theses were successful: Bolshevik Party membership rose from 24,000 in February 1917, to 100,000 in April 1917. People could understand the simple slogans, for example 'Peace, Land, Bread' and agreed with the Bolsheviks' arguments. However, the Bolshevik Party was still much smaller than other parties in the first half of 1917.

The July Days

By July, Lenin thought the Bolsheviks had enough support in Petrograd to overthrow the Provisional Government.
- There were around 10,000 **Red Guards** who were largely loyal to the Bolsheviks.
- Bolshevik propaganda had been spread widely by Bolshevik newspapers (more than 40 across Russia) – the Bolshevik Party had been given money for this by Germany.
- The Provisional Government was in trouble: its limited reforms had not helped solve food shortages and the June Offensive was a disaster, with an estimated 2 million soldiers and sailors deserting the armed forces. Many of these soldiers were revolutionaries.

From 3 to 7 July 1917, there was a **spontaneous** demonstration in Petrograd. With banners demanding that power go to the Soviets, thousands of workers and soldiers took to the streets. The demonstrators called on the Soviets and the Bolshevik Party to help them. This became known as the July Days. However, the Petrograd Soviet did not support the demonstration, and without any leadership or organisation, it was broken up (a thunderstorm helped with this). The Petrograd Soviet believed the Bolsheviks had started the July Days, and did not want to increase Bolshevik popularity by supporting it.

Crackdown on the Bolsheviks

After the July Days, the Petrograd Soviet worked with the Provisional Government to try to crush the Bolshevik Party. Kerensky **denounced** Lenin as a German spy and a traitor. Troops were sent to arrest Bolshevik leaders: Lenin fled in disguise to Finland; 1,000 Bolsheviks were arrested and put in prison; others went into hiding. It appeared as though the Bolshevik Party was over.

> **Revision task** [TESTED]
>
> 'The July Days showed the Bolsheviks were not ready for revolution.'
>
> How far do you agree? Come up with one point that supports this statement and one point you could use to argue against it.

The Kornilov Revolt

By September 1917, Kerensky had been made leader of the Provisional Government. He appointed General Kornilov as the new commander-in-chief of the Russian army. Kerensky's plan was to bring back **discipline** to the army so it could protect Russia's borders from Germany and also crack down on any unrest in Russia's revolutionary cities.

- Kornilov wanted to do more than bring back discipline to the army, however. Local Soviets were taking over from government in many places. Kornilov hated this: he wanted **martial law** across Russia, so he could use the army to break up the Soviets (criminals, in his view).
- On 24 August, Kornilov sent troops to Petrograd with the aim of shutting down the Petrograd Soviet. He claimed Kerensky supported this move.
- Kerensky did not agree (he was a member of the Petrograd Soviet, after all) and dismissed Kornilov as commander-in-chief.
- Revolutionary workers and soldiers in Petrograd rushed to defend Petrograd and the Soviet from attack: many of them were Red Guards with strong links to the Bolshevik Party.
- Kerensky believed that Kornilov wanted to overthrow his leadership in a military **coup**. He therefore called on the Soviet to defend Petrograd, which allowed Petrograd Bolsheviks to arm the Red Guard and free many Bolshevik prisoners (including Trotsky).
- The Bolsheviks organised defences to stop the advancing troops. Bolsheviks also met with Kornilov's soldiers and convinced them to disobey their officers and stop their advance. Kornilov was arrested.

The impact of the Kornilov Revolt

- Kerensky was weakened – he had appointed Kornilov, then his government had to rely on the Petrograd Soviet to defend the city.
- The army was further demoralised – many ordinary soldiers now supported the Bolsheviks and the Germans advanced close to Petrograd.
- The Bolsheviks were strengthened:
  - many of their leaders were out of prison
  - the Red Guards were now an armed force, with many more recruits (about 100,000 in total) from soldiers and workers
  - the Bolshevik defence of Petrograd was a huge propaganda success
  - Bolsheviks had majorities in the Petrograd Soviet and in the Moscow Soviet.

> **Key terms**
>
> **Denounced**: accuse someone of doing something terrible.
>
> **Discipline**: making sure people obey rules by punishing them if they don't.
>
> **Martial law**: when a military government takes power and imposes laws that restrict people's usual freedoms.
>
> **Coup**: overthrowing a government and taking power illegally, usually by force.

Their success in defending Petrograd meant that by the end of September 1917, the Bolshevik Party had over 400,000 members.

> **Revision task** — TESTED
>
> Complete the table below to describe at least two features of the Kornilov Revolt.
>
> | Feature of the Kornilov Revolt | Supporting detail of this feature |
> |---|---|
> | | |
> | | |

The Bolshevik Revolution

Key events of the Bolshevik takeover

Support for the Soviets increased after the defeat of Kornilov. By October 1917, Lenin was sure the time had come for an armed takeover of Russia's government.

- First he needed to convince the other Bolsheviks: Bukharin, for example, did not think Russia was ready for revolution. Returning from exile on 10 October, Lenin won round the Bolshevik Central Committee.
- Kerensky attempted to move Bolshevik-supporting **garrison** units out of Petrograd. This was a mistake since most of the garrison units responded by declaring they would now only obey the Petrograd Soviet.
- Following Trotsky's direction, on 19 October, the Petrograd Soviet formed the Military Revolutionary Committee (MRC) to co-ordinate all the Soviet-supporting troops and armed workers in Petrograd so they could work together to defend the Soviet from an attack from Kerensky.
- On 23 October, Kerensky shut down Bolshevik newspapers and ordered the arrest of leading Bolsheviks. This pushed Lenin to take action.
- On the night of 24 October, following Trotsky's plan, Red Guards took control of key parts of the city. The Winter Palace – which housed the Provisional Government – was surrounded. There was very little resistance. The Government surrendered after a shot was fired from a ship called the *Aurora*. Kerensky fled Petrograd in the morning of 25 October.
- On 26 October, Lenin formed a Bolshevik government called the Council of People's **Commissars**.

> **Key terms**
>
> **Garrison**: troops who are stationed in a city with the job of defending it.
>
> **Commissars**: government ministers, also political leaders in the Red Army.

Reasons for the success of the Bolshevik takeover

The role of Trotsky

- **Leon Trotsky** planned the Bolshevik takeover, and his excellent organisational skills ensured success.
- He was very influential in the Petrograd Soviet and in its MRC (Military Revolutionary Committee), which was important for getting Soviet-supporting soldiers and sailors to accept the Bolshevik takeover.
- Trotsky explained the Bolshevik takeover as having happened in the name of the Soviets, with the aim of passing power over to the Soviets. This meant there was less resistance to the Bolshevik takeover than there would have been if it had been clear from the start that the Bolsheviks had no intention of passing power to anyone else!

Pearson Edexcel International GCSE (9–1) History

> **Leon Trotsky (1879–1940)**
> - Trotsky joined the Russian Social Democratic Labour Party in 1902, but as a Menshevik rather than a Bolshevik.
> - In 1905, he became chairman of the first Soviet, which at the time was called the St Petersburg Soviet.
> - In 1917, after returning from exile in Siberia, he left the Mensheviks and became a Bolshevik.
> - He became chairman of the Petrograd Soviet and played a leading role in planning the Bolshevik armed takeover of 1917.
> - As Commissar for Foreign Affairs, he negotiated the Treaty of Brest–Litovsk with Germany.
> - In the civil war, Trotsky's role as Commissar for War was very important for the eventual victory of the Reds.

The role of Lenin

- Although Lenin did not take part in the takeover himself, he was the driving force behind the decision to overthrow the Provisional Government and take power.
- Lenin's role in persuading the Bolshevik Central Committee to commit to the revolution was important: many of the senior leaders did not think it was the right time (following the failure of the July Days).
- Lenin's April Theses, simple slogans and inspiring speeches were very important in the growth of support for the Bolshevik Party through 1917, from a very small party at the start of the year, to a party with over 400,000 members by October.
- Lenin created the Red Guards and used German money to equip them. By October 1917, there were over 100,000 Red Guards: they were the troops that actually carried out the armed takeover.

The failures of the Provisional Government

Lenin and Trotsky were able to take power so easily because the Provisional Government was very weak by the end of 1917, following a series of dreadful failures.

- Continuing the First World War (especially the disaster of the June offensive) meant that the Provisional Government had no support from many ordinary Russians, who turned to the Bolsheviks instead.
- The Provisional Government was blamed for the food shortages which continued to be a major problem in the big cities.
- Kerensky had armed the Bolshevik Red Guards in order to defeat Kornilov – the Red Guards were the force that carried out the Bolshevik takeover.
- Kerensky acted to shut down the Bolshevik newspapers on 23 October, but this was too late. The Bolsheviks had been spreading propaganda and criticism of the Provisional Government for months.
- When he attempted to round up the Bolshevik leaders on 23 October, Kerensky actually triggered the Bolshevik takeover – Lenin was forced to give the order for the takeover to begin in case they were all arrested.

Historians have different opinions on the main reason why the Bolsheviks were successful in October 1917.

> **Revision tasks** TESTED
> 1. Identify four reasons for the success of the Bolshevik takeover in October 1917.
> 2. Put your four reasons in order of importance and explain why the first was the most important and the fourth the least important.

Exam practice

Study Sources A and B.

How far does Source A support the evidence of Source B about the reasons for the Bolsheviks' success in the Bolshevik Revolution?

Explain your answer. (8 marks)

Source A

An account of the Bolshevik Revolution by Joseph Stalin, written in 1918. Stalin was in Petrograd during the Bolshevik takeover.

The moving spirit of the revolution from beginning to end was the Central Committee of the Party, headed by Comrade Lenin. On the evening of October 24 he [Lenin] was called to the Smolny Institute [headquarters of the Bolsheviks] to take charge of the movement. An outstanding role in the October uprising was played by the sailors of the Baltic Fleet and the Red Guards from the Vyborg District.

www.marxists.org/reference/archive/stalin/works/1918/11/06.htm

Source B

From a speech given by Leon Trotsky in November 1917.

We pointed out that the war was destroying the Revolution, was exhausting and destroying the country …

We desire to live and develop as a free nation: but, for the conclusion of peace, we had to overthrow the power of the bourgeoisie (the middle and upper classes) and of Kerensky. They told us we would be left without any supporters. But … the local Soviet of Petrograd took the initiative upon itself, as well as the responsibility and with the aid of the garrison and the workers accomplished the coup d'état …

Leon Trotsky, The Peace Programme of the Revolution, www.marxists.org/archive/trotsky/1917/11/peace.htm

Exam tips

1. Start by reading the sources twice.
2. Then annotate parts of the sources that are especially important to the exam question to help you identify the reasons given for Bolshevik success.
3. In your answer you should give a judgement on how far A supports B. You could use phrases such as *'totally supports / partially supports / does not support at all …'* to help you do this.
4. You should state any reasons that are the same or similar.
5. Then state any reasons that are different.

4.4 The Bolshevik consolidation of power and the Civil War

REVISED

What you need to know

In this section you will revise the actions of the Bolsheviks after the Revolution, how the situation in Russia deteriorated into civil war and the key events of that conflict, as well as reasons why the Bolsheviks won. This will include:
- The Bolshevik consolidation of power, including the 1917 Decrees, the closure of the Constituent Assembly and the Treaty of Brest-Litovsk.
- The two sides in the Civil War.
- Key events of the Civil War and reasons for the Bolshevik victory.

The Bolshevik consolidation of power

The Provisional Government was replaced by the Council of the People's Commissars, with Lenin as Premier (leader) and Trotsky as Commissar for Foreign Affairs. Lenin had promised that he would then pass power onto the Soviets. He had also promised to hold elections to the Constituent Assembly immediately.

The significance of the 1917 Decrees

The Bolsheviks used *Sovnarkom* – the Council of People's Commissars – to pass several decrees in November and December 1917. They aimed to show how the Bolsheviks would keep to their promises of 'Peace, Land and Bread'.

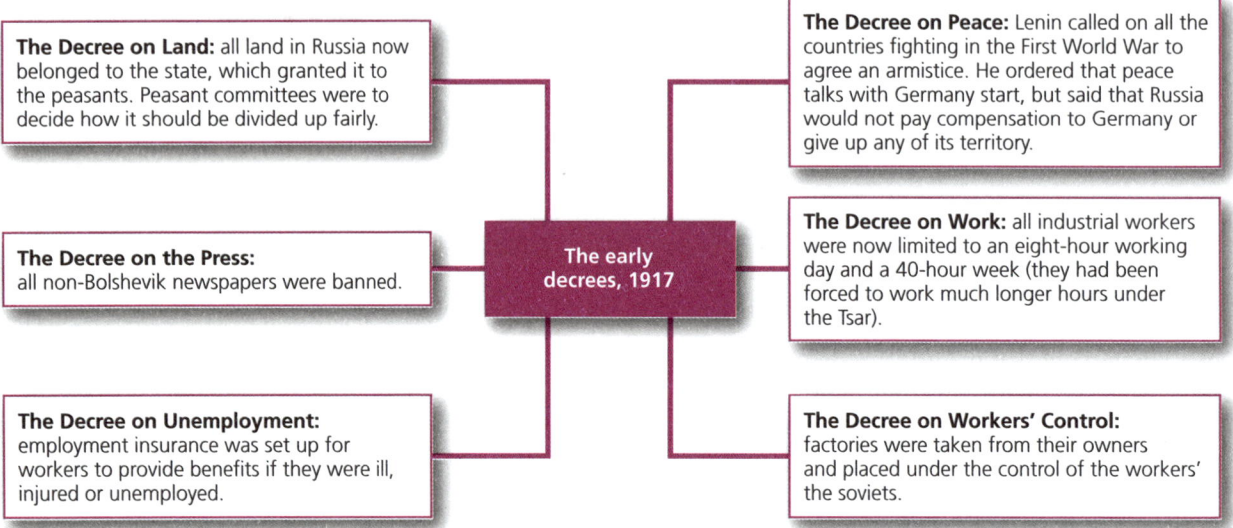

The Decree on Land: all land in Russia now belonged to the state, which granted it to the peasants. Peasant committees were to decide how it should be divided up fairly.

The Decree on the Press: all non-Bolshevik newspapers were banned.

The Decree on Unemployment: employment insurance was set up for workers to provide benefits if they were ill, injured or unemployed.

The early decrees, 1917

The Decree on Peace: Lenin called on all the countries fighting in the First World War to agree an armistice. He ordered that peace talks with Germany start, but said that Russia would not pay compensation to Germany or give up any of its territory.

The Decree on Work: all industrial workers were now limited to an eight-hour working day and a 40-hour week (they had been forced to work much longer hours under the Tsar).

The Decree on Workers' Control: factories were taken from their owners and placed under the control of the workers' the soviets.

Other decrees included the 'All-Russian Extraordinary Commission for Combating Counter-revolution and Sabotage', which set up the **Cheka**; the Decree on Banking which put all Russia's banks under state control; and the Decree on Marriage, which made divorce easier and allowed couples to have non-religious marriages.

The decrees were significant:
- The decrees that applied to employers and workers would bring about big changes to society. This would please some people – mostly those who already supported the Bolsheviks – and anger others.
- The Decree on Land ended private ownership of land, which further alienated all land holders. Peasants had taken the land anyway in many cases so Lenin's decree didn't change a great deal in practice.
- The Decree on Peace called for an **armistice**, but Lenin had no power to persuade other countries to do this. Lenin was also not realistic about a peace treaty with Germany. Russia's position was very weak. A peace treaty with Germany was obviously going to cost Russia dearly.

> **Key terms**
>
> **Cheka**: the first Soviet secret police force.
>
> **Armistice**: an agreement made by opposing sides to end fighting in a conflict.

> **Revision task** [TESTED]
>
> Add supporting details to these two features of the 1917 Decrees:
> a) The Decree on Land abolished private ownership of land …
> b) The Decree on Peace called for an international armistice for the War …

The closure of the Constituent Assembly

Elections for the Constituent Assembly were held in November 1917. The election results were as bad as the Bolsheviks feared. Out of a total of 707 seats in the Constituent Assembly:
- Bolshevik candidates got 175 seats
- the Left SRs (left-wing Socialist Revolutionaries) got 40 seats
- the Right SRs (right-wing Socialist Revolutionaries) got 370 seats.

The Bolsheviks only won around a quarter of the seats, mainly in Russia's industrial cities and among soldiers. The Right SRs won the election with 370 of the seats: 52 per cent (they also won 40 per cent of the vote). The SRs were the peasant party and had split into Left SRs, who supported the Bolsheviks, and Right SRs, who opposed the Bolsheviks. Peasants preferred the Right SRs' policies because the peasants got to keep their land with the Right SRs, while the Bolsheviks and Left SRs wanted to **collectivise** land.

Within the Constituent Assembly, 87 seats went to parties representing different **nationalities**. This was alarming to Lenin because some of these nationalities (e.g. Estonians) wanted independence from what had been the Russian Empire. This would weaken Bolshevik Russia against foreign enemies.

Lenin was not prepared to hand over power to the SRs nor to allow nationalities to break free from Russia. His argument after the election was that the Constituent Assembly threatened the Revolution, because power should be going to Russia's Soviets, not to the Constituent Assembly.
- The Constituent Assembly met on 5 January 1918. *Sovnarkom* (see definition on page 128) put forward its package of decrees for the Constituent Assembly to approve and also said the Assembly should have limited powers compared to the Soviets.
- The Assembly voted these proposals down by a large margin of 100 votes.
- Lenin said this result proved the Constituent Assembly was counter-revolutionary and was trying to bring back **capitalism**. The next day, the Red Guards surrounded the Assembly and stopped its deputies from going in. The Assembly was then shut down.
- Following this, all political parties that opposed the Bolsheviks, including the Right SRs, were banned and their leaders put under arrest.

> **Key terms**
>
> **Collectivise**: to organise farming so that everyone is working together for the state.
>
> **Nationalities**: areas within the Russian Empire in which people felt connected by being the same ethnicity.
>
> **Capitalism**: where trade and industry are owned and run privately rather than by the state.

> **Revision task** [TESTED]
>
> 'Lenin never intended to allow other political parties in Russia.' How far do you agree with this statement? Give one point to support it and one point to argue against it.

The Treaty of Brest-Litovsk

Lenin needed to quickly end Russia's involvement in the First World War for three main reasons:
- The Bolsheviks had promised peace.
- Many Bolshevik supporters were ordinary soldiers and sailors who wanted the war to end – if the war dragged on, this support would quickly be lost.
- If the Germans advanced much further, they would capture Petrograd and Bolshevik rule would be over.

Negotiations at Brest-Litovsk

Peace talks began at Brest-Litovsk (then in Poland) on 22 December 1917.
- Lenin's call for an armistice between all the countries fighting the war did not succeed. The peace talks involved Russia and Germany alone. These two countries did agree a ceasefire while the talks went on.
- Trotsky was Russia's lead negotiator. His main tactic was to drag the talks out over two months. This was because the Bolsheviks believed a German revolution was about to happen and negotiating with another socialist state would be much easier.
- As a German revolution did not happen, Trotsky declared that Russia would not give up any territory to Germany as part of the peace deal.
- In response, in February 1918, the Germans ended the ceasefire and started to advance again towards Petrograd.
- Even though the Germans' terms for a peace treaty were extremely harsh, Lenin ordered Trotsky to agree to what the Germans were offering.

Lenin took this decision because:
- He knew the weakened Russian army would not be able to defeat the Germans. Peace with Germany on any terms was better than war.
- Even if revolution did not happen in Germany, Germany was still likely to be defeated by the Allies, and if Germany was defeated then Russia would not need to keep to the terms of the treaty.

Terms of the Treaty of Brest-Litovsk

- Russia had to give up around 1 million square kilometres of its western territories, with a population of around 50 million people. This area contained over a quarter of all Russia's **arable** land and three-quarters of its iron ore and coal.
- Russia had to pay 3 billion roubles in **reparations**.

Reactions to the Treaty of Brest-Litovsk

The Bolshevik Party agreed to accept the Treaty, but only by a very narrow margin. Lenin was convinced that this was the only way that Bolshevik rule could continue. Russians generally were horrified by the Treaty, because so much was given up to the enemy. This brought together lots of different groups who were determined to bring down the Bolshevik government and overturn the Treaty. The Treaty of Brest-Litovsk was therefore a major reason for the Russian Civil War.

Another impact of the Treaty was that the loss of so much productive land worsened the food shortages in Russia's cities. People began returning to villages where they could grow their own food.

> **Key terms**
>
> **Arable**: land used for growing crops.
>
> **Reparations**: compensation for damage done by war, paid by the defeated country.

> **Revision task** TESTED
>
> Complete the table below of reasons why Lenin accepted the Treaty of Brest-Litovsk. One reason has been given. Add at least two more. For each reason, decide how important it was by giving it a mark out of ten. Then write an explanation of what you think the main reason was.
>
> | Reason why Lenin accepted the Treaty of Brest-Litovsk | How important was this reason out of 10? |
> |---|---|
> | The Bolsheviks had promised to end the war | |
> | | |
> | | |

The Civil War

The two sides in the Civil War

The Civil War was a complex conflict because the Bolsheviks (the Reds) faced a number of different enemy groups, with different enemies being more or less important at different stages of the conflict.

The Whites

The Whites included:
- monarchists, who wanted the return of the Tsar
- gentry landlords who had lost their land
- middle-class industrialists who had lost their factories to the Soviets
- liberals and moderate socialists who wanted a return to the aims of the February Revolution
- Socialist Revolutionaries who had won the Constituent Assembly elections and wanted the Constituent Assembly to be in power.

The only thing these groups had in common was their hatred of the Bolsheviks.

Tsarist army generals and navy admirals led the main White armies, including:
- Admiral Kolchak in Siberia (north eastern Russia)
- General Denikin in the Caucasus (south of Russia)
- General Yudenich in Estonia (east of Russia).

The Czech Legion

The Czech Legion was a force of 50,000 soldiers who had fought with Russia in the First World War. After the Brest-Litovsk Treaty, the Bolsheviks agreed that these soldiers could travel by train (6,000 miles) through Siberia to the port of Vladivostok, to re-join the allies.

As they were on their journey, tensions were high and local Soviets challenged them. The Bolsheviks ordered them to hand over all their weapons and then tried taking them by force. In response, the Czech Legion took control of large sections of the Trans-Siberian Railway. They helped Admiral Kolchak's White army against the Bolsheviks.

The Greens

Other groups were also involved in the Civil War, including peasant armies (called the Greens) who were fighting to keep control of their own areas. These were often not much more than bandit groups, but some were from ethnic groups who wanted independence from Russia. One example was a Green army led by a Ukrainian called Nestor Makhno. Makhno's forces sometimes fought for the Whites against the Reds, and sometimes for the Reds against the Whites.

Other countries

British, French, Polish, US and Japanese forces were also involved in the Civil War.

- Russia's former First World War allies (Britain and France) were furious that Russia had pulled out of the war. They had loaned Russia a lot of money before the Bolshevik takeover, which Lenin's government refused to pay back. For example, France had invested millions in Russian industry, which the Bolsheviks had put into state ownership. These were strong reasons for foreign powers to help the Whites against the Reds. A third reason was that western countries were worried that Bolshevism would spread to their countries.
- Japan sent 70,000 troops to fight against the Bolsheviks because Japan wanted to take territory from Russia in eastern Siberia. The USA sent troops to the same region, mainly to stop Japan from succeeding in taking the territory.

The location of the main participants in the Russian Civil War in 1919

Key events in the Civil War

Date	Event
1918	
January	The Red Army is established.
March	The Treaty of Brest-Litovsk is signed – White opposition unites against the Reds (Bolsheviks) in Russia. Russia's First World War allies begin supporting the Whites: the first British troops arrive in Murmansk (northern Russia). Trotsky becomes War Commissar.
May	Trotsky orders the Czech Legion to give up their weapons.
	The Czech Legion captures a large section of the Trans-Siberian Railway.
	Conscription into the Red Army begins.
July	Nicholas II and his family are executed. They were being held captive in Samara. When White forces (with the Czech Legion) approached Samara, the Bolsheviks shot the royal family in case they were captured by the Whites.
August	Fanya Kaplan, an SR, shoots Lenin, seriously wounding him. This marks the start of the Red Terror, in which the Cheka are used to search out and execute Whites in each area the Reds captured in the Civil War; 300,000 people are killed by the Cheka over the course of the Civil War.
1919	
March	Kolchak's Siberian army crosses the Ural Mountains into European Russia, but the Reds push back their advance.
June	Denikin's southern army captures key cities as it advances from the south.
October	Yudenich's advance almost reaches Petrograd, but the Red Army defeats his army and drives it back.
	Denikin advances to within 300 miles of Moscow. However, Trotsky's skilful tactics force a White retreat back to the south.
1920	
January	Kolchak is captured by the Bolsheviks and executed in February 1920.
April	Denikin is replaced by General Wrangel.
May – July	A Polish army invades Russia and takes control of Kiev. By July, a Red Army counter-attack drives the Poles back to Poland.
August	The Red Army is defeated by the Polish army outside Warsaw.
	Peasant uprisings occur in Tambov province (Green army), following increases in grain taxes by the Bolsheviks.
November	The Red Army defeats the last White army, led by General Wrangel. The Bolsheviks win the Civil War.
1921	
February	The Bolsheviks sends 100,000 troops into Tambov province to defeat the peasant uprising.

> **Key term**
>
> **Conscription:** when it is compulsory for people of certain ages to join the armed forces.

> **Revision task**
>
> Read through the list of key events of the Civil War. Using this and other information on pages 131–32, describe two key features of the Civil War
>
> TESTED

Reasons for the Bolshevik victory in the Civil War

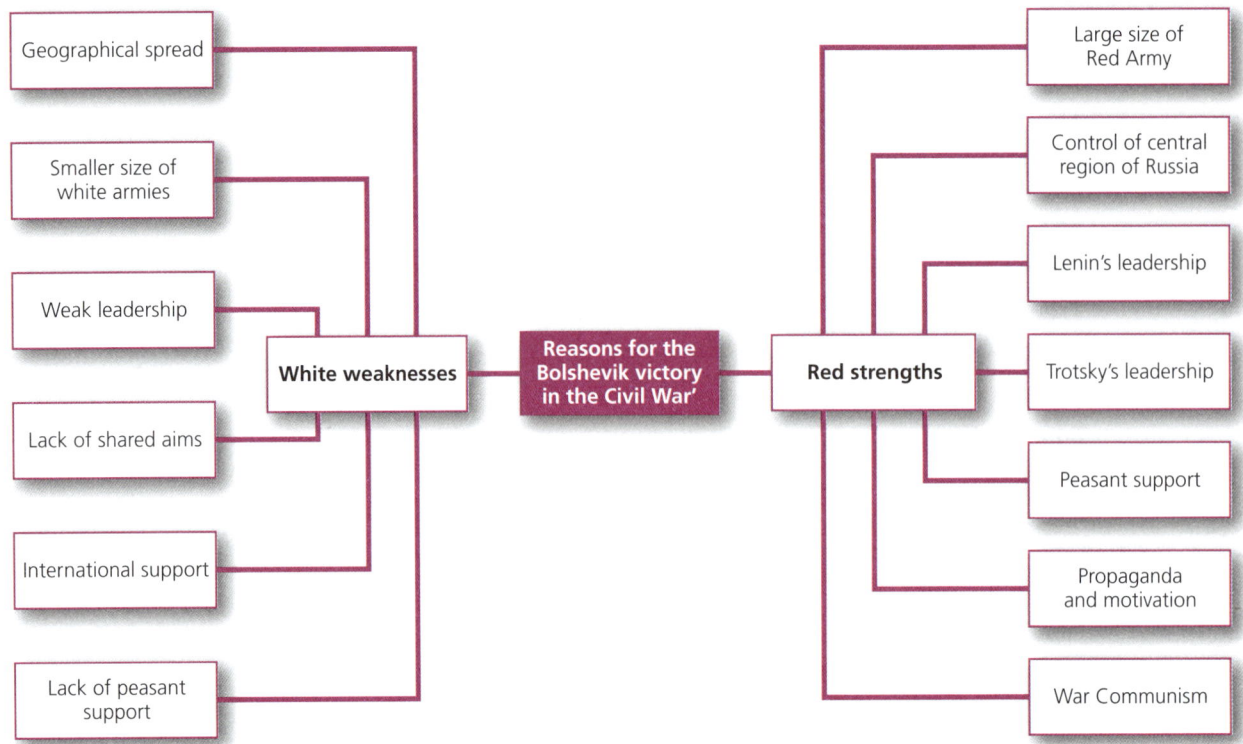

Red strengths

- The Red Army was much bigger than the White armies: by 1921, conscription had increased the Red Army to 5 million men. At most, the White armies totalled 250,000.
- Control of central Russia was a major advantage for the Reds: that was where most Russians lived (so there were more people to conscript from) and where Russia's industries were located. The train network in central Russia meant Red Army forces could be moved quickly to defend central Russia from advancing White armies.
- Lenin's leadership gave the Bolsheviks their inspiration and ruthlessness: Lenin introduced War Communism (see page 137) and he oversaw the creation of the Cheka and the Red Terror which eliminated possible opponents in areas brought under Red control.
- Trotsky created the Red Army and his leadership was vital for imposing strict discipline on his troops and for his strategic thinking, which used the railway system of central Russia to bring Red Army forces together in large numbers where they were most needed.
- Peasant support: although the peasants did not necessarily support either side, they supported the Reds more than the Whites because the Bolsheviks' Decree on Land had given peasants land which the Whites would take away from them again. Peasant support was important because most of the conscripts came from the peasantry.

- Bolshevik supporters fighting for the Reds in the war were highly motivated: they wanted to defend the Revolution from the Whites. Bolshevik propaganda was also important for motivating Red Army conscripts. For example, Bolshevik propaganda showed the Whites as supported by foreign powers who wanted to take control of Russia.
- While Trotsky was leading the Red Army, Lenin introduced War Communism: putting the state in control of factory production and food distribution. This made sure the Red Army had the supplies it needed, and also increased the supply of food: although this came at a terrible cost and reduced peasant support by the end of the war.

White weaknesses

- The White armies were located around the edges of central Russia: this made it hard for the different armies to work together because they were separated by large areas. Also, the Whites were based in areas without industry and with lower population numbers, so there were fewer people to conscript and no factories for making weapons, which meant smaller White armies – White forces were frequently outnumbered by Reds in battles.
- Although the Whites had very experienced leaders – generals and admirals from the Tsarist army and navy – there was no overall leader co-ordinating the White attacks. The White leaders also sometimes refused to work together. It was much easier for Trotsky to fight the White armies one by one than it would have been if they had all attacked together.
- The Whites did not have shared aims: some wanted the return of the Tsar; some wanted a Russian republic; some wanted the Constituent Assembly to be put into power. This meant the White armies did not have the same motivation as the Red Army, which had the clear aim of defending the October Revolution.
- At the start of the Civil War, international support meant the Whites got supplies which gave them better chances of success, but as the war went on, foreign support weakened. For example, many British socialists did not want their government to support the Whites. The Bolsheviks could also say that they were defending Russia from foreign attackers.
- Both the Reds and the Whites used brutal tactics to get peasants to fight for them or hand over food, but the peasants saw the Whites as worse than the Reds. The Whites were also committed to overturning the Bolsheviks' decrees. This included the Decree on Land, which was popular with peasants.

Revision task

TESTED

Historians have different opinions on the main reasons why the Bolsheviks won the Civil War. Which do you think was more important in explaining the Bolshevik victory: Red strengths or White weaknesses? Support your answer with evidence.

Exam practice

Study Extract C.

Extract C suggests that the brutality of the White armies was the reason why peasants supported the Bolsheviks in the Civil War.

How far do you agree with this interpretation? **(16 marks)**

Use Extract C, Sources A and B and your own knowledge to explain your answer.

Source A

From the diary of a White nobleman who joined Admiral Kolchak's army; this diary entry was written in July 1919.

Yet right now, to our disadvantage, the Red Army at the front has been given strict orders not to harm the populace [the peasants] and to pay set prices for everything taken. The Admiral [Kolchak] has given the same orders and instructions several times, but with us they are not worth the paper they are written on, whereas with the Reds they are reinforced by the immediate execution of the guilty.

The Soviet Union: A documentary history, vol. 1, Edward Acton and Tom Stableford, University of Exeter Press, 2005, p.131.

Source B

From the report of a Red Army provisions commissar (responsible for getting army supplies) from Tambov Province, writing in summer 1919.

The government orders, the thousands of party bosses with lists and warrants and orders three yards long who travel around the country terrorising the peasants – all this has placed a heavy burden on the population, and has caused the people to grumble and curse and become bitter. It has even driven some of the peasants to destroy their grain, meat and other foodstuffs rather than give them to the Communists.

Adapted from *Peasant Russia Civil War: The Volga Countryside in Revolution 1917-1921*, Orlando Figes, OUP, 1989, p. 246.

Extract C

[The peasants] were often more inclined to support the Bolsheviks for the reasons below:
- Lenin had introduced the Decree on Land in 1917 which gave the peasants the right to the land, whereas the Whites made it clear that they would restore the land to its former owners.
- The brutality of the White armies drove many peasants to support the Bolsheviks as the lesser of two evils. For example, the Cossacks in the southern White army practised 'ethnic cleansing', driving out thousands of non-Cossack peasants, especially Russians and Ukrainians, from their lands and treating them brutally.

Russia in Transition, 1914-1924, John Wright and Steve Waugh, 2012, Hodder Education, p. 73.

Exam tips

1. Start with the interpretation (Extract C). Read it twice and annotate it to identify what the authors are saying and what evidence they have used to back it up.
2. See how far the first source agrees with the interpretation, and how far it disagrees. Add in your own knowledge here: does what you know support Source A's areas of agreement and disagreement?
3. Do the same for the second source.
4. Write your overall judgement of how far you agree. You can use phrases such as 'I totally / partially / do not agree' ... in your answer.

4.5 War Communism and the New Economic Policy (NEP)

REVISED

What you need to know

In this section you will revise the economic policies of the Communist Party during and after the Civil War, as well as assessing Lenin's achievements at his death. This will include:
- Reasons for, nature and effects of War Communism.
- The Kronstadt Naval Mutiny.
- Reasons for, nature and effects of the New Economic Policy.
- Opposition to the NEP.
- Achievements of Lenin to 1924.

War Communism

In March 1918, the Bolsheviks renamed themselves as the Communist Party. The economic policies of the Communists between 1918 and 1921 (during the Civil War) would come to be given the name 'War Communism'. These policies were brought in for a combination of reasons.

Reasons for War Communism

- **Putting Communist ideology into practice**
  A central idea of Communism was state ownership of land and industry so that the wealth or profits could be shared, making a more equal society. Many of the policies of War Communism were about redistributing wealth – sharing resources among everyone.
- **Supplying the Red Army with food and the necessary military equipment to win the Civil War**
  The Bolsheviks knew that lack of food and especially military equipment were major reasons for Russian defeats in the First World War. Some War Communism policies were aimed at increasing industrial production of military equipment, while others were aimed at making sure the army was fed.
- **Feeding the towns and cities**
  There were still food and fuel shortages in many towns and cities throughout Russia, even before the Civil War started. The Bolsheviks wanted to avoid the huge problems food shortages had caused both the Tsar and the Provisional Government, by improving the supply of food to prevent uprisings. They also wanted to make sure that industrial workers had enough food to work hard to produce the goods and equipment that the country, and especially the army, needed.

Revision tasks

1 Which do you think was the most important reason for the Bolsheviks introducing War Communism?
2 What do you think a Bolshevik would have said was the most important reason at the time? Explain why this answer might change depending on who the Bolshevik was talking to.

TESTED

The nature of War Communism

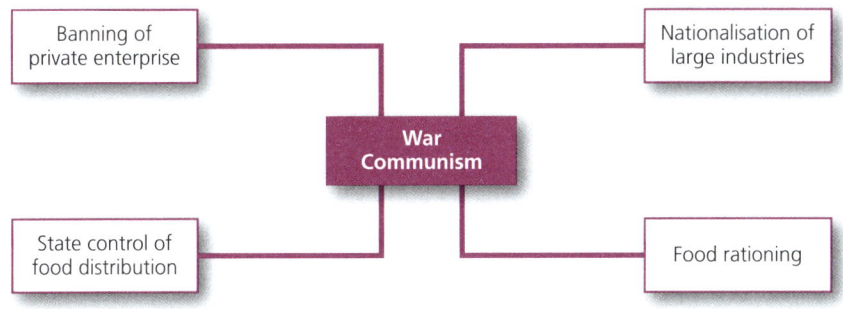

Industry and business

Factories and businesses with over ten employees were **nationalised** and production was planned and organised by the state. Strict discipline was enforced in factories to try to increase the work done by each employee. The railways were also taken over by the state to improve the supply of goods and food around Russia, in particular to the Red Army.

Private trade or making a profit became illegal – all profits had to be handed over to the state. Foreign trade was only allowed by the government.

Agriculture

From 1918, food in the towns and cities was rationed according to the role of each person. The largest rations were given to those working in industries producing weapons and equipment or those performing hard physical labour. The smallest rations were given to professionals such as teachers. However, even those on the largest rations got little food. Therefore, to improve the supply of food to towns and cities (and the army), from July 1918 all surplus food produced by the peasants had to be handed over to local committees run by the government. These committees proved ineffective so armed gangs were sent to the countryside to forcibly take food from peasants. Peasants who resisted were shot.

Effects of War Communism

A major reason for the Reds' victory in the Civil War was that War Communism ensured the Red Army got what it needed. Enough food was supplied and transported to the soldiers, factory production successfully increased production of military clothing, weapons, ammunition and other equipment, while the nationalisation of the railways ensured that these supplies reached where they were needed.

In almost every other aspect, however, the effects of War Communism were terrible.
- The methods for getting the surplus food produced by peasants were brutal. Many were killed. Peasants didn't see the point of producing more food only for it to be brutally taken away from them, so they simply stopped growing more food than they needed for themselves. Therefore, many in the towns and cities did not get the food they needed, particularly those on lower rations.
- Many industrial workers left their jobs and moved into the countryside to grow food to feed themselves. The number of workers in factories and mines dropped by as much as 50 per cent! With fewer workers and little food to feed those that did remain, industrial production fell for everything except the military.
- The economy almost totally collapsed. Many people turned to the **black market** as the only way to get what they needed. At the start of 1921, strikes and urban demonstrations broke out.
- Many areas of Russia were struck with bad weather in 1920 and 1921, causing harvests to fail. As peasants had very little food stored away, famine was widespread. Estimates suggest up to 7 million people died. By 1922, there were even reports of cannibalism.

As a result, support for the Bolsheviks decreased, especially among peasants and the middle classes. Then, in February 1921, some members of the armed forces started to rebel against Bolshevik policies.

> **Key terms**
>
> **Nationalised**: when privately owned companies are taken over by the state.
>
> **Black market**: illegal trade.

> **Revision task** [TESTED]
>
> 1 Complete the following table to help you outline the main policies of War Communism and their effects.
>
> | Policy of War Communism | Effects of this policy |
> |---|---|
> | | |
> | | |
> | | |
>
> 2 What opinions might the following people have had on War Communism?
> - A factory worker
> - A Red Army officer
> - A peasant
> - A Communist Party member
>
> Give reasons for your answer.

The Kronstadt Naval Mutiny

Kronstadt was a Russian military base on a small island near Petrograd. The sailors based there had played a major part in both the 1905 and 1917 revolutions. Trotsky called them 'heroes' of the November 1917 Revolution. They were seen as very loyal Bolshevik supporters.

As members of the armed forces, the Kronstadt sailors were less negatively impacted by War Communism than many other Russians. However:
- many were from peasant families so they heard about the horrors in the countryside from their families
- during their time off, they spent time in Petrograd so saw the impact of economic problems in the cities
- they had seen the Red Terror (see page 133) for themselves.

In late February 1921, the 15,000 Kronstadt sailors formed a Provisional Revolutionary Committee and issued a list of demands for the Communist government, including:
- New elections to Soviets with everyone being able to stand for election (not just Communists).
- Freedom of speech and removal of press censorship.
- The immediate end of taking food from peasants by force.
- The re-establishment of a market economy.

Crushing the rising

Lenin and other Communists responded by saying that it was a plot by the Whites and foreign countries to bring down Communism. Trotsky organised a swift and brutal response. Around 60,000 Red Army troops laid siege to the base while launching minor attacks for nearly three weeks. The troops suffered heavy losses before finally invading the base. Exact numbers are unknown but the Red Army suffered as many as 10,000 casualties and the rebels over 1,500. Many of the rebel sailors fled, most to Finland. Around 2,000 of these were captured and most of them were executed.

> **Revision task** [TESTED]
>
> Write a paragraph describing the reasons why the Kronstadt sailors mutinied in 1921 and why the Communists responded so brutally.

The New Economic Policy

War Communism was replaced with the New Economic Policy (NEP) by Lenin in March 1921, at the Tenth Party Congress.

Reasons for the NEP

By March 1921:
- there were peasant uprisings in most areas of the country
- not enough food was being produced or distributed
- the Russian economy was on the brink of collapse
- the Kronstadt Mutiny was taking place.

In short, War Communism was not working and signs of unrest were growing. Lenin was particularly shocked and worried by the Kronstadt Mutiny because these sailors had been very loyal Bolshevik supporters. He realised that he had to change tack or there was a risk there would be another revolution. He needed a policy that would improve the economy and increase food production, thereby reducing the opposition to his Communist government.

Nature of the NEP

The New Economic Policy brought back capitalism to some parts of society:
- Peasants still had to give some of the food they produced (50 per cent) to the government but they could sell whatever extra they didn't need for themselves. The government would still gain from this as any profits from sales were taxed.
- The taking of food from peasants by force was abolished.
- Private ownership of businesses employing less than twenty people was allowed. Some businesses were returned to their previous owners. People were allowed to get a licence to start a new small business.
- Private trading of small goods was allowed. Profits from sales of these foods were taxed.
- Large industry (such as coal, iron and steel, railways) remained nationalised.

Effects of the NEP

- The new agricultural policies gave peasants a greater incentive to grow more food. This, combined with better weather and an end to the war, saw agricultural production rise significantly from 1922. By the end of 1924, food production was back to the levels of 1913.
- As peasants were producing more food, the threat of famine in the countryside ended.
- Greater food production also ended food shortages in the towns and cities. Moreover, the price of food dropped, so more industrial workers could afford more of it.
- Some peasants, known as kulaks, became fairly wealthy under the new scheme. They were able to buy more land and even hire other peasants to work for them.
- The number of small businesses increased rapidly – by 1923 an estimated 85 per cent of companies were privately owned. Some private traders, known as NEP men, became quite wealthy.
- Industrial output also increased. Wages and working conditions improved for industrial workers but many did not return from the countryside.

- Although industry did improve, it did not match the rate of agricultural growth. This meant that the price of manufactured goods was very high compared with the price of food, which became lower as more was available. This meant that many peasants could not afford the goods being produced.

Opposition to the NEP

To begin with, many Communists were in support of the NEP as they could see that something needed to be done to stabilise the economy, avoid further famine and prevent revolution. Lenin had argued that Russia was not yet ready for a full communist system and many agreed that the NEP would be a short-term measure until more communist measures could be taken.

However, although many Russians were happy with the new system, as time went on there was increasing opposition to the NEP within the Communist Party.
- Many Communists resented any form of capitalism because it was against their beliefs. They viewed the NEP as a betrayal of the Revolution.
- They particularly resented the fact that the NEP had created new classes in society – kulaks and NEP men. Communism was supposed to reduce inequalities in society, not create more!
- The NEP was not solving all of Russia's economic problems – industry only recovered slowly and industrial output was still hugely behind western countries.

Achievements of Lenin to 1924

Lenin suffered a series of strokes in 1922 and 1923 which left him with very limited movement and speech. He died in January 1924. He was only 53 years old but he had achieved much.
- He successfully led the October 1917 Revolution to take power in Russia. He had the intelligence and courage to take the opportunity when it arose.
- Few revolutionaries are successful, yet Lenin not only gained power but played a major role in making sure that the Bolsheviks kept power. The communist regime he created would rule Russia until the end of 1991. A major way he did this was through adapting to situations and adjusting his policies to ensure he kept power – the NEP is a good example of this.
- He not only took and kept hold of power, he played the main role in changing Russian society and its economic system. Although the NEP did bring capitalism back into the Russian economy, the basis of communism – that business and industry should be nationalised – was maintained.
- His leadership played a major part in ensuring victory for the Reds in the Civil War. Some of these policies were ruthless but they made sure Communist rule would continue.
- In 1923, he oversaw a new constitution which changed the Russian Empire into the Union of Soviet Socialist Republics (the USSR, also known as the Soviet Union).

Lenin was, and still is, a controversial figure. However, he was undoubtedly one of the world's most influential people of the twentieth century.

Revision tasks

1 Create a Venn diagram of the positive and negative effects of the NEP. Remember that some effects were both positive and negative! These should be placed in the overlapping circles.
2 Which groups of people were likely to have been:
- strong supporters of the NEP
- mild supporters of the NEP
- critics of the NEP

Give reasons for each.

3 'The NEP shows that Lenin was not committed to communism. He just wanted to retain power at any cost.' Give reasons for and against this view. How far do you agree with this opinion?

TESTED

Revision task

TESTED

What factors enabled Lenin to take and maintain power from 1917 to 1924? Complete the following table.

Lenin's own qualities and actions	The actions of others	Other factors

Exam practice

Describe **TWO** features of **EITHER** War Communism **OR** the New Economic Policy. (6 marks)

Exam tip

1 Decide which policy you are going to pick – you only need to write about one.
2 Then identify two features of this policy. You won't get any more marks if you identify more than two. If you only identify one feature you can only receive a maximum of three marks.
3 Write two paragraphs – one on each feature. For each feature you need to give supporting details to show your knowledge and understanding.

5 The USA, 1918–41

5.1 The Roaring Twenties

REVISED

What you need to know

In this section you will revise the reasons for, and effects of, the economic boom in the USA in the 1920s. This will include:
- How the USA benefited financially from the First World War.
- How changing production methods and consumerism boosted demand.
- Problems for the older industries and for farmers.
- The growth of the leisure industry, especially the cinema, jazz music and sport.
- The changing lives of America women.

The economic benefits of the First World War

America did not join the First World War until 1917, but was involved before then in selling food and weapons to some of the Allied countries. As a result, there was a huge increase in production and exports which helped drive the **economic boom** in the USA during the 1920s.

There were a number of ways in which the US economy benefited from the war:

Key term

Economic boom: a period of time when individual incomes and company profits increase rapidly.

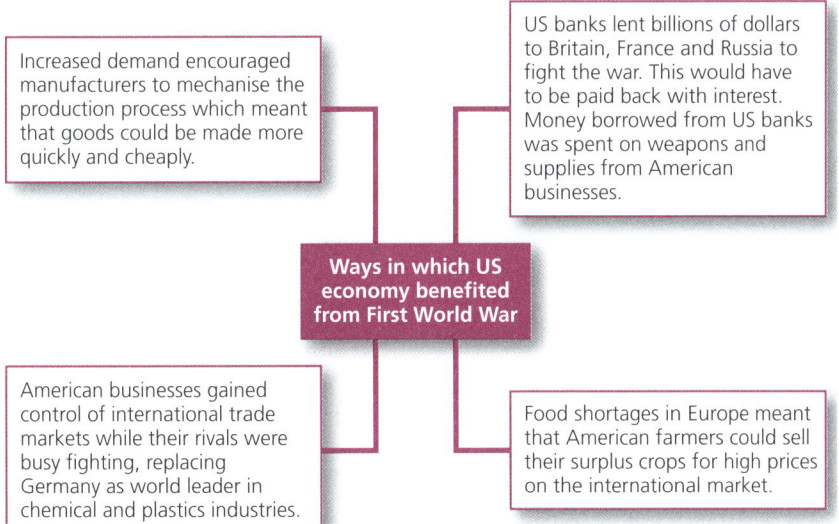

Revision task

Briefly explain why the USA benefited economically from the First World War.

TESTED

Reasons for economic boom in the 1920s

By 1922, the economy was showing signs of recovery from its post-war slowdown and it quickly entered a boom period which lasted until the autumn of 1929.

Between 1919 and 1929, industrial productivity (per worker per hour) increased 72 per cent due to mechanisation. Workers could earn companies more money while being paid the same wage. As well as new mechanised techniques like the production line, there were also new materials from the chemical industry, such as rayon, Bakelite and cellophane, which made products cheaper to produce so more could be sold at lower prices. American businesses bought huge quantities of materials, forcing the price down.

There were also several specific reasons that help to explain why this economic boom happened in the 1920s.

Henry Ford (1863–1947)

- Ford founded the Ford Motor Company in 1903 in Detroit.
- He built the first Model T Ford in 1908.
- He increased workers' pay to $5 a day in 1914 – double what other car-makers paid.
- Ford revolutionised factories with his assembly-line methods, as seen at the River Rouge plant.

Henry Ford and mass production

The car industry played a very important role in the boom of the 1920s, leading the way in technological developments and stimulating growth in other industries.

Henry Ford pioneered new methods of production – the electric conveyor belt and the **assembly line**. The conveyor belt carried the partly assembled car past gangs of men along the line, each gang performing a specific task. The parts they needed were supplied to them by another set of overhead conveyor belts.

- The time to assemble Ford's Model T was reduced from 13 hours to 1 hour 33 minutes.
- Mass production methods caused the cost of the Model T to fall (1914: $850; 1926: $295).
- To offset the boredom of repetitive work, Ford doubled wages to $5 a day by 1914.
- His factory in Detroit operated 24 hours a day, using a system of three × eight-hour shifts a day and employing 80,000 people.
- The Model T, nicknamed 'Tin Lizzie', was the world's first mass-produced car using standardised parts and one colour – black.
- Ford used modern advertising techniques to sell his cars, and also introduced **hire purchase**.
- By 1925, half the world's cars were Model Ts.
- Other firms copied Ford's use of **mass production** – including Chrysler and General Motors.

The mass production of cars:
- stimulated growth in other industries – steel, wood, rubber, leather and petrol
- stimulated road construction and the building of gas stations, motels and restaurants
- encouraged the development of suburbs
- transformed buying habits – hire purchase became the acceptable means of buying costly items
- benefited rural areas, making farmers less isolated and more mobile.

Hire purchase, advertising, consumerism

Americans had more money to spend on consumer items in this period. Wages increased by 25 per cent in the 1920s, while prices stayed the same or fell. There was a craze for household gadgets – radios, telephones, vacuum cleaners, etc. This was known as **consumerism**.

Hire purchase allowed consumers to buy the goods they wanted with a small deposit, and then pay the rest in weekly or monthly instalments. It was a payment method pioneered by the car industry and six out of ten cars in the USA were bought this way in the 1920s.

Advertising became an important way of encouraging consumers to spend their money in the 1920s. Coca-Cola increased their sales by advertising their products nationally. New technology increased opportunities for advertising. America's first full-time radio station, KDKA, in Pittsburgh, was paid for by adverts. Magazines such as *Vogue* associated products with the lifestyles of the rich and famous.

Another marketing tool was the **mail-order catalogue**. Improving roads and the growth of the truck industry lead to the growth of mail-order businesses like Sears, Roebuck and Co. of Chicago.

Key terms

Assembly line: a line of workers and machines in a factory assembling a product.

Mass production: manufacture of goods on a large scale using a standardised mechanical process.

Consumerism: spending money on items which are not essential; the pre-occupation with acquiring consumer goods.

Hire purchase: paying for goods in instalments over a fixed period of time ('buy now, pay later').

Mail-order catalogue: a book containing products that people could send off for and have delivered to their homes.

Revision task

Draw a spider diagram to show the reasons why the development of the car industry benefited the US economy. You should consider the following:
- How the production techniques of the car industry benefited other industries.
- How the growth of the car industry also led to the growth of its supporting industries.
- How the development of the car industry led to the development of services for people who were driving the cars.

Which two features of the US car industry in the 1920s do you think were the most important? Explain your choice.

TESTED

Popularity of the stock market

Investors bought **shares** in companies and got paid a **dividend** in return. This investment allowed US companies to expand and make even more goods. People bought shares in businesses because, as industries made more money, the shares became worth more, so that in future they would have made a profit on the money they had used to buy the shares. This was known as '**speculating**' on the **stock market**. '**Buying on the margin**' also occurred.

Problems in farming, including over-production and mechanisation

The government encouraged farmers to modernise their methods by using machines, better breeds and seeds. The result was over-production as farmers were now easily able to grow more produce than they were able to sell. This lowered prices and profits. It was disastrous for **sharecroppers**, many of whom were black Americans, as they paid their rent as a share of the value of the crops they grew.

There were a number of other problems faced by American farmers in the 1920s:
- economic decline in Europe after 1918 led to falling sales of American food overseas
- **prohibition** destroyed the market for wheat and barley
- high tariffs on imports to the USA forced other countries to impose high tariffs on American wheat which led to a lower demand for it
- farming was hit by diseases such as the boll-weevil that attacked cotton crops.

Total farm income fell from $32 billion in 1919 to $13 billion in 1928. Farms were sold and workers left the countryside to work in towns. Many were forced to borrow money and struggled to keep up with their mortgage payments.

The decline of older industries

The growth of new industries in the 1920s left older industries facing problems caused by competition and new technology:
- The coal industry faced increased competition from oil, gas and electricity; there was falling demand from the railroad industry; there was more international competition from cheap imports; mechanisation led to the loss of many jobs in mining; many mines were forced to close; there was an increase in strikes and industrial unrest within the industry.
- The railroad industry faced increasing competition from the development of a national road network; the growth in car ownership made business very difficult as people preferred using cars to traveling on the railways. Companies found it harder to generate profits.
- The textile industry faced increasing competition from new man-made fibres (e.g. rayon); the change in women's fashions, e.g. with shorter dresses, reduced the amount of cloth needed; there was competition from cheaper imports from abroad; many textile mills were forced to close down.

> **Key terms**
>
> **Share**: a small portion of a business.
>
> **Dividend**: a bonus paid to shareholders when the company makes a profit.
>
> **Speculating**: buying shares, hoping that their value will increase so that the shares can be sold later for a profit.
>
> **Stock market**: the people and organisations involved in buying and selling shares.
>
> **'Buying on the margin'**: borrowing money to buy shares, selling them when they make a profit, repaying the loan and keeping the rest of the money.
>
> **Sharecropper**: a tenant farmer who gives a share of his crop as rent.
>
> **Prohibition**: banning the making, selling and transportation of alcohol.

> **Revision task**
>
> What problems did some US industries face in the 1920s? Why might this have caused a problem for future economic growth?
>
> TESTED

The leisure industry

Entertainment was important in the lives of Americans in the 1920s. Mechanisation and rising wages meant that Americans had more time and more money to spend on leisure activities. Some of the main forms of entertainment before the 1920s included the following:
- Vaudeville – a theatre variety show featuring acts including juggling, tap dancing and singing.
- Dance halls – people danced the Bunny-Hug, the Turkey Trot and other slow-paced dances.
- 'Ragtime' – an upbeat form of music made popular by artists such as Scott Joplin.
- 'Nickelodeons' – cheap cinemas where people could watch early films.
- Baseball and college football were popular sports.

Cinema

Cinema developed in this period from silent black and white films to the first **'talkie'** (*The Jazz Singer*), two-colour films and animations such as those from Walt Disney. Cinema became more popular because there was an increasingly wide range of films on offer. The movie industry worked hard to maintain people's interest, through the publicity of popular film stars through to the introduction of new technology.

US cinemas – numbers

- **1910:** 8,000 cinemas
- **1926:** 17,000 cinemas
- **1930:** 303,000 cinemas

Hollywood in California emerged as the centre of the film industry for several reasons:
- the attractive climate – there were few days of rain
- the variety of landscape locations – desert, mountains, rivers, coast.

New production companies built studios in California, e.g. Paramount, Warner Brothers, Metro-Goldwyn-Mayer (MGM), resulting in movie stars moving to the Los Angeles area. A wide range of films were produced – westerns, crime stories, romantic tales, slapstick comedy.

The most spectacular innovation was the introduction of synchronised sound in 1927. It was first used in the film *The Jazz Singer*, starring Al Johnson. It led to a revolution in film making as companies dropped or altered silent films to add soundtracks. It was the birth of the **'talkies'**.

The popularity of movie stars

Through successful marketing and advertising campaigns, film studios helped to build up the reputations of movie stars, who developed cult followings:
- Clara Bow – famous for films such as *It* (1927) and *The Wild Party* (1929); known as the 'It Girl' because of her sex appeal and her **flapper** lifestyle (see pages 148–49).
- Rudolph Valentino – famous for films such as *The Four Horsemen of the Apocalypse* (1921) (the first film to take $1 million) and *The Sheik* (1921); he was the first male star to be sold as a sex symbol.
- Charlie Chaplin – famous for films such as *The Kid (1921)* and *The Gold Rush (1925)*; his trademark was a tramp-like image, wearing an ill-fitting suit, with his trademark bowler hat and cane.

> **Key terms**
>
> **'Talkies'**: the name given to the first films to have synchronised sound; audiences could hear what the actors were saying as they watched them on the screen.
>
> **Flapper**: a fashionable young woman of the 1920s who wore short skirts, listened to jazz and challenged the behaviour considered acceptable at the time.

The film industry was not popular with everyone. Movies were accused of lowering moral standards, presenting movie stars as sex symbols. The lifestyle of some stars attracted criticism, with stories of wild parties and love affairs. To improve its image, the film industry introduced its own 'Hays Code of Practice' and in 1928 set up the Oscars to celebrate the best of the industry.

Jazz

Jazz developed in the southern states of America from traditional forms of black music such as ragtime and the blues. Jazz became increasingly popular during the 1920s in the new nightclubs and speakeasies (illegal bars where people could get and drink alcohol). Jazz was associated with the new flapper lifestyle and the new fashionable dances such as the Charleston.

> **Key term**
>
> **Jazz**: improvised, rhythmic music developed by black Americans in the 1920s.

Leading jazz artists included:
- Bessie Smith, one of the greatest blues singers of the 1920s
- Duke Ellington, the famous pianist and band-leader
- Louis Armstrong, an influential trumpet player and vocalist.

Older and more religious people objected to jazz, partly because of its association with black Americans and with organised crime, as many of the clubs where it was played were owned by Prohibition-era gangsters (see page 154). They also did not like how it encouraged people to dance closely together in darkened rooms. Some people called it the 'devil's music'.

Dancing

The slow formal dances of the pre-First World War period were replaced by the fast beat jives and rhythmic dances associated with jazz music. New popular dances included the Charleston, the Black Bottom and the Lindy Hop. Dance halls became popular and some, like the Cotton Club in New York, had live jazz bands performing.

These new developments in dancing shocked the older generation and religious groups who blamed jazz music for causing a decline in moral standards. They considered these new dances to be too sexual and nightlife behaviour to be scandalous.

Sport

Many changes occurred in sport during this period. The popularity of spectator sports such as baseball and boxing grew. Tennis and golf were professionalised and the National Football League (NFL) was established.

Matches were broadcast on the radio, which meant people could follow sports teams they could never hope to go to see. As these sports became more popular, attendances grew, the top players became stars and more people were interested in playing sport themselves.

Some of the famous American sportsmen and women of the 1920s included:
- Babe Ruth – a baseball player who moved from the Boston Red Sox to the New York Yankees in 1920; he was a powerful hitter who held records for most runs and most home runs for many years.
- Jack Dempsey – held the world heavyweight boxing title from 1919 to 1926; Dempsey's fights were attended by tens of thousands of people.
- Red Grange – an American football player known as the 'Galloping Ghost' because of his speed on the pitch.
- Gertrude Ederle – the first woman to swim the English Channel in 1926.

Radio

Over 40 per cent of US homes had a radio and listening to it became one of the most popular forms of entertainment by 1929. This was because of:
- the electrification of America – not just the towns and cities but out into the countryside as well
- mass production that made radio sets available at reasonable prices – the accessibility of higher purchase meant people could borrow money to buy them.

The radio enabled people to keep up to date with current affairs and came to replace the newspaper as people's main source of news. It allowed people to listen live to sporting fixtures and to hear the new jazz music coming from the clubs of Chicago and New York.

By 1930, there were over 600 radio stations across America, the largest being the National Broadcasting Company (NBC) established in 1926, and the Columbia Broadcasting System (CBS) established in 1927.

Advertising

With radios in so many American homes, advertisers were now able to reach a wider audience. They persuaded:
- women to spend more money on Max Factor make-up to look more like their favourite film stars
- people to spend more of their spare time on new hobbies such as photography, encouraged by Kodak
- people to buy products they did not really need, such as the advertising for Listerine which made people worry about their bad breath!

Motoring

By 1929, 23 million Americans owned a motor car. As more people owned cars:
- motels, roadside 'fast-food' diners and drive-in cinemas were built
- people moved to the suburbs as they could drive into town centres to work and shop
- people could travel to visit friends, or go to the cinema, theatre or sports stadium, even if they lived in isolated rural communities.

Driving changed from being an occasional necessity to being a leisure activity. Motor racing became a popular sport. Cars stimulated tourism as people were able to go on day trips and could travel further afield if they wanted to – Florida became a popular tourist destination in this period.

Some people blamed the car for making crime easier, and for giving young people too much sexual freedom.

> **Revision task** TESTED
>
> Which do you think was the most important influence on leisure activity in the USA in the 1920s – the cinema, the motor car or the radio? Explain your choice.

The changing position of women, including the flappers

Before the First World War, middle-class and upper-class women led secluded lives:
- single women had to be accompanied by a **chaperone**
- it was considered 'unladylike' to smoke or drink in public.

Key term

Chaperone: a married or elderly lady who accompanies a young woman where men are present.

Women wore tight-waisted, ankle-length dresses and little make-up. Working women occupied low-paid jobs – cleaning, dress-making, secretarial work. No women had the right to vote.

The First World War began to change this for some women – 90,000 women enlisted in the US military, serving in supporting roles as office clerks, radio operators, telegraphers, electricians, chemists, accountants, police officers, mail deliverers and nurses. They also served in the American Red Cross and Salvation Army and worked as farm labourers attached to the Women's Land Army.

However, when the war ended, women were expected to give up these new jobs and return to their former lives.

Changing attitudes after the First World War

During the war, women showed that they were capable of a much wider range of work. New labour-saving devices such as refrigerators and washing machines meant that they had more spare time in which to work. By 1930, 2 million more women were employed than had been in 1920, but many of these jobs were low paid.

Women had gradually been gaining the vote on a state by state basis, starting in Wyoming in 1869. In 1913, Alice Paul started the National Women's Party to gain more publicity for women's right to vote.

Politicians gradually came around to the idea that women should have the vote after women's work in the war was widely recognised. Women's support for prohibition was also appreciated by Congressmen. The Nineteenth **Amendment**, giving all women the vote, was finally passed by Congress in 1919, and came into effect in 1920.

> **Key term**
>
> **Amendment**: a change to the US Constitution, the set of rules for the American political system.

The 1920 presidential election was the first election that women across America were all allowed to vote in. Jeanette Rankin became the first Congresswoman representing the state of Montana. In 1925, Miriam Ferguson in Texas and Nellie Taylor Ross in Wyoming became the first elected female state governors. However, by 1930 only thirteen women had been elected to Congress.

Flappers

During the 1920s, younger middle-class and upper-class women began to challenge traditional attitudes towards women. They wanted a more independent social life and a more liberal lifestyle for women. Women who adopted this new approach were called flappers.

The influence of jazz culture encouraged this independent flapper lifestyle, as did flapper role models – movie stars such as Clara Bow (see page 146), Louise Brooks and Joan Crawford, who famously kissed, drank, smoked and danced the Charleston in films such as *Our Modern Maidens* (1929).

A typical flapper:
- went out without a chaperone
- wore make-up and perfume
- wore short skirts and bright colours
- cut their hair short – the 'bob' haircut became fashionable
- smoked and drank in public
- enjoyed dancing to the new jazz music
- went to the new jazz clubs and speakeasies
- drove cars or rode motorbikes.

Jazz culture provided some women with an opportunity to break free. Jazz clubs, speakeasies and dance halls allowed women to escape from their traditional roles as daughters and mothers. Women also had greater freedom to express themselves in their clothing and behaviour. Women found new employment in the advertising, cosmetic, and clothing industries, all of which were related to jazz culture.

By the standards of the day, this was extremely liberal behaviour for a woman, and not all women themselves supported the more liberal lifestyle of the flappers:
- Traditional groups, especially in rural areas, believed women were supposed to be wives, mothers and home-makers.
- Religious groups thought the flapper lifestyle was too sexual and immoral.
- Older women formed the Anti-Flirt League in protest.
- Poorer women who lacked the money and free time to become flappers.

Some flappers deliberately flouted the law, bringing bad press to the feminist movement.

> **Revision task**
>
> How much do you think the lives of American women changed in the 1920s? Draw a table to show what did and did not change for American women in this period.
>
> TESTED

Exam practice

Describe **TWO** key features of **EITHER** the economic boom of the 1920s, **OR** the leisure industry in the 1920s. (6 marks)

> **Exam tips**
>
> You should break your answer down into two short paragraphs, one for each feature.
> 1. Begin the first paragraph, 'One feature of [topic from the question, e.g. the leisure industry of the 1920s] was …'
> 2. Begin the second paragraph, 'Another feature of [topic from the question, e.g. the leisure industry of the 1920s] was …'
> 3. For each feature, write down at least two pieces of relevant factual detail to show that you fully understand that feature.

5.2 Increased social tensions in the 1920s   REVISED

What you need to know

In this section you will revise the reasons for, and effects of, the growing tensions between different groups of people in the USA in the 1920s. This will include:
- Changing attitudes towards immigration and its impact on immigrants.
- Increasing xenophobia and fear of communism in the USA.
- Increasing discrimination against black Americans as a result of segregation and racial violence from the Ku Klux Klan.
- The clash between religious fundamentalism and modern ideas as seen in the 'Monkey Trial'.
- The introduction of the prohibition of alcohol and the rise of organised crime.

Attitudes and policies towards immigration

The vast majority of Americans were immigrants, from Europe, as well as Asia and Mexico. This resulted in a **melting pot** of different races, cultures, religions and languages. By 1919, 40 million immigrants had arrived.

> **Key term**
>
> **Melting pot**: a mixture of races and nationalities.

The 'open door' policy

To help colonise the country, the US government had traditionally followed an **'open door' policy** towards immigration which was designed to make entry into America as easy as possible. The fact that anybody could enter the country was a key attraction. Immigrants entering the country were processed at Ellis Island, New York.

A combination of push and pull factors caused this mass immigration. Push factors are those which cause people to move away from an area and pull factors are those which cause people to move to an area. In this case, push factors are those which caused immigrants to leave their homelands and pull factors are those which attracted them to America.

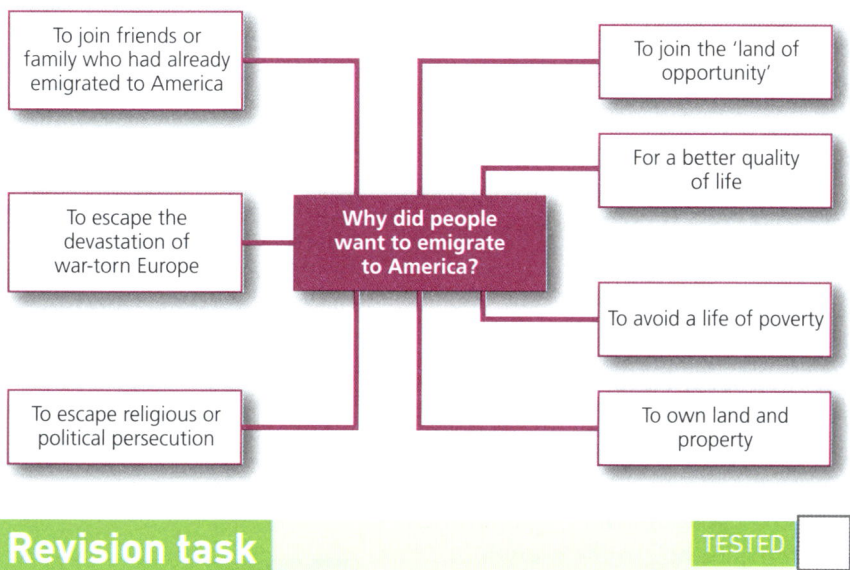

Revision task

TESTED

Study the diagram above. Write down whether each factor is a push or a pull factor. Why would some people argue that the "pull" factors were more important than the "push" factors?

Demands for the restriction of immigration

Many Americans were starting to question the 'open door' policy towards immigration:
- There was a large increase in the number of poorer immigrants arriving from Eastern Europe (13 million between 1900 and 1914).
- The devastation caused by the First World War resulted in a sharp rise in the number of immigrants escaping poverty and persecution.
- Americans increasingly felt 'swamped' by the rising number of immigrants.
- The growth of **xenophobia** and the perception of an ideal citizen being a **WASP** led Americans to look down on immigrants from Eastern Europe and Italy.
- Immigrants were seen as poor, illiterate and unable to speak English.
- The rise of Bolshevism (communism) in Russia following the Revolution of 1917 led to a fear of immigrants bringing **communist** ideas with them into America.

Key terms

'Open door' policy: free admission of immigrants.

WASP: White Anglo-Saxon Protestants.

Xenophobia: an irrational fear or hatred of foreigners.

Communist: a person who believes in the ideas of Karl Marx to create a classless society, with all land and business owned collectively.

Government legislation on immigration

Increasing pressure was placed upon the US Congress to pass measures to restrict entry into America. Four important measures were introduced, each one being stricter than the previous one.

Year	Measure	Key features
1917	Literacy test	Immigrants had to pass a literacy test in English. People from Asia were banned from coming to the USA unless they were from Japan.
1921	Emergency Quota Act	This introduced a 3 per cent quota based upon the total population of each ethnic group in 1910, e.g. if there were 100,000 Germans in total then another 3,000 would be allowed in; it allowed 357,000 immigrants to enter each year.
1924	National Origins Act	This cut the quota to 2 per cent based upon the 1890 census. It allowed more people from northern Europe to enter.
1929	Immigration Act	This restricted immigration to 150,000 per year. No Asian people were allowed. People from countries in northern and western Europe were allocated 85 per cent of places.

Impact on the lives of immigrants

In the 1920s, immigrants lived in overcrowded slums alongside other immigrants from their own country, for example, Little Italy in New York. They worked long hours in poorly paid manual jobs. Immigrants kept to themselves. Living in poverty meant that many became ill, or turned to alcohol and gambling.

The Palmer Raids and the 'Red Scare'

Many Americans were alarmed by the Bolshevik Revolution in Russia in 1917, which led to a Communist government replacing the Tsar. Many feared that immigrants would spread communist and **anarchist** ideas into America. The US government passed the Sedition Act in 1918, making it illegal to criticise or abuse the US government, flag or army. Events during 1919–20 added to these fears, leading to the growth in xenophobia:

- In 1919, 3,600 workers' strikes added to the fear that a communist revolution was pending.
- In April 1919, a bomb planted by anarchists damaged the house of the Attorney-General, Mitchell Palmer.
- In April 1919, a bomb planted in a church in Milwaukee killed ten people.
- In September 1920, an anarchist bomb exploded on Wall Street, killing 38 people.

Such actions gave rise to the **'Red Scare'** – the fear that anarchists and communists threatened America.

The Palmer Raids were organised by the Attorney-General, Mitchell Palmer, head of the US Department of Justice. This involved the arrest of over 6,000 suspected communists in 36 cities across America. Trade unionists, Jewish and Catholic people and black people were particularly targeted. These people were held for several weeks without charge and hundreds were later deported.

The Sacco and Vanzetti case

The case of Sacco and Vanzetti was important because it was a clear instance of racial discrimination and highlighted the unfairness of the US legal system towards immigrants.
- On 5 May 1920, two Italian immigrants – Nicola Sacco and Bartolomeo Vanzetti – were arrested and charged with carrying out a robbery at a shoe factory in Massachusetts in which two people died.

> **Revision task**
>
> Draw a spider diagram to show the difficulties that immigrants into the USA had to overcome. How would you explain why they were prepared to face these problems?
>
> TESTED

> **Key terms**
>
> **Anarchist**: a person who wants to remove all forms of government.
>
> **'Red Scare'**: fear that immigrants from Eastern Europe were spreading communist ideas across America.

> **Revision task**
>
> Create your own spider diagram to show why the 'Red Scare' occurred during the early 1920s.
>
> TESTED

- Their trial opened in May 1921, but the case against them was not strong – 61 eyewitnesses identified the two men, but the defence produced 107 witnesses who said they were elsewhere at the time of the robbery.
- The case aroused mass media attention and the judge, Webster Thayer, seemed determined to find the two men guilty.
- Both Sacco and Vanzetti were self-confessed anarchists. The prosecution focussed mainly on their status as immigrants and their radical beliefs.
- The jury found them guilty and they were sentenced to death; their appeal failed and they were executed by electric chair in August 1927.
- The treatment of these two anarchist immigrants demonstrates the hysteria of the 'Red Scare'.

Attitudes towards black Americans

The 1920s was a period that witnessed a growth in racial intolerance, particularly against black Americans.

The Jim Crow laws

In 1910, some 12 million black people lived in America, 75 per cent of them in the southern states. Slavery had been abolished in the southern states in the 1860s, but the white-controlled state governments soon introduced laws to control the freedom of black Americans.

The **Jim Crow laws** introduced **segregation**, separating black and white Americans in schools, parks, hospitals, swimming pools, libraries and other public places.

Life for black Americans living in the South was very hard. They could not vote and were denied the right to a decent education and a good job. They could not marry white Americans.

In the southern states most black Americans became sharecroppers. White landowners paid black workers a share of the profit when crops were sold.

Between 1900 and 1919, 1,360 black Americans were **lynched**, 281 in the 1920s and 119 in the 1930s. When some black Americans tried to prevent a lynching in Tulsa, Oklahoma, in 1921, a white mob raided the black neighbourhoods, burning 1,256 homes and killing 26 black Americans.

The 'Great Migration'

Segregation did not exist in the northern states, so many black Americans decided to migrate to the industrial cities of the North in search of a new job and a better standard of living. Between 1916 and 1920, almost 1 million people made the trek north into cities like Chicago, Detroit, New York and Philadelphia, in what became known as the 'Great Migration'.

Demand for workers in factories was high as American industry was booming, building weapons for the First World War in Europe. Black Americans worked in dangerous industries such as steel, car-making and meatpacking; female workers became maids.

Black Americans continued to be treated as second-class citizens, even in the North. They were the last to be hired and in bad times, were the first to be fired from jobs. They received low pay and lived in poor neighbourhoods called ghettos, such as Harlem in New York. More workers caused wages to fall and rents to rise, which angered poor white workers. Growing racial tension resulted in the outbreak of riots in twenty US cities in 1919, the worst being in Chicago and Washington DC.

> **Revision task**
>
> 'Sacco and Vanzetti did not receive a fair trial.'
> 1. List arguments for and against the interpretation of the Sacco and Vanzetti case.
> 2. Consider the reasons why some people would argue for and some people would argue against this interpretation.
> 3. How far do you agree with this interpretation?
>
> TESTED

> **Key terms**
>
> **Jim Crow laws**: laws which brought about segregation and discrimination against black Americans living in the southern states of America.
>
> **Segregation**: keeping a group separate from the rest of society, usually on the basis of race or religion.
>
> **Lynching**: when a mob kills someone without a trial, usually by hanging. In this period it describes the actions of mobs of white Americans who killed black Americans by hanging them from trees.

The Ku Klux Klan

Founded after the Civil War, the Ku Klux Klan (KKK) was a racist organisation which aimed to terrorise black Americans in the southern states who had just been freed from enslavement.

- The movement was revived in 1915 by William J. Simmons, following the release of the film *Birth of a Nation*.
- Membership of the Klan was only open to WASPS; members saw themselves as being superior to other races; they were anti-black people, anti-Jewish people, anti-Catholic people, anti-Communist people.
- Concerns over immigration and the 'Red Scare' caused Klan membership to rise sharply in the early 1920s; 100,000 members in 1920, rising to 5 million members by 1925.
- The head of the Klan was the Imperial Wizard – a post held in the 1920s by Hiram Wesley Evans; Grand Dragons were in charge of each state.
- Klan members dressed in white robes and white hoods – the colour symbolising white supremacy; members carried the American flag and burnt crosses during their night-time meetings.
- Klan members carried out lynchings, floggings, brandings, mutilation, tarring and feathering, and kidnapping; they terrorised and evoked fear in non-WASPS.
- Klan members were rarely brought to justice as their 'friends' in the courts would not convict them; politicians resisted speaking out for fear of losing white votes.

The Klan suffered a sharp decline in membership following the conviction in 1925 of David Stephenson, the Grand Dragon of the Indiana Klan, for the rape and mutilation of a woman on a Chicago train. During the trial, Stephenson spoke about illegal Klan activities, which discredited the movement.

Revision task

TESTED

Explain how each of these problems affected the lives of black Americans: the Jim Crow laws, segregation, lynching, the Ku Klux Klan.

Morals and values and the 'Monkey Trial'

The period 1910–29 saw a growing divide between conservative-minded rural areas and modern urban areas of America. The rural areas tended to be very religious, especially those in the **Bible Belt** states of the south east such as Alabama and Tennessee. Many of the people in these states were Christian **fundamentalists** who believed that everything in the Bible had to be taken literally and must not be questioned.

- Traditional and modern America clashed over the 'Monkey Trial', which was an argument about Darwin's theory of **evolution**.
- The Bible Belt states believed in **creationism** and in 1924–25, six states banned the teaching of evolution in their schools.
- A biology teacher called John Scopes from Dayton, Tennessee, ignored the ban. He was arrested and put on trial in July 1925.
- Scopes was found guilty of teaching evolution and fined $100.
- The case was important because it showed how the fundamentalists were trying to curb freedom of thought.

Key terms

Bible Belt: an area of southern America where Christian belief is strong.

Fundamentalist: a religious person who goes to church regularly and believes in the Bible word for word.

Evolution: the theory that living species have developed gradually over time, through a long series of generations.

Creationism: the belief that all living species were created by God, as described in the Bible.

Prohibition and the gangsters

In January 1920, the Eighteenth Amendment made it illegal to sell alcohol and the Volstead Act set down penalties for breaking this law. This became known as prohibition.

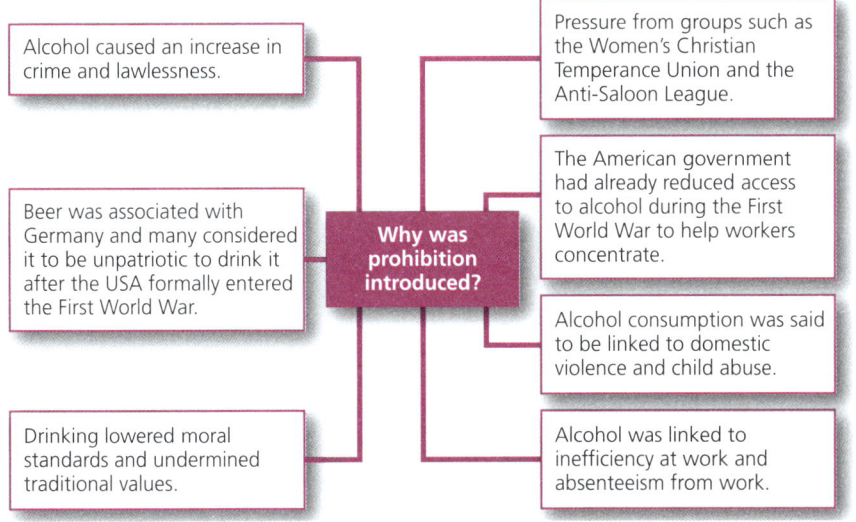

Al 'Scarface' Capone (1899–1947)

- Capone was nicknamed 'Scarface' after being slashed with a knife by the brother of a woman he insulted.
- He controlled organised crime in Chicago between 1925 and 1931, running gambling, sex trade and bootlegging rackets.
- Capone was responsible for the 1929 St Valentine's Day Massacre of the rival Bugs Moran gang.
- He was sent to prison for eleven years for tax evasion in 1931.

Prohibition proved impossible to enforce and the law was openly ignored, particularly in the cities. The alcohol trade went underground and developed into organised crime under the control of powerful gangsters.
- **Bootleggers**, such as **Al Capone**, made large sums of money smuggling alcohol into the country.
- **Moonshiners** distilled their own illegal home brews.
- **Speakeasies** selling illegal alcohol sprang up in large numbers – by 1925, there were over 100,000 in New York alone.

The new law was enforced by prohibition agents. John Kramer was first Prohibition Commissioner. Congress gave him enough money to hire 1,500 prohibition agents. These agents were not well paid, so they often took bribes ('back-handers') and looked the other way, letting the gangsters get away with it. There were lots of trials for breaking the Prohibition law but there were very few convictions.

Key terms

Bootlegger: a person who supplies and distributes illegal alcohol.

Moonshiner: a person who brews or distils their own illegal alcohol.

Speakeasy: an illegal drinking shop.

The growth of organised crime

The 1920s saw rapid growth in the number of criminal gangs. Prohibition provided them with the opportunity to engage in organised crime, providing illegal alcohol through bootlegging schemes. They controlled the speakeasies and diverted into other areas of crime – running protection rackets, gambling dens, brothels and supplying drugs. Gangs increasingly fought each other for the control of this trade.

One of the most notorious gangsters of the 1920s was Al Capone.
- In 1921, Capone followed his gangster leader Johnny Torrio from New York to Chicago and quickly rose up the ranks in the gang.
- In 1925, he took over Torrio's operations in Chicago.
- By bribing senior police chiefs and the city mayor, he was able to build up a vast empire of organised crime.
- His empire included speakeasies, bookmakers, gambling houses, brothels, nightclubs and breweries.
- Capone had over 200 rivals killed between 1925 and 1929.
- The most serious incident was the St Valentine's Day Massacre in 1929. This was an attempt to kill the rival gangland leader Bugs

Moran. The authorities could not find enough direct evidence to prosecute Capone.
- In 1931, Capone was found guilty of tax evasion and sent to prison. This really marked the end of the 'Age of the Gangsters'.

Prohibition proved impossible to enforce and by 1930 there was widespread opposition to it. There was an increase in alcohol-related problems – by 1926, 50,000 people had died from drinking poisoned alcohol. It led to the growth in organised crime and an increase in violence relating to gangster activities.

After the Wall Street Crash, many argued that making alcohol legal again would create jobs in the brewing and service industries, helping to reduce the high unemployment level. By introducing the Twenty-first Amendment, President Roosevelt ended prohibition in December 1933.

> **Revision task**
>
> Make a list of:
> a) the reasons prohibition was introduced
> b) the problems it caused
> c) the reasons why it was ended.
>
> TESTED ☐

Exam practice

Study Sources A and B.

How far does Source A support the evidence of Source B about attitudes towards immigration in the USA in the 1920s? Explain your answer. (8 marks)

Source A

From a speech to Congress by Senator James Heflin from Alabama, in 1921.

The steamship companies haul them over to America and as soon as they step off the decks of their ships, the problem of the steamship companies is settled, but our problem has begun. Thousands come here who never take the oath to support our constitution and to become citizens of the United States. They pay allegiance to some other country while they live upon the substance of our own. They constitute a menace and a danger to us every day.

WJEC GCSE History: Germany in Transition 1919–1939 and USA A Nation of Contrasts 1910–1929, Steve Waugh, John Wright and R. Paul Evans, 2017, Hodder Education, p.103.

Source B

From a speech to Congress by President Calvin Coolidge, in 1923.

We must remember that every object of our institutions of society and government will fail unless America is kept American. New arrivals should be limited to our capacity to absorb them into the ranks of good citizenship. America must be kept American. I am convinced that our present economic and social conditions warrant a limitation of those to be admitted. Those who do not want to be partakers of the American spirit ought not to settle in America.

WJEC GCSE History: Germany in Transition 1919–1939 and USA A Nation of Contrasts 1910–1929, Steve Waugh, John Wright and R. Paul Evans, 2017, Hodder Education, p.103.

> **Exam tips**
>
> Divide your answer to this question into three paragraphs:
> 1. The first paragraph should focus on areas of agreement between the sources – quote material directly from both sources to support the points you are making and clearly explain each area of agreement that you identify.
> 2. The second paragraph should follow the advice for the first paragraph, except that it should focus on areas of disagreement.
> 3. The third paragraph should begin with your judgement of how much you think these sources agree with each other about the topic in the question, followed by your explanation for why you think this.

5.3 The USA in Depression, 1929–33

REVISED

What you need to know

In this section you will revise the reasons for, and effects of, the Wall Street Crash and the Great Depression in the USA. This will include:
- The reasons why the Wall Street Crash happened in 1929, and its immediate effects, as well as the longer-term Great Depression.
- How President Hoover responded to the Depression.
- The impact of the Depression on banking, farming, industry and on the lives of the American people.
- How unemployment and homelessness led to the growth of Hoovervilles and the Bonus March of 1932.

The causes and consequences of the Wall Street Crash, 1929–30

By 1929, the economic boom that the USA had been experiencing came to a sudden end for a variety of reasons. The main problems in the US economy by the end of the 1920s were:
- **over-production** (which flooded the market and reduced prices and therefore profits)
- under consumption (which reduced sales and therefore profits).

The policies of the Republican presidents of the 1920s

Republican presidents in the 1920s believed in:
- **laissez-faire** economics – giving businesses the freedom to do as they wanted
- 'rugged individualism' – anyone could become rich simply by hard work and determination.

They reduced income tax, allowed super-companies called trusts to fix prices, weakened trade unions and workers' rights, and introduced **tariffs** like the Fordney–McCumber Act (1922) to protect US industry from international competition.

The unequal distribution of wealth

Five per cent of Americans earned 33 per cent of all the money so there was only a small number of people who could actually afford the goods being produced. There were many reasons why some people did not prosper during the boom of the 1920s:
- mechanisation resulted in many people losing their jobs
- falling wages in farming, coal and textiles
- discrimination in low-paying jobs, especially for black Americans and immigrants.

By 1929, 60 per cent of Americans lived in poverty. By the end of the decade, the top five per cent of the population owned one-third of the wealth. This was very damaging for the economy as rich people saved rather than spending their money, and poor people had no money to spend.

Over-production

By the late 1920s, American businesses were producing more goods than there were American people who could afford to buy them.

> **Key terms**
>
> **Over-production**: producing too many goods.
>
> **Laissez-faire**: policy of non-interference in the running of the economy.
>
> **Tariff**: a tax on goods coming into a country from overseas.

- Factories produced too much; large companies such as the General Electric Company kept wages low and prices high, so too few workers could afford to buy what their factory made.
- Farm incomes dropped throughout the 1920s because prices for farm products fell; problems in agriculture had a large impact, as 30 per cent of Americans still lived on farms.

The solution to this problem would have been to sell more products abroad. However, at the end of the First World War, European countries owed over $10 billion to the USA and they had no way of paying the money back. The USA insisted that their former allies pay the money back anyway. With so much debt to repay, it meant that Europe could not afford to buy goods from America.

To make matters worse, the 1922 Fordney–McCumber Act imposed high tariffs on imported industrial products. Other countries did the same to American imports and so the USA could not sell its goods abroad, even when countries did have the money.

Speculation on the stock market

With American business protected by tariffs, money easily available through hire purchase and credit, and consumer spending high in the mid-1920s, investors had every reason to believe that share prices would continue to increase.

There were 20 million shareholders by the summer of 1929, and share prices had reached an all-time high – the total value of shares in 1925 was $27 billion, but by 1929 it was $87 billion. It seemed as if the market would never fail.

Revision task TESTED

Make a list of the causes of the end to the economic prosperity of the 1920s. Number your list in order of importance. Give reasons why you think your number one is the most important cause.

The Wall Street Crash

Investors buy 'shares' in a company. The company uses this money to increase the value of its business. Shareholders get paid a dividend, a share of this increased value. Shareholders sell their shares in a company when the price is higher. The more a company is worth, the higher the value of its shares. Speculators made a living just from buying and selling shares. Between 1924 and 1929, the price of shares on the New York Stock Exchange on Wall Street rose by 500 per cent.

People thought prices would keep on rising forever. Many borrowed money to buy shares, hoping to pay back the loan with the profit they made when they sold their shares ('buying on the margin'). As a result, share prices rose faster than the value of the companies. Banks were happy to lend their customers' savings to speculators as they were sure they would make their money back.

Then, people started to lose confidence in how much more money American businesses could make, which began to affect the share prices of those companies. Share prices had been driven up by demand in the 1920s, which meant most shares were overvalued. There was only one way share prices could go ... down!

Events of the Wall Street Crash

In early September 1929, there were repeated warnings of a crash and prices began to fall back down to a more realistic level. The more prices fell, the more people wanted to sell, and so prices fell faster.

- **Saturday 19 October:** 3.5 million shares traded. Prices fell.
- **Monday 21 October:** 6 million shares traded. Prices continued to fall.
- **Thursday 24 October ('Black Thursday'):** 13 million shares sold; because there were few buyers, prices crashed.
- **Friday 25 October:** Bankers bought shares to restore confidence.
- **Monday 28 October:** 9 million shares were sold; prices continued to fall.
- **Tuesday 29 October:** 6 million shares were sold in a panic.
- **November:** Share prices continued to fall until mid-November.

Key terms

Wall Street Crash: the collapse of the American stock market in October 1929.

Great Depression: the economic and social slump which followed the Wall Street Crash.

Gold Standard: when a country's currency is linked to the amount of gold it has.

The **Wall Street Crash** affected the economy, which had a knock-on effect on most Americans during the 1930s. This became known as the **Great Depression**. People were more careful about how they spent their money, but this held back the economic growth that would have solved the situation.

Immediate effects of the Wall Street Crash

- Much of the speculation had been financed by the banks. When speculators failed to pay back their loans, many banks went bankrupt.
- People stopped spending. Sales of essentials did not fall by much, but sales of cars and labour-saving devices, which people could live without, plummeted.
- American banks began calling in loans from abroad, which caused a financial crisis in Europe. Europeans stopped buying goods from America.

Companies closed down factories and laid off workers. This led to the 'cycle of depression':

The government made things worse:
- The US Federal Reserve raised interest rates, which stopped people borrowing.
- The government kept to the '**Gold Standard**', which limited the money that people had to spend.

The cycle of depression
- Falling demand
- Increased unemployment
- Fewer people with money to spend
- Demand falls further

Revision task

What do you think was the most serious effect of the Wall Street Crash? Explain your choice.

TESTED

Hoover's reaction to the Great Depression

The policies of *laissez-faire* and rugged individualism had worked well during the boom years of the 1920s, but left many people poor and starving during the Depression.

Volunteerism

Herbert Hoover believed that it was not the job of government to take over businesses and force them to pay employees decent wages. Instead, he worked with businesses and local government leaders to try to persuade people to take this action, rather than forcing them to.

He also believed that it was not the job of government to help hungry and homeless people. Republicans believed that if the government stepped in to help people in crisis, then people would become dependent on government and would do nothing to help themselves. Instead, Hoover encouraged charities to help people in need. This was known as '**volunteerism**'.

Intervention

Government intervention on this scale had never been needed or attempted before. The interventions that President Hoover felt he could make began the process of solving the crisis but did not go far enough:
- 1929 Federal Farm Board – bought surplus farm produce to keep prices up, but encouraged farmers to grow too much.
- 1930 Hawley–Smoot Act – set a tariff on imported products. When other countries did the same to American products, it damaged US businesses which depended on selling abroad.
- 1931 President's Organization on Unemployment Relief (POUR) – advised charities how to help the unemployed and encouraged fund-raising. Charity donations almost doubled in 1931, but they were overwhelmed with demand for their services.
- 1932 Emergency Relief Act – the government offered $300 million in loans to states to provide unemployment pay, but states did not want to increase their debt.
- 1932 Norris–La Guardia Act – allowed workers to join unions and to strike, but workers did not feel secure enough to try to pressure their bosses.
- 1932 Home Loan Bank Act – twelve regional banks were set up to stimulate house building and home ownership.

Some of Hoover's policies, like the 1932 Reconstruction Finance Corporation (RFC) which offered loans to banks and companies which were struggling, and spending on road-building, public buildings and the Hoover Dam, were similar to those in Roosevelt's New Deal (see page 165) but did not do enough to stop the Depression.

President Hoover's popularity

As the Depression continued, Hoover became increasingly unpopular.

Hoover believed in a 'balanced budget', so he had to increase taxes to pay for his public works. His 1932 Revenue Act introduced an income tax – the rate increased depending on how much money a person earned. This made him unpopular with rich people who now had to pay 63 per cent tax instead of the 25 per cent they had paid before. His proposed Sales Tax made him more unpopular with the poor.

Herbert Hoover (1874–1964)
- Hoover served as Secretary for Commerce for Presidents Harding and Coolidge in the 1920s.
- He became US President between 1929 and 1933, promising 'a chicken for every pot'.
- He attempted to deal with the Depression but was opposed to direct federal relief for the poor.
- Hoover lost the 1932 presidential election to the Democrat Franklin Roosevelt as people thought he was not doing enough to help them.

Key term

Volunteerism: the belief that charities, not the government, should help poor people.

The Democratic Party blamed Hoover for the Depression. They invented a series of 'Hoover' terms that attacked his reputation. For example:
- the 'Hoover blanket' – a newspaper used as a blanket
- 'Hoover leather' – cardboard used to fill a hole in a shoe
- 'Hoover stew' – soup from a soup kitchen.

This created an image of a president who did not care. It gave rise to a popular slogan: 'In Hoover we trusted, now we are busted'. Hoover's measures had little time to work before a presidential election was held in November 1932.

The 1932 presidential election

The two candidates fighting the presidential election in November 1932 were:
- Republican Herbert Hoover
- Democrat Franklin Delano Roosevelt (FDR).

During the election campaign, people booed films of Hoover in the cinema, his train had eggs thrown at it and the Secret Service had to stop a number of assassination attempts. Roosevelt blamed the bankers and rich people, which appealed to poor people.

Roosevelt won a landslide victory, securing 23 million votes and 42 of the 48 states, compared with Hoover's 16 million votes.

> **Revision task** — TESTED
>
> Draw a spider diagram to show the reasons why Hoover lost and why Roosevelt won the 1932 presidential election.

The impact of the Depression

Banking

Banks were needed to protect people's savings, to provide **mortgages** for people to buy homes and to give loans to businesses. When the banks began to fail in 1929, they could no longer guarantee to do any of these things. Many banks had little in the way of cash reserves as they had been investing their customers' money in the stock market. Only one-third of banks were in the **Federal Reserve** scheme, and those who were not could not be helped directly by the Federal Government.

By the end of the 1930s, 10,000 banks had failed. There were 'runs on the banks', where everybody tried to withdraw their money, fearing that the banks were about to go **bankrupt**. One of the worst closures was the New York City Bank in December 1930, which left 400,000 people without their savings.

As banks closed, people lost their savings and businesses were cut off from investment, which made the Depression even worse. By 1933, 5,000 American banks had failed and their customers had lost all of their money.

Agriculture

Agriculture struggled during the 1920s as overproduction drove down the price of food. The hard times of 1929–33 caused a collapse. American tariffs on foreign imports meant that other countries put tariffs on American farming produce. Farmers found it more difficult to sell their produce abroad.

> **Key terms**
>
> **Mortgage**: a loan to buy a property, usually paid back over a long period of time, e.g. 25 years.
>
> **Federal Reserve**: the federal government's central banking system.
>
> **Bankrupt**: when a person or a business no longer has any money and is not able to borrow any more money.

Many farmers had taken out large loans to mechanise their farms. Farmers who had bought shares were ruined by the Crash. Many rural banks failed.

Farmers and sharecroppers experienced many problems:
- Many farmers went bankrupt – farms were foreclosed (taken by a bank when loans could not be repaid) or sold off.
- Large industrial-scale farms replaced smaller farms. Farmer-owners became paid labourers.
- Sharecroppers (see page 145) were badly hit in the southern states, where white workers pressured landowners to give them work instead. Landowners reduced their rates to force black sharecroppers off the land.

In the 1930s, the Midwest saw record summer temperatures and the worst drought in 300 years. In 1935, it rained at harvest time and ruined crops. Pests thrived. There was a plague of chinch bugs in 1933 and grasshoppers in 1936.

During the 1920s, farmers in the Midwest had over-cropped the fields, trying to get more money by growing more. This had drained the soil of nutrients. Crops failed in the drought, which created huge dust storms which blew for hundreds of miles, destroying people's homes and farms. This forced many people to leave these areas.

Industry

Between 1929 and 1932, 100,000 businesses shut down. The number of unemployed rose to almost 13 million (a quarter of the working population) in 1933. The 'old industries' were particularly badly hit – coal production fell back to the level of 1904, and 300,000 coalminers lost their jobs. Textile, car, iron and steel production all fell – car production fell from 4.5 million in 1929, to 1.1 million in 1933, and steel production fell 59 per cent in the same period.

Prices halved, so people who had a job could buy more with their money. The 'new industries' (electrical goods, chemicals, etc.) continued to expand. They invested so they could cut costs and reduce prices. This led to innovations in air conditioning, airline travel and other technical developments that could enable companies to keep on selling more products.

The impact of the Depression on people's lives

America had a very limited **welfare system**, which the poverty of the Depression overwhelmed. Soup kitchens, '**breadlines**' of people waiting for food, and men begging for a job, became common features of American towns.

Between 1931 and 1933, there were hunger marches all over the United States as people demanded government action. The marchers were met with force. For example in 1932, a peaceful march of 5,000 people in Detroit was attacked by police and guards from the Ford Automobile Company.

Depending on who they were, the Depression affected people in different ways:
- black Americans were more likely to lose their jobs than white workers
- immigrant workers lost their jobs to people who had been born in the USA
- women lost their jobs in domestic service as people could not afford help in their home
- older people became increasingly dependent on their relatives to look after them as few states or businesses had pension schemes.

> **Key terms**
>
> **Welfare system**: a government system to make sure that its citizens are not too poor so that they have food to eat, somewhere to live and help to get work; this is paid for from taxes.
>
> **Breadline**: people queuing for free food, often bread or soup, provided by churches or charities.

Many farmers and labourers were driven off the land. Around 2 million people moved from the countryside to the towns in the early 1930s, although this quickly slowed as all they found was more unemployment and terrible living conditions.

Hoovervilles

Hoovervilles were shanty towns, built of packing boxes and corrugated iron sheets, named after President Hoover. There was no sanitation and little access to clean water. The biggest Hoovervilles were in New York City, Washington DC and St Louis. Some became semi-permanent, like those in St Louis and Seattle, and ended up with a mayor and police force.

The Bonus Marchers

In 1924, Congress had voted to give each First World War veteran a bonus to make up for the wages they lost while fighting the First World War. Unfortunately, they would have to wait until 1945 to claim it.

In January 1932, a 'Bonus Army' of 25,000 veterans marched on Washington to claim their bonus. They set up a Hooverville, military-style, with strict hygiene rules and a daily parade. Congress would not pay the full bonus but offered $100,000 to help the marchers get home. Five thousand marchers stayed to demand they be paid the full amount they were owed.

In July, after the marchers had attacked the police who were sent in to empty some of the buildings in the camp, President Hoover sent in 600 troops and tanks to clear the camp completely, burning tents and using tear gas to chase the veterans away. Hundreds were injured. It was very bad publicity for Hoover in an election year.

Unemployment and homelessness

In 1929, 3.2 per cent of the American workforce was out of work, but this rose to 24.9 per cent by 1933. In some places where local industries were particularly hard hit by the Depression, it was much worse and unemployment could be as high as 50 per cent. Those who still had jobs also suffered as they were forced to work part time or for lower wages.

People's living standards fell as they had to cut spending on food and fuel. There was no national benefit system so people had to rely on whatever relief their local town or state provided. Extended families or soup kitchens run by charities were used by many people to get them through. It had long-term effects on family life as the average age at which people got married increased by two years, and the birth rate fell.

When people could no longer afford to pay their rent or their mortgages, they ended up losing their homes. Over 1 million men, women and children travelled the country in cars, on the railroad or even on foot in search of work and a place to live. Sometimes they were referred to as **hobos**.

> **Key term**
>
> **Hoovervilles**: basic temporary housing built on the edges of cities by the unemployed during the Great Depression; named after President Hoover.
>
> **Hobo**: an unemployed wanderer searching for work.

Revision task TESTED ☐

Using your knowledge of this topic, explain the impact of the Great Depression on:
a) unemployment
b) people who lived in towns and cities
c) farmers.
To what extent does this information support the view that the Great Depression affected the lives of all Americans?

Exam practice

Study Extract C.

Extract C suggests that the Wall Street Crash was one of many causes of the Great Depression.

How far do you agree with this interpretation? (16 marks)

Use Extract C, Sources A and B and your own knowledge to explain your answer.

Source A

From a businessman commenting on increasing speculation on the stock market in 1928.

The number of inexperienced speculators is being increased by a great many men who have been attracted by newspaper stories. These stories tell of big, easy profits to be made on the stock exchange. These amateurs have not learned that markets sometimes panic and that there are large falls in prices. These suckers speculate on tips, on hunches. They buy or sell at the slightest notice.

WJEC GCSE History: Germany in Transition 1919–1939 and USA a Nation of Contrasts 1910–1929, Steve Waugh, John Wright and R. Paul Evans, 2017, Hodder Education, p.137, Source C.

Source B

From the New York Times *newspaper, published on 30 October 1929.*

Stock prices virtually collapsed yesterday, swept downwards with gigantic losses in the most disastrous trading day in the stock market's history. Billions of dollars in market value were wiped out. The market on the rampage is no respecter of persons. It wasted fortune after fortune yesterday and financially crippled thousands of individuals in all parts of the world. From every point of view, in the extent of losses sustained, in total turnover, in the number of speculators wiped out, the day was the most disastrous in Wall Street's history.

WJEC GCSE History: Germany in Transition 1919–1939 and USA a Nation of Contrasts 1910–1929, Steve Waugh, John Wright and R. Paul Evans, 2017, Hodder Education, p.140, Source F.

Extract C

The Depression was not caused by the Crash alone. The issues with the economy in the 1920s are vital to understanding what was wrong with the USA at the time. However, the Crash did speed up the approach of the Depression, and its effects were catastrophic for the country and the people during the next decade. Farmers were hit terribly, and when they demonstrated in towns they carried placards attacking the president. One slogan became extremely popular: 'In Hoover we trusted, now we are busted.'

WJEC GCSE History: Germany in Transition 1919–1939 and USA a Nation of Contrasts 1910–1929, Steve Waugh, John Wright and R. Paul Evans, 2017, Hodder Education, p.140.

Exam tips

Divide your answer into three paragraphs.
1. Using quotes from the source and specific relevant information from your own knowledge, explain the ways in which Source A could be said to agree and disagree with the view in Extract C.
2. Repeat this process using Source B.
3. Explain how much you agree with the view in Extract C, backing up your opinion with reference to points that you have made earlier about Sources A and B.

5.4 Roosevelt and the New Deal, 1933–41

REVISED

What you need to know

In this section you will revise how President Roosevelt tried to solve the problems caused by the Depression. This will include:
- Roosevelt's plan to deal with the Depression – the 3Rs (relief, recovery, reform).
- The actions President Roosevelt took in his first one hundred days as president.
- The Alphabet Agencies which were set up to solve the problems of the Depression; the first New Deal (1933–35) and second New Deal (1935–38).
- The successes and failures of Roosevelt's attempt to solve the problems of the Depression.

Franklin Delano Roosevelt (1882–1945)

- Roosevelt was Governor of New York, 1929–32.
- He was elected US President in 1933 (and again in 1936, 1940 and 1944), promising a 'New Deal' for the American people.
- Roosevelt attempted to solve the problems of the Depression through new laws for social security and new federal agencies to help get people back to work.
- He served four consecutive terms as President, dying in office.

Roosevelt's aims

When he took office as President in January 1933, **Franklin D. Roosevelt** introduced a change of policy known as the **New Deal**, which was very different from what President Hoover had attempted. It was based on the 'three Rs'.

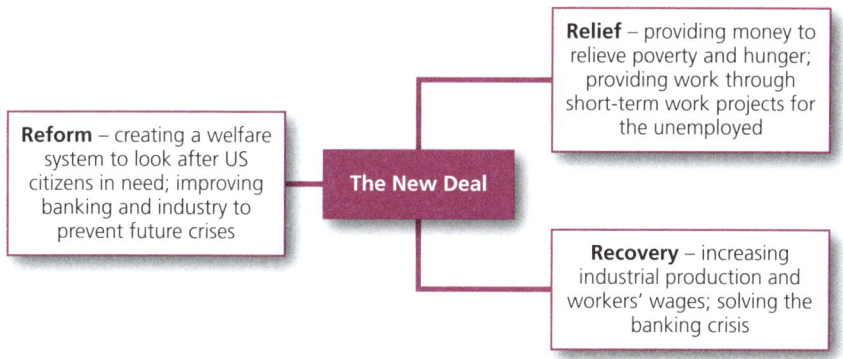

Key term

New Deal: policies introduced by President Roosevelt to deal with the effects of the Great Depression.

As a result, Roosevelt's 'New Deal for the American people' meant:
- public works programmes
- welfare
- support for industry and agriculture
- banking reform.

Roosevelt needed Congress to turn his policies into laws, to use federal money to create jobs and to create new government agencies to get what was needed done. Each step of the way he explained what he was doing to ordinary people through his regular radio broadcasts which were referred to as the 'fireside chats'.

The First Hundred Days

- After taking advice from a group of experts known as the 'Brains Trust', in his first hundred days (9 March–16 June 1933) Roosevelt introduced a large number of government programmes to restore the economy.
- He got Congress to pass the Emergency Banking Act (EBA) which closed all banks for ten days so that the government could determine if banks were safe.
- Roosevelt's government officially backed 5,000 banks, which helped to restore confidence. By the end of March 1933, $1 million had been

deposited in banks again. Another law guaranteed that if banks went bust, people would get up to $2,500 back.
- Once the banking system had been stabilised, Roosevelt asked Congress to pass the laws that would create the government agencies he believed were necessary to promote America's economic recovery from the Depression. These agencies were often referred to by their initials and became known as the '**Alphabet Agencies**'.

> **Key term**
>
> **Alphabet Agencies**: nickname given to the group of organisations set up as part of the New Deal.

> **Revision task** — TESTED
>
> Draw a diagram to summarise the different ways that Roosevelt planned to end the Depression.

The first New Deal 1933–35

The first New Deal focused on relief and economic recovery.

Alphabet Agency	Aim	Effect
Agriculture		
Tennessee Valley Authority (TVA), 1933	Set up across the seven states of the Tennessee Valley to deal with agricultural overproduction, flooding and soil erosion. A huge public works programme built 33 dams to irrigate the land and generate hydroelectric power. Farmers were given loans and training in soil conservation and new forests were planted.	Brought electricity to rural areas, and encouraged industries to re-locate to take advantage of cheap electricity.
Agricultural Adjustment Administration (AAA), 1933	Dealt with rural poverty and low crop prices. Subsidies were paid to farmers to destroy their crops and slaughter animals in an effort to push up prices.	By 1936, farm incomes were one and a half times higher than they had been in 1933. The AAA was declared invalid by the Supreme Court in 1936.
Commodity Credit Corporation (CCC), 1933	Paid farmers to keep excess crops in their warehouses. If prices rose, farmers could buy back their crops and sell them at the new, higher price.	
Farm Credit Administration (FCA), 1933	Provided funds for farmers who were struggling to make their mortgage payments.	One fifth of farmers were kept on their land by the FCA in the 1930s.
Industry		
National Industrial Recovery Act (NIRA), 1933	Aimed to solve the poor economic condition of the USA. Established the NRA and PWA (see below).	
National Recovery Administration (NRA), 1933	Encouraged employers to deal with over-production and poor working conditions. Introduced voluntary codes of practice for minimum wages, limited working hours and improving conditions for workers. Workers were given the legal right to join **trade unions**, although few did until the Wagner Act (see page 168).	As an incentive, companies complying with the code could display the Blue Eagle symbol; 2.3 million businesses were part of the scheme by the end of 1933.

Alphabet Agency	Aim	Effect
Unemployment		
The Federal Emergency Relief Administration (FERA), passed in the Hundred Days	Provided $500 million emergency relief for poor and homeless people in immediate need by providing food and clothing.	
The Homeowners Refinancing Act, 1933	Extended mortgage payment terms from five years to twenty years so people who were struggling were able to keep their houses.	
Civilian Conservation Corps (CCC), 1933	Provided six months of work for men aged between 18 and 25 in conservation projects, such as planting trees to stop soil erosion.	By 1940, over 2 million men had been given work in the CCC.
Public Works Administration (PWA) 1933	Spent $3,300 million of government money on public works projects for the unemployed – **slum** clearance; building schools, roads and hospitals; constructing the Grand River Dam in Oklahoma.	This took time to set up so a temporary agency, the Civil Works Administration, was quickly set up to help 4.2 million workers get through the winter of 1933.

Revision task

TESTED

Which of the measures of the Alphabet Agencies do you think was the most important? Explain your choice.

> **Key terms**
>
> **Trade union**: an organisation that could negotiate better conditions and wages for workers from their employers.
>
> **Slum**: an area of a town or city made up of a lot of poor quality housing, often overcrowded with inadequate sanitation.

The second New Deal, 1935–38

- The Democrats did well in the 1934 elections for Congress, especially in the Senate, and with this vote of confidence, Roosevelt wanted to address some of the criticisms of his first New Deal.
- In January 1935, Roosevelt introduced a Second New Deal which targeted the rights of workers, poor people and people without work.

Alphabet Agency and legislation	Aim	Effect
Help for poor people		
Works Progress Administration (WPA), 1935	Oversaw job creation schemes – manual labourers were given work on road and park building, or planting trees to hold back the ravages of the **Dust Bowl** in the Mid-West; young people were helped to stay at college or join training programmes; women were offered projects ranging from sewing to teaching; writers and performers were employed as researchers or travelling entertainers.	Eight million people were employed on this scheme at a cost of $11 billion.
Resettlement Administration, 1935	Mainly for poor people in rural areas, but also helped to build new houses in the suburbs.	
Housing Act, 1937	Passed to replace **shanty towns**.	
Fair Labour Standards Act, 1938	Aimed to provide fair pay for workers. This tightened up laws against child labour and established a federal minimum wage, as well as defining the working week as 40 hours and requiring overtime be paid for anything worked beyond that.	As a result, 300,000 workers secured higher wages and 1 million had a shorter working week.

Alphabet Agency and legislation	Aim	Effect
Help for farmers		
Resettlement Administration, 1935	Tried to resettle families who had been hit by the Dust Bowl.	Migrant camps were set up to help travelling workers but few were resettled.
Farm Security Administration (FSA), 1937	Replaced the Resettlement Administration. Helped poor people in rural areas to buy land and equipment.	By 1941, $1 billion in loans had been paid to farmers.
Agricultural Adjustment Act, 1938	Used quotas to encourage farmers to limit production and charged heavy taxes to farmers who overproduced.	

The impact of the Social Security Act, 1935

The USA had no national welfare system for pensions or unemployment payments for workers – it was left to individual states to deal with. Some dealt with it well, some very badly and many ignored it all together.

The 1935 Social Security Act aimed to deal with the problem of poverty. It set up a national system of **social security**, providing pensions for the over 65s and aid to widows, orphans and people with disabilities, as well as unemployment benefits jointly funded by federal and state government. These would be paid for through specific taxes paid to the federal government by both workers and employers. Grants would also be paid to help very poor families and people with disabilities.

While it helped in the long run, its immediate effects were limited as people had to pay the taxes first to be able to qualify. Domestic servants and agricultural labourers were not covered by the scheme.

The impact of the National Labour Relations Act (or 'Wagner Act'), 1935

The National Labour Relations Act (the Wagner Act – named after the senator who proposed it) was intended to increase workers' rights, after the Supreme Court had declared the National Industrial Recovery Act of 1933 invalid. This gave workers the legal right to join trade unions and stopped employers sacking union members. The National Labour Relations Board (NLRB) was set up to protect workers against unfair practices and help unions get recognition from employers.

Union membership rose to 9 million and the NLRB had 226 lawyers by 1939. Unfortunately, there were increasing numbers of strikes, many of which became violent as employers tried to stop them.

The impact of the Banking Act, 1935

Roosevelt had rescued the banks in 1933, but without major changes there was a danger that the banking industry could end up in crisis again. Control of the banks was still divided between the Federal Reserve, state governments and big banks.

The 1935 Banking Act gave complete control of banking in the USA to the federal government. The idea was to remove the influence of Wall Street investors and to prevent banks from acting in their own interests, rather than those of their customers. This strengthened the banking system and, as early as 1936, no banks closed. A serious crisis in banking seemed much less likely.

> **Key terms**
>
> **Dust Bowl**: a serious drought that destroyed the crops and soil of some parts of the mid-west of the USA and left large areas where crops could no longer be grown.
>
> **Shanty town**: poor quality, temporary housing, like the Hoovervilles (see page 163).
>
> **Social security**: a government system that gives money to people in need, in order to try to ensure that its citizens are not living in terrible poverty.

The impact of rural electrification

A lot of progress had been made in electrifying towns and cities, but by 1930 only about 10 per cent of farms had electricity – in some of the more remote areas this was as low as 1 per cent. There was no money to be made from providing this service so rural communities were forgotten.

The Tennessee Valley Authority (TVA) began to solve this problem by building dams to provide electricity and lending money to local **co-operatives** to lay cables. The Electric Home and Farm Authority (EHFA) was set up to help farmers buy electrical appliances on credit, and to encourage companies to make cheaper models for sale in the TVA area. This was so popular that it was expanded in the second New Deal and the Rural Electrification Administration (REA) spread these programmes around all of the USA.

By 1941, 35 per cent of farms had electricity and 417 co-operatives had taken loans to lay cables. However, some utilities companies slowed this process down by building cables to richer areas, which meant that the poorer areas did not always qualify for REA help.

> **Key term**
>
> **Co-operative**: a company owned and run by its own members.

Revision task
TESTED ☐

For each of the following Alphabet Agencies, write out its full name and describe what it did to help tackle the problems caused by the Great Depression: CCC, AAA, TVA, EBA, PWA.

Achievements of the New Deal

The New Deal helped to restore confidence and faith in government; it stimulated the economy and put the country back on its feet:
- America avoided the swing towards extremism like the communist and fascist governments that dominated politics in Europe.
- Millions of jobs were created through the Alphabet Agencies – 4 million people were employed on public works schemes created by the PWA and WPA; 2.5 million were employed in the CCC.
- Unemployment was reduced from 12.8 million in 1933, to 9.5 million in 1939.
- The TVA improved the lives of 7 million people with work opportunities.
- The income of farmers doubled between 1932 and 1939 as a result of the AAA.
- The New Deal stabilised the US banking system and restored confidence to the markets.
- Workers were protected by codes of practice and trade unions were allowed.
- It created a welfare state, providing pensions for older people and widows, and help for sick or unemployed people, and people with disabilities.

Shortcomings of the New Deal

Neither unemployment nor the underlying weakness of the economy had been fully solved by 1941, and there was increasing opposition to the New Deal through the 1930s.
- Some believed the New Deal did not go far enough – agencies discriminated against black people, who got no work or received lower wages than white workers; Alphabet Agencies were short-term solutions that provided cheap labour and did not solve the underlying economic problems – this was why there was a further rise in unemployment in 1937.
- Others believed that the New Deal undermined important American values, principles and laws; they felt that the federal government now

interfered too much in the lives of the American people; trade unions were seen as un-American as they were seen to take away the right of choice from workers.
- It was argued that the new social welfare measures encouraged people to live off the state; it went against rugged individualism.
- Work relief programmes were only able to help 40 per cent of those who needed it and direct relief varied from state to state. Little was done to solve the lack of housing.
- The cost of this relief had been underestimated and in 1937, Roosevelt had to ask for a further $3 billion for the programme.
- The NRA codes were not very effective – businesses just ignored them, an approach which was then encouraged by the Supreme Court's decision in the 'sick chicken case' (see page 171).
- Unemployment did fall, but it was America's entry into the Second World War in 1941 that ultimately lifted the country out of the Depression – in 1929 unemployment had been 1.5 million, peaking at 12.8 million in 1933; by 1941 it was still at 5.6 million.
- As social security was paid from people's wages rather than from taxes, the wealth gap between rich and poor was the same in 1940 as it had been in 1930.

Exam practice

Study Sources A and B.

How far does Source A support the evidence of Source B about the aims of Roosevelt's New Deal? Explain your answer. **(8 marks)**

Source A

From the evidence of an ordinary US citizen to the Committee of Labour in Congress 1932.

During the last three months I have visited as I have said, some twenty states of this wonderfully rich and beautiful country. The farmers are pauperised by the poverty of the industrial populations and the industrial populations are pauperised by the poverty of the farmers. Neither has the money to buy the products of the other; hence we have over-production and under-consumption at the same time and in the same country.

Democracies in Change: Britain and the USA in the twentieth century, Robin Bunce, Peter Clements, Vivienne Sanders and Nick Shepley, 2015, Hodder Education, p. 291, Source 1.

Source B

From the Declaration of Policy in the 1933 National Industrial Recovery Act.

A national emergency productive of widespread unemployment and disorganisation of industry, which burdens interstate and foreign commerce, affects the public welfare and undermines the standards of living of the American people, is hereby declared to exist. It is hereby declared to be the policy of Congress to increase the consumption of industrial and agricultural products by increasing purchasing power, to reduce and relieve unemployment, to improve standards of labour, and to otherwise rehabilitate industry and to conserve natural resources.

Adapted from *Democracies in Change: Britain and the USA in the twentieth century*, Robin Bunce, Peter Clements, Vivienne Sanders and Nick Shepley, 2015, Hodder Education, p. 278.

Revision task

1. Which do you think are the three most important successes of the New Deal?
2. What were the three most important shortcomings of the New Deal?

TESTED

Exam tips

Divide your answer to this question into three paragraphs.
1. The first paragraph should focus on areas of agreement between the sources – quote material directly from both sources to support the points you are making and clearly explain each area of agreement that you identify.
2. The second paragraph should follow the advice in Step 1, except that it should focus on areas of disagreement.
3. The third paragraph should begin with your judgement of how much you think these sources agree with each other about the topic in the question, followed by your explanation for why you think this.

5.5 The opposition to the New Deal

REVISED

What you need to know

In this section you will revise the reasons for, and impact of, opposition to Roosevelt's New Deal. This will include:
- Opposition from the judges of the Supreme Court.
- Conservative criticism from the Republican Party, business interests and the Liberty League.
- Radical criticism from Huey Long, Father Coughlin and others.

Opposition from the Supreme Court

Most of the nine **Supreme Court** judges had been chosen by former Republican presidents and could not be replaced, as they could stay on the Court until they retired or died. The judges wanted to protect the US Constitution and the rights of individual states from the power of the President and the federal government. They were led by Chief Justice **Charles Evans Hughes**.

The Supreme Court had the power to stop the New Deal laws from being put into practice. However, the Court could only act if a state, company or individual appealed against an agency or a law.

In 1935, the Schechter Poultry Corporation had signed up to the NRA codes. They were prosecuted by the federal government for breaking rules about wages and animal welfare. They claimed the federal government had no power over trade within a state and the Supreme Court agreed with them. This became known as the 'sick chicken case' and effectively ended the NRA.

This ruling threatened the legal basis of all of the Alphabet Agencies. A similar judgment dealt a blow to the AAA when in 1936, a cotton company challenged the agency's ability to tax the business. The Court ruled that agriculture should be supervised by state not federal government.

The Supreme Court found eleven New Deal laws to be unconstitutional between 1935 and 1936. The 'sick chicken case' judgment was passed on the same day that the Court found the 1935 Farm Mortgage Act to be unconstitutional. The Court was telling the federal government that they could not act in individual states because they only had economic powers over trade between states.

Roosevelt felt the Court was standing in the way of what people had elected him to do. Roosevelt's 1936 Judiciary Reform **Bill** asked **Congress** for the power to replace all Supreme Court judges over the age of 70 – the average age of the nine judges was 71. It would also have enabled him to appoint six new judges who would have been more favourable to the New Deal. This was very unpopular. Congress refused to give its support.

However, the Supreme Court did respond to public opinion. As judges retired or died over the next few years, Roosevelt was slowly able to replace them, as he did when he appointed Hugo Black in 1937. Legal challenges to the New Deal came to an end.

Charles Evans Hughes (1862–1948)

- Hughes was the eleventh Chief Justice of the United States between 1930 and 1941.
- The Hughes Court was very critical of Roosevelt's New Deal to begin with.
- From 1937, Hughes and most of the other Supreme Court judges became more supportive of the New Deal.

Key terms

Supreme Court: the most important court in the USA; it can make judgments on whether laws or the actions of a president have broken the rules set out in the US Constitution.

Congress: makes the laws for the USA; made up of two Houses: the Representatives and the Senate.

Bill: a proposal for a law that has not yet been passed by Congress.

> **Revision task** TESTED
>
> Describe two features of the Supreme Court's opposition to the New Deal.

Conservative criticisms of the New Deal

Opposition to the New Deal came from both ends of the political spectrum – **conservatives** and radicals.

Republicans

Republicans were highly critical of the New Deal, claiming that Roosevelt was changing the role of government in the USA. They said he was now acting more like a **dictator**, like Stalin. The TVA and NRA were compared to the communist Five-Year Plans of the Soviet Union. They argued that the Social Security Act was an attack on 'rugged individualism', that it would make the American people lazy and too dependent on government help.

Republican politicians also objected to the huge amount of money being spent on the New Deal, most of which they considered to be wasted on things that private businesses should be doing, or on things that did not need doing at all.

Republicans struggled to get support for their position to begin with. Alfred Landon, the Republican candidate in the 1936 presidential election, argued that power should be returned to the states and for an end to New Deal regulations. This was not very popular and Roosevelt comfortably won the 1936 election.

In 1937, the Republicans benefited from the **recession** that cost a number of people their jobs, and also from the backlash against Roosevelt's scheme to pack the Supreme Court with judges who supported him.

By the 1938 **mid-term elections**, the Republicans won lots more seats in Congress, and were able to work with the conservative Democrats from the southern states to more effectively oppose the New Deal. Together, they were able to cut spending on relief programmes, block new laws and investigate the Alphabet Agencies. This meant that the New Deal effectively ended with the 1938 Fair Labour Standards Act.

Business interests

In the 1932 election, many businessmen had supported Roosevelt as they thought that he had the best plan for the economy. They quickly became disillusioned when the economy began to recover and yet he continued to introduce more expensive schemes which they were expected to pay for through higher taxes.

Business leaders did not like the government interfering in how they ran their companies. They objected to Roosevelt's support for trade unions, to being made to pay social security contributions for their workers and to putting pressure on them to increase wages. Schemes like the TVA were backed by the government and were considered to give unfair competition to privately-owned businesses. Companies argued that the new rules and regulations from agencies like the NRA were confusing and difficult to put into practice.

> **Key terms**
>
> **Republican**: the Republican Party was an American political party that believed the government should interfere as little as possible in the lives of American citizens or American business.
>
> **Conservative**: someone who does not like change or new ideas.
>
> **Dictator**: someone who rules a country however they like, without having to obey any laws or listen to anyone else's opinion.
>
> **Recession**: a period of falling production and employment; not as serious as a depression.
>
> **Mid-term elections**: elections for Congress that happen two years into a four-year presidential term of office.

The Liberty League

In 1934, a group of business leaders formed the Liberty League to oppose the New Deal. Conservatives from both the Republican and Democrat political parties supported it. The Liberty League:
- spread the message that the New Deal was anti-business using printed leaflets, radio broadcasts and after-dinner speeches
- argued that it was the responsibility of businesses and charities to solve these problems, not the government
- sponsored legal challenges against the Alphabet Agencies and other New Deal legislation.

There was little success to show for 1 million dollars spent. Only 150,000 people were recruited. Republicans did not want to be associated with them in the 1936 presidential election campaign. After 1937, the Supreme Court became more supportive of the New Deal. By 1940, the Liberty League began closing its offices.

Revision task

Draw a spider diagram to summarise criticisms of the New Deal – place conservative criticisms on one side and, in a different colour, add radical criticisms (see below) on the other side.

Radical criticism of the New Deal

Like the conservatives, **radicals** also opposed the New Deal, but for very different reasons.

> **Key term**
>
> **Radical**: someone with new, different ideas and who is often against the ideas supported by most people.

Huey Long's 'Share Our Wealth' programme

Huey Long was elected governor of the poor state of Louisiana in 1928, and increased taxes on the rich to pay for roads, hospitals and schools. He built over 3,000 miles of paved highways, a new airport and set up adult reading and writing programmes. And all of this before the New Deal had begun.

After being elected as a senator in 1932, Long criticised Roosevelt for not sharing out the nation's wealth fairly and proposed his own 'Share Our Wealth' campaign. He wanted to take all personal income over $1.8 million and use it to ensure that all Americans had a minimum income of $2,500 a year. He wanted every American to have the money to buy a house, a car, a radio, and a free college education for all of those who would qualify.

There were not enough rich people to make this plan work. However, his speeches made ordinary Americans feel as if he was speaking for them and soon there were 8 million members of his Share Our Wealth clubs. There was talk about Long running for President in 1936, but he was assassinated in 1935. His successor, Gerald Smith, met with little success, even after campaigning jointly with Father Coughlin's Social Justice campaign (see below) during the 1936 presidential election.

Father Coughlin's 'Social Justice' campaign

Father Charles Coughlin was a Roman Catholic priest whose parish was near Detroit. By 1930, his weekly sermons were broadcast on a large radio network where he attracted over 30 million listeners. He had been a supporter of Roosevelt but became increasingly angry that not enough was being done to help poor people. He believed that the Depression had been caused by Wall Street financiers and that the New Deal would not really help people, as the bankers were still in charge.

Father Coughlin set up the National Union for Social Justice in 1934, to demand banking reform, **nationalisation** of some parts of the US economy, and a fairer taxation policy. He teamed up with Gerald Smith (see page 173) and Francis Townsend (see below). They formed the National Union Party to campaign for their candidate William Lemke in the 1936 presidential election. Lemke got 828,000 votes, while Roosevelt got 27.8 million.

The Second New Deal included some of Coughlin's and Long's ideas so it became more difficult for radicals to criticise Roosevelt. Coughlin lost support as he continued to attack Roosevelt who was still very popular. To make matters worse, his broadcasts became increasingly **antisemitic**. By 1940, his radio broadcasts were banned. He stopped writing when the government threatened to prosecute him for inciting rebellion during the Second World War.

> **Key terms**
>
> **Nationalisation**: when the government takes direct control of a business or industry.
>
> **Antisemitic**: showing hatred of Jewish people.

Other radical criticism of the New Deal

Many other people also believed the New Deal was not doing enough to help people:

- In 1933, Dr Francis Townsend, a retired public health officer, argued that Roosevelt had not done enough to help older people and proposed a pension of $200 a month for everyone over 60 provided they gave their jobs to young people. This way both young and older people would have money to boost consumer spending, which would in turn benefit industry and the economy; he called this the Old Age Revolving Pensions Ltd and planned for it to be paid for by a 2 per cent sales tax. Half a million people joined the Townsend clubs and 20 million signed a petition in support of it. People quickly came to realise that such an expensive benefit could not be paid for by such a small tax – it would have cost 50 per cent of the national US income to make it work.
- In 1934, novelist Upton Sinclair ran for Governor in the state of California using the slogan, 'End Poverty in California' (EPIC); he argued empty land and disused factories should be given to the unemployed to get themselves out of poverty. He was defeated by the Republican candidate.

Revision task

TESTED

Which of the criticisms of the New Deal do you think was the most serious challenge? Explain your choice.

Exam practice

Describe **TWO** key features of **EITHER** Supreme Court opposition to the New Deal, **OR** radical criticism of the New Deal. (6 marks)

> **Exam tips**
>
> You should break your answer down into two short paragraphs, one for each feature.
>
> 1. Begin the first paragraph, 'One feature of [topic from the question, e.g. radical criticism of the New Deal] was ...'
> 2. Begin the second paragraph 'Another feature of [topic from the question, e.g. radical criticism of the New Deal] was ...'
> 3. For each feature, write down at least two pieces of relevant factual detail to show that you fully understand that feature.

Section 2B Breadth Studies

6 Changes in medicine, c1848–c1948

6.1 Progress in the mid-nineteenth century; Nightingale, Chadwick, Snow and Simpson

REVISED

> **What you need to know**
>
> In this section you will revise a period where medical knowledge was very limited and how this impacted on treatment and surgery, but where there were some advances in medical care and public health. This will include:
> - The barriers that caused lack of progress in medicine up to 1848.
> - Florence Nightingale's work at Scutari and how this improved nursing and hospitals.
> - Why surgery was so dangerous and how Simpson's work on chloroform improved surgery.
> - Problems and improvements in public health, including Chadwick's work and the 1848 Public Health Act.
> - The threat of cholera and the work of John Snow.

Barriers to progress

By 1848, there were many different beliefs about what caused disease. A few people still believed that disease was caused by God, but most believed in scientific theories based on what was known at the time.

- The Theory of the Four Humours developed in Ancient Greece. This theory held that there were four humours – blood, phlegm, yellow bile and black bile – and a person became ill when their humours were out of balance.
- People knew there was a link between dirty conditions and disease so the **miasma theory** and the idea of **spontaneous generation** were popular.

None of these theories was correct. The lack of understanding of the causes of disease was the main barrier to progress in medicine by 1848, because treatments for disease and training for doctors were based on these incorrect theories.

> **Key terms**
>
> **Miasma theory**: the theory that 'bad air' caused and spread disease.
>
> **Spontaneous generation**: the idea that rotting matter (from dead plants and animals) produced organisms which cause disease.

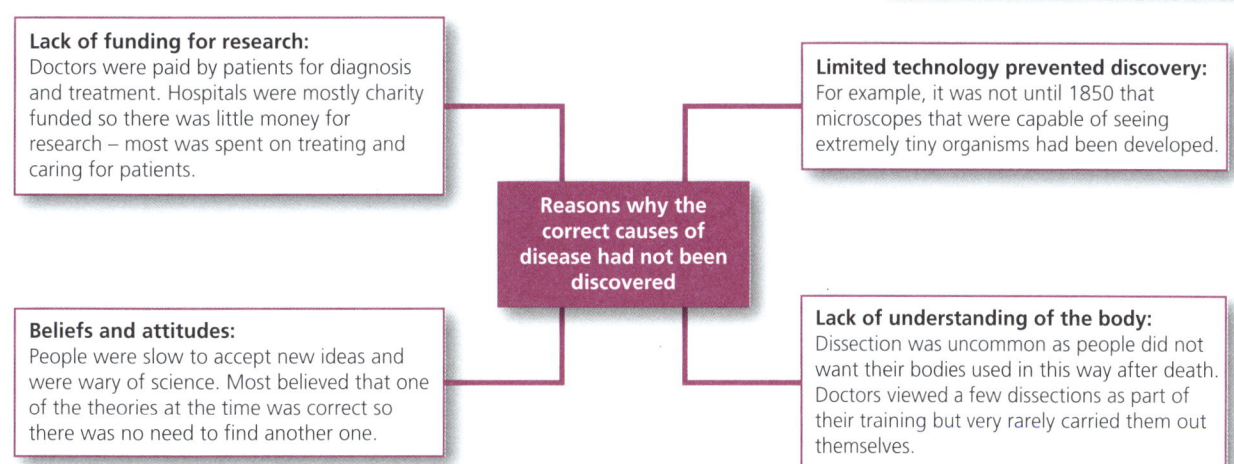

Lack of funding for research:
Doctors were paid by patients for diagnosis and treatment. Hospitals were mostly charity funded so there was little money for research – most was spent on treating and caring for patients.

Limited technology prevented discovery:
For example, it was not until 1850 that microscopes that were capable of seeing extremely tiny organisms had been developed.

Reasons why the correct causes of disease had not been discovered

Beliefs and attitudes:
People were slow to accept new ideas and were wary of science. Most believed that one of the theories at the time was correct so there was no need to find another one.

Lack of understanding of the body:
Dissection was uncommon as people did not want their bodies used in this way after death. Doctors viewed a few dissections as part of their training but very rarely carried them out themselves.

Florence Nightingale and Scutari

In 1848, there were few nurses in hospitals. Most nurses in Britain were poor and had a reputation for drunkenness. They had very little training. Hospitals themselves were often insanitary and diseases spread quickly within them.

Changes in nursing and hospitals at Scutari

The Crimean War broke out in October 1853. Newspapers in Britain reported terrible conditions at the hospital in Scutari, in Istanbul, where British soldiers were being treated. The hospital was dirty, there were few medical supplies and no nurses, and the injured soldiers had little access to adequate food and clean water. Many of the injured were dying of infectious diseases or wound infection.

Florence Nightingale, along with a team of nurses, was sent to Scutari to improve the situation. Her work had a huge impact in reducing the death rate from over 40 per cent to 2 per cent through:
- thoroughly and continuously cleaning hospital wards and equipment
- giving patients separate beds with space between them
- separating patients into different wards by illness or ailment
- ventilating wards so patients had access to fresh air
- ensuring that patients were kept clean and their bedding regularly changed
- setting up a kitchen and organising fresh food for patients
- establishing a clean water supply
- arranging for medical supplies to be sent from Britain
- organising rotas so nurses were always available to help treat and look after all the injured
- frequently cleaning wounds and changing dressings.

Florence Nightingale used her family's influence and her own wealth to provide what was needed. Her success at Scutari was widely reported in Britain. This gave her huge influence and publicity, which meant that her methods began to be copied and her books (the first was published in 1859) were widely read. This helped change attitudes so that people began to see that changes in hospitals could improve medical care. It also began to change the role of women in medicine by showing the positive impact of women working as well-trained, professional nurses.

> **Florence Nightingale (1820–1910)**
> - After much persuasion, her wealthy and influential family allowed Nightingale to train to be a nurse at the first nurses' training school in Kaiserwerth Hospital in Germany and then in Paris.
> - In 1853, she became the superintendent of nurses at King's College Hospital, London.
> - She strongly believed that disease was caused by miasma.
> - She became a national hero due to her work at the hospital in Scutari which helped reduce the death rate of British soldiers in the Crimean War.
> - After returning to Britain, she had an impact on how hospitals were run and designed and helped transform nursing into a profession with proper training.

Revision task

1. Using the information above, complete the table for each example of Nightingale's work in Scutari.

	Helped prevent wound infection	Improved medical treatment	Reduced the likelihood of infectious diseases
Thoroughly and continuously cleaning hospital wards and equipment			

2. Write two paragraphs to briefly explain how:
   - Nightingale and her team of nurses at Scutari helped change the role of women in medicine
   - the Crimean War had an impact on medicine.

Dangers in surgery: pain, infection and bleeding

In 1848, surgery was still very basic because of three major problems: pain, infection and bleeding.

Pain

Patients were often given alcohol during surgery to try to ease the pain, but there was no way to numb the body or make people unconscious so they would not be able to feel anything. This meant that:
- the surgeon had to work extremely quickly to limit pain
- the patient would be held down by several people but it was impossible to keep them still.

Therefore, surgeons often made mistakes and were only able to carry out simple operations.

Infection

As people did not understand how infection occurred, they did not know how to prevent it during or after surgery.
- Surgeons, their assistants and the patient wore their normal clothes.
- The surgeon might wash his hands but did not wear gloves.
- The instruments used and the conditions in which surgery took place were unhygienic.
- Surgical wounds would be covered with unclean bandages that were not changed regularly.

Therefore, those patients who survived an operation often died a few days or weeks later from infection.

Bleeding

All surgery involves blood loss which makes it difficult for the surgeon to see what they are doing, which can lead to mistakes. However, blood loss is a major cause of death in its own right. When a person loses a lot of blood, their body goes into **shock**. If a lot more blood is lost, then their **organs** cannot work and the person dies. There were several methods used to stop the patient losing blood in the mid-nineteenth century but they were all problematic:
- **Tourniquets** were used to temporarily stop the blood flowing during the operation. By 1848, metal clamps were commonly used. This did stop the blood flow and helped the surgeon to see. However, sometimes it caused nerve damage as blood vessels were deprived of blood for too long.
- After surgery, blood vessels were **cauterised** using metal tools heated in fire or boiling oil. This was extremely painful. It did stop the bleeding and the heat reduced the chance of infection. However, it often caused further damage to other body tissue.
- **Ligatures** were another method used to stop blood loss after surgery. This was far less painful than cauterisation. However, it was difficult to do this properly as the patient was not completely still, so sometimes this did not stop the bleeding. It also often led to infection from the ligatures themselves or the surgeon's hands.

These methods might stop the bleeding but did nothing to replace the blood that had already been lost. If the patient went into shock, they needed a blood **transfusion**. This was attempted only sometimes and was rarely successful:
- Blood starts to clot as soon as it leaves the body. During this period of history, it was impossible to store blood outside the body. Therefore only direct person-to-person transfusions were possible. This caused problems as people were not available or did not want to do this because of the risks involved.

Key terms

Shock: when the heart slows down so it can't pump enough blood around the body.

Organs: parts inside the body, such as the heart, lungs, liver, kidneys, which carry out functions so the body can work.

Tourniquets: something tied or pressed around the body part to stop blood passing through blood vessels.

Cauterised: using heat to seal blood vessels to stop blood flow.

Ligatures: threads (usually made from silk at this time) tied around a blood vessel to stop blood flow.

Transfusion: process of transferring blood from one person (the donor) to another (the patient).

- Often the donor's body did not accept the donated blood – their red blood cells would clump together, leading to death. (This is because different blood types had not yet been discovered, see page 190.)

The impact of Simpson and chloroform

In 1846, ether was found to be an effective **anaesthetic**. A small dose could make someone unconscious for days! Also, it could make patients vomit or cough, even when unconscious. **James Simpson** used ether for women in childbirth from January 1847, but wanted to find an anaesthetic that caused fewer problems.

In the summer of 1847, Simpson, along with two assistants, experimented with various different substances. When they tried inhaling chloroform, they quickly fell unconscious. On further testing, they discovered it had fewer side-effects than ether. Simpson began using it on women in childbirth and on patients during surgery. Other medics followed his example.

The impact of chloroform

Simpson's discovery was therefore an important change in surgery but it took time to become widely used because:
- It was difficult to administer chloroform correctly. Too little and a patient could still feel pain, but too much could cause death. (These problems were resolved after John Snow (see page 180) invented an inhaler.)
- Many people believed that childbirth should be painful as that was what God wanted. This view fell out of favour once Queen Victoria praised chloroform after using it during childbirth in 1853.
- It seemed to lead to more deaths during or after surgery. As patients could no longer feel pain and were kept totally still during operations, more complex surgery was attempted. This increased the death rate, largely because the problems of infection and blood loss had not been resolved, as well as the surgery being more complicated.

> **Key term**
>
> **Anaesthetic**: drug used to reduce sensation (and therefore pain).

> **James Simpson (1811–70)**
> - Simpson trained as a physician and then a surgeon at Edinburgh University.
> - In 1836, he became house surgeon at the City Lying-In Hospital, Edinburgh, where he specialised in obstetrics and midwifery.
> - He experimented with different anaesthetics as he wanted to reduce pain during childbirth.
> - He discovered and successfully used and promoted chloroform as an effective anaesthetic, which was quickly accepted by other surgeons but took longer to be accepted in childbirth and by the general public.

Revision tasks TESTED

1. Complete a table like the one below on the three problems of surgery c1848.

	Why it was a problem for surgery c1848	How surgeons had tried to solve it (if they did)	Any new problems encountered
Pain			
Infection			
Bleeding			

2. Write a short paragraph explaining how Simpson's discovery of chloroform as an anaesthetic 'solved' the problem of pain but did not improve the death rate from surgery.

Problems and improvements in public health

From 1750, the **industrial revolution** meant that towns and cities grew rapidly as many people left rural areas in search of work in the new factories. This led to:
- poor quality housing being built as houses needed to be built quickly
- over-crowding as housing was built very close together to accommodate as many people as possible
- over-crowding within houses as families could only afford to live in the poorest parts of towns in just one or two rooms
- unhygienic conditions with few toilets, sewers running into rivers and no rubbish collections.

Disease spread very quickly in these conditions.

> **Key term**
>
> **Industrial revolution**: the changing of society from a rural, farming-based one to an urban, manufacturing-based one.

The work of Chadwick

The Poor Laws stated that local authorities had to provide **workhouses** where those who could not work due to age, illness or disability could live. The laws also stated that Poor Law Guardians had to support widows and orphans. This was becoming increasingly expensive as more and more people became ill with serious, long-term health issues – many were unable to work and were dying young.

The government asked **Edwin Chadwick**, secretary to the Poor Law Commission, to lead an enquiry into sanitary conditions in the whole of Britain. His *Report on the Sanitary Condition of the Labouring Population of Great Britain* (1842), found that the life expectancy of people who lived in towns and cities was much, much lower than those who lived in the countryside. Average life expectancy for labourers in Liverpool was just 15 years, compared with 38 years in Rutland. He argued this was because of the dirty conditions in which people lived. His main recommendations were that authorities should:

- provide clean water
- collect rubbish from houses and streets
- improve drainage and provide sewers
- appoint medical officers.

He tried to persuade the government that this should be done by arguing that these measures would save money in the long run, as fewer people would get ill and die or need the workhouse. The report received a large amount of publicity, but little was done.

Public Health Act, 1848

It was the threat of another **cholera** outbreak (see below) in 1848 that finally made the government act on some of Chadwick's recommendations. The Public Health Act of 1848:

- set up a National Board of Health
- made it possible for the government to force local councils to appoint medical officers, improve water supplies and sewerage and remove rubbish in towns where the death rate was very high
- allowed other councils to do these things as well if they had the approval of local tax payers.

About 160 towns or cities (one-third) acted on at least some of the suggestions, but most did not as it wasn't compulsory. Therefore, public health provision improved only slowly and only in some areas of the country.

> **Edwin Chadwick (1800–90)**
> - Chadwick was educated as a lawyer and was interested in social reform from an early age.
> - In the 1830s, he worked for the government on several investigations, including the working of the Poor Laws, conditions in factories and rural policing.
> - He became secretary to the Poor Law Commission and, in 1848, a member of the National Board of Health.
> - He worked extremely hard and attempted to introduce many public health reforms but was rarely successful, largely because of opponents' views and because he was often rude and personally disliked. He was forced to retire in 1854.

> **Key term**
>
> **Cholera**: a waterborne disease that causes severe diarrhoea and vomiting. In the nineteenth century it led to dehydration and death for most who caught it as there was no treatment.

Revision tasks

TESTED

1. Complete a spider diagram or concept map of the problems in public health in the mid-nineteenth century.
2. Write a list of the ways in which public health provision had improved by 1860.

The cholera threat and the work of John Snow

There were many 'killer' diseases in Britain in the nineteenth century, but none was as feared as cholera which can kill people within hours of them becoming ill. It first appeared in Britain in 1831, spreading rapidly and killing over 26,000 people. Many people believed it was caused by spontaneous generation or miasma, so there were some attempts to clean up houses and streets, but this did nothing to stop the spread of the disease. A second outbreak in 1848–49 claimed over 52,000 lives.

The work of John Snow

John Snow was working as a physician in London when the 1848 cholera epidemic struck. He began work on his theory that it was caught orally – through what someone ate or drank. Another outbreak of cholera in 1854 provided Snow with an opportunity to test his theory.
- He mapped the addresses of people who had died in Soho, London – an area in which over 700 people had died in the first ten days of the cholera epidemic.
- Snow found that most of these people collected their water from one pump – on Broad Street.
- He removed the handle from the pump so people could no longer use it.
- The number of cholera deaths in Soho fell dramatically.

Snow showed the government his findings. He had proven there was a link between the water pump and cholera, but many scientists believed that miasma around the pump had caused people to catch the disease, rather than the water itself. Therefore, Snow's findings led to little immediate action as it did not change people's understanding of the cause of illness. It was only after Pasteur's Germ Theory that more people began to accept that disease could be spread through water.

John Snow (1813–58)
- Born in York, Snow trained as a surgeon at the University of London, and then worked as a physician and surgeon in London.
- He published his idea that people caught cholera through what they ate or drank in his essay 'On the Mode of Communication of Cholera' in 1849. His work on mapping cholera in Soho in 1854 to one water pump seemed to prove his theory, though many did not believe it.
- He was also very interested in anaesthetics and used Simpson's work to invent an inhaler to regulate the dose of chloroform. He was the doctor who gave Queen Victoria chloroform during childbirth in both 1853 and 1857.

Exam practice
Explain **TWO** causes of poor medical treatment c1848. (8 marks)

Exam tips
1. 'Causes' means the reasons why something did or did not happen.
2. You only need two causes – don't include any more as you won't get credit for them. Similarly, make sure your two causes are different – if you only write about one cause you can only get a maximum of four marks.
3. You need to use your knowledge and understanding to include supporting detail for the two causes you select.

6.2 Discovery and development, 1860–75; Lister and Pasteur

REVISED

What you need to know
In this section you will revise a period in which scientific discovery led to developments in surgery and hospitals, as well as advancement of women in the field of medicine. This will include:
- Pasteur's Germ Theory and its effect on medicine.
- The role of Lister and the impact of antiseptics and how this improved surgery.
- Why the Public Health Act of 1875 was significant.
- How Florence Nightingale continued to improved hospitals and nursing.
- How Elizabeth Garrett became the first female doctor to qualify in Britain, and the progress of women in medicine up to 1875.

Pasteur, the development of Germ Theory and its effects

In the 1850s, most scientists and doctors thought that microbes existed but they were unable to see them. They believed the theory of spontaneous generation – that microbes were produced by rotting matter. **Louis Pasteur** was to prove that it was, in fact, the other way around – microbes made the matter rot.

Louis Pasteur was employed by a brewing company to find out why beer turned sour and how this could be stopped. Using powerful new microscopes, Pasteur could observe microbes. He found it was these tiny organisms that were causing the alcohol to go sour. He also believed that these microbes were in the air because when he sealed the alcohol so that air could not enter, the liquid did not go sour. He discovered that these microbes were destroyed by heating the liquid.

Pasteur called his discovery the Germ Theory and published it in 1861. He called microbes 'germs' because he could see them germinating (growing). Pasteur stated his belief that germs were also the cause of disease. He proved this by 1865, but was unable to find which microbes were causing which diseases.

The effects of Germ Theory

In the short term, Pasteur's Germ Theory had little impact on medicine in Britain:

- His work was for the brewing industry so it took time for doctors and medical scientists to pick up on the theory. It was not until 1878 that Pasteur published *Germ Theory and its Application to Medicine*.
- The existing theories of spontaneous generation and miasma were deeply embedded and believed by most scientists and doctors. Most did not believe that Pasteur was correct.

However, in the medium and long term, the effects of the Germ Theory were enormous. This huge change in understanding the cause of illness led to changes in medical treatment and surgery and improvements in public health provisions. It demonstrates the massive impact of science on medicine.

Louis Pasteur (1822–95)

- Pasteur was a French scientist – not a doctor – who worked at various universities.
- His Germ Theory vastly improved understanding of the causes of disease which led to huge steps forward in both preventing and treating disease, therefore saving the lives of many people.
- He developed vaccinations for anthrax, chicken cholera and rabies.
- Today there are thousands of hospitals, institutes, schools, buildings and streets named after him!

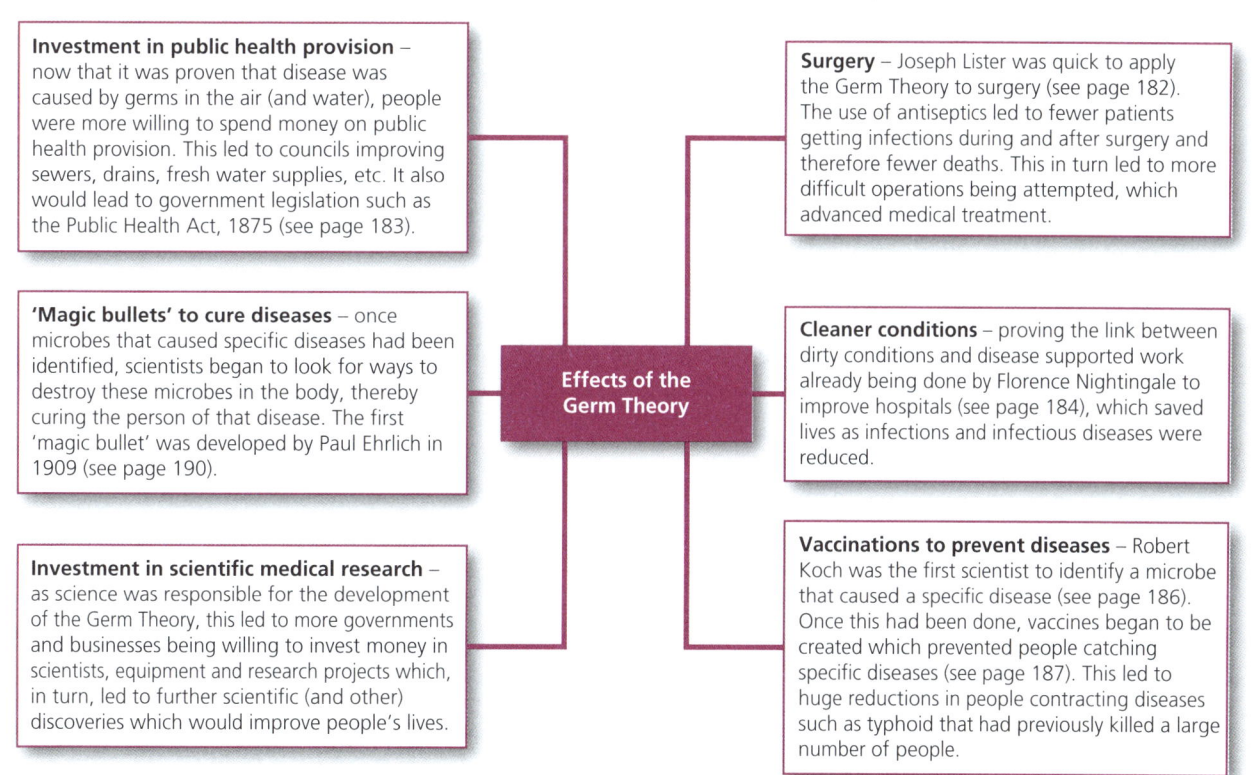

Investment in public health provision – now that it was proven that disease was caused by germs in the air (and water), people were more willing to spend money on public health provision. This led to councils improving sewers, drains, fresh water supplies, etc. It also would lead to government legislation such as the Public Health Act, 1875 (see page 183).

'Magic bullets' to cure diseases – once microbes that caused specific diseases had been identified, scientists began to look for ways to destroy these microbes in the body, thereby curing the person of that disease. The first 'magic bullet' was developed by Paul Ehrlich in 1909 (see page 190).

Investment in scientific medical research – as science was responsible for the development of the Germ Theory, this led to more governments and businesses being willing to invest money in scientists, equipment and research projects which, in turn, led to further scientific (and other) discoveries which would improve people's lives.

Surgery – Joseph Lister was quick to apply the Germ Theory to surgery (see page 182). The use of antiseptics led to fewer patients getting infections during and after surgery and therefore fewer deaths. This in turn led to more difficult operations being attempted, which advanced medical treatment.

Cleaner conditions – proving the link between dirty conditions and disease supported work already being done by Florence Nightingale to improve hospitals (see page 184), which saved lives as infections and infectious diseases were reduced.

Vaccinations to prevent diseases – Robert Koch was the first scientist to identify a microbe that caused a specific disease (see page 186). Once this had been done, vaccines began to be created which prevented people catching specific diseases (see page 187). This led to huge reductions in people contracting diseases such as typhoid that had previously killed a large number of people.

Effects of the Germ Theory

> **Revision task** `TESTED`
>
> Complete the following table.
>
> | Short-term impacts of Pasteur's Germ Theory | Medium-term impacts of Pasteur's Germ Theory | Long-term impacts of Pasteur's Germ Theory |
> |---|---|---|
> | | | |

Improvements in surgery: Lister and the impact of antiseptics

Although chloroform had solved the problem of pain during surgery, it had not reduced the death rate. A major reason for this was that infection continued to cause many deaths in the days and weeks after surgery. Most physicians and surgeons believed that infections were caused by dead and rotting flesh (spontaneous generation). **Joseph Lister** did a lot of research on infections and was not convinced that spontaneous generation was the cause.

- Lister read Pasteur's *Germ Theory*. He thought that if, as Pasteur believed, microbes caused disease then microbes were getting into his patients' wounds during and after surgery and causing infection.
- He began looking for something that would prevent microbes from getting into surgical wounds. In 1864, he learnt that carbolic acid was used to kill parasites in sewage. Cattle that fed on the grass in the path of the sewage were no longer becoming ill.
- Lister experimented to see whether carbolic acid would also prevent infection in people. In 1865, he applied carbolic acid to a compound fracture (where bone breaks through the skin) in a boy's leg and the bandages that covered the wound. Infection did not develop and the fracture healed successfully.
- He continued using carbolic acid, which dramatically reduced the number of infections. He published his findings, recommending that surgeons washed their hands and instruments with carbolic acid before operations, as well as using carbolic acid on wounds and bandages. He designed a carbolic spray which killed microbes in the air while operations were taking place. He also invented a type of ligature ('thread' for stitching wounds) which could be cleaned with carbolic acid and which dissolved, leaving no means for infection to enter the body.

> **Joseph Lister (1827–1912)**
> - Lister studied to become a surgeon in London before moving to Edinburgh.
> - He became Professor of Surgery at the University of Glasgow in 1860, Surgeon at the Glasgow Royal Infirmary in 1861, and Professor of Surgery at King's College Hospital, London in 1877.
> - He discovered, used and promoted the first antiseptic and antiseptic methods, which proved to be a turning point in surgery.

The impact of antiseptics

It took time for Lister's methods and ideas to be accepted because:
- Many people still did not believe that microbes caused disease.
- Infection rates did not always improve, usually because Lister's methods were not being applied properly, so people thought Lister's ideas didn't work.
- Surgeons, doctors and nurses didn't like using carbolic acid because it smelled terrible, caused blisters and soreness on their hands and applying it properly took a long time.
- The equipment needed and the additional time taken meant that operations became more expensive.
- Lister continuously experimented with different techniques and substances so people thought that he was unsure of his ideas and that they didn't work.

However, as more evidence emerged that Pasteur and Lister were correct, **antiseptic** methods during and after operations and in hospitals became more common and infections were reduced. This was a major change in surgery.

> **Key term**
>
> **Antiseptic**: substance that kills germs that cause infections.

Government action on public health: the significance of the Public Health Act (1875)

The period 1860–75 saw the government taking more and more action on public health, culminating in the Public Health Act of 1875. There were several reasons why the government began introducing more public health measures:

- The 'Great Stink' of 1858 in London was caused by hot weather making the sewage in the River Thames smell terrible. Lack of proper sewers and drainage had literally ground Britain's capital to a halt – it was so bad that even Parliament could not meet.
- The beliefs of Edwin Chadwick and John Snow were proved correct by Pasteur's *Germ Theory* (published in 1861). More people understood and accepted the link between unhygienic living conditions and disease.
- The cholera outbreak of 1866 was more severe in those towns that had not acted on the suggestions of the Public Health Act of 1848 to improve water supplies and sewerage, and to collect rubbish.
- In 1867, many working-class men were given the right to vote and became half of the electorate. For the first time, politicians had to try to improve the lives of the poor in order to win their votes.

All of the above meant that more people were willing to pay, through taxes, for public health reform.

The significance of the Public Health Act, 1875

The Sanitary Act of 1866 made town councils employ people to inspect water supplies, drainage and sewerage, while the Artisans Dwelling Act of 1875 allowed councils to demolish slums and build better homes in their place. However, it was the Public Health Act of 1875 which was to bring the most change. For the first time, it was compulsory for local authorities to appoint medical officers to monitor health and for health and sanitary inspectors to inspect public health facilities. Local authorities were also given more powers to raise taxes to:

- provide and maintain clean water supplies
- build and maintain sewers and drains
- remove rubbish.

This was significant because some measures were made compulsory – for the first time, local authorities were forced to do something – and the Act was far more comprehensive than the 1848 Act had been. The years from 1875 to 1905 would begin to see the impact of the measures within the Public Health Act of 1875, but the passing of the Act was significant in itself.

Revision tasks

TESTED

1. Write a paragraph explaining how Joseph Lister improved surgery between 1860 and 1875.
2. Complete a table comparing the Public Health Acts of 1848 and 1875.

	Public Health Act (1848)	Public Health Act (1875)
Measures		
Significance		

Exam practice

Explain **TWO** causes of the Public Health Act of 1875. (8 marks)

Exam tips

1. 'Causes' means the reasons why something did or did not happen.
2. You only need two causes – don't include any more as you won't get credit for them. Similarly, make sure your two causes are different – if you only write about one cause you can only get a maximum of four marks.
3. You need to use your knowledge and understanding to include supporting detail for the two causes you select.

Nightingale and continuing improvements in hospitals and nursing

Florence Nightingale was a very high-profile figure after she returned from the Crimean War. This meant that she became very influential in medical training, particularly nursing and also in the design and running of hospitals.

Nursing

In 1859, Nightingale published *Notes on Nursing*. It was a bestseller and was translated into eleven languages. Using donated money, she set up Nightingale's School for Nurses at St Thomas' Hospital, London in 1860. This was the first professional training school for nurses in Britain. 'Nightingale nurses' then started training schools for nurses all over the world. As well as practical skills in administering treatments and looking after the sick, these training schools taught Nightingale's beliefs on very high standards of cleanliness for patients, hospitals and nurses themselves, to help prevent infection and disease from spreading.

Nightingale's work ensured that by 1875, nurses' training had vastly improved. Nursing had started to be seen as a serious profession and a key part of medical treatment. This helped change nursing into a respectable job for a woman, which attracted more women, particularly middle-class women, to become nurses. Nightingale's work therefore had a big impact on changing the role of women in medicine in relation to nursing.

Hospitals

Florence Nightingale wrote over 200 books, including *Notes on Hospitals* (1863) on the design and organisation of hospitals. Her work influenced how hospitals were run and how new hospitals were built. Some of the effects of her recommendations were:

- Most new hospitals were built in the 'pavilion' style, with separate wards for patients with different ailments and diseases, which helped contain infectious diseases, as well as helping nurses and doctors specialise in certain conditions.
- Wards were made more spacious with separate beds and plenty of room for each patient. There were large windows so there was plenty of light and ventilation.
- Materials used for building new hospitals could be easily cleaned.
- The role of nurses in hospitals became more important and more nurses were employed.

- Sanitation was improved, with good drains and sewers built and maintained.
- Clean water and fresh food were more readily available for patients.
- Proper toilets and washing facilities were available for medical staff and patients.
- Laundry facilities were provided so bedding and clothes could be washed regularly.
- Medical supplies and equipment were better organised so they were available when needed and easily accessed.

There were other things which improved hospitals and access to hospital care at the time:
- Antiseptics started to be used in hospitals due to the work of Lister. This improved hospital care and surgery.
- As more people accepted Pasteur's Germ Theory, others promoted cleanliness, not just Nightingale.
- Developments in engineering and building meant that better hospitals, sewers and drains were built.
- More specialist hospitals such as those for infectious diseases began to appear, improving access to specialised treatment.
- Poor Law Unions used tax payers' money to build infirmaries to treat the poor, which improved access to medical treatment for those without the money to pay for it.

> **Revision task** — TESTED
>
> Draw two spider diagrams, one showing features of hospitals in 1848 and the other showing features of hospitals in 1875.

Elizabeth Garret and the progress of women in medicine

In the 1850s, women could not qualify as physicians, surgeons, apothecaries or midwives because all of these jobs needed a university degree and women were not allowed to attend universities. Women were allowed to work as nurses, but this was not seen as a respectable or professional job until the work of Florence Nightingale and others began to change things from the mid-1850s (see pages 176 and 184).

If women wanted to qualify as doctors then they had to find a way around the rules – **Elizabeth Garrett** was the first to do this!
- After repeatedly being denied entry to medical schools at university, she trained as a nurse at the Middlesex Hospital. While she was there she went to classes for doctors until complaints from medical students forced her to stop. With her father's financial support, she studied to become a doctor in private with medical professors.
- To become a qualified doctor, you had to pass exams from one of three medical boards: the College of Surgeons, the College of Physicians or the College of Apothecaries. The College of Apothecaries was forced to allow Garrett to take their exams after she took them to court. Unlike the others, their rules did not specifically forbid women from taking their exams after private tuition. In 1865, Garrett passed and was issued with a certificate which allowed her to practise as a physician. The College then changed their rules so no more women could do this.

Elizabeth Garrett (1836–1917)
- A well-educated woman from a wealthy family, Elizabeth Garrett was the first woman in Britain to qualify as a doctor in 1865.
- In 1870, she obtained her medical degree in France. She married businessman James Anderson in 1871, and changed her name to Elizabeth Garrett Anderson.
- She set up a new hospital for women, staffed by women, in 1872, and helped set up the London School of Medicine for Women in 1874.
- Garrett campaigned for women's right to vote and for women to be allowed to study for university degrees.

- Garret still wanted a full medical degree from a university so she taught herself French and then obtained her medical degree in Paris in 1870.

Garrett was a pioneer but other women could not become doctors in the same way that she had. Garrett and many other political campaigners put pressure on the government and universities to change the law. In 1874, six more women, including Sophia Jex-Blake, proved that they were capable of becoming doctors by completing the medical course at the University of Edinburgh, but they were not allowed to receive their official degree and went to either Dublin or Switzerland to do so.

In 1876, Parliament changed the law. Finally, women were able to study at and obtain degrees, including medical degrees, from universities in Britain.

Revision task

List ways in which Elizabeth Garrett helped women progress in medicine. List ways in which she did not help women progress in medicine.

6.3 Accelerating change, 1875–1905; Ehrlich, Koch and chemistry

What you need to know

In this section you will revise a period in which there were great developments in science, which led to advances in medical treatment and great improvements in public health provision. This will include:
- The work of Koch and the beginning of bacteriology and its impact on medicine.
- Aseptic surgery and its impact on reducing infections.
- The impact of the Public Health Act of 1875.
- New developments in science and medicine, including blood transfusions, magic bullets and radioactivity.
- The impact of Marie Curie on medicine.

The fight against germs

Koch and bacteriology

Building on the work done by Pasteur (see pages 180–81), **Robert Koch** set about finding a specific microbe that caused a disease, **bacteriology**.
- In 1875, he found the microbe that was causing anthrax, a disease that affected many animals but could also affect people.
- His success led the German government to fund Koch to set up the Berlin Institute of Infectious Diseases.
- Koch and his team at the Institute discovered the microbes causing TB (in 1882) and cholera (in 1883).
- Scientists at the Berlin Institute would go on to make many more important discoveries.

The impact of Koch

Koch's work had more of an immediate impact than Pasteur's work initially had, because:
- it was directly in the field of medicine
- Koch was a doctor himself and was therefore trusted by other doctors.

Robert Koch (1843–1910)

- A German doctor who was the first to discover a specific microbe that caused a disease.
- He is considered the founder of bacteriology.
- His work had huge, long-lasting impacts on treating and preventing disease.
- Pasteur and Koch saw themselves as rivals (France and Germany were at war 1870–71) which led them to 'compete' and drive each other on to more discoveries.

Key term

Bacteriology: the study of microbes (also called bacteria or germs).

Koch's work was important because:
- Finding a specific microbe that caused a disease, Koch proved that Germ Theory was not just a theory but true. Largely due to Koch's work, by 1885 almost all scientists and doctors finally accepted microbes as the cause of some diseases.
- Koch discovered and developed successful methods that other scientists would be able to use to make other discoveries in the future:
  - He developed a way of growing bacteria as solids (Pasteur used liquids which were difficult to work with).
  - He found that chemical dyes could stain certain microbes – therefore it was easier to identify the microbe causing a disease through the microscope.
- He also found a more effective way of killing microbes than carbolic acid – steam. Surgeons would use this to improve surgery (see page 188).
- Koch's work inspired other scientists to work in bacteriology. Most noticeably, Pasteur dedicated himself to studying disease full time from 1877, which led to him developing **vtines** to prevent certain diseases. Pasteur's work also led him to discover that some diseases are caused by **viruses**.

Key terms

Vaccine: a substance, usually injected, to give someone immunity to a disease.

Virus: a tiny infective agent which causes disease.

Revision task

TESTED

Who furthered the understanding of disease more, Pasteur or Koch? Write a list of points for and against each person.

The impact of bacteriology

The work of Koch, Pasteur and their teams was hugely important in providing further evidence that some diseases were caused by microbes. This had an impact on:
- Improving hygiene and cleanliness in hospitals and society in general which reduced disease and infection.
- Convincing governments (and voters) to invest in public health provisions.
- Ensuring that scientific research for improvements in health and medicine would continue and increase.

However, their work did not have an impact on medical treatment at the time – being able to identify the specific microbe causing a specific disease did not help cure people of that disease. But it would do in the future as other scientists continued to use their findings and methods in bacteriology to discover treatments such as magic bullets (see page 190) and antibiotics (see page 199).

Exam tips

1. 'How far' questions are asking you to make a judgement. In this case, how much did something change. You should always remember to answer this question directly as part of your wider answer. For example, 'there was huge / some / little change in understanding of the causes of illness in the years …'.
2. Your answer needs to give examples of what people believed caused illness in 1848. You then need to outline new explanations on what caused illnesses that emerged between 1848 and 1905, giving details on how this occurred.
3. You can, but you don't have to, use the two bullet points of information provided in the question. However, you have to use at least one idea of your own to answer this question well. For example, for this question you could include information on Koch and bacteriology.

Exam practice

How far did understanding of the causes of illness change in the years 1848–1905?

You may use the following in your answer:
- the theory of spontaneous generation
- Pasteur and the development of the Germ Theory.

You **must** also use information of your own. (16 marks)

Aseptic surgery

It took time to accept Lister's methods, but by the 1880s antiseptic surgery (see page 182) was the norm in Britain. This was because:
- Koch's work on bacteriology had helped prove Pasteur's Germ Theory. – that germs cause disease and therefore using antiseptics to kill germs would prevent infection and disease during and after surgery.
- As surgeons began to use antiseptic methods correctly, infection rates fell, helping to prove that the methods worked, so more surgeons used them.
- Koch's discovery that steam was as effective at killing germs as carbolic acid meant that conditions during antiseptic surgery slightly improved. The use of Koch's steam steriliser to remove germs from all surgical equipment also meant that surgeons' skin was not damaged as it was through using carbolic acid.

A German surgeon, Gustav Neuber, used both Koch and Lister's ideas to develop **aseptic** surgery – where rather than killing germs on or around the wound, germs were removed from the whole operating theatre – in his private hospital which opened in Germany in 1886. By 1900, most surgery in Britain was carried out in aseptic conditions.

> **Key term**
>
> **Aseptic**: completely sterile or free from germs.

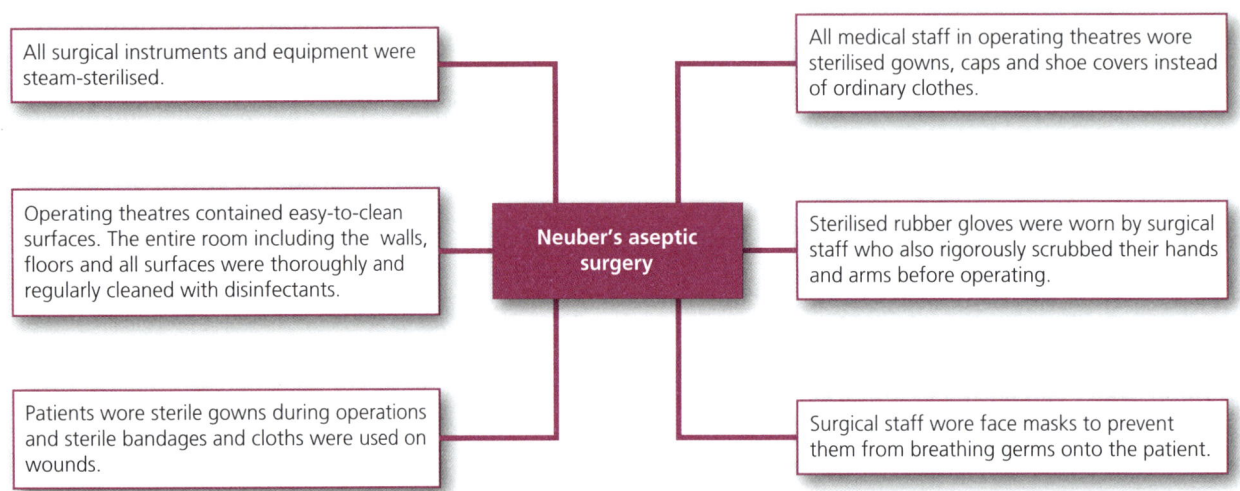

These methods are still used as the basis of aseptic surgery today.

Revision task

TESTED

Complete the following table to show the changes in surgery 1848–1905.

	Surgery in 1848	Surgery in 1905
Where surgery took place and how this place was looked after		
How medical instruments and equipment were treated		
What was worn by medical staff and the patient		
How wounds were treated after surgery		

The impact of the Public Health Act (1875) for improving public health

It took time for the measures of the 1875 Public Health Act (see page 183) to take effect:
- Councils needed to raise the necessary money through taxes to carry out all the measures.
- There had been huge improvements in technology and engineering, but it still took time to find and employ engineers and to design and plan the projects needed.
- Building a complex system of sewers and water pipes took time and a lot of manual labour.

The speed at which councils undertook improvements varied hugely across different towns and cities and progress was not as quick as people had hoped. However, the compulsory employment of health and sanitary inspectors rapidly improved knowledge of conditions in towns and cities. The reports made by these inspectors were published. This led towns and cities to start competing with each other to see who could carry out the greatest or fastest changes. Gradually, towns and cities across the country did become cleaner and the improvements in public health provision began to improve people's health:
- The average death rate per year between 1838 and 1880 had remained about the same. The rate dropped every year between 1880 and 1890, and then remained lower than before 1880.
- Average life expectancy had remained fairly static since 1820 in England and Wales, but it rose from 41 for men and 45 for women in 1871, to 49 for men and 52 for women in 1901.
- Cases of infectious diseases such as cholera and typhoid (both of which are spread through contaminated water) decreased rapidly. There were no more outbreaks of epidemics like these – the last major cholera outbreak in Britain was in 1866.

However, although the Public Health Act did improve public health by 1905, many people, especially the poor, still suffered from disease and poor health.

Exam practice

Explain **TWO** ways in which public health provision in 1848 was different from public health provision in 1905. **(6 marks)**

Revision task

1. List improvements in public health provision between 1848 and 1905.
2. Create a spider diagram of reasons, including public health provision, for the improvements in health by 1905.

TESTED

Exam tips

1. You must write about **two** different ways. Any more than two won't receive any credit and an answer that only gives one way can only receive a maximum of three marks.
2. A good way to answer this question is to write two paragraphs – one explaining one way and another paragraph explaining another way.
3. Remember to focus on 'difference' here. For example, writing about how public health provision varied in different places across the country is a similarity between both years, rather than a difference.
4. You should support each of your two ways with relevant detail to show your knowledge and understanding.

Science and medicine

As more scientific research was taking place towards the end of the nineteenth century, some important breakthroughs in medical understanding and treatment also took place.

Blood transfusions

It had become possible to stop or at least greatly reduce blood loss during surgery (see page 177) but by 1900 there was still no way to effectively replace blood that had already been lost. Human-to-human blood transfusions had first been carried out in Britain in the early nineteenth century by Doctor James Blundell. Sometimes it worked. More often it did not and Blundell could not find out why this was the case.

Karl Landsteiner was an Austrian doctor and chemist who worked in many laboratories across Europe.
- In 1900, Landsteiner first published his findings on his research into blood. He found that while some people's blood mixed together, others caused another person's blood to clot. This explained why person-to-person blood transfusions often led to death.
- In 1901, he identified three different blood groups, A, B and O, and then another, AB, in 1902. He proved that only people with the same blood group could transfer blood to each other, with the exception of the blood group O, which was accepted by all blood groups.
- In 1907 in New York, Landsteiner's findings were used to test the blood of a patient and perform a blood transfusion from someone with the same blood type.

This was a breakthrough because someone who had lost a significant amount of blood could now have that blood successfully replaced. However, transfusions were only possible person-to-person: someone of the same blood type had to sit with the patient while their blood was being transferred. This was because blood clots when it leaves the body so it could not be stored.

'Magic bullets' and the work of Ehrlich

Robert Koch's research team at the Berlin Institute of Infectious Diseases included a number of talented scientists, including **Paul Ehrlich**.
- In 1896, Ehrlich was allowed to set up his own department at the Berlin Institute to develop his ideas. His team began to investigate what he called 'magic bullets' – drugs that would only target the specific germ that caused an illness and would have little or no effect on other parts of the body.
- For years, Ehrlich's team tried to find a chemical that would destroy the microbe that caused syphilis (a sexually transmitted bacterial infection). In 1909, he was finally successful – the 606th compound of Salvarson worked! It was the first chemical cure for a disease.

As the first chemical cure for a disease, this was an important precedent; however:
- Salvarson 606 had many side-effects so it was not widely used. Because of these side-effects, Ehrlich received a lot criticism.
- It was an extremely long and therefore expensive process to develop 'magic bullets'. The second magic bullet was not found until 1932.

Radioactivity and the impact of Marie Curie

The end of the nineteenth century saw huge breakthroughs in physics which would lead to new medical treatments for many types of cancer.
- In 1895, German physicist Wilhelm Röntgen discovered X-rays and invented X-ray machines.
- Other scientists and doctors began experimenting with X-rays and discovered that X-rays damaged biological cells and tissue if they were repeatedly targeted.
- In 1896, French physicist, Henry Becquerel used the work of Röntgen to try to find out where radiation came from – he was the first to work out that radiation came from the chemical element itself.

Paul Ehrlich (1854–1915)
- Ehrlich was a German doctor and scientist who was a member of Koch's bacteriology research team.
- He began his own research into finding chemicals that would kill microbes and therefore could be used to treat a disease.
- His team developed the first chemical cure – Salvarson 606 – which killed the microbe that causes syphilis.

Marie Curie (1867–1934)
- Born in Poland, Curie moved to Paris in 1891, where she met and worked in tandem with her husband, Pierre. After his death in 1906, she continued their work alone.
- She was the first woman to win a Nobel Prize and the only person ever to have won the prize for both physics and chemistry.
- In 1914 she invented 'radiological cars' – vehicles containing portable X-ray machines and photographic darkroom equipment – and trained women in how to use them, which would help many surgeons save soldiers' lives on the battlefield (see page 197).

- In 1898, Marie and Pierre Curie were carrying out research on X-rays and uranium. The Curies discovered two new elements that emitted much stronger levels of radiation – polonium and radium.
- Marie claimed that it was the atomic structure of the elements that produced the radiation. She described the process as 'radioactivity'.
- Eventually, in 1902, **Marie Curie** managed to isolate radium. As radium was much, much stronger than X-rays, it was soon discovered that it had a much greater impact on biological cells and could be used to destroy or reduce tumours. Radiation therapy – soon called radiotherapy – has been used to treat some types of cancer ever since.

The work of Marie Curie and others had a huge and immediate impact on medicine. For the first time, it was possible to successfully treat some types of cancer. Radiotherapy was commonly used as a cancer treatment, with differing degrees of success, from the early 1900s. As research continued, radiotherapy became more successful. Curie also proved the value of women scientists to medical research and inspired more women to become scientists, expanding their role in medicine.

Revision tasks

1 What new medical treatments were available by 1910? Outline the impacts of these treatments.
2 Complete the following table to show the impact of science and technology on medicine in the period 1875–1905.

	Science 1875–1905
Understanding the cause of illness	
Changes in medical treatments	
Changes in surgery	

6.4 Government action and war, 1905–20

What you need to know

In this section you will revise a period of unprecedented public health provision and the huge impact of the First World War on medicine. This will include:
- The impact on public health of the Liberal Government's measures of 1906–11.
- The importance of the First World War for the role of women in medicine.
- How the First World War brought about changes in medical treatment, including surgery, X-rays, blood transfusions and fighting infection.
- The importance of the First World War in bringing about changes in medicine.

The impact of the Liberal Governments' measures (1906–11) on public health

The Liberal Party won the general election of 1906. They promised wide reforms to improve public health. This was because:
- By the twentieth century, most working-class men had the right to vote in elections.
- Surveys and reports by people such as Charles Booth and Benjamin Seebohm Rowntree showed the extent of poverty in Britain and that the causes of this were age (there were no pensions to support people once they were too old to work), unemployment and illness.

- Britain was being economically overtaken by the USA and Germany and people believed a major cause of this was the poor health of British workers.
- One third of men who volunteered as soldiers during the Boer War, 1899–1902, were not allowed to fight due to poor health.

The measures

A wide range of measures were passed (these are detailed in the table on page 193), which had a positive impact on public health:

- The Education Acts of 1906 and 1907 led to improvements in children's health and growth rates (the success of the measures is shown by the increase in children's illness during school holidays).
- Income levels of the poorest workers in society did improve, meaning they were able to afford better housing and food, which improved their health.
- The Old Age Pension Act of 1908 meant that poor older people were slightly more able to pay for food, housing, medicines, etc., which improved their health.
- New planning laws ensured that no more slum areas could develop.
- Measures such as the Education Act of 1907 and the National Insurance Act of 1911 meant that more people could access doctors and medical care if they became ill.

However:

- Wealthier people complained because their taxes were markedly increased to pay for the measures.
- Some workers complained about having to pay into schemes such as the one set up by the National Insurance Act.
- Not all people had access to the benefits and some measures were not enacted across the whole country.
- Access to doctors and medical treatment still depended on the availability of medical care (there were far fewer doctors in poor areas than wealthier ones).
- Many people still had to pay for medical care and could not afford to do so.

Revision tasks

1. How did public health provision change from 1906 to 1911? Make a list of similarities and differences between public health provision in 1911 and 1905.
2. Complete the following table for each of the Liberal Governments' measures in the table on page 193. One example has been completed for you.

Government Act	How it improved public health	Mark out of 10 for its impact on public health
Education (Provision of Meals) Act, 1906	Sometimes poor families couldn't afford to feed their children at all and often couldn't afford to feed them nutritious meals. This Act ensured that children did get more food and the nutrients they needed and so reduced malnutrition and diseases. However, it only worked when children were at school.	6/10

3. Which of the Liberal Government measures did you give the highest mark for its impact on public health? Why?

Government Act	Provisions of the Act	Positives of the Act	Negatives of the Act
Education (Provision of Meals) Act, 1906	Poor children were given one nutritious meal a day at school for free.	Reduced malnutrition and therefore illness in school-aged children.	Didn't apply during weekends or school holidays.
Education (Administrative Provisions) Act, 1907	Children were given free health inspections by a nurse or doctor at school.	Provided some health care and advice and improved monitoring of children's health.	Was only done by some local authorities. Medical treatments still had to be paid for and many could not afford this (this improved as free medical treatments were given to children at school from 1912).
Old Age Pension Act, 1908	Pensions of 1 to 5 shillings per week were paid to people over 70 with low incomes.	Set an important precedent. Provided some security to the poorest older people.	Many people died before 70. Many people could not prove their age. The money given was a small amount.
Coal Mines Regulation Act, 1908	Set maximum working hours of eight hours a day.	Reduced exhaustion (which in turn reduced accidents and illness).	Only applied to coal miners.
The Trade Board Act, 1909	Set a minimum wage for workers in four industries: chain-making, lace finishing, box making, tailoring.	Was the first time a minimum wage was set so it was an important precedent.	Only applied to some industries. Employers could pay less if they could prove someone could not do the work of an average worker.
Housing and Town Planning Act, 1909	Limited the number of houses that could be built on an acre, banned the building of back-to-back housing.	Prevented new 'slums' from developing. Reduced over-crowding. Made rubbish collecting and waste disposal easier.	Only applied to new houses being built.
National Insurance Act, 1911	The government, employer and the worker paid into a scheme for low-paid workers so if the worker became sick they received: • free medical care • a basic income.	Improved access to medical treatment for workers who were insured.	Benefits stopped after 25 weeks so did not help those with long-term illnesses. Only workers themselves were covered – not their spouses or children.
	Provided some money for insured workers who lost their job for up to fifteen weeks.	Provided some unemployment benefit.	Benefits were only for fifteen weeks.

The importance of the First World War for the role of women in medicine

Female doctors

By 1914, there were around 1,000 women with medical degrees in Britain but most hospitals refused to employ female doctors. Most women doctors worked as GPs or in hospitals where only women and/or children were treated. When war broke out:

- The War Office refused to employ female doctors in the Royal Army Medical Corps (RAMC) or in the official charities supporting the military – the British Red Cross and the Order of St John.
- Some British charities that sent medical teams to Europe employed women doctors. A few, such as the Women's Imperial Service League, only employed women doctors.
- Some overseas organisations such as the French Red Cross accepted British female doctors.

For many British women doctors, it was their first time treating male patients! They earned the respect of some of their male colleagues and patients. Because of this, and due to a shortage of male doctors, in 1916, the War Office allowed women doctors to work in official medical units, but only in military hospitals in Britain.

As many male doctors were sent away, many more women doctors who remained in Britain were allowed to work in hospitals, many in positions of authority. However, as with other women workers, once the war was over, many women doctors lost their jobs or were relegated to junior positions, despite their skills and experience.

Nurses

- The number of qualified nurses working for the British army hugely increased from around 300 in 1914, to 10,000 in 1918. Initially, the War Office only allowed nurses to work in base hospitals because it was thought they would not be able to cope closer to the front line. This changed after a few months due to the huge demand.
- The role of nurses increased throughout the war. They had to learn many new skills and were given more responsibility for patient care. By the end of the war, nurses were carrying out minor surgery rather than assisting.
- After the war, many professional nurses found the increased responsibilities and tasks, such as performing minor surgery, were taken away from them.

The huge contribution of nurses was recognised by parliament in passing the Nurses Registration Act in December 1919. This regulated nursing as a profession. Before this, people who worked as nurses did not have to have formal training at a recognised institution.

Volunteers

Many women, some who did not work as nurses in Britain, volunteered to help through two main organisations, where they performed vital roles:

- The First Aid Nursing Yeomanry (FANY) supported medical services on the front line by dressing wounds and transporting supplies of medicine and food. From 1914, it worked with French and Belgium forces, but from January 1916, the RAMC allowed FANY ambulance drivers, including women, to transport wounded British soldiers.

- Voluntary Aid Detachments (VADs) offered a range of support both in Britain and overseas. VADs worked in various jobs such as nurses, stretcher-bearers, cooks and clerks.

Most volunteers were women as men tended to join the armed forces. The organisations demonstrated the capabilities of women, though most women volunteers returned to their homes once the war was over.

The importance of the First World War for improvements in medical treatment

The First World War brought conflict and therefore injuries on an unprecedented scale. Two million British soldiers were treated by medical services, as well as millions of soldiers and civilians from other countries. However, it was not just the number of wounded people that was unprecedented, the types of wounds and associated problems were new as well.

- An estimated 58 per cent of wounds were caused by highly explosive shells. This meant blast injuries, but also huge numbers of injuries caused by shrapnel penetrating deep into the body.
- Most other injuries were caused by bullets fired by machine guns or rifles. Bullets damaged organs and fractured bones.
- Almost all these types of injury led to blood loss and the risk of shock.
- The land on which most British soldiers fought (on the Western Front) was contaminated with gas gangrene and tetanus. These bacteria easily entered the bodies of the wounded, causing infection.
- The war was fought in trenches, meaning that soldiers' heads were the most exposed parts of their bodies. This meant huge numbers of injuries to the brain, head and face.

The types of injury and the huge numbers of people suffering from them led to improvements in many areas of medicine and surgery (see pages 196–98); however, the First World War did not only bring positive change:

- Around 14,000 doctors were taken from their usual posts to care for the wounded soldiers, either overseas or in military hospitals in Britain. This left civilians in Britain with reduced access to medical care.
- Almost all medical resources were ploughed into meeting the needs of wounded soldiers. This meant that medical research into non-war related illnesses and other medical conditions almost completely stopped.

Revision task

Did the First World War improve the role of women in medicine? Write a list of points which suggest it did and another list of points which suggest it did not.

TESTED

Revision task

As you read through the improvements to medical treatment on pages 196–98 complete the following table.

TESTED

Medical treatment	How the First World War improved this treatment	How significant this treatment was for medicine overall
Brain surgery		
Plastic surgery		
X-rays		
Blood transfusions		
New ways of preventing infection		

Improvements in surgery

Two main areas of surgery saw huge leaps forward during the war: brain surgery and plastic surgery. At the start of the war:

- There were very few surgeons or doctors with much experience in either of these areas.
- Removing shrapnel and bullets from the brain or face was very difficult to perform successfully (and without causing further injury), especially as this needed to be done as quickly as possible. Therefore, operations needed to be performed close to the fighting.
- Brain injuries could be difficult to diagnose – patients might appear to have a very minor wound but would actually have a serious, life-threatening injury to the brain.
- General anaesthetics often made the brain swell, which made operating on the brain very risky and frequently caused further injury.
- As for all injuries on the Western Front, the risks of infection were extremely high.

Brain surgery

Soldiers who suffered a brain injury in the early years of the war (1914 and 1915) were highly likely to die. However, improvements to X-ray machines and new methods of fighting infection helped brain injury victims (see below) and ways of successfully treating brain injuries quickly developed:

- All head injuries, however 'minor', were examined as soon as possible. Doctors soon learned the signs of brain injury that was more serious than it initially appeared.
- Some Casualty Clearing Stations were allocated specifically for brain injuries and doctors, and there were surgeons and nurses who specialised in this area.
- Surgeons soon changed to performing most brain surgery under local, rather than general anaesthetic so the patient was conscious but could not feel the affected area. This reduced the risks of error and complications because the brain did not swell.
- Harvey Cushing, an American **neurosurgeon**, developed new brain surgery techniques while working on the Western Front and passed on his findings to other surgeons. He developed the use of magnets to successfully remove tiny metal fragments from the brain without causing damage.

> **Key term**
>
> **Neurosurgeon**: a surgeon who treats disorders of the nervous system (including the brain and the spine).

Plastic surgery

As medical care improved as the war continued, more men survived head injuries. However, many were left with horrific scars or parts of their faces missing. Some were unable to eat, drink, speak or even breathe well.

An ear, nose and throat surgeon from New Zealand – Harold Gillies – become known as the 'father of plastic surgery' due to the methods and techniques he developed to repair and restore parts of the face.

- Facial reconstruction often required many operations and long-term care, which could not be done close to the fighting. Gillies persuaded the army to set up a specialist ward for facial injuries at Cambridge Military Hospital in 1916. Then, as demand increased, in July 1917 he opened a specialist hospital with over 1,000 beds – Queen's Hospital, London.

- He found artists and sculptors to paint and mould likenesses of what his patients had originally looked like to help him reconstruct their faces and therefore help them lead normal lives.
- He developed the use of skin flaps from near the wound, which meant that blood supply was maintained. Where there was not enough skin, he devised new techniques for **skin grafts** – moving tissue and skin in stages using tubed pedicles (stalks made of skin attached to the body), which reduced the risk of infection and maintained blood supply.
- Gillies employed a wide range of doctors, surgeons, nurses and dentists to treat patients. When the hospital closed in 1925, these people took their skills and knowledge with them and developed them further.

Key term

Skin graft: surgery where skin is moved from one part of the body to another.

Exam practice

How far was the First World War responsible for changes in surgery in the years 1860–1920?

You may use the following in your answer:
- Joseph Lister
- Harold Gilles.

You **must** also use information of your own. (16 marks)

Exam tips

1. 'How far' questions are asking you to make a judgement. In this case, how important was the First World War in bringing about change. You should always remember to answer this question directly as part of your wider answer. For example, 'the First World War was hugely / partly / not at all responsible ...'.
2. You should firstly consider the role of the First World War in bringing about changes in surgery and then look at other factors that led to changes in surgery during this period. All your points should be supported with details to show your knowledge and understanding.
3. You can, but you don't have to, use the two bullet points of information provided in the question. However, you have to use at least one idea of your own to answer this question well. For example, for this question you could include information on aseptic surgery.

X-rays

From the start of the First World War, X-ray machines were used in many military hospitals but there were several developments throughout the war:

- More X-ray machines were made and improved. In 1914, X-ray machines were large and heavy so smaller, mobile units were developed which could be taken closer to the front line.
- Use of X-rays was not widespread before the war so far more people were trained to operate machines and huge numbers of doctors, nurses and surgeons learned how to read the X-ray images. Medical staff could soon diagnose fractures and broken bones, and accurately locate shrapnel and bullets, which therefore helped these to be successfully removed during surgery.
- Surgeons soon also became experienced at knowing what X-rays did not show – for example, some objects such as soil or cloth would not show up on X-rays, but surgeons knew to look for these close to where bullets or shrapnel was located during operations.
- More was learned about the damage that X-rays can cause to those exposed frequently. From 1915, screens, gloves and aprons were used to protect people.

X-ray machines saved the lives of hundreds of thousands of wounded soldiers throughout the war. They would become commonly used in hospitals in Britain afterwards.

Blood transfusions

Blood loss was a major problem for many of the wounded in the First World War. This brought about several improvements in blood transfusions:
- In 1914–15 it was discovered that adding sodium citrate to blood delays clotting, and refrigerating blood meant that it could be stored for up to two days. This meant person-to-person transfer was not the only means of transfusing blood.
- Geoffrey Keynes designed a portable blood transfusion kit so medics could carry out blood transfusions very close to the battlefield. This included stored blood but only in small quantities and it only allowed a few hours before it would clot.
- Oswald Hope Robertson, an American doctor, pioneered the first 'blood bank' at the Battle of Cambrai in 1917. He stored blood mixed with sodium citrate and dextrose solution in glass bottles surrounded by ice. The blood kept for 26 days. The blood was transfused into twenty patients with severe shock. All were expected to die, but eleven survived due to blood transfusion.

Therefore, by 1918 it was possible to build up and store supplies of blood so many more people could benefit from blood transfusions.

Fighting infection

Huge numbers of wounded soldiers died from infection at the beginning of the First World War. Aseptic surgery was not possible in war conditions and traditional antiseptics, such as carbolic acid, did not kill gas gangrene. Therefore, the war brought about new and improved methods for preventing and treating infection:
- Surgeons rapidly improved their knowledge and skills so they could remove all dead, damaged and infected tissue and all foreign bodies which could carry infections.
- If the spread of infection could not be stopped, limbs had to be amputated to prevent death. Many surgeons became very skilled at performing amputations and many lives were saved, though by the end of the war around 250,000 men had lost limbs.
- Two doctors developed the Carrel–Dakin method where sterilised salt solution was moved through wounds using tubes to kill and prevent all infections. It was commonly used by 1917.

6.5 Advances in medicine, surgery and public health, 1920–48; the NHS

REVISED

What you need to know

In this section you will revise a period in which there were huge advances in medical treatment and public health provision and the impact of the Second World War on medicine. This will include:
- The roles of Fleming, Florey and Chain in the development of penicillin.
- How the Second World War brought about changes in surgery, including skin grafts and blood transfusions.
- The importance of the Second World War in the role of women in medicine.
- The development of the NHS and the role of Beveridge.
- The importance of the NHS for public health.

The development of penicillin and the roles of Fleming, Florey and Chain

The first **antibiotic** to be discovered was penicillin. It truly was (and is!) a wonder drug that cures many illnesses and infections that had previously killed people.

Penicillin was developed due to many factors, including the work of **Fleming**, **Florey** and **Chain** and their teams of scientists. Since 1945, new antibiotics have been developed which kill other bacteria that cause disease and infection. It is estimated that antibiotics have saved the lives of over 200 million people! The discovery of penicillin was therefore a huge breakthrough in medical treatment.

- For centuries, people ate mouldy bread as a treatment for some illnesses. Joseph Lister used mould to successfully treat a nurse who had an infected wound in 1884.

- Alexander Fleming began research on bacterial infections in 1918. In 1928, on his return to work from holiday, he noticed mould on some petri dishes which contained bacteria. This mould appeared to have destroyed the bacteria around it.

- Fleming carried out further research, confirming that mould killed many kinds of bacteria. He named the mould 'penicillin' and published his findings in 1929. He did not continue with his research as:
  - other scientists did not seem very interested in his discovery
  - penicillin took a very long time to produce and continuing his research would therefore be very expensive.

- In 1936, Howard Florey assembled a team of scientists, including Ernst Chain, to research methods of killing bacteria at Oxford University. In 1938, they decided to continue Fleming's research on penicillin. After failing to secure funding from the British government, they then received enough funding for five years' research from the USA.

- In 1940, Florey and Chain successfully tested penicillin on mice. However, large quantities of penicillin were needed and it took time and space to grow. The team started growing penicillin wherever they could!

- In 1941, penicillin was tested on a policeman who had developed sepsis – an infection from a wound which almost always led to death. After receiving injections of penicillin, the man began to recover. Unfortunately, they then ran out of penicillin and the man died, but it had proved that penicillin worked and did not have serious side-effects that harmed the patient.

- Florey approached the British government and several British companies to try to get penicillin mass-produced. Nobody agreed (they were busy with what was felt at the time to be more important work for the Second World War). In July 1941, he went to the USA.

- The USA entered the Second World War in December 1941. The American government realised the importance of penicillin for treating wounded troops. It agreed to loan money to US pharmaceutical companies to mass-produce penicillin. In 1943, British companies began mass-producing penicillin too. It saved the lives of thousands of wounded soldiers.

- On 1 June 1946, penicillin became available to the British public if prescribed by a doctor. It has saved the lives of millions of people ever since!

Alexander Fleming (1881–1955)

- Fleming began medical research at St Mary's Medical School soon after he qualified as a doctor.
- He served in the Army Medical Corps during the First World War, where he continued his research into infections.
- In 1918, he returned to St Marys, where he discovered the first antibiotic – penicillin – in 1928.

Howard Florey and Ernst Chain

- Florey was an Australian doctor and Chain a German biochemist. They worked together at Oxford University.
- They furthered Fleming's research on penicillin from 1938, including testing it and working out how to mass-produce it.
- Florey, Chain and Fleming won the Nobel Prize for Medicine in 1945 for the discovery of penicillin.

Key term

Antibiotics: a drug that destroys bacteria, preventing them from spreading. These are often used to treat bacterial infections.

Revision task

How important was each of the following to the development of penicillin:
- the work of Alexander Fleming
- the work of Florey and Chain
- accident or luck
- the Second World War?

TESTED

Exam practice

Explain **TWO** causes of improvements in medical treatment in the years 1900–48. (8 marks)

Exam tips

1. 'Causes' means the reasons why something did or did not happen.
2. 'Medical treatment' is anything that involves treating people with injury or illness. It could include drugs, such as penicillin, or surgery such as plastic surgery, or other treatments, such as radiotherapy.
3. You only need two causes – don't include any more as you won't get credit for them. Similarly, make sure your two causes are different – if you only write about one cause, you can only get a maximum of four marks.
4. You need to use your knowledge and understanding to include supporting detail for the two causes you select.

The importance of the Second World War for developments in surgery

The Second World War 1939–45 caused hundreds of thousands of injuries. However, the death rate of injured soldiers during the Second World War was half that of the First World War, largely due to:

- Better preparation – from the mid-1930s, war seemed likely so medical units started getting ready.
- Improvements in medicine – research between 1920 and 1939 had led to many developments, for example, the development of penicillin as the first antibiotic (see page 199).
- Improved organisation of medical facilities.
- The ability to evacuate the injured more quickly – sometimes even by air – and therefore get them to the treatment they needed much sooner.

As in the First World War, the scale and nature of injuries also led to developments in some areas of medicine. The massively increased use of aircraft and bombs caused many burn injuries to those in the military and civilians. Before the war, medical knowledge and treatment of burns was quite limited because few people had burn injuries, which were usually minor. Major burn victims usually died before any sort of plastic surgery became necessary. This changed drastically during the Second World War. Many survived due to advances in medical treatment but were left with scars or life-changing injuries.

Blood transfusions

Blood transfusions were still rarely done by 1939, and a patient's family were the people who usually donated blood when it was carried out. As war loomed, medical authorities realised that blood transfusions would be essential for treating the wounded, both on and off the battlefield. There were several problems that had to be tackled: How could they collect and store enough blood? How could they administer it quickly enough to those who needed it?

The first blood banks

Before the war started in 1939:

- Four blood depots were established on the outskirts of London to treat civilians.
- The Army Blood Transfusion Service was set up at Southmead Hospital, Bristol.

Both advertised for local volunteers to donate blood. There were problems with the system – for example, many people just turned up and were unable to donate – but it did provide some blood which could be used from the start of the conflict. Problems with the organisation of blood donation improved as the war went on. The 'Blood for Victory' campaign, which began in February 1944 to supply enough blood for D-Day, was very successful and unprecedented numbers of people donated.

There still was not enough blood to cope with the numbers who needed it. Therefore, the American Red Cross organised the 'Blood for Britain' campaign where people in the USA donated blood and it was sent to blood banks in Britain, where it saved thousands of lives.

Revision tasks

TESTED

1 Outline at least two ways in which the Second World War improved medicine.
2 Complete the following table to show the different medical treatments available at different times.

Medical treatments available in 1905	Medical treatments available in 1920	Medical treatments available in 1948

The use of blood plasma

Research in the 1930s had uncovered that blood is made up of four components: red blood cells, white blood cells, platelets and plasma. Methods were found to separate and extract the different components. It was found that plasma:
- helps maintain blood pressure and volume
- transports electrolytes and proteins around the body
- is compatible with all blood groups.

In 1934, a patient in the USA was first given a blood transfusion using just plasma. It was found to be successful. It was later discovered that as plasma is mostly made up of water, it could be dried. This made it very easy to transport and store as it didn't need refrigeration. Water could then be added before it was transfused into the patient. US scientist Charles Drew developed the mass production of dried plasma.

The use of plasma saved the lives of thousands of wounded soldiers. It was easily transported close to frontline medical services, where water was added before giving it directly to the patient. It was not as effective as whole blood would have been, but it was impossible to transport and store whole blood close to where it was needed.

Skin grafts

Archibald McIndoe was a plastic surgeon from New Zealand who worked for the Royal Air Force at the Queen Victoria Hospital during the Second World War. He had learned much from his older cousin Harold Gillies (see page 196) and used this as a starting point to experiment and improve the treatment of burns.
- Burns had been commonly treated with chemical creams that protected the area, allowing the skin to heal, but this was painful and caused huge harm for large areas as it would completely dry out skin. McIndoe discovered that covering burns with saline or giving victims saline baths helped heal burned skin.
- For small areas of skin that were completely missing, skin graft techniques were improved. Small areas of skin could be cut from one area of the body and moved to another, for example, to reconstruct eye lids.
- For larger areas, McIndoe developed Gillies' technique of using pedicles and used the 'walking-stalk' skin graft, thereby moving huge areas of skin gradually from one place to another while keeping the skin healthy through maintaining blood supply.

After the Battle of Britain in 1942, Gillies and McIndoe performed some operations on burned airmen at the Queen Victoria Hospital in front of the media. This was widely reported, which helped gain recognition and improve plastic surgery further in the years following the war.

> **Exam practice**
>
> Explain **TWO** ways in which medical treatment in 1905 was different from medical treatment in 1948. (6 marks)

> **Exam tip**
>
> Remember that medical treatment includes surgery, as well as available drugs, etc. You only need to mention two ways but you must include supporting information on each.

The importance of the Second World War for the role of women in medicine

By 1939, women working in medicine had become far more common. During the Second World War, they again stepped up to provide much needed medical care to both soldiers and civilians.

Doctors

The Royal Army Medical Corps included female doctors by 1939. They were allowed to serve overseas for the very first time during the Second World War, though most served in military hospitals in Britain. They had officer status just like male doctors. However, it was still seen as very controversial for women doctors to examine and treat men. Some soldiers objected.

Far more hospitals in Britain employed women doctors by 1939, and this increased during the war as more men volunteered. The number of women who trained to be doctors also increased during the war. However as in 1918, when the war was over, most women doctors who had replaced men had to step aside.

Nursing

The need for nurses in all medical units was not questioned during the Second World War. From the mid-1930s, the RAMC began recruiting more nurses to work for the military. When war broke out, military nurses were sent all over the world wherever British troops were fighting. From 1941, they were given military ranks, equivalent to soldiers. Some nurses were killed, others became POWs (prisoners of war). Many were honoured for their work.

Just as in the First World War, other women volunteered for charities or as VADs and worked providing nursing care for the military. Many of these were not qualified nurses however. This time, qualified nurses tended to remain in their jobs in Britain where there was a massive need due to the civilian injuries caused by bombing raids. Also for this reason, huge numbers of other women volunteered for medical roles in Britain where they worked as ambulance drivers and first aiders and provided support in hospitals by working as cooks or in admin roles.

> **Revision task** TESTED ☐
>
> Draw up a table or diagram to show changes to the role of women in medicine in 1848, 1860, 1875, 1905, 1920 and 1948.

> **Exam practice**
>
> How far did the role of women in medicine change in the years 1905–48?
>
> You may use the following in your answer:
> - the Nurses Registration Act, December 1919
> - military nurses were given military ranks from 1941.
>
> You **must** also use information of your own. (16 marks)

Beveridge, the development of the NHS and its importance for public health

The Second World War brought huge change to Britain.
- Local and national authorities became far more involved in organising hospitals and medical care. Some people received free medical care to ensure they were fit for their roles in the war.
- More people became aware of the poverty in which some people lived due to greater mixing of people in the armed forces and because of the war effort at home.
- Great social change had been promised to help people after the First World War, but didn't happen. Many people wanted the Second World War to bring about this change so that people's lives would actually improve.

Beveridge and the development of the NHS

In 1941, **William Beveridge** was asked by the British government to investigate what measures should be put in place to ensure a better future for everyone. His Beveridge Report recommended huge changes, including unemployment benefit, pensions and sick pay, all paid for by taxes. It recognised the role that ill health and lack of health care played in making and keeping people poor, and recommended a national health service where everyone would be entitled to free medical care at the point of access.

Beveridge's recommendations were very popular with most of the British public. When a Labour Government was elected as the war ended in 1945, it began putting Beveridge's recommendations into practice. On 5 July 1948, the National Health Service (NHS) began. All British citizens were entitled to free:
- GP appointments
- consultations with specialist doctors
- hospital care
- surgery
- medicines
- ambulances
- **maternity** care
- health visitors for young children
- treatment by dentists and opticians.

The NHS also became responsible for medical research and providing teaching hospitals for doctors and nurses.

> **Exam tips**
>
> 1. 'How far' questions are asking you to make a judgement. In this case, how much did something change? You should always remember to answer this question directly as part of your wider answer. For example, 'there was huge / some / little change in the role of women in medicine in the years ...'.
> 2. Your answer needs to explain what roles women had in medicine in 1905 before showing how women's roles changed and/or developed between 1905 and 1948.
> 3. You can, but you don't have to, use the two bullet points of information provided in the question. However, you have to use at least one idea of your own to answer this question well.

> **Sir William Beveridge (1879–1963)**
>
> - Beveridge was an economist who advised the Liberal Governments in their 1906–11 measures.
> - His report became the basis of the **welfare state** begun by the Labour Government in 1945.

> **Key terms**
>
> **Welfare state**: a system where the government protects the well-being of its citizens through providing health care, pensions etc.
>
> **Maternity**: relating to pregnant women and new mothers.

The impact of the NHS on public health

The start of the NHS had a huge impact on improving public health:
- Many of the poorest in society had never seen a doctor before because they could not afford to – access to medical care was improved almost immediately!
- More people sought medical care earlier, therefore improving their chances of getting better.
- Health care became more equal around the country as doctors were all paid the same depending on qualifications and experience rather than where they practised.

The health of the nation improved. Life expectancy started to rise and **infant mortality** dropped drastically. The NHS was funded through tax but the costs rose rapidly, so later on some services had to be paid for.

> **Key term**
>
> **Infant mortality**: the death of children under a year old.

Revision tasks

1. Complete the table below to explain how the NHS improved public health. An example has been done for you.

Before 1948	Free NHS medical care in 1948	How it improved public health
People had to pay to visit a GP. This meant poor people rarely visited one at all and others often put off going to a doctor until their symptoms were very bad.	GP appointments	Far more people went to a GP. This meant more people were diagnosed correctly and prescribed the correct treatment so more were cured. It also meant more people visited the doctor earlier, which increased their chance of survival.

2. Study the table below which identifies possible thematic connections between topics you have studied. For each theme, consider:
   a) Which period/s brought about the greatest change?
   b) What factors brought about change?
   c) How much change was there overall?
3. Pick a theme (or more than one) and use it to explain connections between the topics.

NB 'X' in the table below indicates which theme is covered by which topic.

Topics:	Themes: Changes in medical treatment and in understanding the cause of illness	Improvements in public health provision	Changes in surgery	The changing role of women in medicine	The impact of war, and science and technology on medicine
Florence Nightingale and changes in nursing and hospitals at Scutari	X			X	
The impact of Simpson and chloroform			X		X
The work of Chadwick		X			
The effects of the Public Health Act (1948)		X			
The cholera threat and the work of Snow	X	X			X

Topics:	Themes:				
	Changes in medical treatment and in understanding the cause of illness	Improvements in public health provision	Changes in surgery	The changing role of women in medicine	The impact of war, and science and technology on medicine
Pasteur, the development of the Germ Theory and its effects	X	X	X		X
Lister and the impact of antiseptics	X		X		X
The significance of the Public Health Act (1875)		X			
Nightingale and continuing improvements in hospitals and nursing	X	X		X	
Elizabeth Garrett				X	
The work of Koch and bacteriology	X		X		X
Aseptic surgery			X		X
The impact of the Public Health Act (1875)	X	X			X
Blood transfusions	X		X		X
'Magic bullets' and the work of Ehrlich	X				X
Radioactivity and the impact of Marie Curie	X			X	X
The 1906–11 measures of the Liberal Governments		X			
First World War	X		X	X	X
The development of penicillin	X				X
Second World War	X	X	X	X	X
The development of the NHS		X			X

6 Changes in medicine, c1848–c1948

7 China: conflict, crisis and change, 1900–89

7.1 The fall of the Qing dynasty, warlordism and chaos, 1900–34

REVISED

What you need to know

In this section you will revise the last years of the Qing dynasty, the Revolution of 1911 and the period of disorder that followed when China was ruled by different warlords. This will include:
- The Boxer Uprising and the period of reform that followed it.
- The 1911 Revolution: its causes, main events and results.
- China under the warlords.
- The development of the Guomindang and the Communist Party.
- The attack on the warlords by the Guomindang and the Communists.
- How the Guomindang turned on the Communists.

The impact of the Boxer Uprising: self-strengthening and reform

Causes of the Boxer Uprising

- In 1900, China was ruled by the Qing. This **imperial dynasty** had ruled China since 1644.
- In 1900, the Qing dynasty was in decline and facing many problems. There were internal tensions: rebellions, drought, unemployment and **official corruption**.
- External influences on China, interference by **foreign powers**, were another major problem.
- Foreign powers, such as the British Empire, Japan, Germany and the USA, had forced China to open up to trade. Western powers also insisted that Christian **missionaries** be allowed into China. Foreign interference was strongly resented by many Chinese.
- The Boxer Uprising (1898–1900) was an uprising led by a **secret society** known in the West as the Boxers because they trained in fist fighting and other martial arts.
- The Boxers wanted to force all foreigners out of China: they believed foreigners were evil and were weakening China. The Boxer Uprising saw the massacre of foreigners and those Chinese who had **converted** to Christianity, as well as mass destruction of foreign property. It was not a rebellion against the Qing – the Boxers supported the Qing.
- In June 1900, the Boxers attacked the **foreign district** in Beijing, China's capital city. The Qing rulers said they supported the Uprising. This led to major problems for the Qing dynasty.

Impacts of the Boxer Uprising

A multinational foreign army of 54,000 soldiers invaded China to put down the Boxer Uprising. The foreign powers said the Qing rulers were responsible for all the foreign deaths and damage to foreign property. They demanded that the Qing pay compensation worth £67 million (spread over 39 years): an enormous amount.

Key terms

Imperial: to do with an empire.

Dynasty: a family of rulers going back through several generations.

Official corruption: dishonest behaviour by those in power, e.g. in a government.

Foreign powers: foreign nations, foreign governments.

Missionaries: people sent to another country or region to try to convince people there to join their religion.

Secret society: an organisation whose members keep the society a secret from others.

Converted: when someone is persuaded to believe in a religion that they did not follow before.

Foreign district: these were areas in Chinese cities (also called enclaves) where foreigners were allowed to set up homes, trade freely, convert people to their religion, pay different taxes, etc.

To raise the money, taxes were increased and the state also had to give up more of the money it earned from trade. This meant the state had less money than before.

China's rulers could see that **reforms** were needed. Many of these aimed at social transformation:
- Education reforms meant Chinese students learned about the modern world instead of just Chinese classics.
- Girls began to be educated.
- Old customs such as foot binding were criticised.
- There were bans on the sale of **opium**.
- Industrialisation was promoted and railways were built, with foreign help – aiming at economic transformation.

These reforms looked back to the 'Self Strengthening' movement of the 1870s. The idea was that China needed to build up its resources and become stronger before it could become free of foreign interference and foreign control.

However, the reforms failed.
- Ending the old exam system upset the officials who had spent years training for them.
- Educated Chinese wanted a share in political power, but the leadership did not allow this.
- Educating girls threatened Chinese social traditions and was very unpopular.
- Opium farmers complained about losing money because of the bans.
- To afford the cost of the reforms, the state borrowed money and raised taxes: this increased **inflation** which meant that food became much more expensive for ordinary people.

The state became very unpopular. Disorder increased across China.

The causes, events and results of the 1911 Revolution

Causes of the 1911 Revolution
- By 1911, there were local uprisings in many parts of China – the Qing dynasty was still very unpopular.
- One reason for this unpopularity was that foreign countries were in control of so much of China. In 1911, people were very angry that foreign companies were being sold the right to build railways in China.
- Another reason was that China's middle-classes wanted to have a say in how China was governed, but the dynasty refused to allow more **democracy** in China.
- The Qing had very little control left in many **provinces**. When these provinces decided to stop obeying the government, there was little the Qing could do.

Events of the 1911 Revolution
- In October 1911, in Wuhan, a plot was discovered by police and the rebels acted quickly to seize control of the city. Local troops refused to stop them.
- The rebels declared independence from the Qing dynasty, and other provinces followed suit.
- In November, rebels from all these provinces met together and decided they would form a new Chinese **republic**.
- **Sun Yat-sen** was invited to be the president of the new republic. He returned from the USA to take up this role at the start of 1912.
- The Qing government asked a famous soldier, Yuan Shikai, to put down the rebellions. He agreed and set off with a large army. But when he reached Wuhan, he made a deal with the republican rebels.

> **Revision task**
>
> Explain two reasons why the Qing reforms that followed the Boxer Uprising did not achieve much change.
>
> TESTED

> **Key terms**
>
> **Reforms**: making changes to try to improve something.
>
> **Opium**: an addictive drug made from poppy juice. In the nineteenth century, the British had organised the smuggling of huge amounts of opium in China, which caused widespread addiction.
>
> **Inflation**: when prices go up but the value of money goes down.
>
> **Democracy**: when everyone in a country gets a choice about who is in power.
>
> **Province**: a region of a country, usually with its own provincial administration.
>
> **Republic**: where the people of the country are in charge of it, rather than being ruled by a king or queen.

- Yuan Shikai's deal was that if he was made president instead of Sun Yat-sen, then he would get the Qing rulers to **abdicate**.
- This deal was agreed and on 12 February 1912, the Qing dynasty ended.

Results of the 1911 Revolution

- There were elections to China's first parliament in 1912. Sun Yat-sen set up his Nationalist party: the Guomindang (GMD). The Guomindang won the election.
- However, this result weakened Yuan Shikai. He banned the GMD and democracy ended.
- Yuan Shikai tried to find ways to solve China's financial problems, and also to get back government control over all of China's provinces.
- However, generals in many southern provinces did not want to go back to being ruled from the centre. And Yuan's deals with foreign governments to get massive loans for China looked just as bad as the deals the Qing had done – they gave away control over China to foreign powers, including Japan.
- As a last attempt to assert his control, in 1915 Yuan declared himself emperor, but this was not a popular move: the provinces refused to obey him. In 1916 he died.

> **Revision task** TESTED
>
> Explain two causes of the 1911 Revolution.

China under the warlords

After Yuan Shikai died in 1916, army commanders fought among each other for leadership. The republican government continued, but it had no power.

- The provinces started to be controlled not by the central government, but by independent military commanders and their private armies – the warlords.
- The warlord period lasted for a long time: between 1916 and 1928.
- Some of the warlords were commanders from Yuan Shikai's old army. Others became powerful because they received backing from foreign powers, for example, Japan.
- Some of the warlords were little more than **bandits**, but some were more interested in good government and reform: for example, leading campaigns against foot binding.
- None of the warlords were able to gain control over more than two or three provinces. Sometimes warlords did form **alliances**, but these quickly broke up again.
- The GMD, which was popular in the south of China, was also not strong enough to control all of China during this time.
- The **central government** still continued – in 1917, it decided that China would join the First World War on the side of the Allies. Part of the reason for this was the government's hope that if Germany was defeated, China would get back control of parts of the country controlled by Germany.
- However, the central government had no influence outside a few provinces. China was deeply divided. **Intellectuals** in particular were depressed that China had fallen back into conflict and disorder. **Nationalism** grew stronger.

> **Sun Yat-sen (1866–1925)**
>
> - Sun Yat-sen was from a family of peasant farmers in Guangdong, a province in the south of China. As a young man, he was involved in revolutionary activities against the Qing regime and was exiled from China.
> - Sun lived abroad for sixteen years, organising a series of uprisings against the Qing (all failed).
> - Following the 1911 Revolution, he was invited to be the president of the new republic, then gave up the presidency to Yuan Shikai in 1912.
> - As leader of the Guomindang (GMD), Sun's failed campaign against Yuan led to him having to leave China again; he returned in 1917.
> - With Soviet support, Sun Yat-sen had reorganised the GMD into a strong political and military force by the time of his death in 1925.

> **Key terms**
>
> **Abdicate**: when a king, queen or emperor gives up their position as ruler.
>
> **Bandit**: a robber or outlaw, usually in an area where there is little or no law and order.
>
> **Alliance**: when countries, groups or people join together to help each other.
>
> **Central government**: the government of the whole country. Local government may carry out what the central government decides at a more local level.
>
> **Intellectuals**: highly educated people, thinkers.
>
> **Nationalism**: the belief that your own nation is superior to all other nations and that you should do everything you can to help your nation reach its full potential.

Revision tasks

TESTED ☐

Study this table, which identifies possible thematic connections between topics you have studied.

Topic:	Theme: Civil conflict – order and disorder	External influences on China	Economic transformation	Social transformation	The role of leadership
The Boxer Uprising	X	X	X		X
Reforms after the Boxer Uprising				X	X
The 1911 Revolution	X	X	X	X	X
China under the warlords	X	X		X	X

Pick a theme (or more than one) and use it to explain connections between the topics.

The May the Fourth Movement

- Despite China's support for the Allies in the First World War, at the **Paris Peace Conference** in 1919, German territory in China went to Japan, not to China. China's desire to end foreign control was ignored.
- On 4 May 1919, 3,000 students demonstrated in Beijing against the Peace Conference decision. They marched to the house of a government official who had close links to Japan. They burned down the house and beat up China's minister to Japan.
- More demonstrations and angry protests then occurred across the country, followed by strikes. The government announced that it would not sign the Paris Peace treaty.
- The protests of 4 May 1919 inspired the May the Fourth Movement in the 1920s: a determination to force foreigners out of China.
- Those following the May the Fourth Movement argued that the government had not done enough to pull China free of foreign interference – to achieve this, more radical change was needed.
- Cultural change was also important to the May the Fourth Movement: especially a rejection of **Confucian philosophy**, because it was so closely connected with the imperial government of China.
- Instead of these traditional ways of thinking, the May the Fourth Movement believed in Western scientific thinking and democracy: 'Mr Science' and 'Mr Democracy' were two slogans from the time.
- Mao Zedong was one of many young Chinese who were inspired by the May the Fourth Movement.
- The cultural transformation triggered by the May the Fourth Movement was important for the growth of two revolutionary political parties: the Nationalists (Guomindang: GMD) and the Communists (Chinese Communist Party: CCP).
- Both parties called for a radical social transformation for China that would mean it could finally break free from foreign oppression and regain its place in the world as a strong, independent and powerful nation.

Key terms

Paris Peace Conference: meetings at the end of the First World War in which the Allies decided what terms to set for peace with the defeated Central Powers.

Confucian philosophy: the teachings of the Chinese thinker Confucius (551–479 BCE), which included the idea that people should stay in the part of society that they were born into.

Revision task

Make a link between the Boxer Uprising, the May the Fourth Movement and the aims of the Guomindang (GMD). Explain your answer.

TESTED ☐

Sun Yat-sen, Chiang Kai-shek and the Guomindang

Sun Yat-sen and the Guomindang (GMD)

- Sun Yat-sen returned to China in 1917.
- The May the Fourth Movement helped him build support for his Guomindang Party.
- In 1923, Sun Yat-sen set out his 'Three Principles of the People' for China: nationalism, democracy and social **welfare**.
  - Nationalism was about getting rid of foreign influences so China could become an independent nation again – a **sovereign state**.
  - Democracy was about 'people's power' – the Chinese people should have the right to say what they wanted from their government through national elections.
  - Social welfare was about the Chinese government taking care of its people: to make China more equal and end the terrible poverty many Chinese people suffered.
- These principles were very successful in setting out what the GMD stood for. They were simple to understand and connected strongly with the demands of the May the Fourth Movement.
- Sun Yat-sen also set up a training academy for a GMD army. He said the GMD had to be able to defeat the warlords: they would not submit to anything else but force. Only then could Sun Yat-sen's main aim be achieved: to **reunify** China.
- When the Soviet Union told the Chinese Communist Party (CCP) to join forces with the GMD, Sun Yat-sen reacted positively. An alliance was made in 1923, and the Soviet Union gave the GMD support with money, military supplies and advisors.
- The Soviet advisors were important in reorganising the GMD as a military organisation. They also changed Sun Yat-sen's Three Principles so they were a better fit with **Lenin**'s political theories.

> **Key terms**
>
> **Welfare**: when the state provides help for people who need it, e.g. to pay for health care, unemployment benefit, etc.
>
> **Sovereign state**: a country that governs itself and is not dependent on any other country.
>
> **Reunify**: to bring back together a country that has been divided in some way.
>
> **Lenin**: the Communist leader of the Bolshevik Revolution that changed Russia into the Soviet Union.

Revision task [TESTED]

Explain two ways in which Sun Yat-sen was an important leader.

Chiang Kai-shek and the GMD

- **Chiang Kai-shek** had trained at Sun Yat-sen's military academy. When Sun Yat-sen died in 1925, Chiang Kai-shek became the new leader of the GMD.
- Chiang did not trust the CCP, or the Soviet Union. He opposed communism. In fact, he was not a supporter of the social transformation that Sun Yat-sen had outlined in his Three Principles of the People.
- Instead, Chiang Kai-Shek was more conservative. He did not want to get rid of all China's traditions but looked to bring in moderate reforms (for example, to education and finance) that supported China's middle class.
- However, between 1925 and 1927, the GMD needed the Soviet Union's support, so Chiang kept up a front of accepting the alliance with the CCP – until the warlords had been defeated.

> **Chiang Kai-shek (1887–1975)**
>
> - Chiang Kai-shek came from a well-off family of merchants from Zhejiang province, on China's eastern coast.
> - Chiang entered the military and fought in the 1911 Revolution. He then helped to set up the GMD.
> - As leader of the GMD after Sun Yat-sen's death, Chiang Kai-Shek led the Northern Expedition from 1926 to 1928, and succeeded in defeating the warlords.
> - In 1927, Chiang ordered a purge of Communists, which then led to civil war.
> - In 1949, Chiang Kai-shek lost the civil war and retreated with his Nationalist government to Taiwan.

Revision tasks [TESTED]

1. Draw a spider diagram to represent the leadership of the GMD by Chiang Kai-shek and one for the leadership of Sun Yat-sen.
2. Explain two ways in which Chiang Kai-shek's leadership of the GMD was different from Sun Yat-sen's.

The emergence of the Chinese Communist Party, the United Front and the influence of the Soviet Union

The Chinese Communist Party (CCP) and the Soviet Union

- The Chinese Communist Party (CCP) started in 1921, set up by academics from Peking University, who were inspired by the May the Fourth Movement and by the success of the Bolshevik Revolution in Russia in 1917.
- One of the CCP's first members was a library assistant at Peking University: Mao Zedong.
- The Soviet Union's **Comintern** organisation advised the CCP from the start.
- The Soviet Union thought that the CCP was too small to achieve anything revolutionary, and in 1922, Comintern advised the CCP to join the much larger Guomindang (GMD) to form a **united front**.
- Comintern told the CCP that they should aim to take over the GMD from the inside, and move its policies from nationalism to Marxism.

The United Front and the Soviet Union

- In 1924, CCP members joined the GMD to create the GMD–CCP United Front.
- The GMD included landlords and merchants, i.e. capitalists – the CCP's enemy. But most CCP members agreed with Comintern that only a united front could defeat the warlords and reunify China.
- Soviet advisors helped the United Front reorganise and then develop the GMD army – the National Revolutionary Army (NRA) – into a very disciplined force.
- However, many in the army did not like communist ideas, including Chiang Kai-shek. He recognised that the CCP planned to grow inside the GMD and then take it over.

> **Key terms**
>
> **Comintern**: Soviet organisation that existed to support the development of communism around the world.
>
> **United front**: a group of organisations that share similar goals and work together to achieve them.
>
> **Civil conflict**: conflict between groups within a country rather than between countries.

The Northern Expedition and the Shanghai Massacres

The Northern Expedition (1926–28)

- In 1926, the GMD announced that an expedition to the north would defeat the warlords, bring in Sun Yat-sen's Three Principles of the People, and unify China again.
- The leader of the Northern Expedition was Chiang Kai-shek.
- Although the warlord armies outnumbered the National Revolutionary Army's 75,000 men, the GMD army was very motivated, very disciplined and had plenty of Soviet weapons and supplies. At this point, the CCP and the GMD also worked well together.
- The Northern Expedition's aims to defeat the warlords and reunify China were very popular with many Chinese people. This meant the United Front received support from both local peasants (the CCP were popular with them) and from wealthy Chinese, who gave them money (and who supported the GMD).
- By 1927, the Northern Expedition had defeated the warlords controlling the important cities of Shanghai and Wuhan. By 1928, the Northern Expedition had control of Beijing.
- In July 1928, Chiang Kai-shek announced that the Northern Expedition had achieved its aims and was over. However, **civil conflict** in China was far from finished.

The Shanghai Massacres (1927)

- In 1927, Chiang Kai-shek was confident that he no longer needed the CCP to finish the job of defeating the remaining warlords.
- In April 1927, troops loyal to Chiang turned on the Communists in Shanghai. Five thousand Communists were massacred: shot or beheaded.
- In Shanghai the CCP had helped trade unions to develop and had also formed a workers' army. This was a threat to Shanghai's factory owners and merchants, and they supported the GMD's massacre.
- There were also massacres of Communists in other cities, for example, in Guangzhou province.
- As a result of the Shanghai Massacre, the United Front ended. The Guomindang **purged** CCP members from the Party.
- A period called the **White Terror** then followed: anti-Communist violence that forced surviving Communists to escape to remote regions that the GMD did not yet control.

> **Revision task** TESTED
>
> Identify two factors that caused the Shanghai Massacre (1927).

Key terms

Purge: to remove undesirable people from an organisation or place – often in a very quick and violent way.

White: Communist forces are usually called 'Red', and anti-Communists are called 'White'.

Terror: using brutal tactics to make so people terrified that they do what an organisation wants.

Guerrilla tactics: military tactics that are designed to wear down the enemy instead of defeating them in regular battle.

The Extermination Campaigns

- Between 1927 and 1934, Chiang Kai-shek carried out five campaigns against the Communists.
- The campaigns were masterminded for the GMD by German advisors. The first four did not succeed in defeating the Communists, but the fifth campaign (1934) was successful and led to the Long March (see page 213).
- The Communists had a base in the south of Jiangxi province, which was led by Mao Zedong. It was a large area – about the size of Belgium. The Extermination Campaigns all aimed at destroying this base.
- Mao was successful at resisting the first four Extermination Campaigns because he used **guerrilla tactics**. For example:
  - Mao's Red Army avoided head-on fights, but instead lured the GMD forces into ambushes.
  - By attacking NRA units when they were resting or were tired from pursuing Red Army soldiers.
  - By attacking NRA units when they were retreating.
- In the fifth campaign (1934–35), Chiang Kai-shek raised a huge army of 700,000 men and built thousands of stone forts (called blockhouses) all around the Communist-held area, which the troops used as secure bases, instead of marching around the countryside chasing after the Red Army.
- These forts were very effective: Red Army attacks on them cost many lives without any gains for the Communist side, and the GMD was able to stop supplies getting into the area, so the Communists (and the local peasants) began to run out of food.
- Mao was replaced as military leader. The new leaders of the CCP forces, and their Soviet advisor, decided against continuing guerrilla tactics.
- Instead, they ordered the Red Army to fight a regular battle against NRA, even though the Red Army had fewer men and was not as well trained. The Red Army was badly defeated.

> **Exam practice**
>
> Explain **TWO** causes of the May the Fourth Movement. (8 marks)
>
> > **Exam tips**
> > 1 Make sure you write about two different causes – the maximum mark you can get for one cause is four marks, no matter how good your explanation is.
> > 2 A good way to focus your answer on explaining causes is to use connectors such as: 'because of this', 'this led to', 'as a result of this'.
> > 3 Back up your explanations with knowledge and understanding: key facts and features.

7.2 The triumph of Mao and the CCP, 1934–49

REVISED

> **What you need to know**
>
> In this section you will revise how the CCP, under Mao's leadership, managed to defeat the much stronger Guomindang despite nearly being wiped out in 1934–35. This will include:
> - The events of the Long March (1934–35) and why it was important for the eventual success of the CCP.
> - War with Japan (1937–45) and the roles in this taken by the CCP and the GMD.
> - The Civil War of 1946–49: its key features and reasons why Mao and the CCP won.

The events and importance of the Long March, 1934–35

Events of the Long March

By 1934, the success of the fifth Extermination Campaign meant the Red Army could not hope to hold on in Jiangxi. A decision was made to escape Jiangxi by breaking through at a weak point.

- After fighting for over a month to break out of the encirclement, the Red Army headed for Hunan province. Their Soviet advisor had the 86,000 soldiers marching in a straight line, weighed down by all the supplies they could carry.
- Chiang Kai-shek's forces could predict where they were going and attacked them at the Xiang River. The Red Army lost 36,000 men.
- After this disaster, Mao was put back in charge – in January 1935. He changed the tactics of the retreat:
  - Instead of all marching together, the Red Army broke up into smaller groups.
  - Instead of marching in a straight line, the Red Army groups took zig-zagging routes that were difficult for the GMD to predict.
  - Instead of Hunan province, the Red Army was now heading to remote northern China.
- The Red Army made the 6,000-mile march on foot and it took a year.
- The terrain was very difficult – for example, crossing the Great Snowy Mountains (where hundreds froze to death) and swampy grasslands (where hundreds died from exhaustion and disease).

- Many people were starving on the Long March, but Mao ordered that no one should steal food from local peasants.
- The Red Army had to fight 200 battles against both the GMD chasing after them, and also attacks from local warlords.
- By the time the Red Army reached a safe base in Shaanxi province (north-east China) in October 1935, less than 5,000 of the original 86,000 soldiers were left.

Importance of the Long March

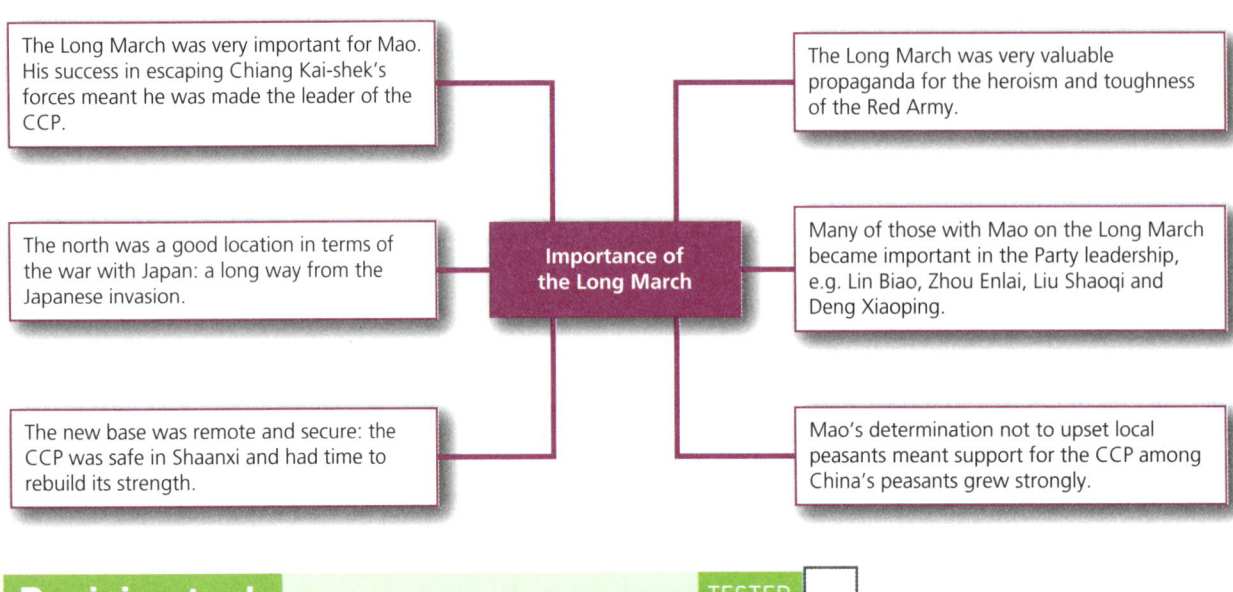

Revision task

TESTED

Identify two ways in which the Long March was a turning point for the CCP in its conflict with the GMD.

War with Japan, 1937–45

Japan had begun taking control over Chinese territory in 1931, when it occupied Manchuria in northern China. The war with Japan began in 1937, when Japan took control over more of China.

- The whole of the eastern coastline of China was occupied – where China's most important industrial and business centres were located.
- Chiang Kai-shek's GMD government retreated to its stronghold in the south west.
- Chiang Kai-shek's strategy was to retreat from Japanese attacks, using China's huge size against the invaders.
- However, this strategy was very unpopular with the Chinese people: it felt like they were giving up their homeland. Chiang's government was also criticised for corruption.
- In 1936, troops angry at being forced out of Manchuria by the Japanese, captured Chiang. They handed him over to the CCP. In return for his freedom, Chiang promised that the government and the CCP would stop fighting each other and instead both fight against the Japanese invaders.

The limitations of the Guomindang
The first phase of the war: 1937–41
- In the first phase of the war, Chiang Kai-Shek experienced serious defeats against the Japanese. The Japanese had a technologically advanced army and the Chinese armed forces could not match them: Chiang knew this.
- By 1938, the GMD had lost Beijing, Shanghai, Guangzhou and Nanjing. The GMD had to retreat to Chongqing, in central China.
- Japanese war crimes (atrocities including hundreds of thousands of rapes) led to millions of refugees from occupied China moving to 'Free China'.
- By 1938, the Japanese controlled 40 per cent of China's population and 95 per cent of its industry. The Japanese stopped advancing and concentrated on strengthening their control over their occupied areas.

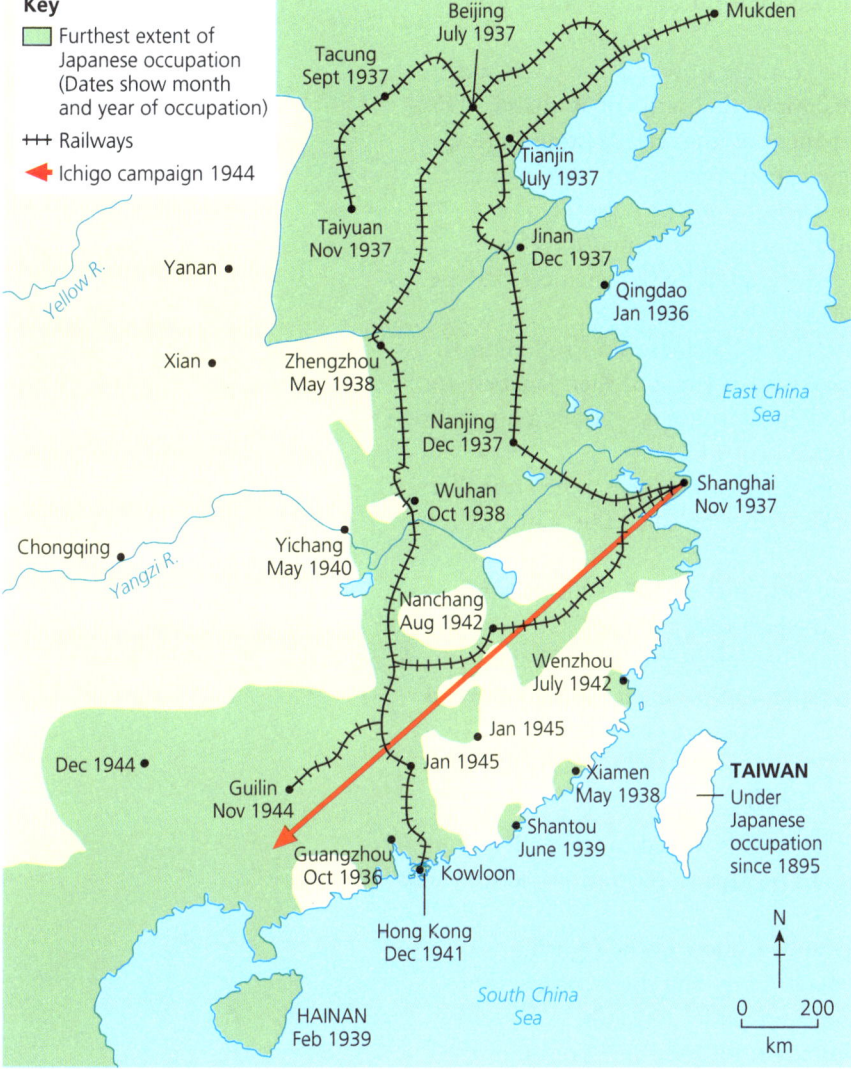

The Sino–Japanese War, 1937–45

The second phase of the war: 1941–45
- In December 1941, the USA declared war on Japan. This significantly changed China's war with Japan.
- The GMD was the government of China, so the USA helped the GMD fight Japan with military equipment worth millions of dollars.
- Now Chiang had US support, the GMD ended its alliance with the CCP. In 1941, GMD troops attacked the Red Army and killed over 3,000 troops.

- At the same time, however, GMD resistance to the Japanese did not increase. GMD troops were not very motivated. Nor was the GMD popular with the peasants. GMD **conscription** was harsh, which meant people were not keen to fight for them. GMD taxes were high and GMD government corruption increased.
- The weakness of the GMD's National Revolutionary Army was shown by the Japanese Ichigo Offensive in 1944. Not only did the GMD fail to stop the advance, the GMD troops were even attacked by Chinese peasants who seized their weapons in order to defend their communities from the Japanese themselves.

The role of the CCP, especially the Red Army

- The Communists, in remote Shaanxi province, were a long way from Japanese-controlled areas. The Japanese **occupation** was good for them, since it bought them time to build up their numbers after the Long March.
- There were some battles against the Japanese in which the CCP and GMD forces fought together, for example, the Battle of Wuhan in 1938.
- Most CCP fighting against the Japanese used guerrilla-style tactics, which the Red Army had developed against the GMD, for example, destroying railway communications.
- The CCP also massively increased the size of its armed forces by recruiting guerrilla fighters in areas occupied by the Japanese. By the end of the war, the Red Army had 900,000 troops.
- In 1940, Peng Dehuai led CCP attacks on Japanese-controlled north and central China. These were successful at first but then Japanese **counterattacks** killed 100,000 Red Army soldiers – about a quarter of all the CCP's forces at that time.
- The Japanese also launched a horrific terror campaign in the areas that had supported the Red Army attacks. This was called the 'Three Alls' – 'kill all, burn all, loot all'.
- The 'Three Alls' helped increase support for the CCP as the peasant population wanted revenge against the Japanese, and the CCP treated them very respectfully: never stealing their crops but instead helping them to harvest them, reducing taxes, making improvements, etc. By the end of the war, well over 1 million people had become members of the CCP.

The end of the war with Japan, 1945

- The USA defeated Japan in 1945: Japan was forced to surrender after the USA dropped two atomic bombs on Japanese cities, Hiroshima and Nagasaki.
- At the time that the war suddenly ended, most of the fighting was in the north of China, between the Red Army and the Japanese. The Communists felt the Japanese should surrender to them.
- Chiang Kai-shek did not want this at all: for then the Communists would look like they had won the war. Chiang had planned that the USA would help him get rid of the Communists.
- Instead, the USA tried to get the GMD and the CCP to find a peaceful way to work together. But neither side trusted the other. In June 1946, civil war began in China.

> **Key terms**
>
> **Conscription**: when it is compulsory for people of certain ages to join the armed forces.
>
> **Occupation**: areas of a country that are taken over by the armed forces of another country.
>
> **Counterattack**: when one side responds to an attack by the other side by attacking them back.

> **Revision task** — TESTED
>
> Explain why the war with Japan helped the CCP become more popular in China.

The Civil War, 1946–49

Key features of the Civil War

- The GMD started the Civil War in what looked like a much stronger position than the Communists:
  - 5 million troops were in the NRA (National Revolutionary Army) compared with 900,000 in the **PLA**
  - better military technology, including aircraft, thanks to the USA's **lend-lease** scheme
  - 55,000 US marines acting as military advisors
  - control of most of China's cities, factories and its most populated regions.
- At first, the GMD succeeded in pushing the Communists back: they even had to abandon their base in Shaanxi. The Communists moved north to Manchuria.
- In 1946, Chiang Kai-shek sent over 500,000 troops to Manchuria to defeat the Communists. Although the GMD captured the cities, the Communists' successful guerrilla tactics wore the NRA down.
- Then the PLA started full-scale attacks on the GMD. Through 1947 and 1948, they captured more and more cities in Manchuria. Lin Biao was a great commander for the PLA.
- The NRA lost 500,000 troops, which meant the Communists now had more troops than them. The NRA had to retreat from Manchuria.
- The Battle of Huai-Hai was a huge Communist victory (see below) that was followed, in January 1949, by Beijing being captured by the PLA. Nanjing, Shanghai and Wuhan followed.
- By September 1949, almost all of China was controlled by the Communists. Chiang Kai-Shek and his government fled to Taiwan.
- The Civil War had high **casualty** numbers: 3 million GMD casualties and 1 million Communist casualties.

The Battle of Huai-Hai (1948–49)

The last major battle of the Civil War, the Battle of Huai-Hai, was where the GMD lost their final chance of stopping the PLA's advance.

- The battle lasted from 6 November 1948 to 10 January 1949.
- Chiang Kai-shek sent 800,000 troops – well-equipped soldiers, trained by USA advisors – to stop the PLA from advancing any further south.
- The Communists had 600,000 soldiers, plus another 600,000 guerrilla fighters and the support of local peasants.
- The NRA's **morale** was low following their defeats. The Communists used **intelligence** to find out which parts of the NRA were particularly vulnerable, then used propaganda to convince them to **desert** and join the PLA.
- The PLA also used guerrilla tactics to cut off supply lines to the NRA and to separate NRA **divisions**, making it easier to surround and defeat them.
- By the end of the battle, the NRA had 500,000 casualties. There were no longer enough NRA soldiers to stop the PLA from capturing the rest of China.

> **Key terms**
>
> **PLA**: the Red Army reformed in 1945 and was renamed the PLA – the People's Liberation Army.
>
> **Lend-Lease**: a programme in which the USA supplied its allies (including the Republic of China) with supplies such as military equipment, food and oil, in return for leases (rights) to set up US airbases in those countries.
>
> **Casualty**: in war, a casualty means someone who can no longer fight: either the dead or injured.
>
> **Morale**: confidence, motivation, belief in winning.
>
> **Intelligence**: military intelligence means secret information captured from the enemy.
>
> **Desert**: in a conflict, to stop fighting for one side and join the opposite side.
>
> **Division**: a large military unit: 10,000–25,000 soldiers.

> **Revision task**   TESTED
>
> Study this table, which identifies possible thematic connections between the topics you have studied.
>
> | Topics: | Themes: Civil conflict – order and disorder | External influences on China | Economic transformation | Social transformation | The role of leadership |
> |---|---|---|---|---|---|
> | The Long March | X | X | X | X | X |
> | War with Japan | X | X | X | X | X |
> | The Civil War | X | X | X | X | X |
>
> Pick a theme (or more than one) and use it to explain connections between the topics.

Military, political, economic and social reasons for the success of Mao and the CCP in the Civil War

Lack of popular support for the GMD

The GMD lost support from the Chinese people because:
- The GMD's economic policies led to unemployment and inflation. Inflation in particular became a massive problem, which convinced many that the GMD was not a good government.
- The government did little to improve the poor working conditions in the factories: this meant the workers did not support them.
- Government corruption was as bad as ever, which people hated.
- The big landlords supported the GMD, so the government refused **land reform**. This meant the peasants did not support the GMD.

As the war went on, the problems got worse:
- **Military decision making**: the decision to send troops into Manchuria was a mistake. The NRA troops were spread out too thinly over a large area, making them and their supply lines an easy target for PLA guerrilla tactics.
- **Military problems**:
  - Morale in the NRA was low, and there were many desertions. Chiang Kai-Shek responded by making discipline in the army even harsher and forcing people to join the NRA.
  - The NRA struggled to attract volunteers because the GMD was so unpopular. Chiang introduced conscription: this involved rounding up peasants and forcing them into the army, where they were treated very badly (for example, not enough food, officers stealing their pay).
  - Chiang also often disagreed with his generals, making military decision making more challenging (and slower).
- **Economic problems**: As popular support fell, Chiang Kai-Shek responded by seizing property and money to fund his campaigns. This was deeply unpopular.
- **Political and social problems**: As protests against his government increased, Chiang Kai-Shek reacted with harsh punishments: protesters were arrested and many executed without any trial. This increased hostility towards the GMD.

Increasing support for Mao and the CCP

Mao Zedong and the CCP won support from the Chinese people because of their political and social policies.

> **Key term**
>
> **Land reform**: dividing up the land owned by just a few rich people and giving it out to many (poorer) farmers.

- The peasants wanted more land, and CCP policies of land reform gave them this. As the PLA took territory from the GMD, they also took away land from big landlords and gave it to the peasants. The peasants knew if the GMD won, they would be forced to give the land back, so this increased CCP support.
- Mao made sure that the PLA treated peasants well (just as on the Long March): never seizing food from them, helping them with harvests, speaking to peasants respectfully.
- The GMD's foreign support was a problem because Chinese people hated the idea of foreigners controlling China. The CCP could claim to be free from foreign control (the Soviet Union had backed the GMD in the Civil War).
- People were very impressed at how good the Communists were at stopping crime and corruption in the cities they captured, and at making sure food was distributed fairly. This contrasted with GMD corruption, food shortages and poor working conditions.

As the war went on, Mao and the PLA got stronger:
- **Military experience**: excellent generals such as Lin Biao and highly motivated troops meant the Communists quickly mastered battle tactics to add to their guerrilla skills.
- **Military success**: Mao worked well with the PLA generals, which meant the PLA acted quickly and decisively.
- **Leadership success**: Mao was an inspiring and determined leader. He had proved his military leadership on the Long March and the PLA trusted him.
- **Political success**: the PLA grew rapidly from deserters from the NRA joining and from armies in Manchuria. CCP propaganda was very effective at convincing new recruits to take on the communist values of the PLA.

Mao Zedong (1893–1976)

- Mao came from a peasant family. He trained to be a teacher and then got a job in Beijing as a librarian.
- He was one of the founders of the Chinese Communist Party in 1921.
- After the CCP's victory in the Civil War, Mao and the CCP set about transforming China into a socialist state.
- Mao's 'Great Leap Forward' (1958) was a disaster, causing a terrible famine.
- After stepping back from China's leadership, in 1966, Mao launched the Cultural Revolution.
- Again, Mao's radical ideas led to a huge loss of life, and the Cultural Revolution ended with Mao having to call on the PLA to restore order.
- After the Cultural Revolution, Mao's health declined. He died in 1976.

Exam practice

How significant was foreign involvement in the changing relations between the Communist Party and the Guomindang in China in the years 1922–49?

You may use the following in your answer:
- Comintern
- land reform.

You **must** also use information of your own. (16 marks)

Exam tips

1. Questions asking '*How far?*' or '*How significant?*' are asking you to make a judgement – to what extent was something the most important reason, or was something else more important?
2. You can start, for this question, by considering how significant foreign involvement was: the importance of the Soviet Union, of German military advisors, of the war with Japan, of US Lend-Lease. One of the stimulus points (bullet points) in the question will be about the significance of foreign involvement, and you can use your own information instead or to add support here.
3. Then consider points against foreign involvement being the most significant reason. The other stimulus point will support this. You should also use your own information to talk about other reasons instead of, or alongside, the other stimulus point.
4. Your answer needs to show your knowledge and understanding, with details to back up your points.

7.3 Change under Mao, 1949–63

REVISED

What you need to know

In this section you will revise the economic, political and social changes brought about by Mao as leader of the People's Republic of China (PRC). This will include:
- Economic changes in agriculture and industry.
- Social changes to the role of women.
- Political changes, including the Anti Campaigns and the Hundred Flowers Campaign.
- The Great Leap Forward: its causes, key features and impacts.
- The influence of the Soviet Union on changes under Mao.

Changes in agriculture

In 1949, 80 per cent of China's population still worked in agriculture: almost all as peasant farmers. Peasants wanted more land.
- The Chinese Communist Party (CCP) supported land reform because doing this meant the peasants supported the CCP.
- Mao also believed land reform would make farming more productive, which China needed to happen in order to develop its economy.

The Agrarian Reform Law and attacks on landlords

- The CCP had already begun land reform in the northern provinces it controlled during the Civil War. After 1949, the CCP rolled out land reform across China.
- In 1950, the Agrarian Reform Law was passed. This gave the state the power to take land away from landlords and give it to peasants.
- Landlords who refused to hand over their land were attacked. Over 1 million landlords were killed. Many of them only owned tiny amounts of land.
- Landlords who were not killed were fined and often beaten. They lost all their land and were forced to leave the village they lived in.

Gradual changes towards co-operative farming

Between 1951 and 1957, the CCP encouraged peasant farmers to work together rather than farm as individuals, by volunteering to join Mutual Aid Teams (MATs) and Agricultural Producers' Cooperatives (APCs).
- In 1950–51, the state encouraged peasants to set up MATs. Peasants in MATs still owned their own land, but they worked together with up to ten other households on large jobs such as harvesting, and they shared machinery. Joining an MAT was voluntary and a peasant could leave if they wanted to.
- Many peasants trusted the CCP because of land reform and were enthusiastic about the next steps in agriculture. By 1952, 40 per cent of peasants had joined a MAT.
- Between 1953 and 1955, APCs were promoted. Up to 30, then up to 300 households combined all their land, creating large fields that could be worked efficiently with modern machinery.
- Again, APCs were voluntary to join and peasants could leave and still keep all their original property.
- By 1957, 90 per cent of peasant households had joined an APC.
- Food production increased by 4 per cent between 1951 and 1957: a modest increase.

Radical change: the communes

- In 1958, as part of the Great Leap Forward, peasants were forced to become part of collective farms called **communes**. Private farming was abolished.
- Communes were huge collective farms – most had around 5,000 households. Peasants gave up everything and worked for the commune. Work was carried out in a military way, with workers organised into brigades.
- CCP officials monitored each commune to make sure it was following CCP orders. The commune police force punished anyone who acted against the commune.
- The communes were set targets for production by the state. Everyone working for the commune had a role to play in meeting these targets.

> **Key term**
>
> **Commune**: huge collective farms in which people shared work, property and produce.

Consequences of radical change – the Great Famine

Between 1958 and 1962, as many as 30 million people in China died from famine. Radical changes in agriculture were certainly an important reason for this famine:

- Peasants got paid the same (not much), whether they worked hard or not. So productivity went down.
- The state introduced new 'socialist' farming techniques for the communes to follow which did not work.
- Rapidly re-organising 400 million peasant farmers into 26,500 communes was too much change. Many communes were not well organised.
- Diverting peasants away from farming and into steel-making in the commune meant a loss of labour power on the farms, not to mention very bad quality steel farming tools.

Wheat and rice harvests declined every year from 1958 to 1962.

Agricultural reforms in response to the Great Famine

In 1960, the state brought in new measures to help rescue food production.

- Peasants could return to individual farms again. They were again allowed to sell whatever they didn't need to feed their own families.
- Communes were split up and workers got more money for doing more work: there was an incentive to work hard again.
- Students, unemployed people and soldiers were sent to the countryside to work on farms and increase food production.
- These measures succeeded in increasing agricultural production. By 1965, agricultural production had reached the level it had been in 1957, before the Great Leap Forward.

> **Revision task**   TESTED
>
> To what extent did Communist rule transform agriculture in China between 1949 and 1965?

Changes in industry

In 1953, Mao decided to implement rapid changes: the first Five-year Plan. Change happened very fast: by 1956, all private industry had been taken over by the state.

The first Five-year Plan

The first Five-year Plan was modelled on the Soviet Union's successful five-year plans.
- The state took over control of industries and decided what they would produce. This meant the state could make sure industries were producing what China needed.
- Ninety per cent of state **investment** went into developing heavy industry, especially iron and steel production.
- There was also a huge investment in infrastructure – roads, ports and railways. This made China better connected so industries could get the raw materials they needed.

> **Key term**
>
> **Investment**: putting money into something to make it grow.

Successes and failures of the first Five-year Plan

Successes	Failures
Coal, steel and electricity production all beat their targets: a huge achievement. Chinese industry expanded by 300 per cent.	Oil production was way off target, meaning China still had to import most of its oil: this was expensive.
Heavy industry expanded by 300 per cent between 1953 and 1957.	Light industry (which made consumer products) grew very slowly.
Around 6,000 kilometres of new railway was constructed – all China's main cities were connected.	Factory wages did not increase. This was unpopular with workers.

Radical change: the Great Leap Forward and industry

Mao named the second Five-year Plan 'the Great Leap Forward'. It had extremely radical aims and was a disaster for industrial production.
- Mao now wanted China to overtake the West in its industrial production.
- Disagreements with the Soviet Union (see page 232) meant Mao also no longer wanted to follow the Soviet model for industrialisation. Instead, he believed agriculture and industry could now develop together, using small-scale industrial production.
- Mao mobilised the communes with targets for industrial production. By the end of 1958, around half of all China's steel production was from the communes' backyard furnaces (see page 227).
- However, the results were very bad. Because peasants had no training in making steel, the backyard furnaces produced such poor quality steel that it could not be used. China's industrial output fell by 50 per cent.

Reforms of industry

Reforms were brought in by Liu Shaoqi and Deng Xiaoping (see page 234) which returned China to a less radical path.
- Small-scale factories were shut down, including the backyard furnaces. Investment went instead into big industrial operations that could specialise and do things well.
- Experts were brought back and put in charge of industrial production. Their expertise meant better quality results.
- Discipline was made stricter in factories, so people worked harder, but workers also got bonuses if they produced more. This meant more incentives to increase production.
- Targets for industrial production were lowered to be more realistic. This meant factory managers did not have to lie about production.
- Industrial production grew rapidly again after 1962: by 1965, industrial production was growing at 20 per cent a year. The reforms worked.

> **Revision task** — TESTED
>
> To what extent did Communist leadership transform industry in China between 1949 and 1989?

Changes in the role of women

Socialism meant equality for women and men. The state needed everyone in China to work together to build socialism – women and men together.

Changes for women before 1949

Qing (in 20th century)	1912 Republic	GMD (1927–48)	CCP areas before 1949
• Attempts to end foot binding – but these failed • Arranged marriages were common • Rich men kept concubines • No education for almost all women	• Foot binding criticised but not ended • Education for girls began • However, women did not get the right to vote	• Foot binding began to disappear • A few women at university • More jobs/careers for women in the cities	• Arranged marriages were banned • Women had the right to vote • Divorce made easier • All elected bodies had to have at least 25 per cent women

The Marriage Law, 1950

The Marriage Law was one of the first new laws introduced by the CCP after it won the Civil War. It aimed to end '**feudal**' marriage laws.
- The law made **arranged marriage** illegal and stopped the payment of **dowries** to the husband or his family.
- It was made illegal for men to keep **concubines**, to marry children, to have more than one wife or to sell a wife – before, husbands could sell wives who had run away or had an affair.
- Domestic abuse became illegal.
- Women were now allowed to own and inherit property – before this time, a wife had no rights to anything: her husband owned everything in their house and all their money.

> **Key terms**
>
> **Feudal**: describing the old imperial system of oppressing peasants.
>
> **Arranged marriage**: when families arrange marriages rather than couples choosing for themselves.
>
> **Dowry**: a payment made by the bride's family to the groom's family.
>
> **Concubine**: men could have a wife but also keep another woman or women in their house to have sex with; these women were concubines.

Impact of changing roles for women

- Women took up their new rights, especially the right to divorce: in some areas up to 25 per cent of all young couples got divorced – getting out of arranged marriages.
- Many more women obtained jobs – however, they tended to be paid less.
- Women took up roles within the CCP – however, over 80 per cent of CCP officials were men.
- Men still expected women with full-time jobs to do all the housework and childcare as well.

> **Revision task** — TESTED
>
> To what extent did roles for women change more under Communism than in the period 1911–49? Use the table above to help you.

Political changes

For the CCP, the political transformation of China was a class struggle: capitalism had to be sought out and destroyed everywhere it might be hiding: including inside people's heads.

Thought Reform

Thought Reform was a set of techniques for getting people to think 'correctly'.

- Thought Reform as a campaign took place between 1951 and 1952.
- During the Thought Reform campaign, 3,000 university teachers were made to **self-criticise** in public about their mistaken capitalist views.
- The Thought Reform campaign also used 'struggle sessions'. The person accused would be confronted by a crowd which would humiliate and physically abuse them to make them confess their political crimes. Struggle sessions often took place at the victim's place of work. Some struggle sessions even ended in executions.
- Struggle sessions were powerful because everyone involved in the crowd would learn what their political views should be, and would be terrified of saying or doing something that would make them the victim of a struggle session themselves.

> **Key term**
>
> **Self-criticism**: being made to publicly confess failures.

The Three-anti Campaign, 1951

- The three 'antis' were: corruption, waste and government bureaucracy (inefficiency).
- The targets of the Three-anti Campaign were CCP officials with Guomindang links – the CCP leadership considered them to be corrupted by capitalism.
- One main reason for the Three-anti Campaign was to remove people from the Party who might not be reliable, and replace them with loyal CCP members.
- Four million people were investigated in the Three-anti Campaign and 1 million were either executed or sent to labour camps.
- The scale of the campaign caused problems: with so many Party officials under investigation, imprisoned or dead, many government jobs were not getting done, for example, tax collection.
- These problems meant the CCP leadership had to stop the campaign after a month, or risk chaos.

The Five-anti Campaign, 1952

- The five 'antis' were: bribery, theft of state secrets, tax evasion, cheating on government contracts and theft of state property.
- The targets of the Five-anti Campaign were business leaders and wealthy capitalists.
- The Five-anti Campaign used propaganda to encourage workers across China to spy on their bosses and report them if they had committed any of the five 'antis'.
- Around 450,000 private companies were investigated in the campaign: almost all of China's private companies. Three-quarters of them were found guilty of one or more of the five 'antis'.
- The companies found guilty were made to pay large fines to the state. Many owners were made to undergo self-criticism and struggle sessions. The fines forced many companies to close.

- One result of the campaign was that the state became much richer because of the fines it was paid. The state also gained control of much more of China's economy.
- There was a lot of popular support for the campaign from workers, which made the state stronger.

> **Revision task** TESTED
>
> Which of these three figures brought the biggest changes to China (positive or negative): Sun Yat-sen, Chiang Kai-shek or Mao? Explain your reasons.

The Hundred Flowers Campaign, 1956–57

Following the Three- and Five-anti campaigns, Mao felt confident that the CCP was in control of China. Its opponents had been removed or intimidated, and there had been huge popular support for these campaigns. Ordinary people had joined in with the Party's campaigns very enthusiastically.

At the same time, the new leader of the Soviet Union, Khrushchev, criticised the harsh leadership of Stalin and was allowing more freedom of speech. This was followed by unrest against Communist Party control in Hungary in 1956.

Events of the Hundred Flowers Campaign

- Following the relaxation of strict control in the Soviet Union, Mao encouraged people to criticise the policies of the CCP.
- The campaign was called the Hundred Flowers because of a Chinese saying, 'let a hundred flowers bloom, let a hundred schools of thought contend' (contend means to struggle against something).
- By the end of 1956, there was only limited criticism, for example, some economists and scientists criticised aspects of the Party's policies and stated how they could be improved.
- Then, in 1957, there was much more criticism of the Party, including criticism that Party officials were corrupt.
- By the summer of 1957, students were openly calling for free elections – as a direct attack on the CCP's right to control China.
- In June 1957, the campaign ended and a new 'Anti-Rightist' campaign began – a terror campaign which purged those who had criticised the CCP. The campaign lasted until 1959.

Reaction to the Hundred Flowers Campaign

- Mass struggle sessions humiliated and punished the students and intellectuals who had criticised the CCP. Between 300,000 and 500,000 people were sent to prison camps for **political re-education**.
- The lack of support for the CCP from ordinary people worried the Party. Education programmes praising the CCP were set up for workers and peasants.
- Mao purged many top CCP officials from their jobs because he said they had failed to keep the Party in touch with ordinary people and their concerns.

> **Key term**
>
> **Political re-education**: imprisoning people who are deemed to have the wrong political views and not releasing them until they have the 'correct' views.

Reasons for the Hundred Flowers Campaign

There are different theories as to why Mao launched the Hundred Flowers Campaign:

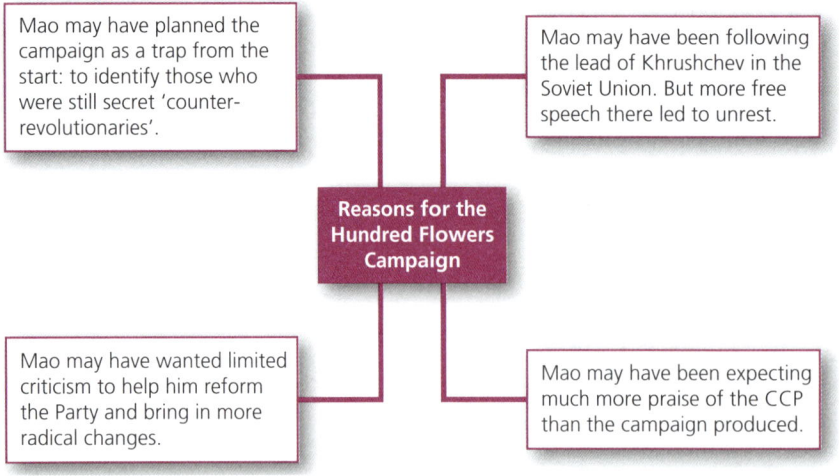

Revision task

TESTED

Explain two possible causes of the Hundred Flowers Campaign.

The Great Leap Forward

The Great Leap Forward was launched by Mao in 1958. It aimed to transform China into a fully communist society that would overtake the western industrial powers in just a few years.

Reasons for the Great Leap Forward

- **Mao's ideology**: Mao believed that there were no limits to what China could do if all its 600 million population followed (his) correct political ideas.
- **Economic**: unless food production could be increased, industrialisation could not increase much more – urban workers needed cheap food, and farm workers needed money to buy modern machinery.
- **Fear**: no one in the CCP dared to argue against Mao because of the Three- and Five-anti Campaigns and the Anti-Rightist Campaign which followed the Hundred Flowers Campaign.
- **Political**: Mao wanted China to stop following the Soviet Union's approach to industrialisation, to end other foreign involvement, and to follow its own, Chinese, path.

Key features of the Great Leap Forward

The Great Leap Forward was China's second Five-year Plan: it was supposed to run from 1958 to 1963.
- **Decentralisation**: instead of the central state driving industries and farming to deliver the Plan, local officials were in charge of mobilising people to deliver the Plan's targets.
  - However, the Plan targets were unrealistic: for example, in 1958 Mao said China would be producing 100 million tonnes of steel by 1962, by the end of the first Five-year plan, it had delivered only 5 million tonnes.

- **Propaganda**: huge resources were put into propaganda to motivate and enthuse the people into meeting and exceeding targets. Everything was done as fast as possible, but without the training or equipment to achieve good results.
- **Backyard furnaces**: 600,000 backyard furnaces were set up in communes to produce iron and steel. Communes melted down everything metal they already had to make iron, and burnt most of their wooden equipment as fuel for the furnaces.
- **Infrastructure projects**: the Great Leap Forward mobilised hundreds of thousands of people to construct new roads, bridges, dams and flood defences – usually by hand rather than with machinery.
- **The Four Noes Campaign**: as part of the Great Leap Forward, Mao urged his people to destroy flies, mosquitos, rats and sparrows – pests responsible for spreading disease and (in the case of sparrows) eating grain in the fields. In fact, sparrows ate bugs that ate crops (for example, caterpillars), so killing sparrows meant more insect pests.
- **Lysenko**: Mao trusted in the Soviet agricultural scientist, Trofim Lysenko, who said that harsh conditions created stronger crops and a bigger harvest. Communes were ordered to follow his techniques, but they did not work.

Effects of the Great Leap Forward

Successes	Challenges
In the first year, almost 50 per cent of China's steel was being produced in the communes.	China's industrial output fell by 50 per cent. The steel produced in backyard furnaces was very poor quality. Most could not be used. In 1959, the backyard furnaces idea was phased out.
All over the country, new bridges, railways, power stations, flood defences and irrigation schemes were built. Most of these were well-constructed and useful.	Many other Great Leap Forward projects were rushed or based on mistaken ideas. For example, seeds planted very deeply or very close together (as Lysenko ordered) failed to grow.
<ul><li>There was a good harvest in 1958, due to very good weather conditions.</li><li>The Party said 375 million tonnes of grain had been harvested.</li><li>A new target of 430 million tonnes was set for 1959.</li></ul>	<ul><li>1959 was the worst harvest for many years – 170 million tonnes.</li><li>In 1960, just 143 million tonnes were harvested.</li><li>There were food shortages in the cities and famine in the countryside.</li></ul>

- Famine from 1959 to 1962 killed an estimated 30 million people. The CCP denied that any famine was happening.
- China was forced to import grain from other countries: from Canada and the USA. This was exactly what the Great Leap Forward was supposed to prevent.
- Peasants lost faith in Party campaigns. There were armed rebellions by peasant groups in some of the worst-hit regions.
- Mao's decision to take a different route from that of the Soviet Union increased tensions between the Soviet Union and China. In 1960, Soviet leader Khrushchev took thousands of Soviet technical advisors out of China.
- The failure of the Great Leap Forward was so obvious that Mao stepped down from being in charge of governing China day-to-day. But he still kept a lot of power and his control of the Party was not weakened.
- When Peng Dehuai, a senior Party leader, criticised the Great Leap Forward, Mao made sure his career in the CCP was finished. Another huge purge was launched to get rid of any opposition in the Party.

Revision tasks

Study this table, which identifies possible thematic connections between topics you have studied.

Topics:	Themes:				
	Civil conflict – order and disorder	External influences on China	Economic transformation	Social transformation	The role of leadership
The first Five-Year Plan		X	X		X
Changes in the role of women		X	X	X	
Political changes, 1949–63	X			X	X
The Great Leap Forward	X	X	X	X	X

Pick a theme (or more than one) and use it to explain connections between the topics.

The influence of the Soviet Union on developments in China

The Soviet Union's influence was very significant at the start of the People's Republic of China's (PRC) development, but grew less as Mao widened the gap between the two socialist countries.

- In 1949, only the Soviet Union supported the PRC. Stalin agreed a $300 million loan for China and set up 50 large-scale industrial projects in China that would develop using Soviet expertise.
- Mao said the peasants could lead a socialist revolution; Stalin said only workers could. This disagreement put strain on the relationship between China and the Soviet Union.
- Whereas the Soviet Union had forced collectivisation on its peasants in the 1930s, resulting in a terrible famine, China used a gradual, voluntary approach until 1958: then forced the change to communes.
- China followed the Soviet Union's approach in the first Five-year Plan: focusing on heavy industry and relying on Soviet technical advisors.
- The Hundred Flowers Campaign (1956–57) was triggered by Soviet leader Khrushchev criticising Stalin.
- In the Great Leap Forward, China took a radically different approach to the Soviet model: trying to combine industrial and agricultural production in the communes – with disastrous results. This radical new approach came from Mao's desire for China to be free of all foreign interference, including Soviet interference. Soviet criticism of the Great Leap Forward angered Mao.

Exam practice

How significant was the Great Leap Forward in changing relations between the CCP and the Chinese people in the years 1934–63?

You may use the following in your answer:
- war with Japan (1937–45)
- famine (1959–62).

You **must** also use information of your own. (16 marks)

Exam tips

1. Questions asking 'How far?' or 'How significant?' are asking you to make a judgement.
2. Consider the reason(s) to support the statement.
3. Consider the reason(s) that argue against the statement.
4. Your answer needs to show your knowledge and understanding with details to back up your points.

7.4 The Cultural Revolution and its impact, 1965–76

REVISED

What you need to know

In this section you will revise the details of the Cultural Revolution and its impact in China. This will include:
- Mao's motives for the Cultural Revolution.
- Key features of the Cultural Revolution.
- The impacts that the Cultural Revolution had on China and on Mao's leadership.
- The split between the Soviet Union and China.

Mao's motives for the Cultural Revolution

- By 1962, Liu Shaoqi and Deng Xiaoping's reforms for farming and industry (see page 222) had ended the famine and the economy was growing again. Mao felt the Party was pushing him into the background.
- Mao felt Liu and Deng's economic reforms took the 'capitalist road' to development: benefiting bureaucrats and industrial experts instead of workers and peasants. For Mao, that meant Liu and Deng were corrupting China's communist revolution.
- Mao wanted 'permanent revolution', not people thinking the revolution had been achieved in 1949 and getting comfortable with how things were. The Cultural Revolution was his attempt to make sure young Chinese people experienced revolution.
- Liu and Deng had enough support in the CCP to block Mao. The Cultural Revolution was motivated by Mao looking for a way to purge the CCP in a way that his rivals in the Party could not block.

Revision task

TESTED

Explain two reasons why Mao wanted a cultural revolution.

Key features of the Cultural Revolution

- Mao launched the Cultural Revolution in May 1966. He mobilised young people to attack 'capitalist roaders' in the CCP – those who followed the 'capitalist road'.
- Propaganda encouraging young people to join the Cultural Revolution was very important. Propaganda was co-ordinated by the Central Cultural Revolution Group, which Mao had set up in 1966, and was led by his (fourth) wife, Jiang Qing.
- Students formed Red Guard groups. Mao gave the Red Guards the power to attack anyone they suspected of being a 'capitalist roader' – even senior CCP officials.
- Mao's ally Lin Biao launched a campaign against the 'Four Olds' in 1966. The Four Olds were: old ideas, old customs, old culture and old habits. This campaign was an attack on counter-revolutionary culture and ways of thinking.
- In response, Red Guards destroyed museums, churches, shrines and art; broke into people's homes to smash traditional objects; and tore up old books and books in foreign languages.

- Red Guards attacked people who looked 'bourgeois' (like capitalists, for example, with Western haircuts), university teachers who had been strict with students, and Party officials. Even very senior CCP leaders were attacked and humiliated, including Liu and Deng. Thousands were purged from the Party, including Liu and Deng.
- The campaign set young people against older people: especially students against teachers and children against parents.
- Red Guard attacks on people often used violent struggle sessions to force their victims to confess to being capitalist roaders. Mao ordered the police not to stop these sessions – even when thousands were beaten to death by the Red Guards.
- As many as 400,000 people were killed in the violence of the Cultural Revolution, and many killed themselves after suffering repeated struggle sessions.
- The Cultural Revolution was out of control by the start of 1967. Red Guards purged local governments and took over their government roles themselves, but then fought with other rival Red Guard groups, including groups of workers. The result was chaos.
- The most radical Red Guard groups then started to demand an end to CCP control over China. This meant they were now challenging Mao for control of China. Mao ordered the Red Guards to disband. Then, in August 1968, Mao ordered the PLA to break up the Red Guard.
- Purges of Red Guard groups took place, with 10 million people investigated. In 1968, nearly 2 million people were arrested, tens of thousands of whom were tortured to death or committed suicide, with most of the rest sent to labour camps.
- After the PLA was used to stop the Red Guard violence, 12 million young people were sent to the countryside (between 1967 and 1972) to 'learn from' the peasants and workers. Many worked on army farms run by the PLA.

> **Revision task** [TESTED]
>
> Identify one similarity and one difference between the Cultural Revolution and the Hundred Flowers Campaign.

The Red Guards, education and the 'cult of Mao'

The 'cult of Mao'

The 'cult of Mao' presented Mao as a perfectly wise and faultless defender of the Revolution, and the ultimate expert on communism, whose guidance could never be wrong.

- Huge portraits of Mao were hung everywhere and 2 billion badges were made featuring Mao. People often started their day by bowing before a picture of the leader.
- Lin Biao collected together sayings of Mao into the *Little Red Book*, published in 1964. The *Little Red Book* was used as a sort of Bible: children studied it at school – there were even stories that doctors had used the book to cure diseases.
- PLA soldiers were ordered to read the *Little Red Book* and follow its guidance. The PLA was trained to be completely loyal to Mao.

The attack on education

- Between May and August 1966, Lin Biao organised a poster campaign attacking the education system for following the capitalist road. The campaign was very effective – students stopped going to classes and attacked their teachers.

- There was a lot of anger about reforms introduced in 1960, which allowed CCP bureaucrats to get their children into the best schools, instead of schools and universities benefiting the children of workers and peasants.
- In August 1966, 1 million high school and university students came to a rally in Tiananmen Square in Beijing. Lin Biao and Mao addressed the students and told them to 'dare to rebel against authority'.
- It was at this rally that Lin Biao launched the 'Four Olds' campaign, in which the students were told that everything that was old was worthless. This included teaching about anything that was not socialist and revolutionary.

The Red Guards

- The Red Guards were groups of school children and university students committed to defending Mao.
- The Red Guards were not one single organisation, although they did tend to dress in the same way (green uniforms, caps and a Mao badge) and shared the same values.
- Following Mao's orders, Red Guards could travel by train to Beijing for free, which is why millions were able to attend rallies. They were trained to march by the PLA.
- As well as teachers, parents were also often denounced by their Red Guard children during the Cultural Revolution.
- The Red Guard was an opportunity for girls and young women to play a leading role in the Revolution, and for young people from poor backgrounds to feel important.

Revision task TESTED

Identify one similarity and one difference between the Cultural Revolution and the Boxer Uprising.

The impact of the Cultural Revolution on Mao's position

The Cultural Revolution increased Mao's importance still further.

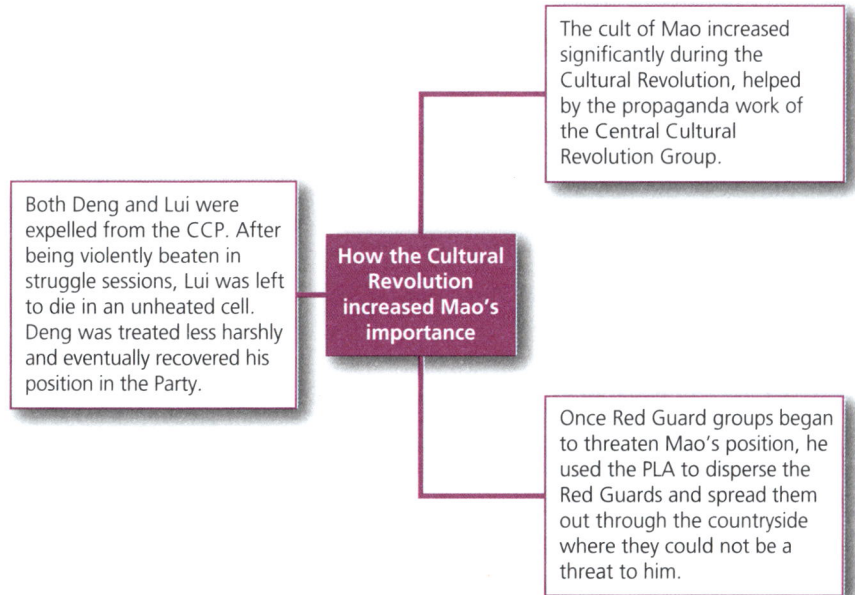

The impact of the Cultural Revolution on China

- Mao's desire to stay in charge nearly caused the destruction of the CCP. By the end of 1968, over two-thirds of the Party leadership (the Central Committee) and 70 to 80 per cent of regional Party officials had been purged.
- The experiences of the Cultural Revolution traumatised many Party workers, who understandably lost motivation. Young people were also disillusioned with China's leadership and the CCP.
- Between 1966 and 1976, industrial production fell by nearly 14 per cent and agricultural production by 2 per cent.
- Education in China largely stopped during the ten years of the Cultural Revolution, which meant a generation of Chinese with lower skills.
- Family life was put under enormous strain, with young people told the traditional values of older people were worthless, encouraged to inform on their parents, and then to move away to work with peasants in remote rural areas.
- The campaign in which 12 million young people were sent to the countryside (between 1967 and 1972) often led to very difficult and depressing experiences because life in remote villages was very hard. These young people didn't have the skills to be useful and there was not much food for them to eat.

> **Revision task** TESTED
>
> Identify three ways in which threats to Mao's leadership changed between the Extermination Campaigns (see page 212) and the end of the Cultural Revolution.

The effects of the Sino–Soviet split on the Chinese economy

The Sino–Soviet split had several linked causes, including China's disappointment that the Soviet Union was reducing tensions with the capitalist West. The split widened from 1958 to 1969, and was at its most serious in 1969, when China and the Soviet Union repositioned nuclear weapons to point at each other, rather than at the West.

- In 1958, the Soviet Union withdrew thousands of experts who had been helping China develop its economic planning and technological development.
- This had a damaging effect on China's economy: 200 projects were cancelled.
- In 1960, the Soviets withdrew all support with developing nuclear technology. They destroyed all the documents that would have helped China develop its own nuclear industry.
- China still owed the Soviet Union for loans: China had to keep paying these back with grain exports, even during periods of famine.
- During the Korean War (1950–53), China had to pay high prices for Soviet-made military technology, which would have been much cheaper if the two countries had remained allies.
- China was keen to develop alliances with other developing socialist countries, especially in Africa. This was expensive: in return for support, China gave $2 billion in loans to African countries.

> **Exam practice**
>
> Explain **TWO** ways in which the Cultural Revolution in 1965 was similar to the May the Fourth Movement in 1919. (6 marks)

> **Exam tips**
>
> 1. Make sure you write about two ways: an answer that only talks about one way (even if in two paragraphs!) can only get a maximum of three marks, however good it is.
> 2. Explain the similarities (or differences if the question is about them) rather than just stating them – 'this was similar because …'.
> 3. Back up your explanations with relevant detail, but keep this concise.

7.5 China, 1976–89

REVISED

What you need to know

In this section you will revise China under the leadership of Deng Xiaoping. This will include:
- The 'Gang of Four' and their fall from influence.
- Economic, social and political changes under Deng.
- The Democracy Movement and the reaction of Deng.

The rise and fall of the 'Gang of Four'

- Mao was often ill in his last years, which weakened his control. A power struggle developed in the CCP between **moderates** and **radicals**.
- The 'Gang of Four' were Jiang Qing (Mao's wife), Zhang Chunquiao, Yao Wenyuan and Wang Hongwen. They were radicals. They were determined that Mao's permanent revolution would not end when Mao died.
- Deng Xiaoping and Zhou Enlai were moderates. Deng had returned to a senior Party role in 1973, and Zhou Enlai was very popular in China.
- The 'Gang of Four' linked Zhou to Lin Biao, who was now seen as a terrible traitor to China after a plot to assassinate Mao failed and ended in Lin's death. Zhou was also accused of wanting to end the Communist revolution in China.
- The 'Gang of Four' had all been promoted to senior Party roles by Mao. When Zhou died in January 1976, they used their influence to ban public mourning for Zhou, and criticised him in newspapers as a 'capitalist roader'.
- Two million people came to Tiananmen Square to mourn Zhou anyway – and demonstrations included criticism of the 'Gang of Four'.
- The army was used to clear the demonstrators from Tiananmen Square. Protesters were arrested as 'counter-revolutionaries', and many hundreds were executed.
- In September 1976, Mao died. The 'Gang of Four' began to gather supporters in Shanghai (100,000 militia troops), ready to take power by force.
- However, in October 1976, the rest of the CCP leadership and the PLA leadership joined together to arrest the 'Gang of Four'. The 'Gang of Four' and their supporters were imprisoned – and blamed for the Cultural Revolution.

> **Key terms**
>
> **Moderates**: people who are generally satisfied but can see ways to improve how things are.
>
> **Radicals**: people who want a complete change to how things are.

Revision task

TESTED

At which of the following points would you say Mao caused the most change in China?
- The Extermination Campaigns
- The Long March
- The war with Japan
- The Civil War
- The first Five-year Plan
- The Great Leap Forward
- The Cultural Revolution

Explain your answer.

Changes under Deng

By 1978, Deng was firmly in control. His reforms took China in the opposite direction to that of the Cultural Revolution.
- Instead of strict ideological control, Deng said China should do whatever worked, and get rid of what didn't.
- Like the self-strengthening movement (see page 207), Deng wanted China to learn from the rest of the world.
- He pushed for 'Four Modernisations': modernisation of national defence, of education (science and technology), of agriculture and of industry.

Changes in agriculture

- Farming had declined during the Cultural Revolution. By 1976, people working for the large farming collectives were earning less than they had in 1970. There was no incentive for them to work hard and grow more.
- Deng's reforms (see page 222) changed farming in China completely. Farmers could now sell whatever they had left after they had met their state quotas. The more they produced, the more they could earn.
- The large communes were broken up into village-sized units called *xiangs*. Instead of farming decisions being made for all the communes in an area by Party officials (often with little knowledge about farming or local conditions), farmers in each *xiang* now produced what they knew grew well and what the market demanded.
- The reforms were very successful: farming productivity increased by up to 10 per cent each year and people in rural areas earned up to 20 per cent more each year between 1978 and 1984.
- The downside of this was that food prices went up, adding to inflation.

Changes in industry

- Wages were increased so factory workers could afford the higher food prices. This created demand for more industrial products and services.
- Individual enterprises were permitted again, so people could set up their own businesses. These businesses could keep their profits.
- Big industrial plants still remained under state control, but their managers were now encouraged to make a profit. Workers received bonuses for hard work.
- A big change came with the setting up of SEZs – Special Enterprise Zones. These opened up parts of China (usually port cities) to foreign investment. Foreign companies shared their technology and in return they got very cheap workers – wages were much lower in China than in western countries or Japan.
- The SEZs started an export boom in China. China's trade with the rest of the world increased by 100 per cent in the early 1980s. China earned a lot of valuable **foreign exchange**. This was used to buy foreign technology and expertise, modernising more of China's industry and leading to more industrial growth, especially in manufacturing.
- Downsides: a big increase in corruption and in inequality; for example, between coastal China and rural China: millions left the countryside to go to work in the industrial cities.

> **Key term**
>
> **Foreign exchange**: currencies from other countries, e.g. US dollars.

> **Revision task** TESTED
>
> Was industry under Deng the same as industry under the Qing? Draw a table detailing features of industry under the Qing and under Deng. Identify one similarity and one difference.

Changes in education

Deng's reforms in education were designed to train up a new generation of scientists and managers who would help modernise and run China's industries. This was the opposite of the Cultural Revolution, which rejected everything that was not revolutionary.
- The number of universities increased and universities also expanded so they could take more students.
- More than 10,000 students were sent to study abroad (80 per cent of them to study sciences) so they could bring back modern innovations to China.
- One impact was that better-educated Chinese people wanted more political freedom (democracy) as well as more freedom to learn.

Emergence of privatisation and Westernisation

Privatisation

The changes in agriculture and in industry meant the return of privatisation:
- farmers had private plots of land and sold some of their produce for profit
- individual enterprises: people in the cities set up small businesses and sold products or services for profit
- export companies in the SEZs were private businesses run to make profits.

Mao had led the struggle for years to get rid of all private ownership and private profits. Deng had been criticised during the Cultural Revolution for being a 'capitalist roader'.

Now he was in power, Deng said it was acceptable if some areas got rich before others – as long as it led to everyone getting richer over time. That view conflicted with core socialist beliefs.

Westernisation

Opening up China to foreign influences meant growing Westernisation:
- The students sent abroad to study, brought back Western fashions and ideas.
- The SEZs attracted investment from Western companies, which introduced Western technologies and ideas to China's industries.
- Making products for Western markets also meant more Western-style products (for example, TVs) became available for Chinese people to buy.

Westernisation was important because:
- Mao had wanted China to be **self-sufficient**. Deng's reforms accepted that Mao's experiment had failed. China had to be open to the world in order to modernise.
- The Cultural Revolution had rejected all Western ideas and wanted only revolutionary culture for China. Deng wanted China to learn from the West.
- However, Westernisation led to conflict. In the West, people had much more political freedom – the right to choose which party to vote for, for example. This threatened the power of the CCP over China.

> **Key term**
>
> **Self-sufficient**: when a country can produce what it needs by itself.

> **Revision task** TESTED
>
> Identify similarities in Chinese attitudes to the West across the following events and leaders:
> - the Boxer Uprising
> - the May the Fourth Movement
> - Sun Yat-sen
> - Chiang Kai-shek
> - the Great Leap Forward
> - the Cultural Revolution.

Changes in birth control

In 1979, the one-child policy was introduced. The state wanted to reduce the birth rate because of China's enormous population (which reached 1 billion people in 1981). As a result:
- Couples in cities were only allowed to have one child.
- Couples in rural areas could have a second child after five years (farms depended on family workers).
- Couples who did not follow these rules faced fines, struggle sessions, compulsory fitting of contraceptive devices, forced abortions and forced sterilisation.
- Propaganda was used to convince people to follow the policy.
- Boys were seen as much more useful to a family than girls. Girls married and then left the family to join their husband's family, while boys stayed to work on the farm.
- The one-child policy led to families aborting girl foetuses and even killing baby girls (infanticide). By 1989, there were 114 males for every 100 females.
- The policy was also not very effective in rural areas. Nearly half of all mothers who had two children went on to have a third child, and a quarter of those mothers went on to have a fourth child.

> **Revision task**
>
> Pick at least two points, and then two facts to back up those points, that you would use to answer this question:
>
> How far did life change for women in China between 1911 and 1989?
>
> TESTED

Deng's opposition to political reform

Deng was strongly opposed to any political reform that might weaken the CCP.
- Deng believed that China must be stable, not rocked by radical political change, if his economic reforms were going to work.
- Deng also did not want China to become a capitalist country. He wanted it to stay socialist, but modernised.
- Deng believed that the CCP needed to stay in control in order to ensure stability and socialism.

Although Deng's economic reforms upset some CCP conservatives, his opposition to political change reassured them.

Origins of the Democracy Movement, 1979

The 'Democracy Wall' movement and Wei Jingsheng

- The 'Democracy Wall' was a long wall near Tiananmen Square. In October 1978, posters appeared on the wall encouraging CCP members to think freely.
- People took this to mean they could post their opinions on the wall. In November, a poster appeared that criticised Mao.
- Deng responded by saying that although he did not want to criticise Mao, it was legal for people to post their opinions.
- In December, however, a poster written by Wei Jingsheng appeared on the 'Democracy Wall'. It called for a 'Fifth Modernisation' – real democracy. He criticised Deng as well as Mao.

- Wei Jingsheng was arrested and imprisoned as a 'counter-revolutionary'. He spent eighteen years in prison.
- Inspired by Wei Jingsheng and other pro-democracy activists, the Democracy Movement began: people (mostly highly educated intellectuals) who wanted political reform to be part of China's modernisation.

University student protests

In the mid-1980s, support for the Democracy Movement spread through universities in China.

- In 1985, there was a student demonstration in Beijing. The students were angry that the government was doing nothing about their poor living conditions, rising prices, corruption and foreigners getting special treatment.
- Hu Yaobang – a close colleague of Deng who had also suffered during the Cultural Revolution – was CCP General Secretary. Hu encouraged the students, saying they should challenge the Party if they thought it was wrong.
- An inspirational intellectual called Fang Lizhi toured universities, calling for more democracy.
- In 1986, demonstrations spread to universities in Hefei, Wuhan and Shanghai.

The students' economic concerns (for example, rising prices) and the political concerns were connected. The CCP, the students said, was too corrupt to govern China well. The students wanted the right to choose between different parties: a democratically elected government.

Reaction of Deng

- Deng's government used the police to pressure the students to stop protesting.
- Fang Lizhi was moved from his job to an unimportant post in a remote part of China.
- Hu Yaobang was criticised for encouraging the student protests. He was sacked from his job as CCP General Secretary (but wasn't purged from the Party).
- Deng said that China was not ready for Western-style democracy because so many of China's huge population were not well educated. The implication was that the Chinese people still needed the government to tell them what to do.

Tiananmen Square, 1989

- In April 1989, Hu Yaobang died. Hu was respected as a supporter of political reform.
- Student demonstrations criticised the CCP for sacking Hu and for blocking reform.
- There were links to the May the Fourth demonstrations of 1919, with student demonstrators again calling for 'Mr Democracy' and 'Mr Science' (see page 20).
- On 13 May, hundreds of students joined a **hunger strike**, demanding to speak to CCP leaders about political reforms.
- Nearly 1 million people demonstrated in Tiananmen Square to support the hunger strikers: students but also workers. There were hundreds of demonstrations elsewhere in China, too.
- The demonstration happened while Mikhail Gorbachev, the Soviet leader, was visiting Beijing. International media broadcast images of the Beijing demonstrations around the world. This embarrassed the CCP leadership.

Revision task

Wei Jingsheng's poster on the 'Democracy Wall' included the following statement:

'Those who worry that democracy will lead to anarchy and chaos are just like those who, following the overthrow of the Qing dynasty, worried that without an emperor the country would fall into chaos.'

What evidence can you find from the period 1911–89 to support Deng's view that China needed stability in order to modernise and develop?

TESTED

Key term

Hunger strike: refusing to eat until political demands are discussed.

- On 19 May, CCP leaders visited the protests. The hunger strike ended.
- On 20 May, **martial law** was imposed in Beijing. However, the demonstrations continued, this time and imprisoned as 'counter-revolutionaries'.
- The government decided to send in the PLA to 'restore order'. Tens of thousands of troops were involved, plus tanks and armoured personnel carriers.
- At first, ordinary citizens of Beijing got in the way of the troops and prevented them from reaching the demonstrations.
- However, on the night of 3 June 1989, troops approached the unarmed demonstrators and opened fire on them. Hundreds, possibly thousands, were killed, and hundreds more arrested and imprisoned as 'counter-revolutionaries'.

> **Key term**
>
> **Martial law**: when a military government is brought in and people's personal freedoms become severely restricted.

What happened after the Tiananmen Square massacre?

- Although there was a crack-down on demands for political reform, economic modernisation continued. China experienced enormous economic success in the 1990s.
- To some extent, the CCP was successful in satisfying the Chinese people enough by raising their living standards.
- Democracy and freedom of speech have not been allowed to develop in China. Discussion of the massacre is not permitted there.
- By the time Deng died in 1997, there were more political prisoners in China's prison camps than there had been in 1976, when Mao died.

Revision task

Study this table, which identifies possible thematic connections between topics you have studied.

Topics:	Themes:				
	Civil conflict – order and disorder	External influences on China	Economic transformation	Social transformation	The role of leadership
The Cultural Revolution	X		X	X	X
The Sino-Soviet split		X	X		X
Changes under Deng	X	X	X	X	X
Tiananmen Square (1989)	X	X		X	X

Pick a theme (or more than one) and use it to explain connections between the topics.

Exam practice

How far were student protests responsible for political change in the years 1911–89?

You may use the following in your answer:
- the Agrarian Reform Law
- the Democracy Movement.

You **must** also use information of your own. (16 marks)

> **Exam tips**
>
> 1. Questions asking 'How far?' or 'How significant?' are asking you to make a judgement.
> 2. Consider the reason(s) to support the statement.
> 3. Consider the reason(s) that argue against the statement.
> 4. Your answer needs to show your knowledge and understanding, with details to back up your points.

Notes